Democratized Generative AI

Principles, Challenges and Applications

nova
science publishers
www.novapublishers.com

The Future of Artificial Intelligence Series

Divine Feminine Energies in Vedic Anthologies: A Scientific Inquiry Using AI and Large Language Models
Chandrasekar Vuppalapati
ISBN: 979-8-89530-583-6
eBook ISBN: 979-8-89530-706-9

Navigating the Future: Embracing Advances in AI and Digital Transformation and Seamlessly Integrating ESG Across Sectors
Michail Chalaris, Christina Patitsa and Stavros Kalogiannidis (Editors)
ISBN: 979-8-89530-461-7
eBook ISBN: 979-8-89530-571-3

Real-World Applications of Artificial Intelligence and Machine Learning in Power Systems: A Code Approach
T. Mariprasath, ME, PhD and V. Kirubakaran
ISBN: 979-8-89530-228-6
eBook ISBN: 979-8-89530-332-0

More information about this series can be found at
https://novapublishers.com/product-category/series/the-future-of-artificial-intelligence/

S. Balasubramaniam
Seifedine Kadry
Editors

Democratized Generative AI

Principles, Challenges and Applications

nova
science publishers
www.novapublishers.com

DOI: https://doi.org/10.52305/NSGY2831

NOTICE TO THE READER

Library of Congress Cataloging-in-Publication Data

ISBN: 979-8-89530-684-0 (Hardcover)
ISBN: 979-8-89530-786-1 (eBook)

Published by Nova Science Publishers, Inc. † New York

Contents

Preface

Democratisation demonstrates the evolution of Artificial Intelligence (AI) from a complex and exclusive technology understood by a select few to a more accessible tool. This suggests that AI capabilities are no longer limited to just big enterprises and specialised researchers, but are readily accessible to small businesses, creative workers, and educators in general. The changes have extensive implications, impacting several aspects of the service delivery process and profoundly changing our interaction with technology. The evolution of AI from a specialised field to a widely available tool is remarkable. The artificial intelligence era was defined by large corporations and advanced research institutions. This undertaking required a significant allocation of resources, and a specialised skill set. There has been a growing democratic movement over time, triggered by numerous factors. Advancements in technology have lowered the cost of AI. Accessible platforms are being developed, reducing the barrier to entry and enabling individuals and enterprises to utilise AI without requiring specific technical expertise. This change is enabled by a growing recognition that AI can accelerate innovation, productivity, and competitive advantage across several industries. AI has expanded and improved its utilisation in the digital economy's healthcare, finance, education, and entertainment industries.

IT leaders are increasingly looking for methods to expand the advantages of AI capabilities throughout the entire organisation. The arrival of new AI-based tools facilitates achieving that goal. This democratisation involves expanding low- and no-code technologies, which allow non-developers to create and launch software, to include AI. It involves exchanging verified data and enhancing data literacy within the organisation. Not every professional is proficient in writing machine learning scripts. commercial experts comprehend the potential of AI, create appropriate use cases, and utilise the results to attain commercial outputs and insights. Facilitating the democratisation of AI in the corporate sector is achievable through decentralised governance structures and the emergence of AI-centric services in the market. However, as with any venture incorporating novel technology, democratisation has advantages and obstacles.

This book covers a wide range of democratized generative AI techniques, algorithms and frameworks, explores the latest advancements in democratized generative AI, practical use cases and applications of democratized generative AI.

Editors' Biographies

Dr. Balasubramaniam S (IEEE Senior Member) is working as an Assistant Professor at the School of Computer Science and Engineering, Kerala University of Digital Sciences, Innovation and Technology (Formerly IIITM-K), Digital University Kerala, Thiruvananthapuram, Kerala, India. Before joining Digital University Kerala, he was a Senior Associate Professor at the School of Computer Science and Engineering, Vellore Institute of Technology (VIT), Chennai, Tamilnadu, India. He has around 15+ years of experience in teaching, research, and industry. He has completed his post-doctoral research in the Department of Applied Data Science at Noroff University College, Kristiansand, Norway. He holds a Ph.D degree in Computer Science and Engineering from Anna University, Chennai, India, in 2015. He has published nearly 25+ research papers in reputed SCI/WoS/Scopus indexed Journals. He has also been granted 1 Australian patent and 2 Indian Patents and published 2 Indian patents. He has presented papers at conferences, contributed chapters to edited books, and has been an editor in a few books published by international publishers. His research and publication interests include machine learning, deep learning, federated learning-based applications in healthcare, and cloud computing security.

Google Scholar: https://scholar.google.co.in/citations?user=1KGLST0AAAAJ&hl=en

Academic url: https://duk.ac.in/personnel/balasubramaniam-s/

Orcid Id: https://orcid.org/my-orcid?orcid=0000-0003-1371-3088
LinkedIn:
https://www.linkedin.com/in/dr-balasubramaniam-s-6873533b/

Professor Seifedine Kadry has a bachelor's degree in 1999 from Lebanese University, an MS degree in 2002 from Reims University (France), an EPFL (Lausanne), PhD in 2007 from Blaise Pascal University (France), an HDR degree in 2017 from Rouen University (France). His research currently focuses on Data Science, education using technology, system prognostics, stochastic systems, and applied mathematics. He is an IET and AAIA fellow. and . He is a full professor of data science at the Department of Computer Science and Mathematics, Lebanese American University, Beirut, Lebanon.

Google Scholar: https://scholar.google.com/citations?hl=en&user=EAVEmg0AAAAJ

Academic url: https://soas.lau.edu.lb/about/people/seifedine-n-kadry.php

LinkedIn: https://www.linkedin.com/in/seifedine-kadry/

Chapter 1

Introducing Generative Artificial Intelligence for Democratic Engagement

S. Aathilakshmi[1,*]
and Ayodeji Olalekan Salau[2]
[1]Department of ECE, Chennai Institute of Technology, Chennai, Tamilnadu, India
[2]Department of Electrical and Computer Engineering, Afe Babalola University, Aye, Nigeria

Abstract

Generative AI is a significant technological advancement that can reshape citizen participation in democratic procedures in fundamentally transformative ways. Generative AI can radically enhance how citizens engage with democratic processes. Traditional ways of civic involvement through public consultations, debates, or policy feedback are generally encumbered by barriers that include limited accessibility, jargon linguistics that are often difficult to understand, and costly analysis. Generative AI could overcome these barriers by automatically analyzing and summarizing lengthy, complex legislative texts and thus making the material available to more readers and understandable by a wider public. Moreover, it can produce various perspectives or scenarios in public debates, which bestow a more inclusive spectrum of voices on civic discourse. Regarding real-time interaction, AI-driven systems can facilitate large-scale citizen dialogues and consultations, creating an interactive feedback loop between citizens and policymakers. These systems can modulate conversations to filter out noise and hone in on actionable insight, making policy discussions more robust and, most importantly, welcoming diverse voices that once were excluded. AI can

* Corresponding Author's Email: me.aathi92@gmail.com

In: Democratized Generative AI: Principles, Challenges and Applications
Editors: S. Balasubramaniam and Seifedine Kadry
ISBN: 979-8-89530-684-0

also generate personalized content that informs citizens about ongoing political developments based on their interests, further enhancing public engagement. However, bias, misinformation, and ethical issues concerning transparency and accountability are risk-laden challenges in using generative AI in democratic systems.

Keywords: generative artificial intelligence, citizenship, social media, big language models, deliberative democracy

1. Introduction

The generative artificial intelligence model is exceptional because it employs "sophisticated models" to produce "better, near-human quality content" [1]. As illustrated by the popular Chat GPT, these models can learn and create multiple input and output types, including text, images, audio, and long-form language models. It is widely used for moderation, paraphrasing, authoring, information retrieval, and content creation. These applications have the potential to catalyze realignments in society and politics that profoundly influence the mode of operating democratic institutions. It may include changes in how the executive dispenses services [2], the formulation and assessment of laws made by the legislative, and the administration of judicial processes [3]. It's necessary to examine the impact of generative Artificial intelligence on the citizens of democratic countries and cognitive, social, and political characteristics to understand the kind of significant societal changes that may be induced. It will be evaluated from the following aspects: We will analyze how generative Artificial intelligence affects an information ecosystem and social media—critical to democratic involvement. Once the paradigm is established, we enumerate several potential beneficial impacts that generative artificial intelligence may have on democratic institutions and some negative implications for them. Our analysis of the possible effects of generative Artificial intelligence on democratic behaviors stems from current deployments and breakthroughs. To that end, this effort to use artificial intelligence to alert various stakeholders—from citizens and regulators to artificial intelligence developers—about these potential consequences. This information will help in today's decision-making, eliminating prospective hazards and employing breakthrough technologies, as shown in Figure 1.

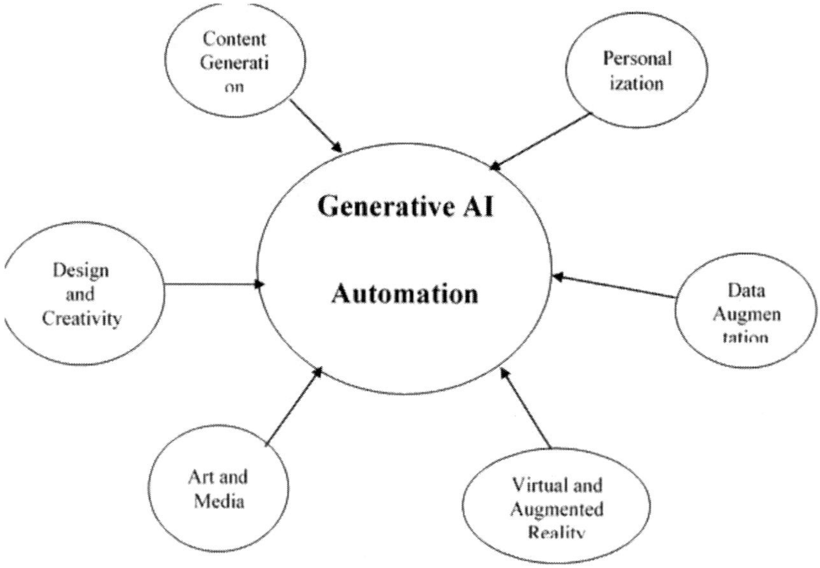

Figure 1. Basic Block Diagram of democratic engagement.

2. Social Media and Informational Ecosystem

One of the normative premises of liberal democracies rests on the assumption that citizens will have access to pertinent and reliable information about political and public policy issues, which they will then evaluate to formulate their political preferences. This core idea recasts the interaction between individuals and the informational ecosystem in which they reside. It includes traditional media networks, digital platforms, political entities, social movements, libraries, and everyday conversations among fellow citizens—this enables the citizens to receive contextually relevant facts and information about their social and political contexts. Whenever such factors continually erode its information environment or otherwise alter it unpredictably, they will exclude citizens from freely participating in democratic politics and cultural activities. The emergence of such generative Artificial intelligence technologies as Chat GPT, Copilot, and DALL-E will challenge and open up opportunities for traditional and digital media and users.

It corresponds to the development of journalistic methodologies and a significant increase in personalization technologies, thus guaranteeing the output corresponding to particular preferences for each user [4]. The advance of our informational ecologies by generative Artificial intelligence, particularly as an emerging trend associated with social media services, has consequential impacts on our democratic organs. Social media are best described as digital intermediaries that "host, organize, and disseminate users' shared content or social interactions," often focus on commercial artificial intelligence. In the last decade, information has fundamentally changed and, thanks mainly to Facebook and YouTube, been altered, particularly through their contributions. Media companies, especially those connected with news-related sources, newspapers, independent organizations, educational institutions, and various governmental agencies, have increasingly used social media to disseminate their content and to promote what they offer. Social media should be seen as instruments that mold and dictate the digital public sphere, which is very important in the greater public sphere. While some researchers often focus on the negative impacts of social media [5], it is essential to recognize that such technologies have also facilitated some changes in better directions, like diversity in information networks [6] and the rise of social justice movements through digital spheres. Social media companies influence users through desirable attributes and undesirable behaviors expressed through social media, thus changing the participation of these users in deliberative conversations with each other [7].

Social media companies have profoundly altered our democratic culture by changing the information landscape. Independent of LLMs, such knowledge might change the information environment outside social media. The exploration of public policy in Chat GPT provokes deep reflection; also ignored is the concurrent loss of attention to the interplay between generative Artificial intelligence and social media, considering the drastic shifts experienced in the information landscape. Of course, a complete understanding requires following the impact of user-generated and consumed content on social media platforms alongside the responses from these companies regarding censorship, demotion, or amplification of such content to appreciate how our democratic culture is changing entirely [8]—artificial intelligence of attention on the scope of content that can be devoted to it. The attention economy focuses on the resourceful consideration of the organizations striving to extract and exploit toward their ends [9]. There needs to be a recognition of the intrinsic limits within attention economics on social media, especially when directly compared to the volume of content that could occupy this space. Here, constituents with the most significant attention may be the most influential in society and political life [10].

If people consume or create content predominantly through generative Artificial intelligence on social media, then generative Artificial intelligence will eventually become a major player in the attention economy. It isn't very accurate to understand the digital world as a sphere that users operate in with a single instrument digitally while interacting with entirely separate worlds—digitally and non-digitally. We envision a hybrid approach [11] in which distinctions between offline and digital borders are blurred and entwined. A teenager uses Copilot to research a current political issue, then types an essay edited by Chat GPT, publishing it on Facebook with an image created visually through DALL-E. The combined [12] method includes a steady conversation on LLM and other social media and face-to-face dialogue, as shown above. It also encompasses scenarios where one of the sub-goals is accelerated by LLM, thus leaving more attention for doing another activity. We are utilizing a hybrid methodology that has proven effective in exploring the complexities of modern digital technologies, intrinsically linked with user preference. Many view their digital identity as a further extension of themselves. For us, it also means assessing the likely positive and negative effects of generative Artificial intelligence on democratic processes.

3. Beneficial Effects of Generative Artificial Intelligence on Democratic Citizenship

First, the concept of citizenship should be defined in order to examine the possible positive effects of generative artificial intelligence on citizenship. There are three elements of [13] democratic citizenship: legal status, identity connected with membership in a particular political community, and an active role through which citizens function as political agents, participating in democratic institutions by voting, deliberating about political issues with other citizens, and so on.

A key tool in understanding the third part is the theory of deliberative democracy, as described by [14]. Deliberative democracy argues that political institutions and practices can be legitimate only if they can be openly justified to all citizens as free and equal members of political society. Therefore, citizen involvement in deliberative activities oriented toward reason-giving is necessary. Deliberative democracy requires that citizens acquire skills. According to [15], key elements include a willingness to recognize each other as peers and to empathetically assess differences in perspectives, and to engage in open, honest, and respectful conversation; norms of deliberative conduct: openness, accountability, and reciprocity; internal deliberative virtues of humility and hope that complement the abilities required to reason and deliberate effectively; and other virtues that advantaged participants might need to develop, specifically the ability to facilitate equitable deliberative interactions among disparate groups[16]. In a democracy, citizens need to have the ability and the will to input into deliberate practices about the leadership of their community. Generative Artificial intelligence dramatically shapes democratic citizenship and the development of relevant virtues and vices. We can evaluate these effects by looking at three forms of interaction between humans and Artificial intelligence. These include: first, Artificial intelligence substituting or replacing human tasks and competencies; second, Artificial intelligence complementing individuals' ability to conduct activities; and third, Artificial intelligence enhancing or improving human skills and abilities [17].

The final two categories align with the concept presented by [18], who defines "information" capabilities as technological tools that provide users with valuable knowledge presented in practical forms, thus enhancing their decision-making and action-taking abilities [19]. These three techniques may have the potential positive ramifications of generative Artificial intelligence toward short-term progress in democratic citizenship. Concerning the automation of replacement, A) promises to alleviate the "tedium" associated with repetition and low-value tasks [20], like drafting boilerplate letters or simply social media comments, freeing citizens from dullness and mental work to focus on more meaningful, politically relevant activities, such as thoughtful discourse with other citizens.

Generative Artificial intelligence could soon substitute in-person and small-sized human-moderated debates and political rallies for a non-artificial intelligence chatbot for the comprehensive study of LLM-based chatbots. It can facilitate hundreds of online talks that are geographically free and enhance political engagement. Building upon our previous discussion regarding the hybrid approach to comprehending the impacts of generative Artificial intelligence, one might anticipate these interactions occurring within a broader informational framework, wherein Artificial intelligence functions not only as an interlocutor but also as a coordinator of online discourse, seamlessly intertwined with offline activities and various political processes such as voting and opinion formation. Its artificial intelligence is connected to the potential of generative artificial intelligence in helping and expanding avenues for information. Generative Artificial intelligence has the potential to enhance and speed up human capabilities in information acquisition and processing.

LLMs can provide much faster, more focused, and carefully selected content to enhance discussions over many topics.

Besides civic consciousness, exposure to LLM might make people better arguers and deliberators. Large language models can be leveraged to present counterarguments, identify flaws in our argumentation, and better understand opposing positions. Evidence emerging evidence comes from non-artificial intelligence chatbots in this context. A study showed that a chatbot's facilitation of web-based deliberative conversations improved discussion quality, and thus, a chatbot could partially replace a human moderator in specific situations. It might make the LLM-based chatbots more effective in this case.

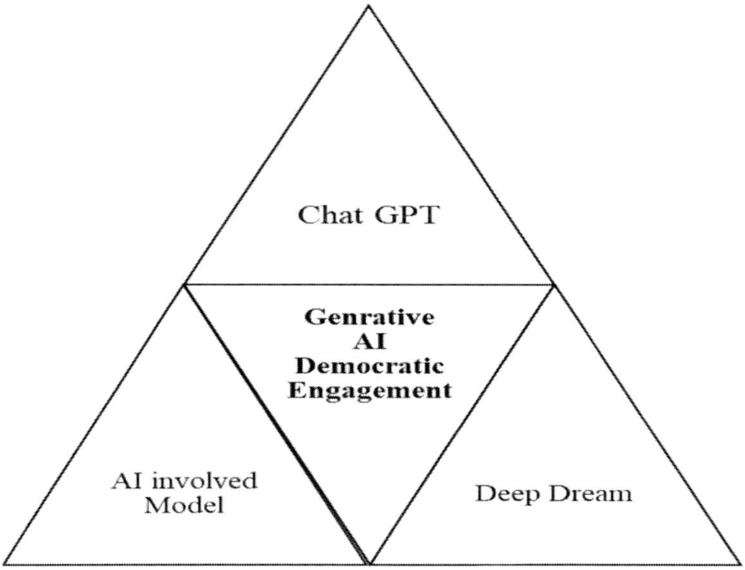

Figure 2. AI involved democratic generative model.

The research used a Generative Artificial intelligence tool, namely the GPT-3 LLM, to show how real-time Artificial intelligence interventions in online discussions improve the quality of perceived discourse, enhance democratic reciprocity, and shift the tenor of deliberation around contentious political issues such as gun control. These interventions assist deliberators in recognizing counterarguments, an essential ingredient in artificial intelligence using the quality of discussions and fostering civility, which may help reduce the polarization so often visible on social media and other digital landscapes.

Generative Artificial intelligence can address two challenges in deliberative democracy: argumentation inequality, referring to inequalities in individuals' deliberative capabilities, and scalability, referring to the challenges of enhancing participatory, deliberative conversations. Argumentative inequality is a problem because discursive democracy is based on equal freedom and the ability to contribute as equal participants in discourse; however, the capacity for reasoning among citizens is starkly unequal. Artificial intelligence can help people with minimal ability to communicate, reason, access existing knowledge, or structure argumentation to expand their political voice and understanding, assisted by large language models (LLM).

It may endow citizens with the eradication of deliberative inequalities. Additionally, the ability of generative Artificial intelligence to provide accurate facts, encourage deep discussion, and act as a critical discussant may help alleviate the significant challenges facing deliberative democracy. There is a need for a national debate day wherein citizens engage in a structured, in-person public discussion facilitated with expert knowledge and moderation, as shown in Figure 2. Such an approach has been regarded as infeasible as a practical solution to the scalability problem, given the significant resource requirements for mobilizing adequate physical and human resources to support extended, high-quality deliberative discussions facilitated by artificial intelligence. -Deliberative polls and citizen juries are only feasible with small groups due to their resource intensity, making them infeasible on a larger scale. Challenges regarding the scalability of generative Artificial intelligence, marked by its capacity for extensive deployment and accessibility via personal devices like mobile phones or laptops, are expected to be surmounted through technological advancement. There are two Artificial intelligence roles of generative Artificial intelligence: information delivery, such as retrieval-augmented generation, in accessing fresh data outside its artificial intelligence dataset and engaging in reasoning discourse with the public, which may involve "fine-tuning" a language model designed explicitly for this purpose. In addition, technology could enable rich civic conversation by providing real-time interventions that promote civility, kindness, and empathy. Such improvements in citizens' capacities for education and meaningful participation in major issues would significantly enhance discussions on numerous imperative political matters. A core assumption of deliberative democracy points out that more engagement with ethical behavior on the part of citizens will improve the quality and, eventually, the equity of political institutions. Generative artificial intelligence has the potential to make debates more fruitful, enriching the informational landscape of communication and content generation in social media. Conversely, these desirable outcomes are neither assured nor imminent because social media encourages polarization and misinformation instead of consensus and informed discourse. Furthermore, the benefits of artificial intelligence might reach only a limited subpopulation because of the observed "technological divide" among various social groupings. It calls for exploring the potential negative consequences of generative Artificial intelligence for democratic citizenship.

4. Negative Influence of Generative Artificial intelligence on Democratic Citizenship

This review of the negative impacts of generative Artificial intelligence on the attention economy of social media identifies three primary risks: the hallucination effect and misinformation, biased or manipulative Artificial intelligence data, and deepfakes, which enable the exploitation of ubiquitous false information. We evaluate these threats before exploring their implications for democratic citizenship and deliberative democracy. This ability of Generation A to produce poor, prejudiced, or even erroneous information because of hallucination and flawed Artificial intelligence data is quite dangerous, especially in political talk. The bias in the generated information is attributed to the Artificial intelligence data used for model development.

Conversely, hallucinations are outputs that are "illogical or artificial intelligence" to the provided source input. They argue in their work that "Chat GPT and other similar models work through the statistical properties of language in massive online text data, which can Artificial intelligence errors, bias, or outdated information. Researchers found that the generative AI tool DALL-E exhibits gender and racial biases, broader than text-based models. If democratic voters rely on generative Artificial intelligence outputs to feed political discourse and make decisions, these biases and errors would be catastrophic. Scholars argue that the rapid pace and high volume of generative artificial intelligence outputs could saturate voters' information environments with misleading content, thereby compromising their ability to critically evaluate the performance of elected representatives. The more advanced generative Artificial intelligence models become in terms of generating text that appears to be written by humans, the higher the chance is that such text will be used in discourse without sufficient checks or scrutiny of its knowledge base. Deepfakes are artificial intelligence-produced videos showing people performing actions or speaking words that they did not genuinely perform or speak.

It is a massive threat to our information ecosystem and democratic institutions. Deepfakes seek to deceive the viewer; as this technology grows, so does the prospect of actual deception. Political leaders have already been targeted in instances of deepfakes, which are widely spread through various media on social networks. Research argues that deepfakes pose a significant threat to epistemic values by further undermining the credibility of data when digitally generated videos and other content are used to mislead audiences. The question of democratic discourse is twofold. Primarily, such misinformation disseminated by sources perceived as credible by democratic individuals leads them astray.

Moreover, citizens may begin to lose trust in information, regardless of its accuracy or value, leading to increased skepticism toward others who share or disseminate information. Another significant concern is the use of generative artificial intelligence to distribute and exploit large-scale misinformation. Studies suggest that the enhanced ability to rapidly and extensively generate seemingly credible falsehoods aligns with the complex and evolving landscape of digital information, making coordinated influence efforts more effective and harder to detect.More dynamic than ever, artificial intelligence demonstrated that a publicly accessible LLM could generate 102 distinct blog entries over 17,000 words of health disinformation regarding vaccines and vaping, incorporating fabricated patient and doctor testimonials, all in 65 minutes. Wealthy actors may leverage this ability, in the form of rival governments, businesses, or oligarchs, to flood the information space and dominate the attention economy.

Based on 80% of the detected false stories related to sensitive and politically volatile topics, the organization concluded that the model could produce false news stories, essays, and television scripts. Additionally, there is fear that Generative A's sheer volume of customized political ads could ultimately be used for micro-targeting voters. Political parties in countries like India, Pakistan, and Slovakia are already using deepfake technologies. Additionally, Iranian hackers are using deep fake news through different foreign streaming services to attract attention domestically as well as internationally. It may foster wrong impressions about controversial political matters or aggravate social tensions and mistrust.

Thus, this may discourage people from engaging in trustworthy and constructive conversation, damaging the very nature of democracy and the quality of the informational environment. The three approaches defined in the previous section can be used to provide a closer view of the possible negative impacts of generative artificial intelligence on democratic citizenship. Using generative Artificial intelligence instead of the investigation, understanding, and critical analysis required to solve specific challenges puts vital democratic deliberate skills at stake.

There is very little research on the effects of generative Artificial intelligence on critical thinking, partly because technology is so new. Nonetheless, experts have warned for decades that over-reliance on technology could lead to the decline of essential cognitive and moral faculties. Studies note that the development of skills necessary for data analysis, logical argumentation, and persuasive reasoning remains crucial, even in the absence of generative artificial intelligence applications. Researchers demonstrate how generative artificial intelligence could undermine users' abilities to deliberate effectively, by a set of experiments, the authors tested the evaluated models—Chat GPT and GPT-4—to see whether these models might be vulnerable to flawed user arguments, often allowing bad reasoning to continue existing even after first corrections when producing the correct response.

The experimental results suggest that the models' response was chosen to fit human tastes rather than improving discursive quality. This finding also reveals another undesirable impact of generative Artificial intelligence on a person: it reduces meaningful communication, perpetuates wrong assumptions, and worsens the spread of false information and disinformation. Face-to-face conversations incorporating generative Artificial intelligence are likely to reduce people's interest in other people's thoughts and opinions. Incorporating generative Artificial intelligence in face-to-face communication is expected to reduce social trust since more people will become artificially intelligent about whom they communicate. The incorporation of generative Artificial intelligence in communication and decision-making would significantly erode citizen interaction.

This strategy would endanger the feeling of belonging to an integrated political community. A) Chatbots, increasingly controlled by artificial intelligence, are assuming the function of virtual communication tools, particularly in contentious online political discussions. Due to its broad capabilities, generative Artificial intelligence has spread conversational bots and their responses on social media sites, making it hard to distinguish imaginary chatter from real individuals. Artificial intelligence-driven chatbots can harm significant human interaction, which is necessary for an intense democratic process. At the same time, users are likely to face ever-increasing challenges in having discussions and organizing political actions given the competition in attention spans by sheer volumes of generative Artificial intelligence-generated information. The discussed risks—prejudiced and false outputs, deepfakes, and misinformation—are gradually shaping the contours of what has been termed a state in which reality can no longer be reliably distinguished from falsehood.

It indicates that individuals will struggle to differentiate between fact and fiction on particular topics modified by generative Artificial intelligence. Substituting trivial and low-value tasks with Artificial intelligence offers significant advantages; nonetheless, it necessitates that we verify and assess the information generated by Artificial intelligence, thereby augmenting our accountability as conscientious citizens. The conversation of economic agents, ChatGPT-3.5 and ChatGPT-4, included wrong references, showing lower accuracy as prompts became more specific. First, we risk the development of an ignorant society, which isolates individuals from direct human interaction and is unable to think critically. The scale of generative Artificial intelligence hits, especially in the Artificial intelligence of social media, where a person surrenders control over and disinformation from the attention market. It may trigger the term "Weaponized Skepticism," defined as the "intentional scattering of landmines in the epistemic commons," in the form of flooding the "epistemic environment with contradictory narratives, making truth only one among many disputed meanings." The ease with which generative artificial intelligence can be scaled allows malicious actors to manipulate ambiguity, contributing to suspicion and social cleavages and eventually to deep loneliness in individuals within the political order and amongst each other.

Conclusion

This study identified various negative and positive impacts of generative Artificial intelligence on democratic citizenship. The development of this technology has significant implications for democracy and citizenship. Generative Artificial intelligence develops through commercially motivated corporations holding substantial power over politics and the economy. It should be optimized, and the adverse impacts must be mitigated to make all Artificial intelligence technologies accessible and equitable. Citizens must be equipped and informed of appropriate skills, receive truthful data to function in this new environment and measure how regulation could limit the harm that generative artificial intelligence poses to functioning democracies. Rules on social media and Artificial intelligence are already underway; however, considering implications for democratic citizenship in this context would help protect the viability of democracies. Artificial intelligence is the growing power of generative Artificial intelligence.

References

[1] Bruce Ackerman and James S. Fishkin. 2002. Deliberation Day. *Journal of Political Philosophy* 10, 2 (2002), 129–152. https://doi.org/10.1111/1467-9760.00146.

[2] Joy Buchanan, Stephen Hill, and Olga Shapoval. 2024. ChatGPT Hallucinates Non-existent Citations: Evidence from Economics. *The American Economist* 69, 1 (March 2024), 80–87. https://doi.org/10.1177/05694345231218454.

[3] Jiawei Chen, Hongyu Lin, Xianpei Han, and Le Sun. 2023. Benchmarking Large Language Models in Retrieval-Augmented Generation. arXiv: 2309.01431. Retrieved from https://doi.org/10.48550/arXiv.2309.01431.

[4] Catalina M. de Abreu. 2024. Artificial intelligence and deepfakes take over Pakistan's elections. *France 24*. Retrieved March 26, 2024, from https://www.france24.com/en/tv-shows/truth-or-fake/20240208-artificial-intelligence-and-deepfakes-takeover-pakistan-elections.

[5] Don Fallis, 2021. The Epistemic Threat of Deepfakes. *Philosophy & Technology* 34, 4 (December 2021), 623–643. https://doi.org/10.1007/s13347-020-00419-2.

[6] Mohammadreza Farrokhnia, Seyyed Kazem Banihashem, Omid Noroozi, and Arjen Wals. 2023. A SWOT analysis of ChatGPT: Implications for educational practice and research. *Innovations in Education and Teaching International* (March 2023), 1–15. https://doi.org/10.1080/14703297.2023.2195846.

[7] Mirko Franco, Ombretta Gaggi, and Claudio E. Palazzi. 2023. Analyzing the Use of Large Language Models for Content Moderation with ChatGPT Examples. In *the 3rd International Workshop on Open Challenges in Online Social Networks*, September 4, 2023, Rome, Italy. ACM, Rome, Italy, 1–8. https://doi.org/10.1145/3599696.3612895.

[8] M. A. Griffin. 2011. Motivating Reflective Citizens: Deliberative Democracy and the Internal Deliberative Virtues. *Journal of Value Inquiry* 45, 2 (May 2011), 175–186. https://doi.org/10.1007/s10790-011-9276-y.

[9] Rafik Hadfi, Jawad Haqbeen, Sofia Sahab, and Takayuki Ito. 2021. Argumentative Conversational Agents for Online Discussions. *Journal of Systems Science and Systems Engineering* 30, 4 (2021), 450–464. https://doi.org/10.1007/s11518-021-5497-1.

[10] Nick Hajli, Usman Saeed, Mina Tajvidi, and Farid Shirazi. 2022. Social Bots and the Spread of Disinformation in Social Media: The Challenges of Artificial Intelligence. *British Journal of Management* 33, 3 (2022), 1238–1253. https://doi.org/10.1111/1467-8551.12554.

[11] Martin Hasal, Jana Nowaková, Khalifa Ahmed SaghArtificial intelligencer, Ussam Abdulla, Václav Snášel, and Lidia Ogiela. 2021. Chatbots: security, privacy, data protection, and social aspects. *Concurrency and Computation: Practice and Experience* 33, 19 (2021), e6426. https://doi.org/10.1002/cpe.6426.

[12] Soomin Kim, Jinsu Eun, Joseph Seering, and Joonhwan Lee. 2021. Moderator Chatbot for Deliberative Discussion: Effects of Discussion Structure and Discussant Facilitation. *Proc. ACM Hum.-Comput. Interact.* 5, CSCW1 (April 2021), 1–26. https://doi.org/10.1145/3449161.

[13] Sarah Kreps and Doug Kriner, 2023. How Artificial intelligence Threatens Democracy. *Journal of Democracy* 34, 4 (2023), 122–131. https://doi.org/10.1353/jod.2023.a907693.

[14] James H. Kuklinski, Paul J. Quirk, Jennifer Jerit, David Schwieder, and Robert F. Rich. 2000. Misinformation and the Currency of Democratic Citizenship. *The Journal of Politics* 62, 3 (2000), 790–816. https://doi.org/10.1111/0022-3816.00033.

[15] Taylor Matthews, 2022. Deep fakes, Intellectual Cynics, and the Cultivation of Digital Sensibility. *Royal Institute of Philosophy Supplement* 92, (2022), 67–85. https://doi.org/10.1017/s1358246122000224.

[16] Taylor Matthews and Ian James Kidd. 2023. The Ethics and Epistemology of Deep fakes. In *The Routledge Handbook of Philosophy and Media Ethics*. Routledge. 342-354. https://doi.org/10.4324/9781003134749-33.

[17] Spencer McKay and Chris Tenove, 2021. Disinformation as a Threat to Deliberative Democracy. *Political Research Quarterly* 74, 3 (September 2021), 703–717. https://doi.org/10.1177/1065912920938143.

[18] Jeremy Pitt. 2023. Chat Sh*t and Other Conversations (That We Should Be Having, But Mostly Are Not). *IEEE Technol. Soc. Mag.* 42, 3 (2023), 7–13. https://doi.org/10.1109/MTS.2023.3299450.

[19] Jared Schroeder. 2018. toward a discursive marketplace of ideas: Reimaging the marketplace metaphor in the era of social media, fake news, and artificial intelligence. *First Amendment Studies* 52, 1-2 (July 2018), 38-60. https://doi.org/10.1080/21689725.2018.1460215.

[20] Carl Mika, Lei Chen, Chengbing Wang, Sean Sturm, Sharon Rider, and Steve Fuller. 2023. Artificial intelligence and the future of humanity: ChatGPT-4, philosophy and education—critical responses. Educational Philosophy and Theory (June 2023), 1–35. https://doi.org/10.1080/00131857.2023.2213437.

Chapter 2

Democratized Generative AI — Development and Major Milestones

Dawn Sivan[1,2]
Veena Raj[3]
K. Satheesh Kumar[4]
and Rajan Jose[1,2,5,*]

[1]Center for Advanced Intelligent Materials, Universiti Malaysia Pahang Al-Sultan Abdullah, Kuantan, Pahang, Malaysia
[2]Faculty of Industrial Sciences and Technology, Universiti Malaysia Pahang Al-Sultan Abdullah, Kuantan, Pahang, Malaysia
[3]Faculty of Integrated Technologies, Universiti Brunei Darussalam, Bandar Seri Begawan, Brunei
[4]Kerala University of Digital Sciences, Innovation and Technology (Digital University Kerala), Thiruvananthapuram, Kerala, India
[5]Battery Research Center of Green Energy, Ming Chi University of Technology, New Taipei City, Taiwan, ROC

Abstract

The evolution of generative AI (GenAI) has transformed creativity and problem-solving by enabling automated content generation. This chapter examines the democratization of GenAI, focusing on its evolution and milestones such as open-source platforms, pre-trained models, and low-code tools that increase accessibility for non-experts and resource-limited individuals. The chapter highlights practical applications in various sectors; GenAI is applied to diagnostics and personalized treatments in healthcare, process automation enhances customer engagement with

[*] Corresponding Author's Email: rjose@umpsa.edu.my

In: Democratized Generative AI: Principles, Challenges and Applications
Editors: S. Balasubramaniam and Seifedine Kadry
ISBN: 979-8-89530-684-0

small businesses, and enhanced creativity in arts. These innovations overcome technical and financial barriers to enable the adoption of GenAI on a wider scale. However, democratizing GenAI brings its own sets of problems: algorithmic bias; ethical misuses; and governance gaps. Thus, the chapter concludes by pointing to the need for ethical safeguards, transparency, and inclusive design approaches to help lower these risks in the future.

Keywords: deep learning, scalability, human collaboration, automated decision-making, deployment, LLM, neural networks, transfer learning

1. Introduction

Generative AI, or GenAI in short, demonstrates a significant shift in the AI ecosystem, leading to a transformational way of technology interacting with the users and our views on creativity, productivity, and the very nature of knowledge creation [1, 2]. In simple terms, GenAI is a subclass of AI models, which uses large datasets to independently generate new data or content by discovering patterns. In contrast to traditional AI which focuses on classifying, analyzing, or retrieving known facts, GenAI models produce new outputs by predicting future items in a set or by combining learned knowledge in new ways [3]. Currently, GenAI can produce human-quality text, stunning visuals, or even music with compositions. For example, Generative Pretrained Transformers (GPTs) are remarkably impactful as they are "pre-trained" on large datasets [4, 5], and could be "fine-tuned" for specific tasks, such as text generation, complex question answering, or creative content drafting [6-8]. This capability to provide high-quality, contextually precise material has resulted in extensive implementation of GenAI in domains such as customer service [9, 10], education [8, 11], and healthcare [12, 13].

Now, imagine a situation of creating highly personalized advertisements in multiple languages for a microbusiness, generating custom art for a brand, or interpreting complex medical imagery to detect diseases becomes as simple as using a mobile app. This is where the democratization of AI comes in — a paradigm shift to make such powerful AI capabilities accessible to everyone, not just the technically sound or financially capable [14, 15]. Thus, powerful tools are freed from the hold of tech giants and AI experts; they are made available to small businesses, individual creators, and everyday users by lowering entry.

The democratization of AI has been driven by the creation of user-friendly, open-source frameworks such as TensorFlow [16] and PyTorch [17], providing the fundamental tools needed to allow almost anyone with an internet connection the ability to test, research, and build with AI [18, 19],. Open-source frameworks serve as an infrastructure layer, allowing both individuals and industries to customize and implement their AI models, which would not only change the way businesses run but also how research would be carried out by scholars. To give an example on the commercial side, small businesses are using apps such as ChatGPT to produce marketing material in a fraction of the time [20], and on the health side, AI-powered apps help clinicians diagnose illnesses from imaging data [12, 21], often without advanced computational skills. Such innovations are restructuring the options for people and organizations that – until now – did not have the capacity or skill set to meaningfully interact with AI technologies.

Recently, the rise of no-code and low-code platforms has significantly made AI more accessible, by letting users with little or no programming experience build and deploy AI solutions. Platforms such as Microsoft's Power Platform [22] and Google's Vertex AI [23] allow users to create AI-based applications through easy-to-use drag-and-drop interfaces, reducing barriers for small businesses, schools, and healthcare providers. Moreover, AI democratization could enable a non-expert to derive his or her customized machine learning models. For instance, Google's AutoML provides small enterprises with accessible interfaces that could easily use AI analytics in applications such as product recommendations or customer sentiment evaluation [24]. Another seminal example is Apple's CoreML, where developers bring AI capabilities natively into iOS applications and bring the execution of AI-driven functions onto mobile with no dependence on special computational hardware [25].

2. Development of Generative AI

This section is devoted to the timeline of Generative AI development, as illustrated in Figure 1.

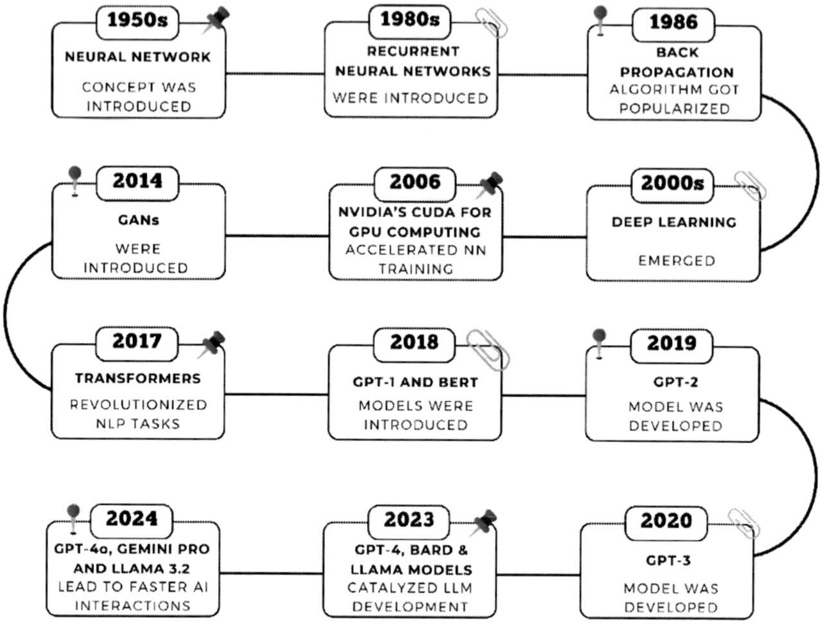

Figure 1. Milestones of Generative AI development.

2.1. Core Concepts in Neural Networks

Neural networks (NNs) build the foundation of generative artificial intelligence. Neural networks are mathematical models inspired by the human brain. These are designed to replicate learning and decision-making as humans [26, 27]. The idea of a neural network was first introduced with the perceptron in the 1950s [28]. The perceptron iteratively changes the parameters to learn and distinguish its inputs. However, the simplicity of the architecture and the high requirement of computational power made it difficult for these to be used in natural language processing and even in image processing tasks. The development of the backpropagation algorithm in the 1980s allowed neural networks to be fine-tuned, based on their errors at different levels to increase their accuracy [29]. Moreover, it enabled such networks to mine granular features of massive datasets [30, 31].

In the 2000s, the emergence of GPUs and their programming, particularly with the introduction of NVIDIA's CUDA toolkit [32, 33], and the development of open-source tools namely PyTorch and TensorFlow, made neural network training much simpler and faster. Additionally, this development made it possible for generative AI models to be creative, a feature that has remained infeasible for NNs thus far. The year 2014 brought a big leap in the form of Generative Adversarial Networks (GANs) [34]. These networks consist of two components: the generator creates outputs while the discriminator rates these outputs as either real or fake and repeatedly enhances the quality of the outputs (see Figure 2). Such an adversarial framework allowed GANs to produce high-quality images, music, and even 3D objects, finding applications in art, entertainment, content creation, marketing, virtual reality, and research [35-37].

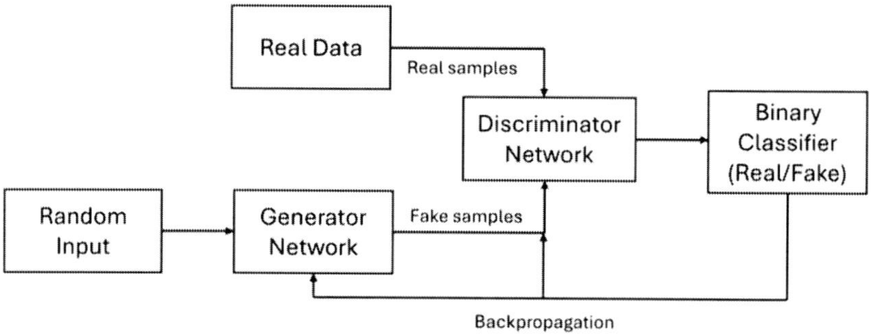

Figure 2. Simple GAN Architecture.

2.2. Transformer Models (BERT, GPT) and Their Significance

Ever since the work by Vaswani et al. [38], Transformer models have been one of the main innovations for AI, especially in NLP applications. The ubiquitously efficient use of models such as BERT (Bidirectional Encoder Representations from Transformers) [39] and GPT (Generative Pretrained Transformer) [40, 41] models led to the achievement of accuracy and effectiveness in language understanding and generation. Instead of sequence processing as in RNNs or LSTMs, these models understand the dependencies between words within a given textual sequence by applying self-attention.

In 2018, Google launched BERT, a model that considers the context on the left and the right of the words in a phrase to understand it. In that way, BERT could model complex language structures, making it useful for problems such as question answering and sentiment analysis. Furthermore, the release of BERT as an open-source model on platforms such as TensorFlow Hub made advanced NLP models widely accessible. This enabled developers and researchers to fine-tune BERT for specific needs with relatively low computational requirements, as in diverse domains such as research, aiding in processing scientific literature [42-44], and finance, helping to analyze textual data from financial reports [45].

The GPT, developed by OpenAI in 2023, expanded the Transformer framework for pretraining vast datasets and fine-tuning for specific tasks. Unlike BERT, GPT works mainly as a unidirectional model, generating text by predicting each next word based on prior context. The public releases of GPT-2 and GPT-3 contributed to its popularity, making these models a staple in chatbots, digital assistants, and content generation tools [46, 47]. Now, GPT-4 is advancing this trend, scaling transformer models to produce and organize information on complex topics [48].

3. Key Milestones in Democratizing Generative AI

3.1. Open-Source Platforms

The open-source AI movement has been the key to making powerful machine learning available to everyone so that they can experiment, create, and apply AI in several domains [49]. Open-source platforms such as TensorFlow (released by Google in 2015) and PyTorch (released by Facebook AI Research in 2016) were the game changers in this movement: industry professionals and researchers could create AI models without proprietary software.

TensorFlow supports neural networks, deep learning models, GANs, and Transformer architecture, thus researchers and developers can build complex models with ease [50, 51]. PyTorch further accelerated this democratization process by being flexible - its syntax is user-friendly and compatible with Python scientific computing libraries, so new researchers and students could learn and experiment with different AI models. PyTorch evolved by adding advanced features and simplifying model deployment in production environments, bridging the gap between research and applications [52-54].

Both TensorFlow and PyTorch have community-driven documentation, help forums, and tutorials, letting users of all levels use them. Moreover, these platforms keep evolving fast by incorporating user feedback and comments. Learning resources on GitHub and Hugging Face platforms have pre-trained models and tools working on these frameworks, so the users could experiment with GenAI models without heavy computational complexity [55, 56]. Furthermore, the extension of these platforms to enable cloud-based integrations – TensorFlow Extended (TFX) [57] and PyTorch Lightning [58] – made them more accessible and provided scalable resources for training and deployment of large models.

The availability of open-source datasets has also been a key milestone, providing large, diverse, and curated data for training robust AI models. Datasets such as ImageNet were the foundation for computer vision [59], while public datasets in healthcare such as EyePACS for diabetic retinopathy enabled diagnostic models [60, 61]. Beyond datasets, GitHub and Kaggle platforms foster community engagement through competitions and collaborative projects that accelerate AI research and applications.

In summary, open-source systems have been the key to GenAI democratization. By providing flexible, scalable, and community-supported frameworks, these have enabled everyone to access, create, and apply AI models. Open-source programming, easily available resources, and community-driven projects, all together, have made these platforms the catalyst for GenAI adoption, so that small organizations could automate tasks and researchers could build impactful solutions.

3.2. Case Study: Siemens and Democratization in Industry

Siemens is one of the best examples showing how big companies in traditional engineering and industrial fields could lead the way in making GenAI more accessible to everyone. When Siemens added AI to its digital environment, it made advanced analytics and GenAI available to itself as well as to other companies in the same field [62]. The cloud-based, open Internet of Things (IoT) platform developed by Siemens, called MindSphere (now known as Insights Hub), enables businesses to link their data and machines on a single platform [63]. It offers businesses solutions to use predictive maintenance, real-time monitoring, GenAI, and machine learning in quality control, thereby lowering the technological obstacles usually related to AI development in industrial environments. Thanks to this accessibility, AI democratization in industries enables even factory workers to employ AI technologies to make data-driven decisions and to ensure operational effectiveness. Using GenAI models taught on past data, for example, operators could forecast equipment breakdown in advance, increasing output and lowering expensive downtime.

Moreover, to promote an open innovation environment, Siemens has switched to working with start-ups and universities in the development of AI technology. Projects such as the Siemens AI Lab and partnerships with universities such as Carnegie Mellon University help research and development in GenAI. In turn, it provides the opportunity for smaller businesses to utilize modern tools. Democratizing AI in business focuses on inclusion and teamwork, allowing professionals to come up with new ideas, maintain long-term growth, and to adjust rapid technological changes.

3.3. Effects of Cloud Computing and Low-Code Tools

Cloud computing and low-code platforms have made GenAI more accessible, especially to non-technical audiences and small-sized businesses. Cloud computing enables users to use enormous computational capabilities when needed, thus eliminating the need for investing in expensive high-performance infrastructure. Key cloud service providers such as Google Cloud, AWS Sagemaker, and Microsoft Azure provide customized AI solutions in a single application, making it less complicated for small organizations, financially and technically, to manage large amounts of data sets and build generative models and execute applications [64, 65]. In addition, these cloud GenAI applications come with advanced auto-scaling and managed platform features which allow businesses to deploy applications capable of real-time data processing [66].

In short, low-code and no-code enhances the accessibility of GenAI by allowing users to create programs using drag-and-drop interfaces as opposed to having to write complex codes. As AI advances, the integration of low-code platforms with cloud computing will probably fuel further innovation and enable a broader audience to explore the applicability of AI in multiple fields.

4. Applications of Democratized GenAI

Several sectors are getting transformed with the widespread democratization of GenAI. This section investigates the three major fields where GenAI is applied – (i) health services, (ii) small and medium enterprises, and (iii) creative domains.

4.1. Health Services: Progress in Diagnosis and Treatment with AI Technology

GenAI is now an important part of modern healthcare and is rapidly changing the diagnoses and treatment techniques. By making AI more accessible, doctors could use modern diagnostic tools without much expense or learning complicated codes [67]. For example, with artificial intelligence (AI) powered medical imaging devices, doctors could easily and accurately interpret complex tests such as MRIs and X-rays. Medical imaging systems driven by artificial intelligence let doctors interpret, for example, sophisticated tests including MRIs and X-rays with more speed and accuracy. Enormous amounts of diagnostic radiology imaging data could be examined with deep learning, enabling radiologists to prioritize high-risk situations by producing quicker diagnostic predictions [68, 69]. Furthermore, pre-trained generative models could find patterns in images that human eyes might miss, aiding in the early detection of conditions including cancer, diabetic retinopathy, and cardiovascular disease [70]. This also helps resource-limited healthcare environments — including community hospitals and rural clinics — to offer quality diagnostic services.

Another significant application of GenAI in healthcare is the creation of synthetic medical data for the training and validation of AI models without endangering patient confidentiality. Artificial intelligence models could be developed using synthetic images or records that maintain the statistical characteristics of real data, even in the absence of extensive, well-labeled datasets [71, 72]. This approach solves one of the main challenges in healthcare AI adoption — the lack of high-quality labeled medical data — which facilitates the development of AI systems for several diagnostic tasks on a global scale.

Apart from diagnosis, GenAI is also advancing customized treatment plans. Artificial intelligence models could simulate possible reactions to various treatments by assessing the medical history, genetic profile, and real-time health data of the patient, thereby enabling clinicians to more precisely target interventions. Moreover, AI-driven drug discovery platforms make use of generative models to forecast novel medicinal materials, hastening the progress toward personalized treatments [73-75].

Democratized GenAI also supports telemedicine and virtual healthcare solutions, which have grown ever more crucial during global health catastrophes such as the COVID-19 epidemic [76, 77]. Generative models built with NLP and conversational artificial intelligence allow virtual assistants to engage with patients, answer medical questions, and even do symptom-based assessments [78, 79]. These solutions not only make healthcare more accessible, but they also make it easier for healthcare workers by automating routine questions and follow-up.

To sum up, democratized GenAI is changing healthcare by making diagnoses more accurate, letting patients choose their treatments, and making it easier for people to get good care. Using these apps, healthcare workers could improve patient outcomes, cut costs, and make clinical processes easier by incorporating AI into their daily work. This would make healthcare fairer.

4.2. Small and Medium Enterprises (SMEs): Democratized AI as a Catalyst for Innovation

AI democratization has revolutionized SMEs as now organizations with fewer technologies can innovate, improve the overall consumer experiences, and optimize standard operations without the need for in-house AI experts or investing in massive infrastructure [80]. By using low-code AI solutions and pre-trained AI models hosted on cloud platforms, SMEs could utilize AI for various applications such as customer service, marketing, content generation, and predictive analytics. For example, chatbots and virtual assistants built with generative models and cloud services allow SMEs to offer effective customer support round-the-clock to address repetitive questions and to target consumers with personalized recommendations based on their browsing history. GenAI could also help in diversifying advertisements, creating appropriate descriptions of goods and products, and other marketing and social media content for various market segments faster, easier, and cheaper than required previously [20, 81]. Moreover, AI predictive analytics allow SMEs to make predictions on asset trends and demands and enable them to control the stock level [82]. The SMEs could hence react readily to anticipated changes in marketing strategies or sales volumes and adjust their inventory, resulting in enhanced efficiency and competitiveness in a fast-changing marketplace.

In summary, democratized GenAI allows SMEs to streamline processes, improve involvement from consumers and investigate new market opportunities. With GenAI technologies, SMEs could compete more effectively, promoting a dynamic business environment that is devoid of constraints on innovation due to size or resources.

4.3. Creative Domains: The Role of AI in Artistic Pursuits, Music Composition, and Media Production

The democratization of GenAI helps artists, musicians, and producers by allowing them to change styles of artistic content and inspire creativity [83]. Artists could use GenAI tools to innovate and create multimedia content using tools such as DALL-E (images), GPT (text), and Jukedeck (sound or music) without much effort. Such tools push artists forward to merge digital innovation with traditional artistry, facilitating a new hybrid creative age.

Visual arts tools, with DALL-E and Midjourney as examples, allow visual artists to draw images from a given text and to experiment with their concepts, style, or compositions [84]. For music composition, AI tools such as Jukedeck and OpenAI's MuseNet give musicians the ability to create novel works spanning several genres [85, 86]. Such generative tools allow producers and musicians to create background music, experiment with configurations, or develop harmonies fit for specific moods, all of which could be modified for advertising, movie scores, and contents of social media. These tools democratize content creation by helping independent artists with limited resources from expensive settings or extra collaborators.

Generative AI has also revolutionized material creation in the media and entertainment sectors by automating processes such as audio editing, video generation, and scriptwriting. Advanced artificial intelligence models could create realistic speech, narratives, and even whole video sequences based on basic input cues, enabling artists to develop multimedia content rapidly and at scale. Particularly, AI helps creators create storyboards or script drafts, letting them effectively visualize scenarios and plan shots accordingly. Media industries also use GenAI to simplify tasks such as dubbing subtitling, and language translation, making content available to a worldwide audience at less expense. These tools enable independent producers — such as podcasters and developers of YouTube content — by granting them access to advanced media creation skills once limited only to sophisticated labs with lots of resources.

In short, generative AI in creative fields has unlocked immense opportunities in the world of artistic discovery and experimentation. This fusion not only redefines conventional creative processes but also makes a new generation of artists improvise their artistic vision, thereby shaping new heights in entertainment and culture.

5. Challenges and Risks in Democratizing Generative AI

While the democratization of generative artificial intelligence enables access to a larger spectrum of users and encourages innovation across sectors, this also poses complicated ethical, social, and technical problems and threats [87, 88]. Democratized AI, without careful consideration and responsible governance, could unintentionally feed biases, allow misuse, and undermine public trust. Dealing with these issues calls for a balanced strategy that promotes accessibility and inclusion while using protections to stop damage. This section explores the ethical and governmental aspects related to democratizing GenAI, stressing the need for transparency, fairness, and responsibility.

5.1. Ethical Considerations: Bias, Misappropriation, and AI Transparency

Bias is an important ethical challenge for generative artificial intelligence, stemming from training data, model architecture, and/or deployment settings. Generative models, especially those extensively utilized in open-source platforms, are trained on vast datasets that may reflect societal biases. For example, a model trained on primarily Western data might tend to favor Western linguistic patterns, cultural practices, or viewpoints. These biases could result in unwanted misconceptions among some populations, particularly in applications such as job recruitment, healthcare, and customer service [89-91]. To address bias, communities should be involved effectively in the development of these models, training datasets have to be carefully curated, and robust measures should be introduced to measure inequalities.

Misuse of content generated by GenAI is another ethical issue. Even though these tools are capable of generating realistic images, text, and music, the output content could be vulnerable to abuse, as in the deepfake technology [92, 93]. Videos could be fabricated convincingly to spread false information, to defame individuals, and to enter into privacy. It undermines the confidence of the public in media as fabricated content could even create risks of political harassment. Democratizing GenAI should include putting together clear usage guidelines, and technical safeguards such as watermarking and authenticity cheques, to prevent its misuse.

To address these ethical issues, transparency is essential, ensuring that the sources of training data, model behavior, and decision-making procedures are easily and publicly accessible. Improving transparency with GenAI includes creating explainable models, using interpretable metrics, and sharing model capabilities and constraints of GenAI with the public. Moreover, developers and companies should educate users, exposing the potential biases and risks to promote ethical use.

5.2. Governance: Who Regulates Democratized AI?

With the democratization of GenAI, challenges have risen in its governance as well, which requires effective systems to ensure responsible use [94, 95]. Currently, the responsibility of AI governance is shared among governments, international organizations, industry stakeholders, and AI developers. However, unlike other technologies, there are no global standards to regulate the ethical, social, and legal implications of GenAI, resulting in inconsistencies in its practice among countries [96, 97]. Notably, governments in certain countries have taken policy measures to protect user privacy, prevent bias, and enhance accountability while using GenAI. For example, the European Union's Artificial Intelligence Act [98] categorizes AI applications based on risk, imposing greater restrictions on high-risk uses such as law enforcement and healthcare.

Responsible AI development could also be driven by industry self-regulation. Companies such as OpenAI, Google, and Microsoft have set ethical guidelines and published transparency reports focusing on fairness, accountability, and transparency. Though similar business companies are capable of putting forward norms to regulate themselves, it is voluntary. Hence it is necessary to strike a balance between official control and self-governance to safeguard the unethical use of AI.

Global agencies such as the United Nations [99] and the OECD [100] have been developing global ethical frameworks for AI beyond national boundaries. However, AI governance on a global scale is still difficult to harmonize due to the cultural, political, and economic differences among countries. To sum up, democratization in GenAI calls for a hybrid approach of governance that integrates local, industrial, and global oversights to deal with its ethical and social issues while promoting innovation and responsible use.

Conclusion and Future Aspects

The democratization of generative AI has now changed the technological scenario by being accessible to people, small companies, and businesses all over the world, hence promoting innovation in medical, educational, and creative sectors, and so on. The milestones in the path of generative AI, particularly the developments of GANs and LLMs, have further expanded the scope of democratizing AI such that the tasks that required technical expertise earlier could now be achieved with simpler interfaces or through straightforward API calls. It has also increased the involvement of international communities with diverse cultural and linguistic backgrounds to employ and apply AI tools. The rise of open-source resources, the development of collective datasets, and the introduction of collaborative platforms also led to building AI systems serving varied needs and perspectives. However, the complexity of the questions on ethics, governance, and accessibility that democratizing AI brings needs careful attention to ensure its responsible use to the maximum.

The future of generative AI would be determined by a balanced ecosystem guided by the lights of responsibility, inclusiveness, and effective governance. Most importantly, processes for governments to strengthen initiatives that help align artificial intelligence with sustainable development goals have to be fostered in specific disciplines such as environment sustainability, agriculture, and education, among others. For example, these models could be used to ensure lean operations for industries, improve agricultural harvests, and deliver personalized education. However, the new issues that might arise as AI democratization progresses, including data ownership for generative AI models and responsibility in autonomous decisions, require more structured approaches and cooperative initiatives from users, industry stakeholders, and the government. Using the principles of collaboration, innovation, and ethical stewardship, generative artificial intelligence is indeed a catalyst in global advancement, ultimately leading to sustainable solutions and equal opportunities for everyone.

References

[1] Banh, L. and G. Strobel, Generative artificial intelligence. *Electronic Markets,* 2023. 33(1).

[2] Rafner, J., et al., Creativity in the age of generative AI. *Nat Hum Behav,* 2023. 7(11): p. 1836-1838.

[3] Feuerriegel, S., et al., Generative AI. *Business & Information Systems Engineering,* 2023. 66(1): p. 111-126.

[4] Zha, D., et al., Data-centric artificial intelligence: A survey. arXiv preprint arXiv:2303.10158, 2023.

[5] Gunasekar, S., et al., Textbooks are all you need. arXiv preprint arXiv:2306.11644, 2023.

[6] Engelbach, M., et al., Fine-tuning and aligning question answering models for complex information extraction tasks. arXiv preprint arXiv:2309.14805, 2023.

[7] Yang, X., et al., A large language model for electronic health records. *NPJ Digit Med,* 2022. 5(1): p. 194.

[8] Li, C., et al., Generative AI meets 3D: A Survey on Text-to-3D in AIGC Era. ArXiv, 2023. abs/2305.06131.

[9] Brynjolfsson, E., D. Li, and L. Raymond, Generative AI at Work. *SSRN Electronic Journal,* 2023.

[10] Townsend, D., Leveraging Generative AI Tools Like ChatGPT for Startups and Small Business Growth. Entrepreneur and Innovation Exchange, 2023.

[11] Dickey, E. and A. M. Bejarano. GAIDE: A Framework for Using Generative AI to Assist in Course Content Development. 2023.

[12] Shokrollahi, Y., et al., A comprehensive review of generative AI in healthcare. arXiv preprint arXiv:2310.00795, 2023.

[13] Abbasian, M., et al., Foundation Metrics: Quantifying Effectiveness of Healthcare Conversations powered by Generative AI. ArXiv, 2023. abs/2309.12444.

[14] Robertson, J., et al., Game changers: A generative AI prompt protocol to enhance human-AI knowledge co-construction. *Business Horizons,* 2024.

[15] Seger, E., et al., Democratising AI: Multiple Meanings, Goals, and Methods. *Proceedings of the 2023 AAAI/ACM Conference on AI, Ethics, and Society*, 2023.

[16] Abadi, M., et al. TensorFlow: A system for large-scale machine learning. in *Proceedings of the 12th USENIX Symposium on Operating Systems Design and Implementation, OSDI* 2016. 2016.

[17] Paszke, A., et al. PyTorch: An imperative style, high-performance deep learning library. in *Advances in Neural Information Processing Systems*. 2019.

[18] Lomonaco, V., et al. AI-Toolkit: A Microservices Architecture for Low-Code Decentralized Machine Intelligence. in *2023 IEEE International Conference on Acoustics, Speech, and Signal Processing Workshops (ICASSPW)*. 2023.

[19] Pati, S., et al., GaNDLF: the generally nuanced deep learning framework for scalable end-to-end clinical workflows. *Communications Engineering,* 2021. 2.

[20] Chuma, E. L. and G. G. de Oliveira, Generative AI for Business Decision-Making: A Case of ChatGPT. *Management Science and Business Decisions,* 2023.

[21] Pinto-Coelho, L., How Artificial Intelligence Is Shaping Medical Imaging Technology: A Survey of Innovations and Applications. *Bioengineering,* 2023. 10.

[22] Hodel, B., Microsoft Power Platform, in Beginning Microsoft Dataverse: Exploiting Microsoft's Low-code Database for the Power Platform, B. Hodel, Editor. 2023, Apress: Berkeley, CA. p. 1-20.

[23] Nawalgaria, A., et al., Operationalizing Generative AI on Vertex AI.

[24] Thirunavukarasu, A. J., et al., Democratizing artificial intelligence imaging analysis with automated machine learning: tutorial. *Journal of Medical Internet Research,* 2023. 25: p. e49949.

[25] Thakkar, M., Introduction to Core ML Framework, in Beginning Machine Learning in iOS: CoreML Framework. 2019, Apress: Berkeley, CA. p. 15-49.

[26] Andina, D., et al., Neural Networks Historical Review, in *Computational Intelligence: for Engineering and Manufacturing,* D. Andina and D. T. Pham, Editors. 2007, Springer US: Boston, MA. p. 39-65.

[27] Gurney, K., An introduction to neural networks. 2018: CRC press.

[28] Rosenblatt, F., The Perceptron: A Probabilistic Model for Information Storage and Organization (1958), in *Ideas That Created the Future: Classic Papers of Computer Science,* H. R. Lewis, Editor. 2021, The MIT Press. p. 0.

[29] Werbos. Backpropagation: past and future. in *IEEE 1988 International Conference on Neural Networks.* 1988.

[30] Simon, G., et al., Applying artificial intelligence to address the knowledge gaps in cancer care. *The oncologist,* 2019. 24(6): p. 772-782.

[31] Zaharchuk, G. and G. Davidzon. Artificial intelligence for optimization and interpretation of PET/CT and PET/MR images. in *Seminars in Nuclear Medicine.* 2021. Elsevier.

[32] Kirk, D. B. NVIDIA cuda software and gpu parallel computing architecture. in *International Symposium on Mathematical Morphology and Its Application to Signal and Image Processing.* 2007.

[33] Harris, M. J. Many-core GPU computing with NVIDIA CUDA. in *International Conference on Supercomputing.* 2008.

[34] Goodfellow, I., et al., Generative adversarial nets. *Advances in neural information processing systems,* 2014. 27.

[35] Striuk, O. and Y. P. Kondratenko, Generative Adversarial Neural Networks and Deep Learning: Successful Cases and Advanced Approaches. *Int. J. Comput.,* 2021. 20: p. 339-349.

[36] Alqahtani, H., M. Kavakli-Thorne, and G. Kumar, Applications of Generative Adversarial Networks (GANs): An Updated Review. *Archives of Computational Methods in Engineering,* 2019. 28: p. 525 - 552.

[37] Mukhiddin, T., W. Lee, and S. Lee, Generative adversarial networks and their application to 3D face generation: A survey. *Image Vis. Comput.,* 2021. 108: p. 104119.

[38] Vaswani, A., et al., Attention is all you need. *Advances in neural information processing systems,* 2017. 30.

[39] Devlin, J., et al. BERT: Pre-training of deep bidirectional transformers for language understanding. in *NAACL HLT 2019 - 2019 Conference of the North American Chapter of the Association for Computational Linguistics: Human Language Technologies - Proceedings of the Conference.* 2019.

[40] Brown, T., et al., Language models are few-shot learners. *Advances in neural information processing systems,* 2020. 33: p. 1877-1901.

[41] Radford, A., et al., Language models are unsupervised multitask learners. *OpenAI blog,* 2019. 1(8): p. 9.

[42] Sivan, D., et al., Advances in materials informatics: a review. *Journal of Materials Science,* 2024: p. 1-42.

[43] Olivetti, E. A., et al., Data-driven materials research enabled by natural language processing and information extraction. *Applied Physics Reviews,* 2020. 7(4): p. 041317-041317.

[44] Gupta, T., et al., MatSciBERT: A materials domain language model for text mining and information extraction. *npj Computational Materials,* 2022. 8(1).

[45] Araci, D., Finbert: Financial sentiment analysis with pre-trained language models. arXiv preprint arXiv:1908.10063, 2019.

[46] Lund, B. D. and W. Ting, Chatting about ChatGPT: How May AI and GPT Impact Academia and Libraries? *SSRN Electronic Journal,* 2023.

[47] Hakiki, M., et al., Exploring the impact of using Chat-GPT on student learning outcomes in technology learning: The comprehensive experiment. *Advances in Mobile Learning Educational Research*, 2023.

[48] Baktash, J. A. and M. Dawodi, Gpt-4: A Review on Advancements and Opportunities in Natural Language Processing. ArXiv, 2023. abs/2305.03195.

[49] Costa, C. J., et al., The Democratization of Artificial Intelligence: Theoretical Framework. *Applied Sciences,* 2024. 14(18): p. 8236.

[50] Pang, B., E. Nijkamp, and Y. N. Wu, Deep Learning With TensorFlow: A Review. *Journal of Educational and Behavioral Statistics,* 2019. 45: p. 227 - 248.

[51] Goldsborough, P., A Tour of TensorFlow. ArXiv, 2016. abs/1610.01178.

[52] Li, S., et al., PyTorch distributed. *Proceedings of the VLDB Endowment,* 2020. 13: p. 3005 - 3018.

[53] Fenaux, L., T. Humphries, and F. Kerschbaum, Gaggle: Genetic Algorithms on the GPU using PyTorch. *Proceedings of the Companion Conference on Genetic and Evolutionary Computation,* 2023.

[54] Boschin, A., TorchKGE: Knowledge Graph Embedding in Python and PyTorch. ArXiv, 2020. abs/2009.02963.

[55] Ait, A., J. L. C. Izquierdo, and J. Cabot, HFCommunity: A Tool to Analyze the Hugging Face Hub Community. *2023 IEEE International Conference on Software Analysis, Evolution and Reengineering (SANER),* 2023: p. 728-732.

[56] Dan, Y., et al., EduChat: A Large-Scale Language Model-based Chatbot System for Intelligent Education. ArXiv, 2023. abs/2308.02773.

[57] Baylor, D., et al., TFX: A TensorFlow-Based Production-Scale Machine Learning Platform. *Proceedings of the 23rd ACM SIGKDD International Conference on Knowledge Discovery and Data Mining,* 2017.

[58] Falcon, W. A., Pytorch lightning. *GitHub,* 2019. 3.

[59] Deng, J., et al. Imagenet: A large-scale hierarchical image database. in *2009 IEEE conference on computer vision and pattern recognition.* 2009. Ieee.

[60] Long, F., H. Xiong, and J. Sang. A Classification Method for Diabetic Retinopathy Based on Self-supervised Learning. 2024. Singapore: Springer Nature Singapore.

[61] Tariq, M., V. Palade, and Y. Ma. Transfer Learning Based Classification of Diabetic Retinopathy on the Kaggle *EyePACS Dataset.* 2023. Singapore: Springer Nature Singapore.

[62] van Giffen, B. and H. Ludwig, How Siemens Democratized Artificial Intelligence. *MIS Quarterly Executive,* 2023. 22(1).

[63] Interface News. *Measurement and Control,* 2016. 49: p. 298 - 305.

[64] Rajendran, P., et al., Comparison of Cloud-Computing Providers for Deployment of Object-Detection Deep Learning Models. *Applied Sciences,* 2023.

[65] Alla, S., et al., What is mlops? Beginning MLOps with MLFlow: Deploy Models in AWS SageMaker, Google Cloud, and Microsoft Azure, 2021: p. 79-124.

[66] Edward Korot, M., et al., Democratizing Clinican-driven AI: Self-training with Code-free AutoML and Public Data.

[67] Reddy, S., Generative AI in healthcare: an implementation science informed translational path on application, integration and governance. *Implementation Science,* 2024. 19(1): p. 27.

[68] Kermany, D. S., et al., Identifying Medical Diagnoses and Treatable Diseases by Image-Based Deep Learning. *Cell,* 2018. 172: p. 1122-1131.e9.

[69] Moawad, A. W., et al., Artificial Intelligence in Diagnostic Radiology: Where Do We Stand, Challenges, and Opportunities. *Journal of Computer Assisted Tomography,* 2022. 46: p. 78 - 90.

[70] Negi, A., et al., RDA-UNET-WGAN: An Accurate Breast Ultrasound Lesion Segmentation Using Wasserstein Generative Adversarial Networks. *Arabian Journal for Science and Engineering,* 2020. 45: p. 6399 - 6410.

[71] Ten Dam, W., et al., Representative Data Generation of Diabetic Retinopathy Synthetic Retinal Images. *Proceedings of the 2023 Conference on Human Centered Artificial Intelligence: Education and Practice,* 2023.

[72] Umer, F. and N. Adnan, Generative artificial intelligence: synthetic datasets in dentistry. *BDJ Open,* 2024. 10(1): p. 13.

[73] Shanehsazzadeh, A., et al., Unlocking de novo antibody design with generative artificial intelligence. bioRxiv, 2024.

[74] Bordukova, M., et al., Generative artificial intelligence empowers digital twins in drug discovery and clinical trials. *Expert Opinion on Drug Discovery,* 2023. 19: p. 33 - 42.

[75] Gao, K., et al., Generative Network Complex for the Automated Generation of Drug-like Molecules. *Journal of chemical information and modeling*, 2020.

[76] Bharti, U., et al., Medbot: Conversational Artificial Intelligence Powered Chatbot for Delivering Tele-Health after COVID-19. *2020 5th International Conference on Communication and Electronics Systems (ICCES),* 2020: p. 870-875.

[77] Huang, J. A., et al., Telemedicine and artificial intelligence to support self-isolation of COVID-19 patients: Recent updates and challenges. *Digital Health,* 2022. 8.

[78] Kini, N., et al., Improvement in medical consultation by using an AI-powered symptom assessment application (SAA). *European Journal of Public Health,* 2023. 33(Supplement_2).

[79] Falak, P. D. L., A Survey on Healthcare Virtual Assistant Using Generative AI. *International Journal for Research in Applied Science and Engineering Technology,* 2023.

[80] Rajaram, K. and P. N. Tinguely, Generative artificial intelligence in small and medium enterprises: Navigating its promises and challenges. *Business Horizons,* 2024.

[81] Baek, T. H., Digital Advertising in the Age of Generative AI. *Journal of Current Issues & Research in Advertising,* 2023. 44: p. 249 - 251.

[82] Pal, S., Advancements in AI-Enhanced Just-In-Time Inventory: Elevating Demand Forecasting Accuracy. *International Journal for Research in Applied Science and Engineering Technology,* 2023.

[83] Bengesi, S., et al., Advancements in Generative AI: A Comprehensive Review of GANs, GPT, Autoencoders, Diffusion Model, and Transformers. *IEEE Access,* 2023. 12: p. 69812-69837.

[84] Fathoni, A. F. C. A., Leveraging Generative AI Solutions in Art and Design Education: Bridging Sustainable Creativity and Fostering Academic Integrity for Innovative Society. *E3S Web of Conferences,* 2023.

[85] Sexton, T., MuseNet. *Music Reference Services Quarterly,* 2023. 26(3-4): p. 151-153.

[86] Dredge, S., Jukedeck hopes artificial intelligence can 'democratise music'. URL: https://musically. com/2017/08/09/jukedeck-artificial-intelligence-music (дата звернення 07.12. 2019), 2017.

[87] Wach, K., et al., The dark side of generative artificial intelligence: A critical analysis of controversies and risks of ChatGPT. *Entrepreneurial Business and Economics Review,* 2023.

[88] Kuck, K., Generative Artificial Intelligence: A Double-Edged Sword. *2023 World Engineering Education Forum - Global Engineering Deans Council (WEEF-GEDC),* 2023: p. 1-10.

[89] Ferrara, E., Fairness And Bias in Artificial Intelligence: A Brief Survey of Sources, Impacts, And Mitigation Strategies. ArXiv, 2023. abs/2304.07683.

[90] Weissglass, D. E., Contextual bias, the democratization of healthcare, and medical artificial intelligence in low-and middle-income countries. *Bioethics,* 2022. 36(2): p. 201-209.

[91] Akter, S., et al., Addressing Algorithmic Bias in AI-Driven Customer Management. *J. Glob. Inf. Manag.,* 2021. 29: p. 1-27.

[92] Shoaib, M. R., et al., Deepfakes, Misinformation, and Disinformation in the Era of Frontier AI, Generative AI, and Large AI Models. *2023 International Conference on Computer and Applications (ICCA),* 2023: p. 1-7.

[93] Ferrara, E., GenAI Against Humanity: Nefarious Applications of Generative Artificial Intelligence and Large Language Models. *J. Comput. Soc. Sci.,* 2023. 7: p. 549-569.

[94] Kenthapadi, K., H. Lakkaraju, and N. Rajani, Generative AI meets Responsible AI: Practical Challenges and Opportunities. *Proceedings of the 29th ACM SIGKDD Conference on Knowledge Discovery and Data Mining,* 2023.

[95] Allen, D., E. G. Weyl, and J. Bryant, The Real Dangers of Generative AI. *Journal of Democracy,* 2024. 35: p. 147 - 162.

[96] Hagerty, A. and I. Rubinov, Global AI Ethics: A Review of the Social Impacts and Ethical Implications of Artificial Intelligence. ArXiv, 2019. abs/1907.07892.

[97] Li, J., X. Cai, and L. Cheng, Legal regulation of generative AI: a multidimensional construction. *International Journal of Legal Discourse,* 2023. 8: p. 365 - 388.

[98] Meltzer, J. and A. Tielemans, The European Union AI Act. Bruselj: Brookings Institution, 2022.

[99] United Nations Educational, S. and C. Organization, Recommendations on the Ethics of Artificial Intelligence. United Nations Educational, Scientific and Cultural Organization, 2021.

[100] Galindo, L., K. Perset, and F. Sheeka, An overview of national AI strategies and policies. 2021.

Chapter 3

The Essential Concepts of Generative AI Democratization

M. Keerthana*
R. Sejana
Hemambika Krishnakumar
and D. Karthiga Priya
Department of Artificial Intelligence and Data Science, Easwari Engineering College, Chennai, Tamilnadu, India

Abstract

The Democratization of Gen AI: Changes in the method of developing, accessing, and applying cutting-edge artificial intelligence technologies by many users across different industries. The better understanding of these concepts is found in this chapter that is related to the essence underlying the democratization of Gen AI. The heart of Gen AI democratization lies such high-level, complex AI models like open-source platforms GPT (Generative Pre-trained Transformers) and GANs (Generative Adversarial Networks) that lead to a cloud service low-code/no-code environment. The chapter centres around the necessity to lower the hurdles imposed by computational cost. Technical knowledge and access enable individuals, small enterprises, and non-technical individuals to take advantage of the capabilities of Gen AI for many different tasks. Main drivers are open data sets. The pre-trained models and intuitive interfaces have fueled the spread of AI generation tools across the creative sectors such as healthcare, education, and so much more. The research also raises ethical issues and opportunities for

* Corresponding Author's Email: keerthum2003@gmail.com

In: Democratized Generative AI: Principles, Challenges and Applications
Editors: S. Balasubramaniam and Seifedine Kadry
ISBN: 979-8-89530-684-0

democratization. This chapter seeks to discuss the economic and social aspects of technological advancement. It also provides a balanced perspective of risk. Democratizing Gen AI is a significant stride toward making AI Innovation all-inclusive to provide creativity, productivity, and problem-solving ability among users across the globe.

Keywords: artificial intelligence, generative pre-trained model, generative adversarial networks, democratization, problem-solving

1. Introduction

Generative Artificial Intelligence (Gen AI) is a branch of artificial intelligence that generates content and synopses based on prompts or queries that resembles human-generated data. In contrast to traditional AI models that primarily analyze existing data to interpret outcomes, Gen AI creates original outputs, such as text, images, audio, and complex simulations, by learning patterns from training data [1, 2]. This technology has evolved from aiding small projects to revolutionizing businesses by providing comprehensive solutions, including expenditure analysis and planning. Core technologies behind Gen AI are Generative Pre-trained Transformers (GPT) and Generative Adversarial Networks (GANs), which have introduced novel perspectives and fostered innovations across various fields [3, 4]. These models have pushed the boundaries of AI, achieving feats once thought beyond human ingenuity. However, until recently, access to Gen AI models has been limited to organizations with substantial computational resources and technical expertise, creating a gap between technology and its potential beneficiaries [5, 6].

The democratization of AI aims to bridge this gap by making advanced AI tools accessible to the broader public, including individuals, small businesses, and non-technical users. The open-source models, cloud-based platforms, and low-code/no-code environments are key enablers of this democratizing influence, reducing technical and financial barriers. By broadening the access, democratized AI fosters Innovation, diversity, and the application of AI tools to solve complex societal challenges.

For example, in healthcare, democratized AI aids in early disease diagnosis and improved patient care. In education, it enables personalized learning experiences and public access to real-world knowledge [7]. Furthermore, democratization contributes to economic growth and societal well-being by ensuring that advanced AI tools are available to all. However, this democratization push also presents challenges, such as data privacy concerns, intellectual property rights issues, and biases in AI models [8]. Addressing these ethical concerns requires responsible use and robust frameworks to mitigate risks. This chapter explores the importance of democratized generative AI and examines its core concepts, accessibility factors, and ethical considerations, highlighting how it can promote innovation while navigating its inherent challenges.

2. Understanding Key Concepts in Generative AI

Generative AI is an advancement of Artificial Intelligence that produces new content from existing data by learning new patterns using machine learning algorithms to make predictions or classifications rather than analyzing existing data and extracting patterns to make predictions. In other words, Gen AI creates new data rather than interpreting the existing data. This technology covers a range of areas such as writing text pieces, crafting visual art pieces, making music, and coming up with product designs imitating human creativity by generating outputs that are fresh, logical, and sometimes challenging to tell apart from what humans create.

2.1. What Is Generative AI?

Generative AI refers to a group of algorithms capable of producing data points that were not present before by grasping and interpreting the patterns and relationships within the data it has been trained on. For example, when trained with thousands of landscape images, Gen AI models can craft a new and realistic landscape image. Hence, unlike the traditional machine learning model that merely predicts outcomes or categorizes existing data, this Gen AI model generates content that focuses on creativity, making it uniquely powerful in tasks where originality is key. In traditional machine learning, the tasks would be discriminative. These discriminative tasks are called categorizing or classifying the existing data points into predefined classes. For example, let us consider a model for image classification, which detects whether the given picture has a cat or a dog. Unlike classification models that classify a given input (a dog vs. cat image), generative ones create new data points resembling the training data. For example, it is not only recognizing an image of a dog, still the generative model learned about many images with dogs, it will create a new imaginary image of a dog that looks like a part of the same dataset. The generated image will be unique and won't exist in the real world. The functionality to create own data is the sole reason that generative AI is considered a creative and innovative technology.

The strength of generative AI is that it can understand the hidden patterns and relationships within the dataset instead of only memorizing the training data. For example, let us consider a model trained on handwritten digits. Gen AI learns the entire structure instead of just learning the pixels of each digit, like how the number 5 looks different from the number 2 and what makes them both unique yet similar in various contexts. By grasping these foundational structures, the model can generate new digits that preserve the characteristics of the original data, although they are fundamentally novel. This concept of pattern recognition and structural understanding enables generative AI to produce data that is coherent and plausible in its context. For example, the AI absorbs the grammar, context, and associations between words. Consequently, it can generate sentences that are not only syntactically correct but also contextually meaningful (which is essential) in a given language [9]. Generative AI depends on deep learning, a branch of machine learning that learns complex dataset representations by using multiple layers of neural networks. In a neural network, different features can be extracted from each layer of input data, enabling the model to understand the patterns at various levels of abstraction. In a deep neural network designed for image generation, the basic shapes or edges can be focused on in the initial layer. At the same time, features like color and textures are more complex and can be captured by the later layers. As complex datasets with complicated patterns can be easily handled by deep neural networks, they are well-suited for generative AI tasks like writing text pieces, crafting visual art pieces, making music, or generating realistic images [10].

Generative AI can be applied across various fields, such as:

- Natural Language Processing

Content generation, text summarization and completion, conversational agents

- Computer Vision

Image generation, image enhancement, video generation

- Art and Music

Style transfer, creative design, music composition [11]

2.2. Core Technologies: GPT and GANs

Generative AI falls under several architectures notably Generative Pre-trained Transformers (GPT) and Generative Adversarial Networks (GANs), both which are incredibly prominent. Novel applications abound for various technologies that converges on a common objective, yielding innovative and high-quality outputs [12].

2.2.1. Generative Pre-Trained Transformers (GPT)

The GPTs represent a revolutionary technological leap in the development of natural language processing – the ability to generate and comprehend language like never experienced. GPT was created by OpenAI. In contrast with the latest models of neural networks, GPT is built on the architecture of a transformer designed by Google in 2017. It works more effectively by processing the sequential data using mechanisms like self-attention. This architecture has utterly revolutionized AI models' handling sequential data in tasks such as machine translation and text generation [13]. GPT models leveraging transformer architecture excel at grasping language's intricate structure and nuanced meaning, generating remarkably human-like text. Traditional models such as recurrent neural networks (RNNs) had limitations while handling long text sequences. As the data is processed sequentially, it cannot handle long-range dependencies, i.e., remembering the words at the beginning of the sentences.

To overcome such limitations, the entire sequence can be processed by the transformers at once. GPT can grasp the connection between words despite their distance in the text [14]. Hence, the modern forms of natural language processing tasks are more advanced and less intensive than traditional models. The primary purpose of GPT is to construct text. The constructed text will appear as if it is composed by a human being. This work will be done by understanding how to predict the next word or the placement of a new word or a statement in relation to the preceding words. For example, if the input "Apple is a" is given to the GPT, the next word can be predicted as "fruit." It will be accomplished through pre-training by using vast datasets collected from various sources such as websites, books, and articles. GPT learns the context, structure, and patterns in pre-training, then the model is fine-tuned on smaller datasets or specific tasks to improve performance in areas like question-answering, summarization, or translation [15].

2.2.2. Generative Adversarial Networks (GANs)

Generative Adversarial Networks (GANs), developed by Ian Goodfellow and his collaborators in 2014, have been a game changer in the field of artificial intelligence and more specifically in deep learning because they allow for the generation of synthetic data that is highly realistic which resembles the original data. In contrast to typical machine learning approaches that seek to understand a problem based on available data or even predict some outcome, GANs are built to create data that does not exist but can very well be fabricated to seem real. The primary strength of Generative Adversarial Networks lies in creating remarkably realistic fake images, tapes, sounds, and even texts that one would have a tough time distinguishing from the actual authentic versions. This advancement has transcended several industries, including but not limited to arts, entertainment, and medicine, where quality synthetic data is in great demand. For example, GANs allow the designer to create images of people or objects that do not exist, which enhances the video game industry, computer graphics creation, or augmenting datasets for other ML models.

There are two main networks in GANs: the generator and the discriminator. As implied in the name, each of the two networks competes and collaborates in the training process. The generator network's primary objective is to generate artificial data like actual data. Such synthetic data can be an image, text, audio, or any other class of data that the respective GAN is supposed to produce. Initially, the generator makes a lot of poor-quality data, which, gets better over time as the network receives corrections from the discriminator. The generator aims at integrating data within a 'fake' audience such that even the best 'discriminator' cannot separate it from genuine data. A discriminator network must examine the input data and derive whether the data corresponds to the objective set (the actual dataset) or was instead created by the generator (the fake data). As time goes by, the discriminator becomes keener, hence developing its skills towards distinguishing real and fake data. In this way, it helps the generator refine its techniques because the generator's goal is to make the discriminator believe that the counterfeit data generated depicts reality [16].

3. The Role of Open Source in AI Democratisation

Open sources make the techniques and tools available to vast audiences, not limited to organizations or groups, with the democratization of AI sources that really breaks down barriers and demolishes monopolism of a single group taking over the advantages of the business and market by innovative and proprietary technology, enabling every participant to be involved in AI development.

3.1. Key Dimensions

3.1.1. Availability of Advanced AI Tools and Frameworks

Now, because of this free availability, the basic implementation of any such project may use open-source software essential for building and launching complex models. What are TensorFlow, PyTorch, and Keras, for instance? These tools helped many sophisticated hardcore coders to work with AI technology without the prohibitive associated costs. Any developers with the necessary skills can experiment with AI without licensing fees. Apart from the technical framework, these systems carry huge libraries, documentation, and pre-trained models that significantly reduce the difficulties for a newcomer to learn and help him build his own AI applications.

3.1.2. Enhancing a Collaborative Research Ecosystem

Wherever one tends to look, there are many collaborative platforms that aid in sharing knowledge, and that brings in a new order of creation in AI. Rather than working alone, the people engaged in research can help by working with developers and putting everything out in the open to tackle issues in AI much better and faster. This community approach facilitates quicker breakthroughs to crack solutions for the problems of the organizations. It is done by making available the existing work done by one group to be available for many shared communities. For example, hugging face transformers encourage a community around NLP (natural language processing). Developers add models and enhance the domain of NLP by saving time and resources, thus lowering the overall costs and carbon footprints. These models support everyday tasks in multiple modalities and researchers with various backgrounds to build up from one another's work in an iterative cycle of improvement.

3.1.3. Reducing the Entry Barriers and Promoting Experimentation

Quite a few startups, people, students, and specific organizations in economically underprivileged nations cannot experiment with AI since it is too expensive for them. This is because open-source AI makes advanced technology more accessible so everyone can explore and experiment with AI. For instance, OpenAI published its GPT-2 model so that people from all over the world could see how generative AI works and experiment with other models. This way, users can generate text and images with only a prompt. This made the technology accessible for the smaller companies and individual developers to incorporate powerful language models into their applications, thus countering and diminishing the dominance of some big AI providers. Democratizing generative AI also enables people to work on personal projects that would not be feasible in the first place when proprietary models are used since those often come with usage restrictions or costly cloud services. Prototyping new ideas becomes possible, and people see the complexity of AI without going into financial pressure.

3.1.4. Translations of Trust and Transparency in AI Systems

The other problem with AI is that it is not transparent about its operations. This lack of transparency creates a potential risk of bias and ethical dilemmas and fuels public mistrust. Making AI open-source lends itself to the support of transparency since users can view and be enlightened about the workings of the AI systems. Closed-source proprietary models confine insight, and the users find it challenging to learn how the models work. Transparency is what helps detect biases and fair treatment of AI systems. For instance, Google offers TensorFlow and IBM's AI Fairness 360 Toolkit, both of which have tools for bias detection and mitigation in datasets and models. Using the said open-source tools by researchers and developers would help audit models for their problematic aspects and allow better fairness within AI applications.

3.1.5. Compliance with Ethical Practices and Guidelines

While embarking on open-source AI developments, developers strictly observe certain ethical principles, which allow them to regulate the use of any model they seek to implement. The development of Open-Source AI systems, in sequel, includes broad and deep information on their algorithms. It also serves other purposes such as compliance with regulations like GDPR and the EU Ethical Guidelines for Trustworthy AI. Organizations guarantee that their application is ethical through re-architecting, sometimes entirely rearchitecting some parts of the model that meet particular criteria. The requirement of turning out to agree with the needs of standards is highly vital within medical sectors, such as for example, where organizations would need to adopt some standards so that they can protect the safety and privacy of patients more effectively.

3.1.6. Foster Local Development and Satisfy the Demands of Small Market Segments

Due to the availability and accessibility of the tools, even sectors that multinational companies would hesitate to develop any commercially inclined tools for because of their non-viable nature stand to benefit from the increasing use of creativity which many open-source systems encourage. It is particularly so since such a strategy is very much merited in areas that provide unique challenges or are otherwise under-serviced in terms of demand. For example, AI in agriculture-related studies was developed by some researchers to develop open-source AI models that help in recognizing crop diseases and controlling them as well as optimizing irrigation systems and application of pesticides. The outcome of this research is an enhancement in the quality and security of food globally. It also brought a change to the open-source tool within the education sector; it enabled the education sector to assist schools and other learning institutions in developing applications designed for the students to learn without making use of expensive goods.

3.1.7. Promote and Leverage Global Network for Assistance and Knowledge Sharing

GitHub, GitLab, Kaggle, and others offer software engineers the platforms to upload their code, datasets, and the structures of the models. It enhances the technology of bringing people together from various fields in a beneficial way. Global collaboration benefits the direct local developers by loaning the best practices and adjusting them to other regional contexts. For instance, Mozilla Common Voice and related endeavors represent the significant crowdsourcing potential that may be seen with speech data in enabling improvements to AI language models. Thus, taking audio samples for speech recognition technology improves performance and functionality in various languages and dialects, which, by and large, are left open for commercial solutions that are narrow in scope.

3.1.8. Ongoing Improvement in Quality and Security

AI tools and models in an open-source environment are constantly peer-reviewed. This facility allows bugs to be determined and corrected promptly.

Further on, more security and quality are brought into the system. Issues getting dealt with quickly make these models stronger and more reliable in the long run. Security improvements are also critical in AI because models can become susceptible to adversarial attacks or data leakage when not developed. Apache MX Net and OpenCV also make global contributions. Generally, there are three areas: safety updates, performance optimization, and bug fixing. These AI models are constantly improved, hence becoming a much more reliable source compared to proprietary technologies.

3.2. Advantages of Open-Source Software

- Cost-Effectiveness: The open-source tools and models avoid licensing fees and save long-term costs while investing in technological advancement for more people.
- Accelerated Innovation: Community-led development accelerates Innovation because developers can contribute for free inputs, modify, or improve existing work.
- Quality and Reliability: Peer review enhances quality since mistakes and weaknesses are addressed in the early stages, hence result in dependable and trustworthy software.
- Security and Privacy: Open source encourages open checking of the system by public which in turn helps reinforce security and faster improvements without compromising the user's privacy over his or her data.
- Customizability and Flexibility: The code can be freely taken and modified so that specific requirements are fulfilled without having to depend on a particular vendor.
- Collaboration and Information Sharing: The open-source nature has given way to a culture wherein developers share knowledge in very helpful ways in choosing what will improve performance.
- Interoperability and Standardization: Open standards allow for better integration which increases the usability acceptance and adoption of different systems.
- Scalability: Open source ceases to be an impediment growth of the organization which makes it applicable in both small and large deployments without straining.

- Transparency and Trust: It opens out a way for promoting transparency, and one can assess functionality, thereby earning trust, especially in sensitive industries.
- Digital sovereignty: Organizations will be able control over their data, when utilizing open-source solutions, and simultaneously, they are not too dependent on the large providers of tech services.

3.3. Open-Source AI Case Studies

3.3.1. TensorFlow (Google)

- TensorFlow is an open-source machine learning framework which is developed by the Google Brain team and released in 2015, that steadily risen to become one of the most popular and well-known machine learning frameworks in the world.
- Deep learning finds a reliable base in TensorFlow. It allows both the developers and the researchers to go to the next level and create complex models like image identification, processing visual or audio data and even in the field of robotics.

3.3.2. OpenCV (Open-Source Computer Vision Library)

- OpenCV is a computer vision/image processing library, which was made public in the year 2000. It is among the most frequently used libraries worldwide. OpenCV is capable of providing all the services required for activities like face detection, object motion monitoring, virtual reality and several other projects aimed at enhancing security, controlling robots, carrying out automobile-related functions and many more.

3.3.3. Apache MXNet

- MXNet is a deep learning framework by the Apache Software Foundation. It is an open-source adaptive and scalable framework for deep learning. This efficient and scalable structure was ideal for large-scale applications such as recommendation engines and voice recognition systems.

3.3.4. PyTorch (Facebook)

- The framework was released in open-source mode in 2016 and quickly became popular especially among the researchers.
- Dynamic computation graphs, which are very helpful to developers to try out advanced models without much difficulty, have become a hallmark of PyTorch.
- PyTorch is currently a common framework in both research and production, with applications ranging from academia.

3.3.5. OpenAI GPT Models

- The inception of GPT-2 by OpenAI and subsequent research studies involving GPT-3 has revolutionized the field of language modeling by providing 'complex' text generation models for use.
- The ability to freely operate GPT-2 enabled many people across the world to play with and incorporate generative language models in applications such as chatbots, automated content creation, and virtual assistants.
- Models inspired by GPT are now used in various industries and are helping boost customer service automation, media, and education.

4. Cloud Services and Low-Code/No-Code Environments

The advancements in cloud computing and the rise of low-code/no-code platforms have changed AI for the better by increasing its accessibility and diminishing the development and its integration obstacles. Historically, the process of constructing AI models required sophisticated hardware and were highly technical which meant only the well-resourced and knowledgeable organizations could afford AI. In various fields, cloud computing turned out to be a game changer with simple and easy to use development systems that targeted the end users of technologies. Thus, as most of these developments came over the internet, AI became used by a several users without the need to have any technical expertise. Therefore, by using cloud and low code/no code technologies, individuals and companies can develop, test, and deploy AI solutions in a short period and at a low cost.

4.1. Impact of Cloud Computing on AI Accessibility

Cloud-based solutions have revolutionized the world of artificial intelligence by enabling anyone with an internet connection to access high-quality computing resources. Previously, designing AI systems depend on some physical infrastructure which was expensive and more often out of reach for small and medium-sized businesses. This limitation can be mitigated through cloud services as they allow access to flexible resource management without the worries of investment in infrastructure. Amazon Web Services, Google Cloud Platform, and Microsoft Azure are the most notable examples as they provide an array of services for AI deployment on a pay-as-you-go basis allowing companies to build and run AI applications without significant hardware spending before the business begins. Most importantly, cloud services IaaS and PaaS afford the users the ability to be flexible in their computing needs which also increases accessibility of using AI. For instance, in case there is a model whose training needs more processing power, the user gets to change the resource allocation to more powerful resources temporarily and correspondingly get back after the training is over so that they only pay for resources that are used. This outweighs the cost factor enabling even the smallest of businesses to play around with AI technologies and implement them. Moreover, many cloud vendors have developed readymade solutions and tools, e.g., image recognition, language understanding, and data visualization, which allow users to turn on AI features quickly instead of having to create any models. Another vital effect of cloud computing on the availability of AI to users is its geographical scope. The introduction of cloud services removes such boundaries as location and makes it possible for developers and businesses from any place to work with complex artificial intelligence hardware and software. It is especially advantageous for areas that lack either the proper local infrastructure or talent in terms of AI creation. Resources are made available for everyone, and cloud computing enhances building an inclusive AI ecosystem in which AI can be created and enjoyed by all. In addition, most cloud AI services have inbuilt features available for data handling, training, and application of the model which eases the management workload for the users across the entire step of AI development process. These tools ease complex processes such as the preprocessing of data, training of models and tuning of hyperparameters that required skills specific to certain tasks. Due to the presence of such cloud services, companies can utilize ready-to-use processes that cut down the time of development thus increasing productivity making it impossible for only small teams to develop better artificial intelligence.

4.2. Exploring Low-Code/No-Code Platforms for AI Development

In the sphere of AI development, where the creation of various applications is active, low-code and no-code systems serve as a paradigm shift as they allow even the most non-technical of people to create AI applications. Development toolkits include drag and drop, readymade templates, and development cycle process automation features, which enable a non-programmer to build an AI application by piecing together components rather than writing copious amounts of code. The likes of the Microsoft Power Apps, Google's AutoML or Salesforce Einstein are examples of low-code/no-code solutions that bring AI to business analysts, marketers, and other types of non-engineer end-users. By removing the complex coding requirements and sophisticated technical structures, which would have otherwise held many users back, low-code/no-code platforms enhance the incorporation of AI. In this way, users can relate to AI in terms of what it can do and what it can achieve rather than how it functions. For instance, a business user only needs to provide the necessary data, choose an existing model, and indicate the results they need to create a predictive analysis model. This paradigm shift helps in reducing the time taken in understanding and developing such technologies, making it easy for people who are not technically inclined to use row AI within their processes. Ease of use is not the only quality of low-code/no-code platforms—these platforms encourage rapid testing and prototyping. Companies can research and test AI-dependent concepts, collect data, and improve investments without spending much. This flexibility is primarily helpful for small and medium enterprises when they have ideas that need to be verified before expanding them. In low-code/no-code contexts, teams can make an operative AI prototype in a few hours or days instead of weeks or months, enabling quicker decision-making and Innovation. Cross cutting teams are encouraged in the organizational set up of the low-code/no-code development platforms which allows teams with different capabilities to work on AI projects. It is because these platforms require less or no programming at all hence other personnel from various areas like marketing, finance, customer care etc. can also participate in the AI projects without having to know much of the technical aspects involved. This inclusion of many people helps in eliminating the hierarchy of technical teams and non-technical teams because everyone has a role to play thus the tailored

AI applications better fit the business and its users. Finally, numerous low-code/no-code solutions also fit perfectly into other existing software systems, making it easier to implement AI systems in practice. There is a simply explainable economic shift on these technologies as they tend to eliminate the classical limitations and encourage a far greater number of people and companies to utilize AI through cost savings, access to scalable infrastructure and more straightforward plastics.

5. Reducing Barriers: Computational Costs and Technical Knowledge

The emergence of artificial intelligence (AI) democratization has opened a new window of opportunities for numerous innovations targeting, in particular, non-technical end-users of AI. Historically, the design, development, and deployment of any AI-based systems was purely reserved for persons with professional training in data science, machine learning, computer science, engineering, and so on. Nevertheless, looking at the trends in the market for sustainable AI solutions, the time has come to remove such barriers to enable everyone, including individual users and organizations, to incorporate AI technologies into their regular practices for various purposes. The advancement of user-friendly interfaces forms one of the key approaches to minimizing such hurdles. These interfaces enable individuals who are not technically inclined, for instance, businesspersons, marketers, and product managers, to interact with AI without the need to understand the complicated workings of the technology. Such users get to play with AI models, change their parameters, and incorporate the models into their systems with very little code using visual programming tools and a drag-and-drop approach. Moreover, automation also contributes significantly to the democratization of AI. For instance, automation tools allow non-coders to build and deploy AI models without dealing with the complexities of model training, data preprocessing, or hyperparameter tuning. In so doing, rather than worrying about the technicalities, the users are concerned with the results and implementation of the AI system. At last, simplified workflows are being rolled out in a number of tools developed for AI and aims to improve the whole AI pipeline. With present templates and easy steps, users are able to move from raw data to useful information without much technical help. This has made it possible for many people, including those without extensive data science knowledge, to embrace AI within their daily tasks and business activities. By reducing these entry barriers, AI democratization guarantees that small firms, freelance creators, and individuals across different sectors can leverage the advantages of AI technologies irrespective of their level of technical expertise.

5.1. Challenges of Computational Costs in AI Development

One of the biggest challenges experienced in the growth and application of artificial intelligence (AI) technologies is the associated computational cost, which is prohibitive to many individuals and organizations. Complex AI models take a lot of time to train, meaning they require huge computational power, often involving high-performance, expensive hardware such as Graphics Processing Units (GPUs) and Tensor Processing Units (TPUs). These purpose-built resources are costly and energy consumers, thereby increasing the cost of working on AI projects. For instance, when it comes to the training of large architectures such as GPT-3 from OpenAI, it consumes an enormous amount of computing resources for a very long time, rendering it impractical and often beyond the capacities of many small and medium-sized companies. Another factor that contributes to operational costs is the scale and complexity of the datasets that are needed when training AI models. The sophistication of the models goes up, meaning that more training data is required to recognize the patterns and generalize them. Managing such a vast amount of information carries significant requirements for storage and data processing capabilities, which creates more costs. Bandwidth costs, on the other hand, tend to rise significantly, even though these costs may not be directly related to storage, primarily where data is handled on cloud-operated infrastructure, which charges for the transfer and storage of the data processed. In addition, it should be noted that the computational expenses are not confined to the initial training stage. The machine learning models also need to be frequently updated and retrained. New information that comes in requires this for precision and relevance. The bigger and more complex the AI models get, the more energy they will need, resulting in increased costs and undermining political and social causes for protecting the environment. For sustainability-centered organizations, the energy outlay associated with the development of AI can be pretty discouraging, as it goes against green strategies and promotes carbon emissions. As a result, it has become an important area of research to develop energy-efficient solutions for AI systems. Eventually, as AI technologies reach new heights, businesses need to follow the hardware pace as well, which is why they upgrade their infrastructure regularly. This phenomenon also often degenerates into long-term operational costs and aggravates the complexity of the systems. Bumping up the existing hardware also requires investing in the hardware and resources for optimizing the management processes of novel systems. Moreover, as processes become advanced, they usually require additional computing power than what is already available, which creates an upward spiral of expenditure for businesses with an ambition of leading in the AI frontier.

5.2. AI Democratization Strategies for Non-Technical Users

Considering the problem of computational expenses and the necessity of skills, numerous strategies towards AI democratization have been embarked upon to allow for the rise of non-technical users of AI technologies. These strategies aim at providing easy to use tools and services that limit the extent of expert knowledge required and thus lowers the costs of using AI. Increased popularity of cloud-based AI services is one of the most striking strategies. There are hundreds of such cloud services: Amazon Web Services (AWS), Google Cloud, and Microsoft Azure, all of which provide AI technology and infrastructure that are scalable, flexible, and affordable. Users can pay for access to exceptional computing facilities, thus avoiding the need to make significant equipment purchases. In cloud systems, options are scalable enough for training and deploying AI initiated by even the smallest enterprises without much expense. Additionally, these systems also have numerous standard trained models and various APIs for tasks such as image processing, speech & text recognition, and forecasting that even simple users can use and make AI solutions without much technical establishment required. Apart from cloud computing, the advent of low-code and no-code platforms has further expanded the reach of AI to its users. These platforms feature a user-friendly graphical interface enabling users to build, teach and put AI models to work using a drag and drop mechanism. This allows a person who is not versed in programming to build machine learning models, manage data processes, and even design an application that relies on AI algorithms. Google AutoML, Microsoft Power Platform, and IBM Watson represent of the growth of no-code/low-code means of developing AI solutions and enabling most people irrespective of their work; be it business, marketing or education to come up with AI tools relevant to their industries. Moreover, AI commercialized services and applications are being specifically intended for use by non-programmers hence they can use AI without the technology of coding. These applications come with readymade processes designed to make the complicated tasks easy to use, for example, sentiment analysis, predicting sales, dividing customers into groups matrix and others. Moreover, embedding AI features into other business applications is yet another approach being implemented to popularize AI. Businesses can apply AI features without requiring additional training or technical resources by integrating AI functionalities into typical software applications such as Microsoft Excel, Google Sheets or even CRM systems. These integrations allow users to conduct complex works such as predictive analytics or anomaly detection straight in their respective tools, thus democratizing the use of AI and making it less scary. These strategies are enabling AI democratization which ensures that both individuals and organizations can use AI tools and solutions in ways that were previously available only to IT specialists, thus opening up new ideas and innovations for a more enormous spectrum of users.

6. The Importance of Open Data Sets

6.1. What Is an Open Dataset?

Open datasets refer to the collections of data that are publicly accessible with minimal or no restrictions on usage. These datasets can be freely used, reused and redistributed by anyone with the exception of sharing-alike and attribution requirements. The terms "attribute" and "share-alike" are frequently used in Creative Commons licensing, denoting resharing in the same format and acknowledging the creator, respectively.

6.2. What Makes Data Open?

Open data must meet three criteria:

1) Accessibility: The data must be freely and easily accessible, such as through an open data portal, formatted, and in its entirety.
2) Reuse and redistribution: Permission should be clearly stated regarding reuse and redistribution, typically through a license.
3) Availability: Refers to the frequency with which data users or processors can access and use a dataset.

"Openness" spans free access to the data but its accessibility, understandability, and reusability, made possible by data platforms that enable easy downloading, good documentation, and friendly user interfaces.

6.3. Fair Data Principles

The FAIR principles were initially developed by the FORCE11 community in 2016, which have since gained popularity and attracted recognition from researchers, institutions, and data repositories across the globe over the years. FAIR refers to a set of guidelines that guide research to enhance data management and stewardship. Open data refers to the public availability of data. In contrast, FAIR principles suggest that in addition to being available, the data should be accessible and usable, integratable with other data and systems. Well-structured metadata achieves the significance of the FAIR principle with a preference for standard formats of a definite nature and proper documentation so that others may easily find, understand, and reuse.

6.4. Importance of Open Datasets in GEN AI Democratization

Open datasets will democratize generative AI, as it opens the gates for any researcher, developer, entrepreneur, and hobbyist in various fields to work with first-class data for testing, training, and generating AI models. It is an openness that could be seen in datasets that fosters innovation, equality, and transparency within the AI application landscape-all factors needed to ensure that a vast and diverse population will be impacted by generative AI. Gen AI models require humongous data to learn the pattern and generate new content. The expensive proprietary data needs to be completely wiped out, something that can pose a challenge for smaller firms, academic researchers, and individual developers. Using open datasets, developers can create AI models without the high-cost implications of data acquisition, enabling developers to experiment, innovate, and extend existing AI technologies. This makes the space of AI open to many participants, including those from resource-limited backgrounds or underserved communities.

6.5. Case Studies of Open Datasets Driving Innovation

6.5.1. Common Crawl: Powering NLP and Language Generation Research

Common Crawl is a non-profit that regularly collects petabytes of web data and publishes it as open datasets. Its data has become crucial for generative language models and natural language processing (NLP) because it includes a wide variety of web pages in several languages.

Democratisation and Innovation: Common Crawl has made possible the training of the vast NLP models like Facebook's RoBERTa and OpenAI's GPT series that involve massive and diverse datasets for generalization purposes. Common Crawl democratized the development of the generative language models, mainly on the access to resources available to small businesses and researchers alike, paralleling that which is accessible by the larger tech firms. It has enabled academics to study multilingual models and language comprehension more easily.

6.5.2. Leading Geographic Generative AI Applications: OpenStreetMap

It's an open community-driven project that has provided free and open geospatial data through community contribution and a freely editable world map. That's one of the sources of comprehensive geographic data available worldwide.

Democratization and Innovation: OpenStreetMap enabled the development of generative AI models for environmental monitoring, driverless cars, and many other applications for research, startups and developers. Notably, it has enabled research scientists to develop the models for navigation, urban planning, and disaster response without expensive geospatial data. Because open and collaborative, OSM also allows the data to be crowdsourced from people in various regions, along with community-driven research and innovation, democratizing the process of developing AI models with geographic awareness.

6.5.3. COCO (Common Objects in Context): Enabling Contextual AI in Image Generation

COCO is an open dataset containing photos of complex scenes and annotated with object labels, instance segmentations, and contextual information as shown in Figure 2. It was designed specifically to move contextual understanding forward in computer vision; it provides for a more nuanced Labeling of data than object labels alone.

Innovation and Democratization: COCO revolutionized the way people approached object detection, segmentation, and image captioning, and it led to more excellent accuracy models that could generate images in much greater detail. These rich COCO annotations have been utilized to increase contextual awareness in a large number of generative models and applications in augmented reality and autonomous driving, among others, while also creating accessible data for students and researchers in an academic setting to develop and benchmark generative models with contextual understanding that would otherwise require high resources to produce or access privately.

7. Ethical Considerations in AI Democratization

Ethics in AI usage concern the principles of fairness, accountability, and transparency. These aspects prevent biases, ensure that the decisions made by AI are accountable, and make the whole operation of AI systems transparent and explainable to the users. Fairness prevents discriminatory practices to the users, ensures that human oversight is confirmed by accountability, while transparency enables trusting and verification of outcomes by AI. Governance of AI involves creating and implementing frameworks, policies and best practices that guide the ethical use of AI technologies. This includes establishing standards for data collection, addressing biases in AI systems, complying with regulations and fostering inclusive development practices. As AI becomes more embedded in critical processes, from healthcare to finance, the risks associated with bias, lack of transparency and accountability failures become more pronounced.

7.1. Fairness and Bias

Issue: With increased accessibility of AI tools and large datasets to people, there, a danger that the resultant AI models inherited social biases or even worse is a mechanism to perpetuate those biases if the AI is trained on less diversified or even skewed datasets. AI systems may inadvertently perpetuate stereotypes or unfairly treat marginalized groups.

Implications: The democratized AI efforts will have to build their foundations on diverse, representative datasets, thus creating fair and equitable AI systems. Moreover, it is also a necessity to be transparent with regard to the data sources, data collection practices, and model biases as well so that the developers can see these potential concerns of fairness issues and take the necessary action.

7.2. Data Privacy and Protection

The problem with open data and open-source models is that the data might be extensive and sensitive in nature, thus raising issues of privacy. Standard practice with data anonymization, although it doesn't necessarily eliminate risks of re-identification or use, becomes less effective as models grow increasingly complex.

Implications: Responsible AI democratization should come with clear privacy standards, anonymization techniques, and consent practices. It is upon the developers to have straightforward guidelines on how to handle data responsibly-mostly in terms of information that may pertain to individuals within the dataset. Furthermore, regulatory frameworks such as the EU GDPR have much to do with making sure these standards are enforced.

7.3. Intellectual Property and Plagiarism

Issue: Accessible generative AI models raise questions about who owns AI-generated content and whether producing such content could result in plagiarism. Without clear guidelines, the democratization of AI is likely to enlarge infringement of IP rights, as it certainly will once "generative models" produce "work" that simulates copyrighted material.

Implications: the legal and ethical frameworks should be established to spell out ownership in AI-generated content, mainly if we are talking about art, music, or literature. In addition, such development of responsible training models should prevent the learning from copyrighted materials without permission to respect IP rights while making possible innovation.

7.4. Autonomy and Human Supervision

Issue: As access to systems-as-a-service becomes more effortless, people will cede decisions that previously required human judgment to AI systems. That will further blur and potentially diminish individual control over personal or organizational choices without proper oversight.

Implications: Ethical AI democratization demands considering the salience of human oversight and maintaining systems that respect individual autonomy. Human intervention mechanisms and being open about how the AI model arrives at its decisions will ensure that users are still in control of the AI output and consequences for personal and professional lives.

7.5. Misinformation and Social Impact

Issue: Democratization of generative AI raises a set of concerns on the spreading of misinformation, as wider accessibility will open doors to hyper-realistic forgeries and customized ones from pictures to words, and it leads to erosion of trust in information, entrenchment of polarization and manipulation.

Some of the above effects can be prevented by educating the users on responsible content development and AI literacy. Other design features that observe whether the AI contents are artificially generated and labelled can stop AI-contents. Partnership between AI providers and social media platforms can also be used to check and control the distribution of the generative content in attempts to ward off harmful effects.

Implementing Ethical AI governance involves overcoming several challenges:

- Dynamic Regulation: AI technology evolves rapidly, making it challenging to create regulations that keep pace. Adaptive and flexible regulatory approaches are needed.
- Global Standards: Establishing global standards for AI ethics and governance helps support consistent practices across different regions and industries.
- Stakeholder Engagement: Engaging a wide range of stakeholders, including technologists, ethicists, and the public, is crucial in developing comprehensive governance frameworks.

These are some examples of the real-world application of AI ethics and governance:

Healthcare: systems employing AI systems must respect and ensure the privacy of patients, with their consent being upheld so that the data should be used ethically and transparently.

Finance: In finance, the AI could identify crime like fraud and avoid settling a blame on specific persons.

Employment: There must be an oversight of the use of AI in recruitment such that it is not discriminatory in nature based on gender, race, or another protected characteristic.

8. Social and Economic Impacts of AI Democratization

The social and economic implications of AI democratization reach far beyond the ethical sphere, implying significant changes like work, industry structure, and accessibility of knowledge and resources.

8.1. Job Creation and Transformation

Impact: With the general availability of AI resources and tools, this brings innovation opportunities with new job creation, mainly in tech-intensive areas like AI design, data science, and ML engineering. Democratization further allows people from other disciplines to access AI technologies for applications across fields, creating hybrid roles that can bridge AI skills with industry-specific expertise-for example, AI in agriculture or education.

Challenge: The establishment of new jobs, thereby creating new job opportunities, makes democratization speed up automation that can threaten existing industries and eliminate jobs. Additionally, AI tool usability also can enhance adoption under freelance and gig-based employment models within technology industries, affecting stability in jobs and employee benefits.

8.2. Enhanced Education and Skill Development

Impact: Democratized AI will open access to education through open-source tools, online tutorials, and web courses-so learners from almost any part of the world will be able to learn AI skills. There will be a fantastic enabler to enable people to acquire competencies in machine learning, data science, and AI ethics and translate that into something as valuable as building a better workforce with a lifelong learning mindset. The democratization of AI tools will enable educational institutions to open up this learning opportunity to flow into their curricula and provide much more experiential learning.

Challenge: AI growth might take place so rapidly that skill gaps emerge where workers must constantly upskill to remain relevant. Access to educational resources to learn about AI in many places requires digital literacy and access to the internet, leaving out some sections of society.

8.3. Empowerment of Small and Medium Enterprises (SMEs)

Impact: Democratization of AI will enable small and medium enterprises to make provisions for AI in their operations at affordable costs with efficiency, productivity, and competitiveness. For example, marketing, customer service, analytics tools that are powered by AI enable the small enterprises to give levels of service that others could only achieve with more prominent companies. This helps SMEs scale more rapidly, driving innovation on the ground.

Challenge: The fact that democratization brings a lot of advantages also leads to the market becoming saturated from excessive adaptation of similar AI-driven strategies and diluted differences. Small business companies will also face problems with the implementation and the maintenance of the AI tool, failing which they cannot manage these tools that are technically beyond their level.

8.4. Enabling Local Problem-Solving and Providing Unique AI Solutions

Impact: AI democratization allows communities and local organizations to focus on region-specific problems with AI's help. For instance, it can be used by a rural community for local conservation of the environment, health, or education initiatives. Local actors can tailor solutions that meet local needs through access to open AI tools and datasets, which might not even be noticed by more extensive, centralized models for those specific problems.

Challenge: The local AI solutions can be done with a good intent. However, proper education on how to use AI ethically and how to protect their data would be a need for individuals. At times, a community may face funding or sustainment issues concerning project funding or sustaining AI activities.

8.5. Support for Humanitarian and Non-Profit Sectors

Impact: AI openness can scale the possibilities to very easily use AI for humanitarian purposes without heavy resources among NGOs and non-profits. For example, open AI tools may be used in the analysis of data related to disaster response, disease prediction, or poverty reduction scenes and contribute toward solving societal issues in data-driven ways.

Challenge: Non-profits and humanitarian organizations might have to address some problematic ethical dilemmas related to using AI in specific sensitive areas, such as health or crisis management. And to crown it all, since these free resources are based on an abundance of cutting-edge AI capabilities, their complexity or extent will likely be relatively restricted compared to entities with proprietary access to more advanced AI.

Democratizing artificial intelligence holds enormous potential for social and economic transformation but only where there is serious contemplation to optimize gains without increasing the difficulties associated with the exercise. Democratized AI brings robust empowerment elements to the fingertips of individuals and communities worldwide through equalizing measures that uplift education, embolden local problem-solving, and decentralize innovation. Equitable access, sustainable infrastructure support, and responsible practices in deployment are crucial to ensure that democratized AI is only a wholesome force in society.

9. Balancing Risks and Opportunities

To navigate the challenge of AI democratization, one must also pay attention to the benefits and threats that AI accessibility affords. On the positive side, the inverse scaling of AI access allows many people and organizations, including small businesses, researchers, and the creative sectors, to use resources available only to large corporations. This facilitates innovation and enhances efficiency, as well as providing alternative methods of tackling challenges within, for example, health systems, addressing global warming and education. Nonetheless, when such phenomena as non-expert end-users of AI tools are experienced, the risk of adverse effects also increases. To achieve this, it is essential to have detailed rules and educational programs as well as structures that facilitate the use of AI without causing damage. In such an instance, designing tools that are easy to use and understand and introducing restrictions will help to ensure that the goals of AI application for the masses are achieved without the adverse effects of disregarding morals or privacy of individuals.

9.1. Identifying Potential Risks in Democratizing AI

In hiring trends and even in criminal justice systems, such flawed models may lead to outcomes that harm society by subjugating already marginalized classes. The bias addressing is not only from employing diverse sets of training data but also routine checks on the models, installing and incorporating fairness metrics to monitor the damages caused by the skewed models. The widespread adoption of AI may cause overreaching personal boundaries or expose system vulnerabilities to hackers. Organizations need to practice and emphasized the very best practices of management of data, safe keeping and use of encryption in storage of data to safeguard user data and ensure that rules such as GDPR and CCPA are complied with. Another major challenge is posed by the ownership of intellectual property. As AI system approaches tend to be more open and available to users sharing their works with such systems, the notions of ownership of such works and originality begin to waver. Using generative AI to create and share content like copyrighted material without authorization may result in copyright infringement cases and hate towards AI. There must be some mechanism for fixing these issues, for example, defining ownership of AI-created content and implementing watermarking and licensing. Issues of explainability problems and transparency of algorithms are also important in the context of AI democratization. For those users who lack expertise, AI models are frequently "black boxes" because it is impossible to understand the reasoning behind their predictions. The absence of such transparency can diminish trust in the AI system in question, particularly in sensitive areas such as healthcare, finance, and the legal profession. To address this, the developers should include explainable AI (XAI) techniques, so that the end-user can understand the processes and the reasoning behind the AI decisions and provides means of explaining the level of agreement and the trust in the model. Additionally, there exists the concern that AI would be misused or weaponized. Generative models' risk being employed to make deep counterfeit, synthetic media, and misinformation which could endanger public security, social order and democracy. The ability of individuals to create realistic images, sounds and moving pictures that do not exist is a readymade tool for many fraudulent and injurious operations. This problem needs to be resolved by introducing restrictions on the use of artificial intelligence coupled with ethical principles and their enforcement. Finally, disruption in the economy and workforce will likely rise as an unavoidable risk. The risk of unemployment increases even more as more industries automate tasks with their hands, especially those that do repetitive tasks. Quite the opposite, the democratization of artificial intelligence is likely to create more inequalities because it will streamline more jobs in quick adaptive sectors. There must be systems put in place by the state, educational institutions, and enterprises exhibiting a joint effort to retrain people to change their occupations to those which AI will not easily invade; occupations that will involve human effort, abuse of natural creativity and emotions. In the final analysis, it is possible to view the attempt to highlight the risks associated with the democratization of artificial intelligence as the first step toward developing rational policies, ethical norms, and legal regulations. On the one hand, broad access to AI technologies must be encouraged; on the other, measures must be implemented to ensure that such technology is used fairly, safely, and responsibly so that its benefits are maximized, and its adverse effects are contained.

9.2. Strategies for Mitigating Risks while Promoting Innovation

The widespread use of artificial intelligence encourages creativity and, as a result, bears inherent dangers. To manage these threats, mitigation of both acute and systemic issues should not be considered one-dimensional. In this regard, an essential element is the establishment of ethical limits using of AI through formulation of appropriate policies. The principles call for justice, openness, and responsibility which are the vital components in the creation of reliable AI systems. Such approaches should be integrated within the AI creation and utilization phases to assist AI developers and users in assessing the effects of their innovations on society and reducing the adverse side effects. A further strategy worth mentioning is the investment in explainable AI (XAI) technology. XAI enhances the interpretability of AI models, enabling the users, even non-users, to appreciate the reasoning behind the output produced by the AI systems. This is paramount in health, financial and legal services because the areas deal with high-risk decisions that necessitate clarity. In addition, giving users the capabilities to see and understand the logic in the AI decision-making enhances confidence in its use responsibly as well as decision-making. Data governance and privacy protection measures have an essential role in addressing the risks of both data misuse and privacy breaches. Implementing measures to ensure the privacy of individuals such as the General Data Protection Regulation or the California Consumer Privacy Act requires compliance of these systems with AI. In this way, organizations should consider installing protective measures, such as safekeeping, concealing sensitive data, and making the data ready for use only in an encrypted form. In addition to this, embedding privacy-by-design principles into the AI systems at the start helps in managing compliance and reducing any breach risks, thus widening the use of AI without fear of insecurity. Frequent auditing and bias alleviation measures help seek to address the likely fairness and bias problems that arise with AI. This entails constant monitoring of the models for potential bias, training the models on representative datasets, and including fairness metrics in the development process. Such evaluation by external parties helps to ensure that the integrity and fairness of the AI are maintained, especially in sensitive applications such as employment or justice. Further inclusion of bias mitigation tools and employment of inclusive datasets reduces even further chances of any discriminatory outcomes, hence fostering innovation for the good of all. Encouraging joint efforts and engagement in public-private partnerships may alleviate risks associated with the advancement of AI.

For example, governments, industry, and academia can work together to establish standard norms, provide access to databases, and conduct research on the responsible usage of AI. Such exercises, however, facilitate diffusion of knowledge and promote faster developments, while reducing the likelihood of abuse by focusing the expertise on the creation of beneficial AI. They also encourage accountability and enable governance by allowing interested parties to oversee the progress of AI and its conformity to social standards. Another significant approach is to educate and empower the users, particularly the non-technical users. They will be more inclined towards using AI responsibly without abusing it and will promote creativity safely and ethically. Accessibility to these resources, AI democratization is on the rise, thus reinforcing security measures against illegal access and use like the creation of deepfakes is reasonably necessary. Developers in AI need to employ security measures such as content-aided technologies, watermarking, and detection techniques to help restrict abuse but at the same time encourage creativity and education through use of such technologies. Finally, encouraging ongoing regulatory enforcement and adaptive measures ensures that the movement of artificial intelligence in democratizing society is in line with the demands of society as technology advances. In addition, it is also essential that the government and other advisory authorities have such rules, which can change with the advancement of the trend in regulations on artificial intelligence, to avoid policies that are too aggressive and adventurous, which inhibit creativity and innovation for safety reasons. This allows for controlled and integrated development of new AI applications within specific boundaries, which enables innovators to play around and develop responsibly without hindering growth and use. These measures, when implemented, help find common ground between providing access to AI technology and making sure that the associated dangers are contained. Promoting appropriate practices, embracing openness, and focusing on the education and safety of users allows the responsible development of AI that opens new therapeutic possibilities without crossing certain ethical thresholds and risking society's mission in the diverse users' interest.

10. Future Trends in Generative AI

The democratization of AI presents enormous opportunities and challenges, the effects of which vary from one individual to another. For over two decades now, the diffusion and rapid evolution of AI systems have been a blessing, and in the past decade, the democratization of AI systems has developed positively. Out of many causes that shape the attitude towards AI democratization, the most prominent are the position of a person, the sector of the economy, and the level of knowledge about artificial intelligence. The future of AI will be more inclusive, as there are likely to be more people able to get and use AI-related tools in different sectors. From an economic standpoint, the progression of the democratization of AI is expected to bring about gains in productivity and promote innovation. More and more corporate players are adopting AI technology thus it will be easier for organizations to enhance operational efficiencies, reduce the costs and make better data-based decisions. Furthermore, as even the low-cost competitors start using the high-end AI tools, the landscape will shift leading to more innovation and growth of the market. Such universal absorption is predicted to not only enhance the economy's expansion but also increase the level of employment in advanced technological development including AI, the latter self-evidently stimulating the growth of business activity and the prospects of its diverse branches. In the end the democratization of AI will help create a more competitive, effective and inventive world economy.

10.1. Emerging Technologies and Their Potential Impact

10.1.1. Quantum Computing and AI

Quantum computing greatly influences the area of artificial intelligence by enabling the faster and more complex processing required. This progress might elevate AI applications such as implementing more complex challenges in healthcare, transport, or even science.

10.1.2. Edge Artificial Intelligence

As a result of the increased usage of devices like cellular handsets, Internet of Things (IOT) devices, wearables, etc. can perform AI processing on the edge. The development of applications that are driven by short time-to-market and emphasize privacy more will emerge. This tendency is almost ready to spur the creation of clever, region-specific solutions in a managed or decentralised environment such as, without limitation, healthcare, automotive engineering, smart cities, etc.

10.1.3. The Role of AI Technologies in Biomedical and Life Sciences

The application of generative artificial intelligence (AI) and machine-learning (ML) tools and techniques is on the rise in sectors like analysis of health records for patients, personalized medicine, drug discovery, and genomics. These technologies have made it possible for researchers and clinicians to provide treatment specific to patients based on their genes, background, or their medical history. This model includes the drug design of compounds that do not exist, the classification of data to reveal unseen predispositions to diseases, and the construction of treatment strategies that maximize their benefits to the patients. This trend in the healthcare system is not only beneficial in improving the outcomes of the treatment of patients, but it is also functional in improving the processes involved in the development of drugs.

10.1.4. Brain-Computer Interfaces (BCIs)

The brain-computer interface (BCI) signals the turning point in human-machine interaction. These systems are already sophisticated and yet growing as they help an individual communicate by appreciating brain functions which in turn work at transforming pictures into movements which can control equipment such as computers, prosthetic limbs, or even fantasy-loaded video games. The BCI hierarchy is endless; in particular, they provide beneficial options for disabled people and strive for their development increasing autonomy and accessibility of assistive devices. Likewise, the entertainment and gaming industries are anticipated to be heightened by the evolution of BCIs for a better and more satisfying experience. Use BCIs to enhance medical rehabilitation by integrating patients into the process of restoring motor functions using neurofeedback training; BCI therapies have evolved for further improvement of patients suffering from stroke and spinal cord injury.

10.1.5. Synthetic Data Generation

Considering the increasing demand for quality data and the need for more robust design data in different sectors, the exploration of synthetic data creation has emerged as a significant activity. This new perspective focuses on generating artificial data sets that vary from real data sets in many ways except for individual features. Synthetic data generation results in the production of data, which is used to train algorithms or statistical models without revealing private information. This method aids not only the repeated training cycle of the machine learning systems but also accelerates the development of AI technologies in all spheres.

Conclusion

The democratization of generative AI is reshaping technological innovation by making advanced AI tools accessible to diverse industries and communities. Open-source platforms, cloud services, and low-code/no-code environments are breaking technical barriers, empowering individuals and businesses to harness AI's transformative potential. Despite challenges like bias, intellectual property concerns, and data privacy, robust frameworks can ensure fairness and ethical use. Generative AI has the potential to boost creativity, productivity, and economic development while making its advantages accessible to small businesses, entrepreneurs, and underrepresented communities. By promoting equitable access and addressing disparities, the goal of "AI for all" can be realized, empowering AI to tackle global challenges effectively and pave the way for a more inclusive and fair future.

References

[1] Vaswani, A., Shazeer, N., Parmar, N., Uszkoreit, J., Jones, L., Gomez, A. N., ... & Polosukhin, I. (2017). Attention is all you need. *Advances in Neural Information Processing Systems,* 30.

[2] Brown, T. B., Mann, B., Ryder, N., Subbiah, M., Kaplan, J., Dhariwal, P., ... & Amodei, D. (2020). Language models are few-shot learners. arXiv preprint arXiv:2005.14165.

[3] Goodfellow, I., Pouget-Abadie, J., Mirza, M., Xu, B., Warde-Farley, D., Ozair, S., ... & Bengio, Y. (2014). Generative adversarial networks. *Communications of the ACM,* 63(11), 139-144.

[4] LeCun, Y., Bengio, Y., & Hinton, G. (2015). Deep learning. *Nature,* 521(7553), 436-444.

[5] Benaich, N., & Hogarth, I. (2021). The State of AI Report 2021. State of AI.

[6] Yang, Q., Liu, Y., Chen, T., & Tong, Y. (2019). Federated machine learning: Concept and applications. *ACM Transactions on Intelligent Systems and Technology (TIST),* 10(2), 1-19.

[7] Choi, J., Schuetzler, R., Woo, J., & Huh, J. (2022). Democratizing artificial intelligence: Opportunities, challenges, and implications. AI & Society.

[8] Floridi, L., & Cowls, J. (2019). A unified framework of five principles for AI in society. *Harvard Data Science Review,* 1(1).

[9] Gauthier, J., & Smith, B. (2017). Exploring the creative potential of generative algorithms. *Computational Creativity and Artificial Intelligence.*

[10] Kingma, D. P., & Ba, J. (2015). Adam: A method for stochastic optimization. *International Conference on Learning Representations (ICLR).*

[11] Elgammal, A., Liu, B., Elhoseiny, M., & Mazzone, M. (2017). CAN: Creative Adversarial Networks, Generating" Art" by Learning About Styles and Deviating from Style Norms. arXiv preprint arXiv:1706.07068.

[12] Parikh, A., & Tsvetkov, Y. (2017). Deep generative models. *Synthesis Lectures on Artificial Intelligence and Machine Learning,* 11(2), 1-182.

[13] Vaswani, A., Shazeer, N., Parmar, N., Uszkoreit, J., Jones, L., Gomez, A. N., ... & Polosukhin, I. (2017). Attention is all you need. *Advances in Neural Information Processing Systems,* 30.

[14] Brown, T. B., Mann, B., Ryder, N., Subbiah, M., Kaplan, J., Dhariwal, P., ... & Amodei, D. (2020). Language models are few-shot learners. arXiv preprint arXiv:2005.14165.

[15] Kingma, D. P., & Welling, M. (2014). Auto-Encoding Variational Bayes. International Conference on Learning Representations (ICLR).

[16] Thankaraj Ambujam, S. (2024). Power quality enhancement in the wind energy distribution system using HHO algorithm based UPFC. *Journal of the Chinese Institute of Engineers*, *47*(6), 732-752.

Chapter 4

The Democratic Route to Generative AI: Balancing Ethics and Innovation

A. Ashwini[1,*]
V. Kavitha[2,†]
S. Balasubramaniam[3,‡]
and Seifedine Kadry[4]

[1]Department of Electronics and Communication Engineering, *Vel Tech* Rangarajan Dr. Sagunthala R&D Institute of Science and Technology, Avadi, Chennai, Tamil Nadu, India
[2]University College of Engineering, Kancheepuram, Tamil Nadu, India
[3]School of Computer Science and Engineering, Kerala University of Digital Sciences, Innovation and Technology, Digital University Kerala, Thiruvananthapuram, Kerala, India
[4]Department of Computer Science and Mathematics, Lebanese American University, Beirut, Lebanon

Abstract

Generative AI technologies have become the most promising future applications in various fields, including arts and entertainment, healthcare, science, etc. However, the growth of these technologies has now accelerated, posing ethical questions such as bias, privacy breaches, fake news, and the control of power. This chapter mainly explores the democratic principles that can be effectively integrated with generative AI, thereby creating and fostering innovation and creativity. The

* Corresponding Author's Email: a.aswiniur@gmail.com
† Corresponding Author's Email: kavinayav@gmail.com
‡ Corresponding Author's Email: baluttn@gmail.com

In: Democratized Generative AI: Principles, Challenges and Applications
Editors: S. Balasubramaniam and Seifedine Kadry
ISBN: 979-8-89530-684-0

democratic values integrated into this AI system ensure progress, thereby nurturing the platform that can be designed, governed, and deployed for many applications. The chapter explores the real-world uses of democratic oversight in the framework of artificial intelligence and puts forth a strategy that encourages accountability, inclusion, and integrity. It looks at how individuals, governments, businesses, and civil society may work together to create laws that protect AI from adverse effects while promoting innovation. Participatory methods of decision-making, as well as broad policy structures, may be used to promote a more fair distribution of AI. It accelerates the advantages while reducing dangers like biased algorithms and privacy violations. The chapter also outlines new legislative initiatives that show how democratic approaches might effectively guide the further development of AI technology. It also outlines how responsible AI deployment is where human rights and social wellness are prioritized and can arise from creating an appropriate equilibrium among ethical concerns. This chapter can effectively drive technological advancement. In the end, the chapter concludes that democratic governance gives the most robust and flexible framework for negotiating the intricacies of generative AI, guaranteeing that the more general objectives of justice, equity, and prosperity for everyone are in line with powerful technology.

Keywords: bias, decision-making systems, democratic governance, ethical balance, generative AI, human-centered design, privacy, technological advancement

1. Introduction to Democratic Generative AI

Generative AI is an innovative concept of artificial intelligence that generates new content ranging from texts, images, music, and even scientific solutions. It has recently exploded onto the scene of technological advancement. According to the present writers and authors, the innovation generated by generative AI is revolutionary. It offers opportunities to create something new that washes out the issues of ethics, governance, and technology management at a societal level. Within this changing landscape, there appears to be a unique need for a democratic approach to generative AI. It helps build a generative AI that is in the public's interest. Democratic generative AI generally refers to the values of democracy, which are inclusiveness, responsibility, and openness, and are incorporated into the decision-making systems surrounding AI generation and deployment [1].

Democratic generative AI represents a new way for that massive power to be distributed, away from the hands of giant corporations and governments and towards solutions that are open and democratic instead. Reflective of this approach is a submitted contention that implicated stakeholders such as policymakers, technologists, civil society, and interested citizens be engaged in setting appropriate improvements for new AI technologies that do not worsen existing systemic methods. It aims to achieve a better synergy between demand for technological advancement and provisions for limited rights, and rightly so, to utilize generative AI when its decision-making benefits are set to be less biased across society. Future democratic models can assist in preventing inevitable social risks in AI technologies, ranging from bias to misinformation and privacy invasion. In this way, democracy can ensure openness and responsibility when using generative AI in development, increasing people's confidence. Furthermore, this approach offers a structure for putting up protection measures, government surveillance, and a code of conduct that reflects societal norms.

2. Role of Democratic Values in AI Development

The global population based on democratic values like openness, responsibility, cooperation, and justice defines the principles of artificial intelligence technologies. Because AI systems are virtually creeping into some of the most sensitive sectors of society, including healthcare and criminal justice, it is essential to ensure that principles that will safeguard the rights of all residents are used when designing and implementing such systems [2]. Democracy offers significant insights into the types of AI systems that should be developed to serve society, and it restricts who makes them from leveraging too much power. It is especially crucial, as the learning systems can amplify existing bias or introduce new types of discrimination.

Accountability is a democratic idea that ensures AI systems are transparent and then be examined by the public. In application, this also implies that the foundations of how a decision is made, why it is executed, and in what structures AU commences its decisions must be shown. Transparent models also have the advantage that the models can be audited systemically for potentially harmful biases. An AI system is designed when it functions with its algorithms, where the decision-making process is often unclear to the public, which may cause harm at one time or maybe unethical [3]. Democratic governance of AI development would entail openness by design, providing a framework in which oversight bodies can determine if the AI system in place conforms to ethical benchmarks or societal norms. This contribution is equally vital to democracy as it consists of two intertwined values: inclusiveness and fairness. AI systems ought to be created in a way that encourages them not to perpetuate the forms of social bias from minority groups. Decision-making should be best as a democratic process that invites many participants and lifts the biases of many voices. The various roles of the democratic generative AI are shown in Figure 1.

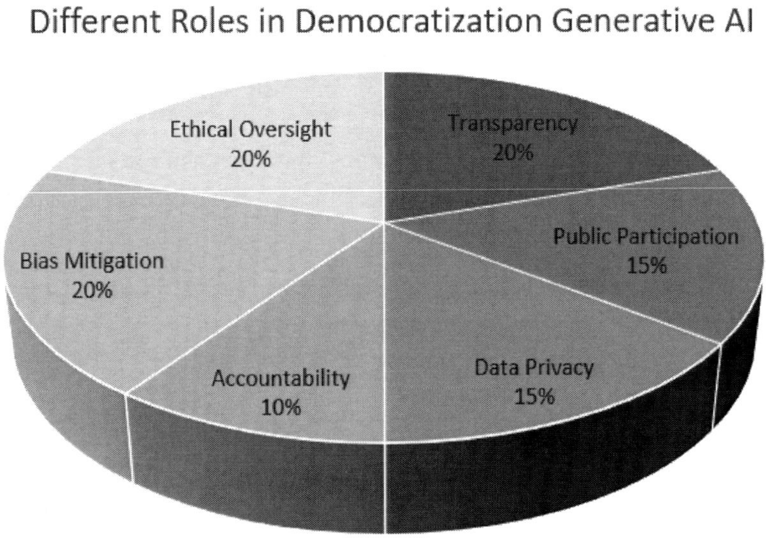

Figure 1. Various roles in Democratic Generative AI.

It does not make it fair if a democracy generates legal obligations, making unfair treatment illegal and granting equal access to the technical advancements of artificial intelligence in economic, social, and political terms [4]. When these values are maintained, the advancement of AI can advance in a particular direction that can capture the overall objectives of giving justice to all via generally acceptable changes to human society.

2.1. Transparency

Transparency ensures that AI decision-making is transparent so the public can easily comprehend it. It helps detect bias, errors, or adverse effects in audits.

2.2. Accountability

Accountability intends to hold developers and organizations accountable for AI outputs [5]. It allows for the setup of correcting errors or undue bias in the application of artificial intelligence. It limits ethical distortions about control bodies and regulatory standards.

2.3. Inclusivity

Inclusivity encourages participation from various groups within the development of AI and from underrepresented parts of society. It ensures that full advantage of all AI technologies is fully embraced by equally distributing them across society's strata.

2.4. Fairness

Fairness promotes the development of distinctive AI systems that address individuals and groups of individuals. It eliminates bias, which means AI algorithms cannot negatively impact specific vulnerable populations in society. Benefits focus on improving and closing the gaps between the various groups that lack the resources to access developments in AI technology fully.

2.5. Public Participation

It engages discussions and decision-making processes concerning the regulation and governance of AI by citizens and civil society. It primarily contributes to the more inclusive discussion of relevant policies for AI's effects on society that make up the populace. It also ensures that artificial intelligence is developed while keeping societal values in mind and for the well-being of the populous, not just for a few at the top.

2.6. Ethical Safeguards

It creates the foundations for integrating requirements for AI systems about human rights and relevant ethical norms [6]. Safeguards ensure that the AI interventions are constructive and respect their privacy, autonomy, and other freedoms. It proposes mechanisms balancing powers to avoid improper use of AI.

2.7. Equitable Innovation

Innovation introduces checks and balances that make it impossible for society to be overridden by attempts to advance technology [7]. It also prevents AI power from being overly concentrated in a single set of hands like one company or Government. It also develops beneficial AI reinforcement to societal objectives, reducing harms that may tip the scale against democracy or human rights.

3. Need for Democratic Generative AI in Balancing Ethics and Innovation

With the advancement of generative AI, new possibilities of change in industries or sectors such as Creative Arts, Healthcare, Education, etc., are generally considered. Nevertheless, these developments also pose significant ethical concerns regarding themselves and their application, such as distributional bias, invasion of privacy, anonymity and responsibility, and the use of AI innovation [8]. The generative AI should be developed in such a way that it should benefit society, as shown in Figure 2.

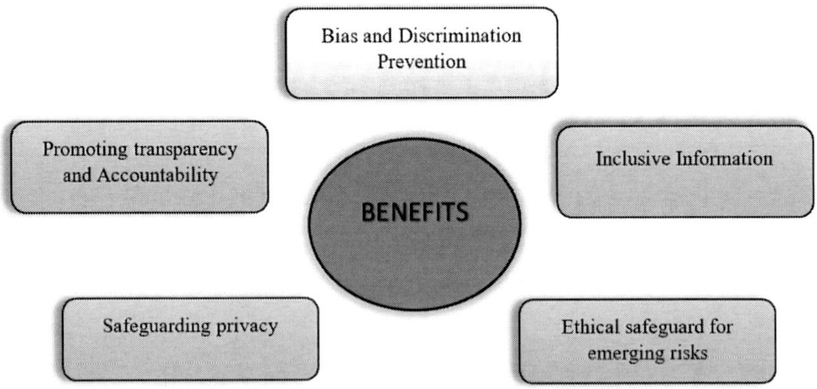

Figure 2. Benefits of Democratic Generative AI.

3.1. Preventing Bias and Discrimination

Biases can also be frozen into the generated AI models when trained on biased and selective data sets as a machine. Democratic are marginalized communities that are primarily composed of racial and ethnic minorities that are systematically oppressed by AI-driven technologies [9]. It proves that building AI develops a highly diverse society.

3.2. Promoting Transparency and Accountability

Democratic AI directly implies that, for AI decisions, the user or the regulator must be able to know how the technology works. Discovery AI models eliminate the problem of opacity of the AI model, where the decision-making logic behind AI outputs is unclear [10]. The democratic approach creates responsibility concerning AI developers and deployers so that they are answerable for the results of its systems.

3.3. Safeguarding Privacy

One striking aspect of generative AI is its ability to create highly targeted content. However, it requires the usage of private information. Wherever a democratic system of Government is adopted, the dignity of an individual's privacy is protected by the Constitution [11]. Rules, norms, and laws should be established to protect the freedom of data subjects in the context of AI systems and ensure that their data is not misused or handled insecurely.

3.4. Inclusive Innovation

The democratic approach to generative AI creation is considered an invention for the general good of society. It has several advantages because the development of AI technologies has become more diverse and dependent on creativity and viability, which are responsible for the public good. This guards against the monopolization of applying AI by either the large technology firms or nations alone.

3.5. Ethical Safeguards for Emerging Risks

As generative AI enhances complexity, novel ethical issues like AI-generated fake news and copyright infringements are featured. A democratic approach supplements the moral requirements for handling these challenges by establishing the structural measures for utilizing artificial intelligence and preventing deleterious impacts and technological advancements. Ethical considerations allow innovative processes that contribute to the betterment of society without compromising society. The proposed democratic approach in generative AI provides a safe midpoint in the fight between ethics and innovation. Through the indoctrination of principles of democracy in developing AI governance tools, the world can prime itself for a generation in which such powerful tools will be universally advantageous.

4. Principles for Democratic Generative AI Governance

The growing use of Generative AI needs to be governed by a set of principles that will conform to the democratic advantages of the technologies, which the entire society will feel. Democratic AI governance is for the efficiency of AI regulation based on open and participatory methods, integrity, and accountability [12].

4.1. Transparency and Explainability

Transparency is another core competencies approach that is applicable based on the principles of democracy. AI systems must also be transparent to the people to achieve the desired transparency and honesty. This implies that the processes involved with AI systems should be explained to the engineers who develop the systems and non-specialists who are on the receiving end. People, customers, and authorities should be able to track how data is gathered, analyzed, and used to make decisions, mainly when such decisions affect people or communities. Explainability enables scrutiny of the outcomes produced by AI systems, leading to an understanding of the results of AI decisions [13]. It helps to be questioned, reviewed, or adjusted if needed to build trust in the AI systems.

4.2. Inclusivity and Participation

Democratic AI governance tries to get as many people involved as possible, including technology experts, policymakers who may or may not be technologically literate, and the general public [14]. AI is only as objective as the people or datasets, including the members of marginalized groups of AI, and is involved in creating and implementing these systems. It can be done by addressing a broad range of domestic issues within the democracy, thus enhancing regulatory equity utilization of AI and protection against discrimination or harm to individuals.

4.3. Accountability and Ethical Oversight

Accountability is a foundational aspect of any democratic rule system. It also ensures that the people who design, implement, and decide on the use of AI are accountable. An organization should have guidelines on how to avoid bias in the algorithm, privacy infringement, or other negative externalities [15]. Ethics must be empowered to regulate and make mandatory guidelines for human rights and ethics in AI systems.

4.4. Fairness and Equity

Generative AI is, therefore, beneficial when appropriately applied; if not regulated well, it will deepen other societal vices. In the case of the democratic model of AI governance, it is necessary to observe two principles of equality of access and the representation of the AI's benefits [16]. Specifically, the generation of ethical artificial intelligence would generate new or existing prejudices based on race, sex, and economic class. It also means ensuring the financial benefits of AI technologies go to the general public. If governance allocation in AI is done fairly, it may also help prevent societal rifts from widening further. The key principles of democratic generative AI governance are shown in Figure 3.

This approach merges the dual agenda of innovation and risk prevention so that AI will be a double-edged sword, leading only to desirable outcomes relying on AI as an instrument that will support society while steering away from making its calamity.

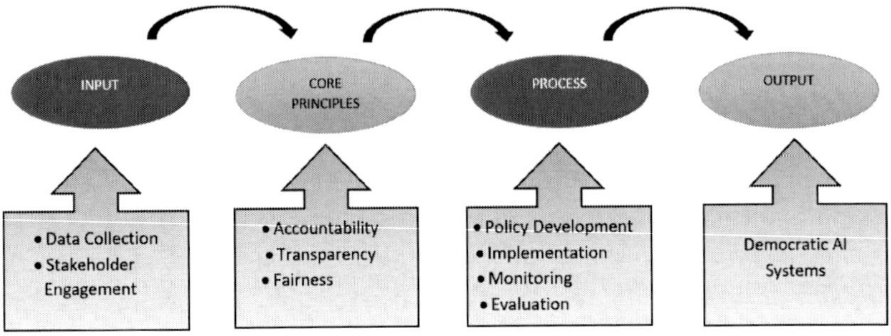

Figure 3. Principles of Democratic AI Governance.

5. Regulatory Frameworks

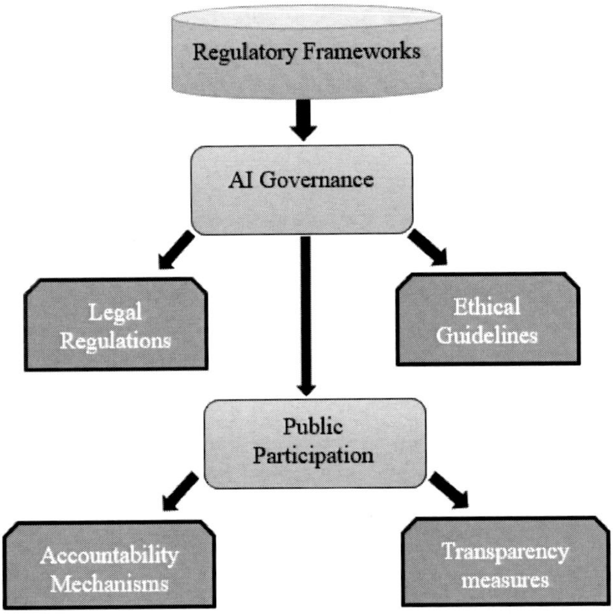

Figure 4. Regulatory frameworks.

Regulative measures are crucial to guarantee that the creation and use of AI solutions, including generative AI, are compatible with democratic standards of openness, participation, non-discrimination, and answerability [17]. These legal and regulatory frameworks help to encourage responsible innovations. They are designed so that AI solutions can be operated, as shown in Figure 4. This can decrease the harm caused by the development of AI systems to the public.

5.1. Transparency Regulations

Democracy in AI requires that the architectures of regulation compel manufacturers to design explainable AI systems so that the public can understand how Artificial Intelligence works. It could be done through an algorithmic reporting model that compels the developer to explain how AI works regarding source data, structure, and decision-making. Regulations can also include an obligation to carry out an impact assessment before using AI systems, which would be a replicant of environmental or human rights impact affecting ethical flaws such as bias or discrimination, among others. Such measures in practice may involve writing descriptions of AI models and algorithms that would be comprehensible to specialists and ordinary users [18]. These explainability requirements enable the user to understand the AI output simply, especially in sensitive areas like health, justice, and finance. Also, transparency requirements cannot require organizations to use AI systems to justify specific AI decisions where such decisions have implications for the rights or interests of individuals. It also means that the regulation will guarantee the liability of AI systems and their transparency in case of the assessment of adverse or prejudiced results.

5.2. Ethical Oversight and Accountability Mechanisms

Democratic AI governance ethical supervisory structures include independent regulatory agencies or the ethics council. It can be adopted under the supervision of AI to adopt the set ethics. These bodies could be able to investigate AI systems, review cases of abuse, and penalize organizations that have strayed away from the stated and recognized principles of ethics [19]. For example, if an organization adopted an AI system that discriminates against candidates in recruitment, such an organization can be prosecuted for breaking the antidiscrimination laws. Secondly, rules and regulations may compel organizations operating with AI systems to log their performances in a manner that can be audited, including information on the frequency of errors, biases, or decisions made. It places responsibility assemblage where artificial intelligent systems are not operating in the dark legally or ethically [20].

Frameworks may also suggest the inclusion of an ethics review committee within organizations that would double-check the proposed AI systems before they are rolled out to consumers.

5.3. Inclusivity and Public Participation

The rules that will help build a clear and coherent concept of a democratic AI regulation system must address the issue among civil society, academia, community, and the general public that can contribute to regulation creation and implementation. The first option is using citizens' committees or meetings to discuss the problems of artificial intelligence and its regulation by ordinary people. Protection policies can also prescribe compulsory affirmative action in forming the development teams for artificial intelligence products, balanced by gender, ethnic, and income diversities. This helps prevent the perpetuation of existing bias in an AI system or the exclusion of some people from accessing a particular AI tool. Furthermore, public participation frameworks could require government departments and agencies that regulate AI. It provides civil society organizations and advocacy groups an opportunity to give feedback about the social implications of AI systems. A more legitimate process would assure them that their policy choices concerning AI will represent a broader spectrum of social values instead of strictly corporate and administrative interests [21].

5.4. Data Privacy and Security Regulations

Generating AI systems mostly depends on big data; most data sets will likely have personal data. Data privacy regulations should also cover the security dangers of artificial intelligence for surveillance to avoid the abuse of civil liberties. Policies will cap the extent to which AI can be employed for surveillance or include rigorous regulation and the need for lawful permission of the state or organization to utilize AI in the communal arena. In addition to that, data security regulations should also protect AI systems from hacking, data breaches, and cyber-attacks. This includes provisions that include encryption policies in the event of a security breakdown.

5.5. Anti-Bias and Fairness Regulations

There is a need to establish some standards so that AI systems do not have a negative bias. The policies introduced by the law must ensure that any organization that develops or deploys AI systems can undergo public bias tests to ensure that their AI does not enshrine discrimination based on race, sex, age, or other proscribed categories [22]. Such regulations may include algorithmic fairness testing, in which cases of bias in AI systems are checked and allowed to be used. Anti-bias policies might commit to a set of data labels that help hedge against biased AI models. Fairness regulation rules like antidiscrimination remedies are used for AI with biased judgment.

5.6. Innovation and Ethical Design Regulations

As for the most critical challenge of AI governance democratization, one of the significant goals is to keep the optimal ethical inventive ratio. The AI regulation should, therefore, promote this technology, but at the same time, it should set foundations. This could be done through early innovation in which the AI developers are allowed with increased autonomy to use the technologies in experimentation, provided the agencies monitor the development [23]. Ethical design regulations can also require that the providers of Artificial Intelligence technologies use human-centered design principles and act in the best interest of users. For instance, the utilization of AI systems must be backed with protection protocols if the system fails or yields adverse results. Ethical design also means that such technologies should be available for people with different cultures or languages. The use and application of regulations concerning Democratic AI are essential in ensuring and safeguarding the rights and moral objectives. Specifically, by having a set of broad rules that govern practical approaches to transparency, accountability, inclusion, privacy, and fairness, as well as embracing innovation, the correct use of AI systems has to be developed [24].

6. Integrating Ethical Values in AI Design

Ethics of AI design means that AI must be contextually appropriate based on societal, ethical frameworks for behavior, giving everyone an equal chance, respecting people's rights, and refraining from causing harm. Applying ethical values within the integration of design throughout the development and execution of AI involves several strategies aimed at human approach, bias, and accountability of the entire life cycle of the AI.

6.1. Human-Centered Design

Human-centric AI design pursues goals from the human perspective, as well as their protection and welfare, and not simply efficiency for a technique or to serve business interests. This means that when AI systems are developed, these technologies assist end-users and improve their lives, the confidentiality of their rights, and the equality of their status. Incorporation of AI in human day-to-day activities requires developers to factor in the relationship between AI and human end users and determine how it will minimize risks and enhance the utility of the systems developed. For instance, when designing AI systems in the healthcare industry, designers should consider the effects of such technology based on the patient and doctor's sides. This means creating tools that help in medical decisions but are not equal to human physicians, accumulating the patients' information while maintaining their confidentiality, and designing AI systems that would not aggravate current health discreteness [25]. Another aspect of human-centered design is performing cultural accommodation and usability testing to make AI usable to prospective end-users and utilizers.

6.2. Addressing Bias and Promoting Fairness

One of the most significant issues in designing AI systems is that they may be prejudiced in one of the worst ways possible. This means that AI systems are trained on large datasets that contain problematic underlying assumptions related to race, gender, or class for the associated AI systems that will inherently reproduce these issues. Designing ethical capabilities into AI requires developers to manage bias as a question of effort and promote fairness equally in sampling data, forming features, and evaluating results. This may be done using bias checkpoints at the various steps in the AI-making process, where both datasets and the various algorithms used are checked for bias effects [26]. For this, developers need to ensure that the training data taken for AI models contains content from all population segments and does not sum up more from one segment. Furthermore, the post-processing method of algorithmic fairness, including adversarial constraints in the post-processing step, helps to mitigate possible bias tendencies. Other elements of fairness in AI design include creating explainable AI (XAI), where the reasons for chosen decisions made by an AI system are clear. However, to increase the acceptability of AI, fairness also has to apply to who benefits from it and who bears the risks. The ethical approach to AI must assign the benefits and the burdens of the intelligence systems to people in society regardless of whether the benefits of the AI systems are enjoyed [27].

6.3. Accountability and Ethical Oversight

To integrate ethical values into the design of AI, it is just as important to define specific accountability measures. Responsibility entails consequences whereby the parties involved in AI development, AI firms, and end-users face consequences regarding the positive or negative impacts of the deployed AI systems. AI systems need to be intrinsically traceable so that the decision-making process by the AI is documented and potentially auditable. The above traceability is important in auditing or checking AI systems to see whether they are also compliant with some ethical principles and the law [28]. To ensure compliance so that the right results are provided, the design of AI has to incorporate methods by which mistakes, scruples, or overlays within AI can be detected. For instance, the risk reduction in the case of unsatisfactory results obtained from the implemented AI systems must also be designed. The ethical supervision bodies or committees set in organizations or independent regulatory organizations should probably be allowed to oversee the use of AI during the developmental and implantation aspects. In addition, principles of AI systems have to include measures for review and reconsideration of detrimental decisions regarding a particular individual or group [29]. For example, if an AI-based recruitment tool disqualifies a candidate, then fingerprinting the candidate so that the application can be reviewed again should be possible.

6.4. Privacy and Data Protection

Privacy is another basic ethical issue that should not be weakened, especially because many AI applications involve collecting or processing personal data. AI technologies work with large amounts of data that can be of various types:

personal, organizational, or even classified, and many have criticized the ways the data gathered and processed by them are used. Both privacy and data protection components of ethical AI design would provide data minimization and principles, such as informed consent, that are part of the process from the ground up. It implies that the AI system will only collect more data while excluding collecting data about people. The first element of informed consent is to inform users of how their data will be utilized and get their permission to process personal data.

Protecting individual privacy is a critical ethical value that must be integrated into AI design, mainly since many AI systems rely on vast amounts of personal data. AI technologies often collect, store, and analyze sensitive information, raising concerns about how this data is handled, who has access to it, and how it may be used. Ethical AI design requires privacy and data protection in every stage of AI development.

Data minimization ensures that AI systems only collect the data necessary for their specific functions, avoiding unnecessary data that could put individuals at risk. In addition, AI systems are bound by GDPR, which applies to the European Union area and has a rigorous level of data protection. AI designers should ensure that their furnishing is done with securities such as encryption and anonymization to avoid cases of either exposure or hacking. Ethical data handling consideration in artificial intelligence design guarantees privacy rights.

6.5. Safety and Security by Design

A second important ethical consideration in the design of AI involves checking that created AI systems have adequate parameters of safety measures that prevent negative impact. It is especially important in fields like self-driving vehicles and the medical and banking sectors, where the work of an AI goes along with high consequences. Safety by design means creating safe AI systems that function with safety as a default and do not require moving to high-risk, high-stress domains [30].

In diagnostic healthcare using AI, the suggested diagnostic tools are required to give the proper diagnostic findings with maximum certainty. They must not involve a lot of wrong possibilities. Again, for the ethical design of these applications, the procedures go through testing, validation, and verification to meet appropriate safety measures. Security by design entails adding great security measures to the AI systems to counter hacking, data invasion, or cyber-attacks. Since AI can be dangerous and manipulated by wrongdoers, designers have the challenge of including security measures for the technologies. Discretionary access control, encryption, and anomaly detection cover inherent risks that threaten the security of AI systems. Thus, making safety and security the major priorities in AI design can ensure that many concerns currently attributed to AI technology will not be realized and that losses will not be suffered from using the same technology. Incorporating values of right and wrong into AI design is not only about functionality; it is an ethical need. The new elements of the ethical framework include human-centered design, the concept of fairness and bias, and the principles of preserving data privacy and information security. This way, these values become a long-term part of AI development, while AI technologies will protect people's rights, be safe from harm, and mitigate risks. The ethics-driven approach is one of the main questions to answer to have more trust in artificial intelligence systems as well as in democracy and human values.

7. Global Cooperation on AI Ethics and Governance

AI is advancing at an alarming rate, depending on the global society, and it operates at the national level only in many cases. The use of AI technologies, particularly generative AI, is already common in healthcare and financial services, education, and administration occupations that generate significant ethical and social dilemmas [31]. Because of such a broad effect and high intertwining of nations, the countries agreed to develop a comprehensive set of norms that will allow the safe use of AI. Cooperation in AI governance follows the need to combat global challenges and set international ethical principles, thus avoiding fragmented and uncoordinated approaches in the governance of AI, which can develop ethical divergence or deepen ethical inequalities. Table 1 shows the key considerations in balancing ethics and Innovation in Generative AI.

AI technologies present a set of generic ethical dilemmas that need collective intervention across the globe. For example, AI models developed using data from one country may eliminate persons of color globally. At the same time, decisions made by artificial intelligence in one region may affect different international supply chains, global financial markets, and the world's laws. In this case, cooperation facilitates the coordination of activities, exchange of best practices, and development of joint approaches that may help combat these challenges across the globe. Moreover, potential institutional discussion spaces by international forums for economic cooperation and development include areas where countries can deliberate on forming additional ethical standards to regulate AI usage. These combined ones are useful in dealing with problems a single country cannot solve.

Table 1. Key considerations in balancing ethics and Innovation in generative AI

Aspect	Stakeholder Involvement	Impact on Policy Development	Innovation Focus	Ethical Focus
Bias	Researchers, marginalized communities, ethicists	Development of standards	Outputs are inclusive	Leveraging large datasets
Transparency	End-users	Establishing standards	Proprietary algorithms	Explainable and understandable
Regulatory Flexibility	AI developers, Lawmakers	Dynamic regulatory frameworks	Adaptive regulations to increase innovation	Safeguard ethical standards
Workforce Displacement	Unions, government	Retraining labor transitions	Automation for gains	Ethical responsibility
Data Privacy	Tech companies, civil society	Data protection laws	Improving AI capabilities	Protecting user data, transparency
Accountability	Government, judiciary	Liability frameworks	Avoiding liability risks	Assigning decisions
Public Trust	Citizens, media	Promotion of trust-building initiatives	Gaining public support	Ethical AI practices
AI in Healthcare	Healthcare professionals, AI experts	Sensitive sectors	Diagnostics and treatment	Patient safety
Environmental Impact	Environmentalists, legislators	Green AI technique	Promote sustainability	Minimizing carbon footprint

7.1. Addressing Shared Ethical Challenges

AI technologies share a set of ethical concerns that are global in nature and demand combined global solutions. These are not problems defined by national boundaries, which include data privacy, algorithms and bias, autonomy of weapon systems, and the prospects of mass surveillance [32]. AI models developed in one country continue to exhibit diverse forms of bias that discriminate against persons in other parts of the world. AI decisions made within one part of the world affect supply networks, financial systems, and legislation in numerous different countries around the globe.

7.2. Establishing Global Standards and Ethical Frameworks

International work allows countries to pool resources, share knowledge, and work together internationally to solve these issues. Collaboration concerning research concerning the ethical issues of the use of AI can go a long way in providing guidelines on how to avoid some of the discriminative features in an AI system algorithm that does not consider fair, equal, and objective representation of aspects of the society in the system. However, there are global platforms that allow countries an opportunity to deliberate on ethical issues of AI. Such collective actions are useful in presenting solutions that cannot be solved individually.

To avoid this, global collaboration is desirable to establish a common ethical standard that can be implemented in all jurisdictions. EU's general data protection regulation (GDPR) maximizes generalized international data privacy by creating a model that compels other nations to qualify for their data protection measures. Furthermore, there is a need to develop joint technical standards for protecting AI, its reliability, and transparency, which can be achieved only with international collaboration. This also means tagging AI to become auditable for fairness and accountability in ethical concerns. AI has to operate with recommendations applicable to any country to guarantee that the technologies do not harm anybody anywhere in the world.

7.3. Balancing Innovation with Ethical Safeguards

International coordination in AI management is also highly relevant in providing an interface between the emerging AI approach and the right level of regulation for society's benefit. AI can help create new jobs, improve healthcare, and even solve problems such as climate change [33]. Multilateral cooperation between international organizations helps support a context in which creativity can be exercised within simple morality to prevent the development of AI systems that erode human dignity, equality, or justice.

Overall, countries can create an innovative environment where artificial intelligence is both efficient and ethically sensible. These ways of cooperation contribute to maintaining the fact that new AI technologies would be proactive and governed by international ethical standards rather than being subsequently regulated once negative impacts have been revealed. Moreover, international cooperation is critical for ensuring AI technology development outcomes are distributed appropriately across different regions of our world. Approaches of partnership, forming schemes of the target programs, and tendencies of the exchange of information-communication technologies will be required for all countries to receive an overall plus from artificial intelligence in the humanitarian classification.

7.4. Preventing AI-Driven Conflicts

Besides regulating ethics issues and advancing AI development, international cooperation is significant for preserving global peace and security. AI's role in self-aging weapons, AI-driven cyber war, and AI surveillance are areas where AI may contribute to worsening geopolitical tension or even violate a nation's laws. Thus, countries must come collectively to shape peaceful uses of AI and sign various international conventions.

There is a need for a combined global effort to ensure that AI is not used maliciously for cyber warfare, where computer science attacks can virtually paralyze any country's infrastructure. AI is posing a range of ethical challenges on an international level.

8. Challenges and Future Directions

One of the most significant concerns is that the evolution of AI is faster for policymakers and regulators. Laws and regulations are slow to change, and AI technologies advance far more rapidly, which leaves a large gap between what has been developed and what has not been addressed. For example, the legal gap often exists with changes in AI, such as facial recognition technology, self-driving cars, and deepfakes. The challenge that policymakers face is setting rules that can effectively mitigate new risks related to introducing AI technology and promoting innovations. There is a need to develop and actively enforce more stringent source-correct legal provisions that can pressure the companies to bear the ethical impacts of AI solutions they are selling and deploying in areas such as privacy, bias, and information exclusion.

In the future, therefore, international collaborations will be essential for setting the next course for AI regulation. The issues that arise with AI include unemployment due to Automation, algorithm inequality, and the ability to become universal. As a result, multi-stakeholder international cooperation will be required to develop more feasible, complex global standards for the ethical use of AI. It becomes evident that the future developments of AI's ethical and governance mechanisms must be collectively solved by strategic, diverse multi-stakeholder approaches to make AI safe, equal, and beneficial to every individual in humanity.

Conclusion

AI technologies are fast emerging as a potential space for an innovation breakthrough related to privacy, fairness, and accountability have emerged as well. With AI operating and having a growing impact beyond individual countries, the world must be attempting to have a unified ethical code. Therefore, global societies need to foster international cooperation to solve the problem of AI. AI must be governed to incorporate innovation aspirations and prevent harm to international AI governance. It implies that coming up with standards for regulation encourages people to engage more than ever in defining what AI policies should be and ensuring that these systems are for everyone, not just the chosen few. Hence, the ethical governance of AI systems helps make the application of AI helpful to people and fair for society as sociological society adapts to a technologically progressive age.

References

[1] Wang, X., & Wu, Y. C. (2024) Balancing innovation and Regulation in the age of geneRative aRtificial intelligence. *Journal of Information Policy*, *14*.

[2] Ovadya, A. (2023). Reimagining democracy for ai. *Journal of Democracy*, *34*(4), 162-170.

[3] Al-kfairy, M., Mustafa, D., Kshetri, N., Insiew, M., & Alfandi, O. (2024, August). Ethical Challenges and Solutions of Generative AI: An Interdisciplinary Perspective. In *Informatics* (Vol. 11, No. 3, p. 58). MDPI.

[4] Sabherwal, R., & Grover, V. (2024). The societal impacts of generative artificial intelligence: A balanced perspective. *Journal of the association for information systems*, *25*(1), 13-22.

[5] Weldon, M. N., Thomas, G., & Skidmore, L. (2024). Establishing a Future-Proof Framework for AI Regulation: Balancing Ethics, Transparency, and Innovation. *Transactions: The Tennessee Journal of Business Law*, *25*(2), 2.

[6] Tsai, L. L., Pentland, A., Braley, A., Chen, N., Enríquez, J. R., & Reuel, A. (2024). Generative AI for Pro-Democracy Platforms.

[7] Ashwini A, J. Jency Rubia, H. Sehina, B. Sundaravadivazhagan (2024). 1 Unveiling the power of Generative AI: A Journey into Large Language Models. *Generative AI and LLMs: Natural Language Processing and Generative Adversarial Networks*, 1-22.

[8] Tuzov, V., & Lin, F. (2024). Two paths of balancing technology and ethics: A comparative study on AI governance in China and Germany. *Telecommunications Policy*, 102850.

[9] Wakunuma, K., & Eke, D. (2024). Africa, ChatGPT, and Generative AI Systems: Ethical Benefits, Concerns, and the Need for Governance. *Philosophies*, *9*(3), 80.

[10] Farina, M., Yu, X., & Lavazza, A. (2024). Ethical considerations and policy interventions concerning the impact of generative AI tools in the economy and in society. *AI and Ethics*, 1-9.

[11] Ashwini, A., Kavitha, V., & Balasubramaniam, S. (2024). 2 Early Roots of Generative AI Models and LLM: A Diverse Landscape. *Generative AI and LLMs: Natural Language Processing and Generative Adversarial Networks*, 23.

[12] Chimbga, B. (2023, November). Exploring the Ethical and Societal Concerns of Generative AI in Internet of Things (IoT) Environments. In *Southern African Conference for Artificial Intelligence Research* (pp. 44-56). Cham: Springer Nature Switzerland.

[13] Gollagi, S. G., & Balasubramaniam, S. (2023). Hybrid model with optimization tactics for software defect prediction. *International Journal of Modeling, Simulation, and Scientific Computing*, *14*(02), 2350031.

[14] Capraro, V., Lentsch, A., Acemoglu, D., Akgun, S., Akhmedova, A., Bilancini, E. & Viale, R. (2024). The impact of generative artificial intelligence on socioeconomic inequalities and policy making. *PNAS nexus*, *3*(6).

[15] Ashwini, A., Kavitha, V., & Balasubramaniam, S. (2024). Deep Biometrics: Exploring the Intersection of Deep Learning and Biometric Applications. In *AI Based Advancements in Biometrics and its Applications* (pp. 68-84). CRC Press.

[16] Delacroix, S. (2024). Sustainable Data Rivers? Rebalancing the Data Ecosystem That Underlies Generative AI. *Critical AI*, *2*(1).

[17] Díaz-Rodríguez, N., Del Ser, J., Coeckelbergh, M., de Prado, M. L., Herrera-Viedma, E., & Herrera, F. (2023). Connecting the dots in trustworthy Artificial Intelligence: From AI principles, ethics, and key requirements to responsible AI systems and regulation. *Information Fusion*, *99*, 101896.

[18] Hall, R. (2024). Generative AI and re-weaving a pedagogical horizon of social possibility. *International Journal of Educational Technology in Higher Education*, *21*(1), 12.

[19] Dautov, R., Husom, E. J., Sen, S., & Song, H. (2023). Towards Community-Driven Generative AI. In *Position Papers of the 18th Conference on Computer Science and Intelligence Systems*. Polish Information Processing Society.

[20] Balasubramaniam, S., Sumina, S., Kumar, K. S., & Prasanth, A. (2024). Machine learning-based models for implementing digital twins in the healthcare industry. In *Metaverse Technologies in Healthcare* (pp. 135-162). Academic Press.

[21] Illia, L., Colleoni, E., & Zyglidopoulos, S. (2023). Ethical implications of text generation in the age of artificial intelligence. *Business Ethics, the Environment & Responsibility*, *32*(1), 201-210.

[22] Amini, M., Tewari, V., Morande, S., Kukreti, M., & Mishra, A. (2024). Steering Generative AI Toward Beneficence: A Review of Constructive Deepfake Applications. *Navigating the World of Deepfake Technology*, 283-294.

[23] Reshmi, L. B., Vipin Raj, R., & Balasubramaniam, S. (2024). 12 Generative AI and LLM: Case Study in Finance. *Generative AI and LLMs: Natural Language Processing and Generative Adversarial Networks*, 231.

[24] Bayer, J. (2024). Legal implications of using generative AI in the media. *Information & Communications Technology Law*, 1-20.

[25] Budhwar, P., Chowdhury, S., Wood, G., Aguinis, H., Bamber, G. J., Beltran, J. R. & Varma, A. (2023). Human resource management in the age of generative artificial intelligence: Perspectives and research directions on ChatGPT. *Human Resource Management Journal*, *33*(3), 606-659.

[26] Cole, M., Cant, C., Ustek Spilda, F., & Graham, M. (2022). Politics by automatic means? A critique of artificial intelligence ethics at work. *Frontiers in Artificial Intelligence*, *5*, 869114.

[27] De Gregorio, G. (2023). The Normative Power of Artificial Intelligence. *Ind. J. Global Legal Stud.*, *30*, 55.

[28] Correa, N. K., Santos, J. W., Galvao, C., Pasetti, M., Schiavon, D., Naqvi, F. & Oliveira, N. D. (2024). Crossing the principle–practice gap in AI ethics with ethical problem-solving. *AI and Ethics*, 1-18.

[29] Carter, D. (2020). Regulation and ethics in artificial intelligence and machine learning technologies: Where are we now? Who is responsible? Can the information professional play a role? *Business Information Review*, *37*(2), 60-68.

[30] Wood, A. Dark echoes: The exploitative potential of generative AI in online harassment. In *Cybersecurity* (pp. 90-129). CRC Press.

Chapter 5

The Challenges and Risks of Generative AI Democratization

J. Reji[1,*]
Dhanya S. Pankaj[2,†]
Dawn Sivan[3,4,‡]
and K. Satheesh Kumar[4,‖]

[1]Indian Institute of Science, Technology and Education, School of Data Science, Government of India, Thiruvananthapuram, India
[2]Department of Computer Science and Engineering, Government Engineering College Idukki, Kerala, India
[3]Centre for Advanced Intelligent Materials & Faculty of Industrial Sciences and Technology, Universiti Malaysia Pahang Al-Sultan Abdullah, Kuantan, Pahang, Malaysia
[4]Kerala University of Digital Sciences, Innovation and Technology (Digital University Kerala), Thiruvananthapuram, Kerala, India

Abstract

Generative AI has transformed human creation by assisting the creative process in various fields such as generating predictions of protein structures for drug discovery, composing music, generating novel clothing patterns, and automating knowledge discovery. Its ability to produce highly naturalistic materials by providing simple prompts has made it popular even among non-experts. Along with its substantial benefits, the uncontrolled integration of generative AI has led to several

[*] Corresponding Author's Email: rejivipin@gmail.com
[†] Corresponding Author's Email: dhanyaspankaj@gmail.com
[‡] Corresponding Author's Email: dawnsivan91@gmail.com
[‖] Corresponding Author's Email: satheesh.kumar@duk.ac.in

In: Democratized Generative AI: Principles, Challenges and Applications
Editors: S. Balasubramaniam and Seifedine Kadry
ISBN: 979-8-89530-684-0

hazards and risks that should be assessed and managed. This chapter discusses the challenges and risks related to the widespread usage of Generative AI and their social consequences such as the impact of algorithmic bias, the privacy of data, and the conflict with intellectual property. The legal challenges associated with content produced by artificial intelligence, including concerns over authorship and intellectual property, highlight the need for effective governance. In addition, the ethical implications of Generative AI's widespread adoption require further research, including the role of digital literacy bias and internet accessibility challenges. Constructive advisers, inventors, legal experts, legislators, and communities need to come together to discuss these issues if generative AI has to benefit societies and lower negative consequences. The power of generative AI can be leveraged to help society by improving ethical development, protecting privacy, and guaranteeing objective access.

Keywords: generative AI, democratic AI, AI governance, AI misuse, disinformation, privacy protection, algorithmic bias, ethical implications, legal challenges

1. Introduction

Generative AI represents a generational paradigm shift in how we access, interact with, and leverage information. Historically, information access has focused on retrieving existing data or content from search engines, databases, or similar structured data resources. This technology has also opened up new ways of solving problems and producing useful solutions. This transformative change is now being adopted at all levels of technical expertise, leading to its democratization due to the availability of cloud platforms and a range of easy-to-use tools. However, generative AI comes with significant challenges and potential risks that we need to address adequately for its beneficial implementation. For instance, generative AI applications built with large training datasets collected from different sources could be prone to biases such as racial and gender bias [1]. Such biases could reinforce stereotypes, widen social disparities, and cause devastating effects. Data privacy is another major concern [2], as users may exploit generative AI tools to create deepfakes or extract unauthorized data. Another concern is the unauthorized and uncompensated reproduction of the work of writers and creators. Writers and creators raise valid concerns about such expropriated reproduction of their work. Hence, the legal ownership of AI-generated content remains unresolved, challenging traditional copyright frameworks.

Moreover, the primary control of generative AI technology is in the hands of major corporations, and wealthy institutions having access to vast amounts of data, challenging its democratization. Infrastructure limitations and digital literacy gaps further worsen inequalities, leaving communities without these resources behind in an AI-driven economy. To apply generative AI with maximum benefits and minimal harm, a collaborative policy framework is required from stakeholders across technology, governance, and civil society to ensure its equitable and responsible use.

2. Challenges of Democratizing Generative AI

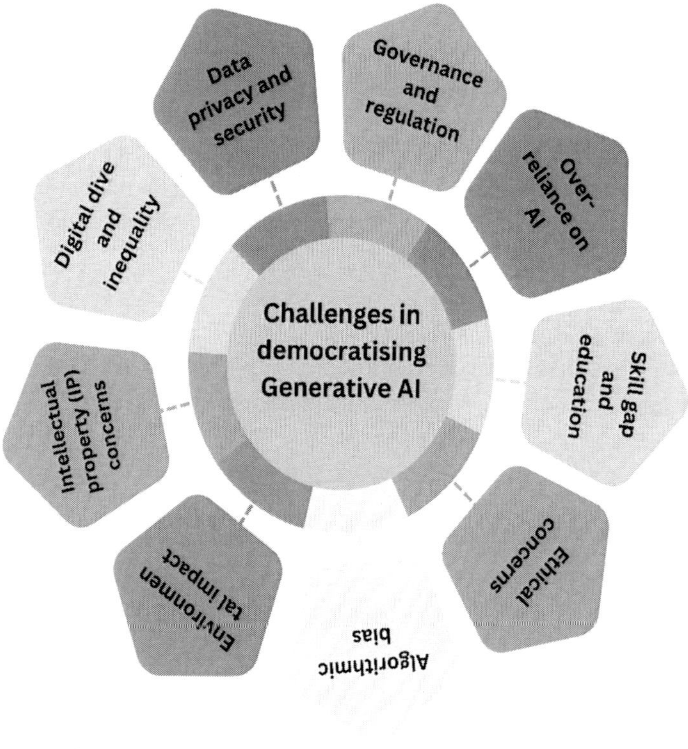

Figure 1. Various challenges and risks involved in the democratization of Generative AI.

Several challenges that inhibit the widespread adoption of generative AI applications include algorithmic bias, data privacy concerns, intellectual property issues, governance challenges, expanding digital divide, over-reliance on algorithms, ethical quandaries, skill gaps, and environmental consequences (Figure 1). Notably, many of these factors are intertwined. This section addresses each of these challenges in detail.

2.1. Algorithmic Bias and Fairness

The algorithmic bias of generative AI systems arises when AI models produce outputs that reflect or amplify existing societal prejudices in their training data. When such models are used for decision-making, it could lead to the unfair treatment of individuals in a society. Ensuring fairness requires careful curation of the data set, diverse representation, and ongoing evaluation of AI systems. Above all, it demands active participation in the database creation of various stakeholders, including those directly affected by AI decisions. Transparent evaluation methods and ethical guidelines tailored to specific applications can help reduce social bias in AI models, but solutions must go beyond technical fixes. In short, we need an ongoing dialogue between developers, regulators, and communities to ensure that AI applications are fair, accountable, and beneficial to everyone.

2.1.1. Sources of Algorithmic Bias

Algorithmic bias stems from multiple sources, typically divided into biases in data collection, model design, and human decision-making.

2.1.1.1. Data Collection and Representation Bias

The most common bias source in AI systems is the training data. AI models learn patterns from large datasets, but if these datasets do not adequately represent the population or context for which the AI will be used, the model may yield biased outcomes. For instance, facial recognition systems often have higher error rates for individuals with darker skin tones due to under-representation in training data. Similarly, large language models trained predominantly on Western data may struggle to interpret or process non-Western languages, leading to biases, inaccuracies, or limited functionality for diverse linguistic contexts. This can lead to biased outcomes for minority communities in criminal justice applications.

2.1.1.2. Model Design and Objective Function Bias

The model bias can also arise from the design of the AI model. AI models are trained mainly to reduce the loss value and maximize the accuracy which does not depend on the model neutrality. For example, an AI-based system trained on historical data having biases toward lending practices might falsely discriminate against certain groups on creditworthiness [3]. The "black box" character of the AI models makes it more complex to detect and address biased outcomes.

2.1.1.3. Human Bias in AI System Design

Generative AI has significantly assisted the human decision-making process, but its influence is often tainted by biases embedded within the models. The bias creeps into the model at various stages starting from model development, as developers make subjective decisions on model selection, selecting training data to define model features. Rigorous data auditing is required for balanced training data selection. Including data from a specific group could bias the model toward that group. Similarly, caution must be exercised when selecting an appropriate model framework. These factors need further attention when democratizing AI since non-experts would increasingly employ and develop AI applications. Apart from developing crippled models, the selection of improper models for a specific requirement can also lead to devastating consequences.

2.1.2. Implications for Fairness

The model-driven algorithmic bias in the Generative AI system has seriously affected the fairness of AI-based decision-making on people's well-being. Some of the important areas are highlighted here.

2.1.2.1. Hiring and Employment

Currently, AI-based tools are used to identify talented individuals seeking employment. However, inevitable bias in these tools can unintentionally affect the hiring process. An AI system trained on historical hiring data is likely to favor candidates who resemble previous hires, leading to biases related to race, gender, social status, and economic background. This might result in the rejection of real qualified candidates in the underrepresented groups, which affects equal employment opportunities for everyone, irrespective of any biases.

2.1.2.2. Criminal Justice

The AI system could be used in criminal justice to predict recidivism or to support sentencing. Studies reveal that these systems often exhibit biased results, especially for minority groups. This results in harsher punishments even if they are innocent, which could affect the public trust in the justice system and the AI.

2.1.2.3. Healthcare

AI has stepped into the healthcare field, bringing remarkable changes in disease diagnosis, personalized treatment procedures, and robotic surgery. Healthcare is highly sensitive to the outcome of the diagnosis, which is crucial for a patient's future well-being. For instance, a model trained on female patients for a certain lifestyle disease may produce an entirely different diagnosis for males and children. This raises ethical concerns about ensuring fair play in AI-based systems in the healthcare sector calling out for the development of models that equally benefit everyone.

2.1.2.4. Financial Services

The involvement of the AI system in financial services is noteworthy. It is used to learn creditworthiness, set the insurance premium, and manage investments and shareholdings. According to research from the USA, mortgages given to different people differ based on the population data used in the AI system [4]. If training data do not adequately represent all demographic groups, the AI model may produce biased outcomes, favoring some groups. As a result, biased AI models not only worsen the existing inequalities but also raise ethical concerns regarding fairness and transparency within the system.

2.2. Data Privacy and Security

As Generative AI becomes more accessible, it presents significant challenges regarding data privacy and security, alongside exciting opportunities for creativity. With AI systems becoming more widely available, concerns are growing about the handling of personal and sensitive data. What's particularly concerning is that AI systems can analyze vast datasets, and the source of these data is crucial, as they may be publicly available or obtained without authorization from private sources. Proper measures must be implemented to secure sensitive personal data. In what follows we discuss the key data privacy and security concerns related to the democratization of Generative AI, particularly in sensitive areas like healthcare, finance, and education. The main focus is on the challenges of collecting, processing, and securing data.

2.2.1. The Role of Data in Generative AI

The quality and amount of data used for training the AI is a key factor in the performance of generative AI models. Therefore, developers tend to collect maximum data to gain better model performance. Unfortunately, many databases contain sensitive information, which causes grave privacy and security issues. In the healthcare domain, patients' vital information is used to improve the detection-treatment mechanism. Without proper safeguards, this data is at risk of exposure or misuse. Similar is the case of financial services, where personal finance details are at risk if necessary security measures are not taken.

2.2.2. Key Challenges in Data Privacy and Security

The key challenges faced by the democratization of Generative AI are discussed below.

2.2.2.1. Unauthorized Access and Data Breaches

AI systems hosted on various cloud platforms are exposed to hacking and unauthorized data access. Unauthenticated access to sensitive information such as defense, medical, or financial records, might result in privacy violations, as highlighted in the data breach in 2019 that compromised millions of patient records [5]. The expansion of AI through accessible cloud platforms heightens these risks.

2.2.2.2. Insufficient Data Anonymization

Anonymizing data for training AI is ineffective in many scenarios. The data thus generated can be identified when compared with other available data leading to privacy issues. This can be further worsened due to the lack of technical expertise to securely manage this data, considering that democratic AI has access to large datasets.

2.2.2.3. Opacity and Lack of User Control

The inherent nature of many AI systems acting as "black boxes," often exhibit ambiguity about how data that requires privacy is collected, processed, and applied. This opacity and lack of user control can lead to ethical and legal issues.

2.2.2.4. Data Ownership and Consent Issues

The ownership of data and informed consent are still unsolved problems in AI. Users of such systems are unaware of the ownership of the data. At the same time, many are unaware that their data is also vulnerable to such exposure.

2.2.3. Mitigating Data Privacy and Security Risks

Following are some ways to mitigate data privacy and security risks.

2.2.3.1. Use of Technologies

Technology plays a significant role in protecting data from unauthorized usage. Several technologies have been developed for this purpose. Technologies such as strong encryption and differential privacy allow the sharing of statistical information, safeguarding the privacy of individuals involved [6]. Another approach could be the employment of federated learning, in which data remains in the devices where it is collected. The training process is decentralized and the decentralized models are trained at the data source. The aggregated insights gathered by the model at the source device are only shared across the global model situated elsewhere. This collaborative learning approach allows the development of AI models without sharing data but the insights gathered at the source level [7]. This privacy-preserving method is particularly effective when dealing with sensitive data as it limits data exposure.

2.2.3.2. Transparent Data Governance and Regulatory Compliance

The General Data Protection Regulation (GDPR) is a European Union law enacted in 2016. It regulates the collection and use of personal data by organizations [8]. Similar laws at the global level would be desirable to protect personal information. This would help organizations to adopt transparent data management practices while keeping the individuals from whom data are collected, informed of how their personal information is utilized.

2.2.3.3. User Education and Awareness

Users should be educated about how the generative AI models collect the data, process and use it. They should understand the risks associated with data misuse, model leaks, and identity theft. It is equally useful to promote best practices for secure data handling. For responsible AI usage, users can be trained on model bias, verification skills to check the credibility of the outputs, and critical thinking for evaluating where generative AI is appropriate to be used.

2.3. Intellectual Property (IP) Concerns

The rapid advancement of generative AI has also created challenges for intellectual property (IP) laws, especially concerning the ownership and authorship of AI-generated content. Traditional IP frameworks were designed with human creators in mind, aiming to protect human innovation and creativity. However, as AI systems now produce original works — such as images, music, text, and even inventions — questions about ownership and authorship have emerged. Should the creator be the AI, the developer who built it, or the user directing it? What rights, if any, do developers or users hold over AI-generated content [9]? These questions are more relevant than ever when AI systems are widely available to individuals and small businesses. This section explores the issues related to ownership of generative AI model outputs, its associated disputes, and the broader impact on creativity and innovation.

2.3.1. Uncertainty in Ownership and Authorship

AI models are trained with existing data. The question is whether the author of the original work used to train the AI model would retain the rights of AI-generated content. Another question is whether AI can legally be an inventor. It is a grey area. Under conventional intellectual property laws, the author of an original work gets sole rights. With AI, it is unclear whether the "creator" is the AI itself, the developer, or the user who generated the content. For example, a visual artist using AI to create artwork might struggle to claim ownership of the artwork if the AI played a substantial role in its creation. Similarly, a company using AI for product design may struggle to clarify its legal rights over the product. This issue has already made its way to the court of law, as seen in the case of Device for the Autonomous Bootstrapping of Unified Sentience (DABUS) [10], where DABUS was listed as the inventor on patent applications. DABUS is an AI system that can make inventions. For example, it has designed a food container using fractal geometry for quick reheating. The UK Supreme Court has dismissed the appeal by DABUS to allow AI to be treated as the inventor. Although multiple courts decided that only humans can hold patents, the case underscores the growing tension between traditional IP laws and AI-driven creativity.

2.3.2. Risk of IP Disputes and Litigation

As Generative AI becomes available to a wider audience, the potential for intellectual property disputes increases. With more users generating content through AI, questions of ownership and copyright are likely to arise, especially when AI-generated works resemble existing copyrighted material [11]. For example, an AI model trained on a music library may generate a new composition similar to an existing one. This could lead to a copyright dispute. This risk is intensified by the unawareness of the IP law by the AI users creating accidental copyright violations. Moreover, corporate sectors having more access to legal systems and resources can circumvent the challenges, which in turn cause a digital divide between such big players and niche AI users.

2.3.3. Impact on Creativity and Innovation

The inadequacy of explicit IP rights for AI-generated content is a major obstruction to creation and innovation, specifically in fields where IP rights are necessary. For example, a designer might be confused about selling designs partly generated by AI due to uncertainty in ownership rights. Similarly, a startup company developing an AI-generated idea-based product may struggle to obtain a patent without clear authorship. This uncertainty in legal matters could deter individuals and small-scale businesses from adopting AI, thereby stifling creativity and innovative ideas.

2.3.4. Ethical Concerns Around AI's Role in Creation

Another issue concerns the ethical concerns associated with the nature of creativity. Traditional legal and IP laws operate under the basic assumption that creativity is the brainchild of the human race and deserves protection. This assumption is challenged, as AI systems are equally capable of content creation and design. There are hot debates on granting IP rights to AI-generated content, claiming the diminishing value of human creativity. At the same time, there are similar claims about this restriction affecting AI's contribution to innovation and culture.

2.3.5. Global Variations in IP Law

Challenges in IP law of Generative AI are further complicated by the geolocation-based difference in regulations worldwide. Some regions protect AI-generated content, while others do not, creating new challenges for individuals or groups looking to commercialize the content internationally. Without consistent standards, the benefits of democratized AI may be unevenly distributed. Due to the ever-evolving nature of AI, intellectual property concerns will require ongoing legal and ethical discussions. A framework developed for this purpose must ensure that the benefits of AI are accessible to all while protecting intellectual property rights.

In summary, the democratization of Generative AI presents major IP challenges, particularly around ownership, authorship, and protection for AI-generated content. These uncertainties can discourage smaller creators, startups, and organizations from using AI, while larger corporations with legal resources may gain a disproportionate advantage. One of the options is to develop a hybrid authorship model of giving credit to both AI and human operators [12]. An alternative proposal is to consider the human operator as the custodian of the AI-generated work [13]. However, both these methods have merits and demerits. A good framework should strike a balance between freedom for creativity and protection of IP in a democratized AI environment for the benefit of society at large.

2.4. Governance and Regulation

This section deals with the challenges in the governance of democratized Generative AI.

2.4.1. The Need for Governance in Democratized Generative AI

Managing the wide variety of AI applications has become essential to mitigate unforeseen outcomes through proper governance. The rapid development of Generative AI and LLMs does not necessarily comply with the current regulatory policies, which are mostly industry-specific. This calls for a more comprehensive approach to ensure AI is responsibly used across sectors [14].

2.4.2. Challenges in Regulating Democratized Generative AI

Global AI presents another significant challenge that needs to be addressed. Given the worldwide reach of AI technologies, no single country or region can effectively regulate them in isolation. For instance, while the European Union is exploring the implementation of comprehensive AI legislation, other areas often lack comparable regulatory frameworks, resulting in a fragmented and inconsistent approach to AI governance globally. Seeing this from a global perspective puts regulators in an unfavorable position as there is a high chance developers and users are likely to operate in areas with fewer restrictions. However, generative AI makes this harder to achieve. After all, content such as false information generated in a specific region has the potential to impact communities all over the world as target audiences for spreading false narratives. Political environments, digital competencies, and even regulations differ greatly between countries, so it is quite a challenge to expect countries to agree on a common action or in this case, legislation [15].

2.4.3. Balancing Innovation and Accountability

The governance of Generative AI must maintain the right balance between innovation and accountability. Stricter restrictions may prevent small developers or individuals from realizing AI's potential. Conversely, if AI is not regulated, its negative uses will flourish, resulting in the spread of falsehoods, bias, and violations of privacy. There is a need for a regulatory framework adaptable to technological changes yet comprehensive enough to cover the important issues. One such approach that has been proposed is the incorporation of regulatory sandboxes, which enable the controlled use of AI systems without compromising accountability or hindering innovation [16]. Moreover, as generative AI can easily create false information, fake accounts, or fake videos, regulatory bodies must take the responsibility of generating and implementing strategies to combat such malpractices. It is clear that for generative AI democratization to avoid facilitating offenses such as identity theft or disinformation campaigns, technical means of protection (e.g., content filters) paired with legal ones should be in place [17]. However, imposing these measures is not straightforward, as there seems to be a fine line between curbing misuse and enabling genuine usage. Excessive governance could stifle creativity and innovation.

2.4.4. Ethical Considerations in Generative AI Governance

Fairness, transparency, justice, nonmaleficence, privacy, and responsibility are some ethical considerations that should be applied in managing democratized AI. AI adaptation requires individuals or institutions to understand how the algorithms work and how they affect their decisions. For example, the AI recruitment tool might adversely favor those trained on certain data if there was a bias in the data training. Potential users of AI products and algorithms may not be aware of these biases in the absence of accountability and such assumptions will only amplify the existing social disparities. Equally important is inclusivity in AI governance. Although inclusive AI has the potential to empower a variety of audiences, it can also lead to the disempowerment of individuals who do not have the appropriate tools or knowledge to participate. AI governance frameworks should embrace inclusiveness by facilitating further education and skill development opportunities and enabling discussions on AI governance among underserved groups [18].

2.4.5. The Role of International Cooperation

Given the worldwide reach of generative AI, efficient governance depends on international cooperation. Cross-border effects of AI technology are common; thus, abuses—such as misinformation or invasions of privacy—can have global ramifications. Promoting consistent, ethical, and legal AI use internationally depends on harmonized norms across nations. International agencies such as the Organisation for Economic Co-operation and Development (OECD) and the United Nations are already developing policies to address transparency, fairness, and accountability. However, establishing global legal guidelines for democratized generative AI is still underway. As noted earlier, the main issue is that democratizing AI will enable more people from diverse backgrounds across society to access AI tools. Imposing regulatory laws might adversely affect innovation due to restrictions on accessing AI technology components. Therefore, the focus should be on developing control mechanisms without stifling innovation [19]. The regulatory framework has to be grounded in ethics, transparency, and inclusivity while fostering innovation.

2.5. Digital Divide and Inequality

Irrespective of the objective of making advanced technologies more accessible to the public, the democratization of generative AI runs the risk of widening the digital divide due to gaps in access to sophisticated technologies, technical skills, infrastructure, and resources [20]. Care should be taken to avoid further widening disparities due to the democratization process. Necessary steps can be taken to equip marginalized or disadvantaged communities with various skills and access to tools for adapting AI technologies for their benefit. As generative artificial intelligence models are resource intensive, many industrialists may be unable to afford them. Apart from affordability, basic technical knowledge is required to employ these tools, even though many are becoming user-friendly. Real democratization of artificial intelligence calls for tackling structural disparities that impede fair participation in an AI-driven economy.

2.5.1. Affordability of AI Technologies

Many AI tools are cost-prohibitive for people in economically underdeveloped areas, as many of them require membership fees or large hardware investments [21]. The availability of generative artificial intelligence models offered by some cloud providers is sometimes subscription-based or comes with expensive usage costs, limiting access for people with fewer means of affordability. This economic barrier accentuates the digital divide, as some users cannot afford to benefit from artificial intelligence, while wealthier users can. Advanced generative artificial intelligence models are sometimes proprietary and demand significant subscription costs, presenting cost barriers and unequal access to them. This restricts access to wealthier individuals and well-funded companies [22]. Free or less expensive substitutes may be less powerful or lack key features, creating an unfair playing field. Fine-tuning or customizing generative models for particular needs or cultural settings is costly and requires resources and technical knowledge. Artificial intelligence depends on high-quality, pertinent data, although access to such data is unequal [23]. While smaller businesses in underdeveloped areas may not be capable of gathering and analyzing massive amounts of data, large companies frequently have the means to do so, thereby restricting the AI development capacity of smaller businesses.

2.5.2. Content Misinformation and Vulnerability to Manipulation

Areas or populations with low digital literacy could find it difficult to tell real from artificial intelligence-generated content, so they are more prone to false information. Democratizing generative artificial intelligence capabilities without sufficient digital literacy might aggravate information disparity and raise vulnerability to manipulation and false news [24].

2.5.3. Exploitation by Those with Generative AI Access

Individuals or companies with access to generative AI technologies can create enormous volumes of generated material that can impact public opinion or culture [25]. Communities devoid of these instruments could lack the means to refute false information. This can aggravate power disparities and impede a fair presentation of several points of view. Those who lack access to generative AI are economically disadvantaged hence they could find themselves unable to compete with companies who can lower-cost automate creative jobs. For creatives and employees in areas without access to sophisticated artificial intelligence capabilities, this could cause job displacement [26]. Organizations without access to generative artificial intelligence suffer in innovation and entrepreneurship, perhaps worsening the economic disparity between areas or communities with and without generative AI capacity. Dealing with the digital gap and guaranteeing fair Generative AI democratization calls for a multifarious strategy involving infrastructure, education, legislative change, and worldwide cooperation.

Governments and international organizations can lead the expansion of Internet and cloud services and provide reasonably priced computing tools in underdeveloped regions. These steps will enhance access to AI technologies. Governments and technology firms could grant free or subsidized access to cloud platforms with generative AI capabilities. For instance, platforms like Google's TensorFlow Research Cloud or Microsoft's AI for Good may offer computational subsidies, especially to small firms and underprivileged groups.

2.5.4. Encouragement of Digital Literacy and AI Education

Governments, businesses, and educational institutions could offer training on Generative AI technologies [27]. This training could be multilingual to incorporate cultural diversity. This inclusion guarantees that generative artificial intelligence remains relevant and efficient for consumers everywhere. Dealing with the Generative AI digital gap calls for world cooperation. To help low-income areas and guarantee inclusivity, governments, international organizations, and technology businesses should exchange best practices and tools. Generative AI democratization runs the danger of aggravating inequality even if it has possibilities for inclusivity and creativity by not addressing the digital divide. Leaders and companies have to help close the digital divide and build an inclusive, AI-driven future so that fair results may follow.

2.6. Over-Reliance on Generative AI

As Generative AI became more accessible through democratization efforts, advanced AI tools once used exclusively by experts became readily available to a wider range of users. While this unveiled great opportunities for general users, it also raised the risk of over-reliance on these systems [28]. When the general users trust the AI outputs too much without adequate examination, it results in over-reliance on AI. As the AI tools became more user-friendly as part of democratization, the non-expert users tend to trust the AI outputs as accurate, while overlooking the assumptions made in developing the AI models. Such over-dependence affects human creativity and skills development and makes the public susceptible to misinformation. It also raises the question of accountability of AI-generated content and results. The perpetuation of existing bias is another major concern. This section discusses some of the challenges surrounding the over-reliance on Generative AI.

2.6.1. Erosion of Human Creativity and Skills Development

Generative AI systems often produce outputs based on the existing patterns in the data used for training. Therefore, too much dependence on these technologies could stifle human creativity and lower the variety of artistic output [29]. This could thus influence the originality of the produced work using AI techniques without enough human control.

2.6.2. Accountability and the Black Box Challenge

Another issue with excessive dependence on Generative AI is responsibility. Comparable to "black boxes" for non-expert users, many Generative AI models have complicated constructions and operations, making it challenging for users to understand how decisions are made [30]. Users who rely too heavily on these systems may shift decision-making responsibility to artificial intelligence, believing its outputs to be objective or unbiased. Furthermore, it can be difficult to determine who is liable if an error or damage results from AI-generated output—the AI provider, the user, or the company utilizing the system—presenting complex ethical challenges.

2.6.3. Susceptibility to Misinformation

Generative AI can create reasonable content that is challenging to separate from original facts. Because people may find it difficult to confirm the accuracy of AI-generated text, photos, or videos, over-reliance on generative artificial intelligence can make individuals more susceptible to false information. Growing reliance on generative artificial intelligence exposes weaknesses for malevolent actors who might exploit it to produce phishing material, false information, or deepfakes.

2.6.4. Risk of Reinforcing Bias and Errors

Generative AI systems can reinforce biases and errors within AI models and the training data. Since AI systems rely on data, any biases in that data can lead to biased outputs. If users rely on AI without questioning its biases, those biases can spread more widely. For example, financial AI systems may reinforce socioeconomic biases if users unquestioningly accept AI-generated recommendations.

2.6.5. Dependence on Proprietary Models

The most advanced generative AI models are developed and controlled by a few leading technology companies. Over-reliance on these proprietary models can result in a concentration of power, where a handful of corporations control the narratives, outputs, and tools accessible to the public. This over-dependence can make it challenging for users to comprehend, audit, or modify how these systems operate, leading to a lack of transparency in AI-generated outcomes. To mitigate over-reliance on generative AI, fostering human-AI collaboration could serve as a solution. [31]. Organizations can advocate for practices where AI aids in generating ideas or automating routine tasks but necessitates human oversight and input for final decisions or creative contributions. A human-in-the-loop approach ensures that AI is utilized responsibly, with human guidance refining and directing AI outputs.

2.7. Skill Gaps and Education

To build, implement, and run Generative AI systems, and to effectively use Generative AI calls for a basic knowledge of technology and particular technical talents. A major problem emerges as artificial intelligence tools get more accessible to non-experts: the skill gap [32]. This discrepancy draws attention to the differences between the general availability of artificial intelligence tools and the lack of the necessary expertise and skills to apply them effectively.

From a lack of fundamental digital literacy to advanced technological abilities in Generative AI creation and deployment, the skill gap covers a spectrum of problems. Many consumers lack the basic knowledge of data, coding, or ethical technology use. Even with technical credentials, people may lack the necessary skills to create AI models, assess data, or apply artificial intelligence unethically [32]. Though democratization seeks to make AI tools more user-friendly, even low-code and no-code platforms depend on baseline knowledge to be effective. On a no-code platform, a non-expert might create a basic model, for instance, but still find it difficult to evaluate model performance, analyze ethical consequences, or handle data. It is a difficult task to close the skill gap.

2.7.1. Access to Education

Availability and affordability of quality education are also critical factors. Though many major universities offer AI courses, they are not affordable to people from low-income areas with inadequate educational support. Although online courses are available in this field, advanced certifications can be expensive. Moreover, gender, racial, and socioeconomic inequalities also affect equal access to AI education and hence targeted initiatives are required to make AI education more accessible.

2.7.2. Rapidly Evolving Technologies

One critical factor associated with AI technologies is the rapid changes happening. Therefore, the workforce should be trained continuously to be in the front. The dynamic nature of this area has significant implications for workforce management.

2.7.3. AI Adoption and Productivity

For businesses, especially small and medium-sized enterprises (SMEs), the skill gap limits Generative AI adoption. Without skilled employees, businesses miss the productivity and innovation gains that generative AI can offer. This slows down the potential economic benefits of generative AI.

2.7.4. Job Displacement and Reskilling

Generative AI automates more tasks, creating a need for reskilling among workers in affected sectors. However, access to reskilling programs is often limited, especially in rural or low-income areas, putting these workers at risk of job displacement and economic hardships.

2.7.5. The Role of Lifelong Learning

Given AI's rapid pace, lifelong learning is essential for remaining competitive. Governments, educational institutions, and businesses should create flexible learning opportunities, such as modular courses and workplace training, to help workers upskill over time [33]. Strategies for addressing the Generative AI skill gap and making generative AI democratization truly inclusive may be adopted.

2.7.6. Expanding Access to Generative AI Education

Governments and educational institutions should invest in accessible Generative AI education through affordable online courses, school curricula, and AI training in underserved regions. The foundational skills can be integrated into the early stages of education.

2.7.7. Public-Private Partnerships

Collaborations between government, academia, and industry can help design courses for industry requirements and further development. Governments can offer funding or incentives to make these programs widely accessible. Governments can also offer tax credits, grants, or subsidies for businesses to provide AI training to employees.

2.8. Environmental Concerns

Developing AI models is computationally intensive and energy-consuming, particularly for large-scale models like image, video, and text generators. As these systems become increasingly accessible, their huge computational demand leads to massive energy consumption, which raises energy concerns due to a larger carbon footprint [34]. This paper examines various aspects of energy concerns.

2.8.1. Energy Consumption and Computational Requirements

Generative AI models are among the most resource-intensive types of AI due to the complexity of their tasks. Training a model like GPT-4 or large-scale image generation models can take thousands of hours of GPU processing time, consuming huge amounts of electricity [35]. Training these models can demand thousands of petaflop/s-days of computing power—equivalent to powering hundreds of homes for a year. As more people and businesses access Generative AI, energy consumption is expected to rise.

2.8.2. Carbon Emissions and Environmental Footprint

The high energy demands of Generative AI systems contribute directly to carbon emissions, especially when data centers rely on non-renewable energy sources. A 2019 study found that training a large AI model could emit as much carbon as five cars' lifetimes [36]. As AI democratization enables more widespread AI use, cumulative carbon emissions risk further increasing.

2.8.3. Data Centres and Resource Consumption

Data centers are the backbone of generative AI, handling the intense computing and storage requirements these models need. However, generative AI models consume vast amounts of energy for computing and cooling, and they require large quantities of water in regions already facing scarcity. As demand for Generative AI increases, the growth of data centers in environmentally sensitive areas could worsen these issues. Utilization of renewable energy sources could significantly lower carbon emissions. Another potential solution is prioritizing certification through the Leadership in Energy and Environmental Design (LEED) program.[37].

2.8.4. Research in Green AI Practices

Developing more sustainable approaches for training and implementing generative artificial intelligence models depends on ongoing research on "green AI" [38]. Democratising Generative AI presents environmental problems even as it creates new opportunities. Dealing with them calls for sustainable hardware practices, cloud solutions, energy-efficient algorithms, and renewable energy for data centers. We can build an AI-driven future promoting innovation and sustainability through technical development with environmental stewardship.

3. Critical Risks

Figure 2. Critical risks involved in Generative AI.

Although generative artificial intelligence presents substantial hazards with major social and ethical consequences, it also has the power to revolutionize sectors and democratize innovation. Making these strong tools generally available might have unanticipated effects including dissemination of false information, weaponizing, loss of control over uses, and possible corporate exploitation. Here we investigate these main hazards together with the requirement of sensible actions to control them. The risks involved in Generative AI are shown in Figure 2 as nodes connected to the major subject, clearly illustrating their interactions.

3.1. Misinformation and Deepfakes

Particularly with deepfakes, the emergence of generative artificial intelligence has heightened the danger of false information. The possibility for harmful use increases as methods for producing highly realistic images, films, and audio become more easily available. Deepfake movies, for instance, might be exploited to make videos of popular personalities for disseminating bogus claims or behaviors ascribed to them [39]. This might affect elections, change world relations, and destroy media credibility. Generative AI techniques make it easier to produce convincing false information, thus undermining societal stability and confidence.

3.2. Generative AI Weaponising

Generative artificial intelligence is more likely to be used for detrimental purposes such as cyberattacks, spying, and autonomous weapons as it is more widely available. Generative artificial intelligence's democratization facilitates the access of criminal minds to sophisticated tools with destructive intent. for instance, fake identities could be developed for political propaganda or cyberattacks [39]. Public security and safety might thus be threatened.

3.3. Loss of Control Regarding Artificial Intelligence Uses

The simplicity of generative artificial intelligence applications can have unexpected effects as non-experienced users might produce models that act erratically. In high-stakes fields like healthcare or driverless cars, this could cause damage even if the inventors themselves find it challenging to justify the surprising outcomes. Lack of openness and control could undermine faith in artificial intelligence systems.

3.4. Large Companies' Ethical Exploitation

Large firms still have a monopoly over extremely complex generative AI models despite efforts at democratization because of their vast data and massive processing capability. Open-source and subscription models still lack the accuracy and features of these models even if they are accessible. This could result in a day when large businesses, by stifling competition and polarising economic power, entirely control the advanced generative AI research. Since these businesses potentially put profits above social welfare, this situation could generate ethical questions. Such centralized authority can limit the general advantages of artificial intelligence availability.

3.5. Unintentional Social Commentary

The democratization of Generative AI can potentially aggravate social inequality. Generative artificial intelligence can revolutionize creative sectors such as media and design, therefore causing an employment displacement in related disciplines. Customer service bots might take the place of customer service executives. Although new employment may result from these innovations, they usually call for some technical knowledge absent in the current unskilled workforce. Concerns regarding fairness and exploitation also surround the Generative AI-driven industry [40]. Proper responsibility for any possible bias is not precisely established when Generative AI algorithms create task assignments, job schedules, and pay rates. Without proactive steps, the democratization of generative artificial intelligence could result in a workforce split and concentration of power and money only among the people with talents and resources.

3.6. Control and Sovereignty of Data

Large volumes of data needed for training the Generative AI models generate serious questions about data sovereignty. This data, likely gathered from third parties without express permission, might cause privacy problems. The lack of defined worldwide rules around data use can result in government or company exploitation. This puts individual rights and privacy in great danger. When generative artificial intelligence gets ingrained in public services, a lack of proper regulations can cause possible conflicts [41].

3.7. Social Media Generation and Manipulation

Generative AI helps more and more applications to be customized, thus increasing the risk of gently affecting individual behavior. Social media content produced using generative AI has been used to manipulate public opinion. Proper recommendation systems may help restrict the viewership of social media content. Entities' adverse motives shall disseminate extreme views and support destructive behavior by establishing echo chambers. We need to consider the influence of AI on personal autonomy and behavior by repeated exposure to AI-generated media. To check this, various steps including comprehensive governance, ethical development, and public awareness are to be taken.

Conclusion

The democratization of generative artificial intelligence demands careful consideration from policy builders, technologists, and the public. Although this technological breakthrough promises more accessibility, innovation, and creativity, its possible misuse cannot be neglected. Therefore, generative artificial intelligence has to be democratized sensibly, striking a compromise between responsibility and inclusiveness.

Firstly, it is important not to consider the hazards of algorithmic bias and intellectual property conflicts as mere technological issues. They indicate more general systematic inequalities and unresolved legal complexity. Dealing with these issues calls for proactive industry cooperation and grounding ethical AI systems with strong intellectual property policies and inclusive design approaches. Secondly, concerns about depending too much on generative artificial intelligence highlight the need for encouraging human-AI interaction instead of replacement. Artificial intelligence has to be a tool that enhances human creativity and decision-making. The main emphasis of educational programs should be on people engaging creatively and critically with AI. Thirdly, one cannot ignore the environmental expenses of artificial intelligence, especially as the technology grows. Aligning artificial intelligence democratization with global climate goals depends on active research on energy-efficient models and motivating sustainable practices in AI development. Finally, governance structures must shift to guarantee the appropriate application of generative artificial intelligence. These systems should be dynamic and flexible enough to fit the fast pace of artificial intelligence development. The development of generative models should be grounded on ethical values including justice, openness, and responsibility. Promoting international cooperation to reduce the worldwide hazards caused by artificial intelligence use—from disinformation campaigns to cyberattacks—is also critical.

In short, the democratization of generative artificial intelligence should ensure that the increased availability results in fair, ethical, and sustainable outcomes rather than only making the technology generally accessible. Unlocking AI's potential for social benefit and mitigating its hazards demands a cooperative strategy including many stakeholders. Generative AI can be a transforming agent for good only by such intentional and inclusive initiatives.

References

[1] Manduchi, L., Pandey, K., Bamler, R., Cotterell, R., Däubener, S., Fellenz, S., ... & Fortuin, V. (2024). *On the challenges and opportunities in generative ai.* arXiv preprint arXiv:2403.00025.

[2] Golda, A., Mekonen, K., Pandey, A., Singh, A., Hassija, V., Chamola, V., & Sikdar, B. (2024). Privacy and Security Concerns in Generative AI: A Comprehensive Survey. IEEE Access.

[3] Garcia, A. C. B., Garcia, M. G. P., & Rigobon, R. (2024). Algorithmic discrimination in the credit domain: what do we know about it? *AI & Society,* 39(4), 2059-2098.

[4] Steil, J. P., Albright, L., Rugh, J. S., & Massey, D. S. (2018). The social structure of mortgage discrimination. *Housing studies,* 33(5), 759-776.

[5] Seh, A. H., Zarour, M., Alenezi, M., Sarkar, A. K., Agrawal, A., Kumar, R., & Ahmad Khan, R. (2020, May). Healthcare data breaches: insights and implications. In *Healthcare (*Vol. 8, No. 2, p. 133). MDPI.

[6] Seeman, J., & Susser, D. (2024). Between privacy and utility: On differential privacy in theory and practice. *ACM Journal on Responsible Computing,* 1(1), 1-18.

[7] Zhang, Z., Rath, S., Xu, J., & Xiao, T. (2024). Federated Learning for Smart Grid: A Survey on Applications and Potential Vulnerabilities. arXiv preprint arXiv:2409.10764.

[8] Zaeem, R. N., & Barber, K. S. (2020). The effect of the GDPR on privacy policies: Recent progress and future promise. *ACM Transactions on Management Information Systems (TMIS),* 12(1), 1-20.

[9] Kirakosyan, A. (2024). Intellectual Property Ownership of AI-Generated Content. *Digital Law Journal,* 4(3), 40-50.

[10] Carlson, E. K. (2020). Artificial intelligence can invent but not patent–for now. *Engineering,* 6(11), 1212-1213.

[11] Gillotte, J. L. (2019). Copyright infringement in ai-generated artworks. *UC Davis L. Rev.,* 53, 2655.

[12] Teixeira da Silva, Jaime A., and Panagiotis Tsigaris. "Human- and AI-based authorship: Principles and ethics." *Learned Publishing* 36, no. 3 (2023).

[13] Yanisky-Ravid, S. (2017). Generating Rembrandt: Artificial intelligence, copyright, and accountability in the 3A Era: The human-like authors are already here: A new model. *Mich. St. L. Rev.,* 659.

[14] Seger, E., Ovadya, A., Siddarth, D., Garfinkel, B., & Dafoe, A. (2023, August). Democratising AI: Multiple meanings, goals, and methods. In *Proceedings of the 2023 AAAI/ACM Conference on AI, Ethics, and Society* (pp. 715-722).

[15] Scherer, M. U. (2015). Regulating artificial intelligence systems: Risks, challenges, competencies, and strategies. *Harv. JL & Tech.,* 29, 353.

[16] Díaz-Rodríguez, N., Del Ser, J., Coeckelbergh, M., de Prado, M. L., Herrera-Viedma, E., & Herrera, F. (2023). Connecting the dots in trustworthy Artificial Intelligence: From AI principles, ethics, and key requirements to responsible *AI systems and regulation. Information Fusion,* 99, 101896.

[17] Jobin, A., Ienca, M., & Vayena, E. (2019). The global landscape of AI ethics guidelines. *Nature Machine Intelligence,* 1(9), 389-399.

[18] Sey, A., & Mudongo, O. (2021). Case studies on AI skills capacity building and AI in workforce development in Africa. Research ICT Africa.

[19] Larouche, P., & Yu, Y. (2024). Between Permission and Protection: AI as a Challenge to Established Approaches to Law and Innovation. Available at SSRN 4981681.

[20] Capraro, V., Lentsch, A., Acemoglu, D., Akgun, S., Akhmedova, A., Bilancini, E., ... & Viale, R. (2024). The impact of generative artificial intelligence on socioeconomic inequalities and policy making. *PNAS nexus,* 3(6).

[21] Mannuru, N. R., Shahriar, S., Teel, Z. A., Wang, T., Lund, B. D., Tijani, S., ... & Vaidya, P. (2023). Artificial intelligence in developing countries: The impact of generative artificial intelligence (AI) technologies for development. *Information Development,* 02666669231200628.

[22] Adams, R. (2024). The new empire of AI: the future of global inequality. John Wiley & Sons.

[23] Fisher, A., & Streinz, T. (2021). Confronting data inequality. *Colum. J. Transnat'l L.,* 60, 829.

[24] Chu-Ke, C., & Dong, Y. (2024). Misinformation and literacies in the era of generative artificial intelligence: A brief overview and a call for future research. *Emerging Media,* 2(1), 70-85.

[25] Wach, K., Duong, C. D., Ejdys, J., Kazlauskaitė, R., Korzynski, P., Mazurek, G., ... & Ziemba, E. (2023). The dark side of generative artificial intelligence: A critical analysis of controversies and risks of ChatGPT. *Entrepreneurial Business and Economics Review,* 11(2), 7-30.

[26] Amankwah-Amoah, J., & Lu, Y. (2024). Harnessing AI for business development: a review of drivers and challenges in Africa. *Production Planning & Control,* 35(13), 1551-1560.

[27] Cetindamar, D., Kitto, K., Wu, M., Zhang, Y., Abedin, B., & Knight, S. (2022). Explicating AI literacy of employees at digital workplaces. *IEEE transactions on engineering management,* 71, 810-823.

[28] Zhai, C., Wibowo, S., & Li, L. D. (2024). The effects of over-reliance on AI dialogue systems on students' cognitive abilities: a systematic review. *Smart Learning Environments,* 11(1), 28.

[29] Atkinson, D. P., & Barker, D. R. (2023). AI and the social construction of creativity. *Convergence,* 29(4), 1054-1069.

[30] Adadi, A., & Berrada, M. (2018). Peeking inside the black-box: a survey on explainable artificial intelligence (XAI). *IEEE Access,* 6, 52138-52160.

[31] Wang, D., Churchill, E., Maes, P., Fan, X., Shneiderman, B., Shi, Y., & Wang, Q. (2020, April). From human-human collaboration to human-AI collaboration: Designing AI systems that can work together with people. In *Extended abstracts of the 2020 CHI conference on human factors in computing systems* (pp. 1-6).

[32] Sidhu, G. S., Sayem, M. A., Taslima, N., Anwar, A. S., Chowdhury, F., & Rowshon, M. (2024). AI and workforce development: A comparative analysis of skill gaps and training needs in emerging economies. *International journal of business and management sciences,* 4(08), 12-28.

[33] Niyomves, B., Kunacheva, N., & Kenaphoom, S. (2024). The Role of Lifelong Learning in Navigating the Future of Work. In *Modern Management Science Practices in the Age of AI* (pp. 297-316). IGI Global.

[34] Chien, A. A., Lin, L., Nguyen, H., Rao, V., Sharma, T., & Wijayawardana, R. (2023, July). Reducing the Carbon Impact of Generative AI Inference (today and in 2035). In *Proceedings of the 2nd workshop on sustainable computer systems* (pp. 1-7).

[35] Bashir, N., Donti, P., Cuff, J., Sroka, S., Ilic, M., Sze, V., Delimitrou, C., & Olivetti, E. (2024). The Climate and Sustainability Implications of Generative AI. *An MIT Exploration of Generative AI.* https://doi.org/10.21428/e4baedd9.9070dfe7.

[36] Van Wynsberghe, A. (2021). Sustainable AI: AI for sustainability and the sustainability of AI. *AI and Ethics,* 1(3), 213-218.

[37] Kubba, S. (2009). LEED practices, certification, and accreditation handbook. Butterworth-Heinemann.

[38] Schwartz, R., Dodge, J., Smith, N. A., & Etzioni, O. (2020). Green ai. *Communications of the ACM,* 63(12), 54-63.

[39] Vaccari, C., & Chadwick, A. (2020). Deepfakes and disinformation: Exploring the impact of synthetic political video on deception, uncertainty, and trust in news. *Social media+ society,* 6(1), 2056305120903408.

[40] Kenfack, P. J., Arapov, D. D., Hussain, R., Kazmi, S. A., & Khan, A. (2021, August). On the fairness of generative adversarial networks (gans). In *2021*

International Conference" Nonlinearity, Information and Robotics"(NIR) (pp. 1-7). IEEE.

[41] Balasubramaniam, S., & Kumar, K. S. (2022). Fractional Feedback Political Optimizer with Prioritization-Based Charge Scheduling in Cloud-Assisted Electric Vehicular Network. *Ad Hoc & Sensor Wireless Networks*, *52*(3-4), 173-198.

Chapter 6

Exploring the Applications and Practical Examples of Democratized Generative AI

Aditi S. Pai[1]
Natasha Jennifer Easu[2]
Himanshu Khajuria[1,*]
Chintan Singh[1]
and Biswa Prakash Nayak[1]
[1]Amity Institute of Forensic Sciences, Amity University, Noida, UP, India
[2]Department of Forensic Science, Teesside University, Middlesbrough, England, United Kingdom

Abstract

Democratized generative Artificial Intelligence (AI) is basically the process of making advanced AI tools available and accessible to a larger number of individuals. Initially, AI models were confined to trained personnel or experts in programming, machine learning and data science to be able to use the features. However, with the democratization of AI, even amateurs can effectively make use of the AI models with great ease. Due to the development of user-friendly platforms and pre-trained models for tasks like generating texts and images and for solving complex problems in seconds, its application across various fields has increased drastically. As a result of this shift, industries like content creation, education, healthcare, entertainment and other small businesses have had a drastic transformation. From helping businesses create personalised promotional content to summarizing the patient's data and

* Corresponding Author's Email: hkhajuria@amity.edu

In: Democratized Generative AI: Principles, Challenges and Applications
Editors: S. Balasubramaniam and Seifedine Kadry
ISBN: 979-8-89530-684-0

generating diagnosis in the healthcare industry, AI can be firmly relied upon. AI also allows teachers and students to create customized learning materials to make learning more effective and easier to understand as AI can simplify complicated sentences. The use of AI-driven chatbots like Open AI's ChatGPT for time-consuming tasks like coding, simplifying large amounts of data, solving complex calculations and tricky questions, etc, reduces human effort and errors and saves time. Therefore, the growth in democratization of generative AI promotes innovation and efficiency among various industries thereby enhancing human interaction.

Keywords: pre-trained models, generative AI, AI powered tools, natural language processing, machine learning, data science, application programming interface

1. Introduction

1.1. Artificial Intelligence

Artificial Intelligence (AI) is basically getting machines to mimic human intelligence to perform various tasks. AI can perform complex tasks with greater efficiency than humans, they can understand human language and respond to it, they can learn from experiences and give detailed recommendations and explanations to users [1]. The creation of AI begins with defining the issue, determining the results, organizing the data, selecting the right technology and testing the solution. First, data is gathered from a variety of sources, ranging from text to audio and videos. It is then divided into groups, such as those that the algorithms can read and those that they can't. After that, a criteria and protocol will be developed that will determine how data is processed and applied to achieve specific outcomes. During the next phase, AI makes decisions about the data that has been collected and entered. AI then classifies and interprets data using patterns that it has been trained on. After processing the data using complex algorithms, it determines outcomes that are used to make decisions. The last phase before AI completes a task is assessment [2]. Figure 1 shows How AI works.

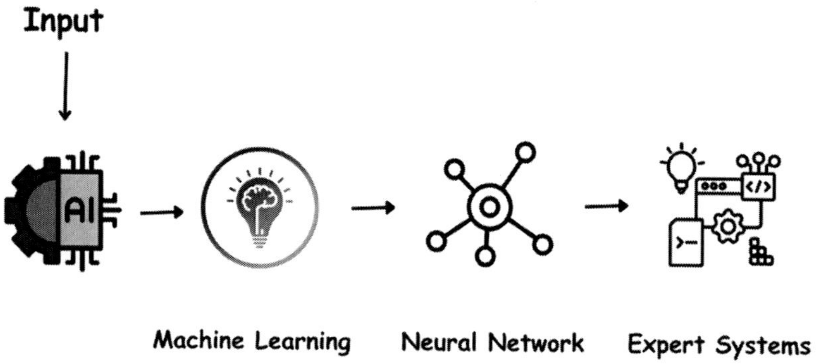

Figure 1. How AI works.

AI plays a significant role in our day-to-day lives, starting with anticipating the weather for the day to showing the best route to reach our destination. It has also improved our day-to-day life by making it more convenient and quicker by using voice-assisted smartphones, performing repetitive tasks such as adjusting the thermostat before reaching home, and providing personalized content and services based on the user's search history. The availability of AI 24x7, mostly at free of cost makes it an exceptional tool to rely on, unlike humans, who need a minimum 2-3 hour break. AI has significantly contributed to the field of education, by providing free access to a wide range of content and making personalized study materials based on the student's capacity. Machine learning algorithms help in detecting fraudulent behaviour and flag suspicious transactions occurring in the banking sector. In the medical field, AI powered tools has helped doctors and researchers analyse the patient's data to detect potential health risks and provide a personalized treatment plan which in turn helps in speeding up the process in hospitals. It has also been a valuable tool in the business sector by enhancing customer experience by providing personalized recommendations of products [3].

AI can be classified based on their capabilities and functionality. Types of AI based on capabilities include Narrow AI (Weak AI), that are designed and trained on a specific task like voice assistants like Siri and Alexa, facial recognition systems etc.; General AI (Strong AI), hat are skilled at understanding, applying and adapting to a wide range of tasks like humans, for example, diagnosing and solving a complex medical issue.; and Superintelligent AI that surpasses human intelligence in creativity and solving problems [4]. Types of AI based on functionality include Reactive Machines, that operate purely on present data and does not store or learn from previous data, such as IBM's deep blue which defeated the world chess champion;

Limited Memory AI, which learns from previous data to improve future performances like Tesla's self-driving cars and chatbots like ChatGPT; Theory Of Mind AI that understands human emotions and beliefs and adjusts its behaviour accordingly; and Self-Aware AI that has the ability to not only understand and react to emotions but also have its own awareness.

Though there are numerous advantages and applications of AI across various sectors, it also has disadvantages such as economic disruption due to loss of jobs, lack of transparency in how AI takes decisions, its impact on privacy and security of the user's data and its high cost to develop and maintain [5].

1.2. Generative AI

Generative AI is a subset of AI that creates new content like images, music, texts, videos, etc., with the help of pre-trained data. Deep-learning models, which are complex machine learning models that imitate the learning and decision-making processes of the human brain, are the foundation of generative AI [6]. These models understand the user's natural language requests or questions by identifying and encoding patterns and relationships in large amounts of data. The rise of generative AI is largely affected due to the fact that humans can use natural language to prompt AI into generating new content, has led to a significant rise in its usage.

The process begins with initiating a prompt that the system can process, such as a text, an image or a video, etc. Then, to respond to the prompt that was initiated, various AI algorithms generate new information based on the request. The generated content ranges from solutions to problems, essays, music composition, images, imitations of people's voices, etc. [7]. Figure 2 shows how generative AI works.

Earlier, data submission in generative AI required the deployment of Application Programming Interface (API) or some other complex processes. These days developers acquire knowledge about how to write programs in other sophisticated languages like python and utilize specialized tools. Due to the simple, robust and user-friendly model of generative AI, the users can express their request in as simple words as possible. This makes it easier for the user to convey their requirements. Also, after receiving a response, the user can also customize the request regarding aspects of the generated content that has to be changed.

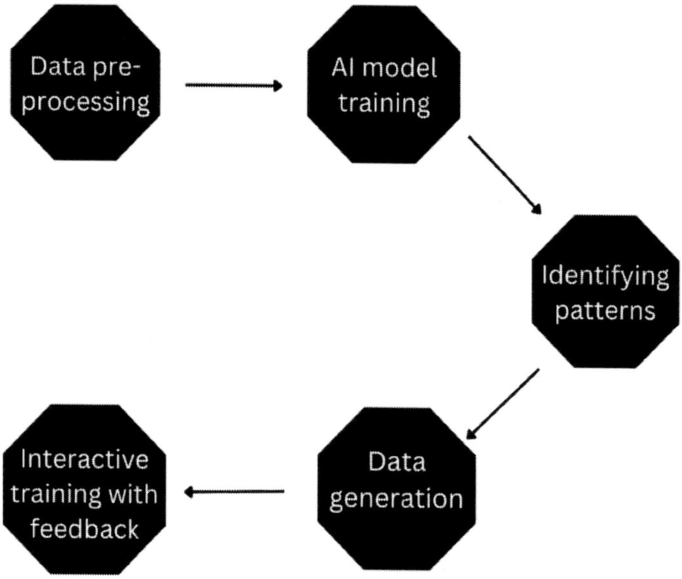

Figure 2. How Generative AI works.

Generative AI models combine various AI techniques to represent and analyse content. For example, many natural language processing techniques transform unprocessed characters such as words, letters, and punctuation into sentences in order to generate text. A range of encoding methods are then used to represent these as vectors. Developers use specialised neural networks like Generative adversarial networks (GANs), Variational Autoencoders (VAEs), neural networks with an encoder and a decoder, and other techniques to generate AI training data, realistic human faces, or even personalized human idols. Neural networks that can create new content in addition to encoding text and images have been developed as a result of recent advancements in transformers, such as Google's Bidirectional Encoder Representations from Transformers (BERT), OpenAI's GPT, and Google AlphaFold [8].

There are a wide range of applications of generative AI. Using generative AI, law firms may be able to generate arguments, deduce facts, and draft and interpret contracts, entertainment agencies can produce material more cheaply and use actors' voices to convert it into other languages, manufacturers can identify the faulty item and determine the underlying reason much more accurately and economically, financial transactions can be tracked to enhance fraud detection systems etc.

Next-generation AI tools include GPT, Lex, Jasper, and AI-Writer. Examples of image-generating tools are Dall-E 2, steady diffusion, and Midjourney. Code generating tools include Code Starter, Codex, GitHub, Copilot, and Tabnine [9].

Generally, generative AI and traditional AI have a lot in common. However, there are also some clear-cut differences between AI and generative AI. Generative AI uses neural network techniques like transformers, GANS, and VAEs, whereas traditional AI uses reinforcement learning, recurrent neural networks, and convolutional neural networks as their methods for realizing their functions. While generative AI generates unique data by utilizing human input and analytical data, traditional AI performs certain tasks, finds patterns, and makes predictions by analysing data. Generative AI is mostly used in content creation processes, including image generation, music composition, and writing whereas traditional AI is mostly applied in fraud detection, spam filtering, and recommendation systems.

Generative AI can be less transparent since its learning mechanisms are complex, making it challenging to understand how it appears at outputs, whereas traditional AI often follows preset guidelines, which makes decision-making easier to understand and more transparent [10].

Benefits of generative AI include automating the time-consuming content creation process, lowering the amount of work needed to reply to emails, increasing the speed at which certain technical questions are answered, creating human depictions that are lifelike and simplifying the production of material in a particular way.

However, there are certain challenges of using generative AI. It doesn't always identify where the content came from, determining the bias of sources might be challenging at times, it may be more difficult to spot false information in content that seems realistic, it can be difficult to figure out how to adapt to new situations. The results can hide bias, prejudice and hatred.

Accuracy, transparency, and usefulness are crucial factors to consider while using generative AI. Users and customers should be able to easily identify all generative AI material. When necessary, use primary sources to confirm the content's correctness. Recognize how bias could be included into the AI's output. Make use of extra tools to confirm the correctness of code and content produced by AI. Learn about the advantages and disadvantages of each generative AI technology. Describe the typical ways that result in failure and come up with techniques to avoid them [11].

1.3. Democratized Generative AI

"Democratized generative AI" (Gen AI) is the process of making modern artificial intelligence readily available to the layperson, irrespective of the level of technical skill he/she possesses. As artificial intelligence expands, the term "Democratized Generative AI" has gained great popularity. Democratized Generative AI is basically a change from AI being a tool for just a few, to a resource for a large number of people, creating new paths for inventiveness, modernization, and problem-solving. The most disruptive developments of this decade being GenAI promises to lift efficiency and creativity which enables a broad variety of users, including those in non-technical background to use advanced AI capabilities. This includes giving people with different needs, access to technologies like ChatGPT, Google Colab and Open AI [12]. Democratizing Generative AI is not as easy as it may sound. Releasing this technology without structure is harmful though it's exciting it could be in the end destructive. It is therefore very important to remember that democratizing AI doesn't mean full freedom. There is a need to balance between individual autonomy and organizational control to ensure the accountable and principled use of Generative AI. Gen AI leads to increase in productivity as it can automate repetitive tasks, streamline workflows and provide insights as it is about opening new horizons of information and skill acquisition. It includes invention of new products and services which enables faster ideation, prototyping and experimentation. Gen AI helps the public to obtain specialized knowledge and training in the new field. This expansion signifies a shift towards more inclusive, efficient, and innovative business practices. It has benefitted small business owners using AI for marketing, artists and designers are leveraging these tools for generating unique visuals and concepts and the researchers and scientists use them for data analysis and hypothesis generation. The collaboration of small business owners promotes a spirit of entrepreneurship and allows the exchange of ideas and creativity among them. The tasks which took a huge lot of time are now completed quickly in minutes thereby people get more time for solving more complex problems. GenAI automates a broad range of tasks, from writing emails to coding, thereby boosting productivity and reducing costs. Using Gen AI irresponsibly may lead to accidental moments which could cause harm to the individual and the public in general. Without proper guidance, democratized Gen AI can feel more like a wild, free-for-all than a productive workplace. Further, as there is a vast amount of data, the privacy and data security are vulnerable and the chances of spreading misinformation, or the unethical use of the data is high. On one hand these tools help in creative thinking while on the other hand skills like critical thinking and decision-making abilities deteriorate. Further, one would have to face legal and ethical implications with respect to the generation of the content [13].

2. Examples of Generative AI

2.1. Text Generation

2.1.1. ChatGPT

ChatGPT is an artificial intelligence (AI) chatbot that simulates human communication by using natural language processing. The language model can answer questions and create a variety of written materials, such as emails, articles, essays, social media postings, and codes. The GPT stands for "Generative Pre-trained Transformer," which describes how ChatGPT interprets questions and creates answers. ChatGPT is trained with reinforcement learning through human feedback and reward models that rank the best responses. This input enhances ChatGPT's machine learning capabilities to provide better results in the future. ChatGPT was developed by the artificial intelligence research firm OpenAI, which released the tool in November 2022 [14]. It was created in 2015, by a group of researchers and entrepreneurs, including Elon Musk and Sam Altman.

ChatGPT creates human-like text using transformer neural networks and deep learning, a branch of machine learning. The transformer anticipates text, including the subsequent word, sentence, or paragraph, based on the regular pattern of its training data. Training begins with generic data, then moves to more tailored data for a specific task. After training ChatGPT on human language through online text, it used transcripts to learn the basics of conversations. Human trainers provide conversations and rank the responses. These reward models help determine the best answers. By clicking on the thumbs-up or thumbs-down symbols next to the response, people can upvote or downvote the chatbot's response, continuing to train it. To enhance and refine subsequent conversations, users can also submit more written input [15]. People use ChatGPT to code computer programs and check for bugs in code, describe complex topics more simply, compose music, draft emails, summarize articles, podcasts or presentations, solve math problems, create articles, blog posts and quizzes for websites, formulate product descriptions, assist with job searches, including writing resumes and cover letters, generate art, etc. ChatGPT has numerous benefits including efficiency, cost-effectiveness, improving quality of the content, instant responses, increased availability, multilingual support, natural language understanding and scalability [16].

However, ChatGPT has few drawbacks like lack of a thorough understanding of how complicated human language is, its responds may sound artificial and robotic, although it summarizes content, no sources are cited, irony and sarcasm are beyond its comprehension, it may not be able to adjust and instead focus on the incorrect portion of a query. Though ChatGPT is highly reliable in generating content, it raises concerns related to privacy, plagiarism and unethical usage and has bias in training data. Its biggest drawback is that it is replacing jobs which is leading to economic instability [17].

2.1.2. Jasper.ai

Jasper AI is an artificial intelligence system that was developed in 2021. Its goal was to either completely replace or significantly accelerate the writing process required for different roles. This powerful model can produce written content in 26 more languages. It is designed to understand and generate human-like writing based on a given stimulus. It is trained on vast amounts of text data to improve its language proficiency and expertise and uses deep learning techniques to generate responses that are logical. It is also known as the robotic writer and can write up to ten times as quickly as an ordinary human [18]. Jasper's technology ensures that the outputs are free of plagiarism and do not show any biases, such as political or religious preferences. It has proved to be a good choice for corporate workers and digital marketers due to its ability to create matter. To begin with, users can choose from several themes which provide Jasper with the context it needs to ensure the system understands the target audience, appropriate tone, and style. The user must then specify their goals which will help Jasper to generate content [19]. Jasper AI is predominantly used in the field of e-commerce, by writing product descriptions and generating creative content for advertisements. In the field of real estate, brokers can benefit from Jasper's ability to create material that presents their properties in a visually appealing way. Educational institutions can use Jasper AI to create interactive learning resources for students. Jasper can also be used by medical professionals to inform individuals about any illnesses they may have along with their potential remedies. Private healthcare practitioners might also use Jasper to create content that effectively highlights their products and services [20].

2.2. Image Generation

2.2.1. DALL-E 2

OpenAI launched the Dall-E project in June 2020 and was first known as Image GPT. It was an effort to show how a neural network could produce high-quality photographs. Later, Dall-E improved the original idea of Image GPT by allowing users to create new images with text prompts with the help of Natural Language Processing techniques [21]. Additionally, OpenAI developed the Contrastive Language-Image Pre-training (CLIP) model, which was trained on 400 million labelled photos, to prove that the Dall-E model could produce images accurately. To evaluate Dall-E's output, OpenAI implemented CLIP, which determined which caption matches most accurately with a generated image. Its potential benefits include speed, accessibility, flexibility and customization. While Dall-E has plenty of benefits, it does come with several important concerns which include copyright issues, image legitimacy and bias. However, it is a reliable tool, giving accurate results and is hence widely used by individuals and organizations to create graphics that are useful for advertising, to generate pictures and explain different concepts, to design new concepts [22].

2.3. Code Generation

2.3.1. GitHub Copilot

GitHub Copilot is an AI coding assistant that can be integrated into a programmer's development environment. It automates the development process, thereby helping developers to write code and resolve errors that occur [23]. Due to the collaboration between OpenAI, Microsoft and GitHub, it was made publicly available on June 29, 2021. The OpenAI Codex, which enabled GitHub Copilot, was created using the same GPT-3 model as ChatGPT-3. However, ChatGPT and the OpenAI Codex, were designed with different objectives in mind. While the OpenAI Codex was trained on more source codes to make it a more effective tool for software developers, ChatGPT was created as a generalised chatbot. Code completion, function writing, unit test development, and commenting on programming code are some of GitHub Copilot's significant abilities. Due to its exposure to huge amounts of data during training, it helps developers write programming codes, build algorithms, implement best practices and create data structures efficiently [24]. GitHub Copilot has significantly helped programmers to save time, increase productivity and improve the quality of the code. It can also explain codes that are unfamiliar to the developers and suggest new approaches. However, there are certain drawbacks concerned with its use, which include code inaccuracy as GitHub Copilot writes codes based on the patterns it is trained on, which may also result in its bias towards a certain result [25].

2.4. Music Generation

2.4.1. Riffusion

Seth Forsgren and Hayk Martiros created the neural network Riffusion, that utilizes sound photographs in place of audio to generate music. It was created as an enhancement on Stable Diffusion, an open-source model which was already in operation for creating graphics on spectrograms in response to text cues. This leads to a template which generates image files using text prompts, which are further transformed into audio files by using an inverse Fourier transform. Even though these files are only a few seconds long, the model may interpolate many files together using the latent space between outputs [26]. The imaging feature of the Stable Diffusion model is used to accomplish this. The music derived from this is called “de otro mundo" (otherworldly). However, it is very unlikely to replace music made by human creativity [27]. Riffusion can be classified within a subset of AI text-to-music generators. The core repository for Riffusion image and audio processing code are diffusion pipeline that performs prompt interpolation combined with image conditioning, conversions between spectrogram images and audio clips, Command-line interface for common tasks, Interactive app using stream lit, Flask server to provide model inference via API and various third-party integrations [28].It was created as an enhancement on Stable Diffusion, an open-source model which was already in operation for creating graphics on spectrograms in response to text cues. This leads to a template which generates image files using text prompts, which are further transformed into audio files by using an inverse Fourier transform. Even though these files are only a few seconds long, the model may interpolate many files together using the latent space between outputs [26]. The imaging feature of the Stable Diffusion model is used to accomplish this. The music derived from this is called "de otro mundo" (otherworldly). However, it is very unlikely to replace music made by human creativity [27]. Riffusion can be classified within a subset of AI text-to-music generators. The core repository for riffusion image and audio processing code are diffusion pipeline that performs prompt interpolation combined with image conditioning, conversions between spectrogram images and audio clips, Command-line interface for common tasks, Interactive app using stream lit, Flask server to provide model inference via API and various third-party integrations [28].

2.5. Video Generation

2.5.1. Synthesia

Synthesia is a powerful artificial intelligence platform that uses synthetic characters to convert text into a realistic-looking video. This technology detects a particular text type and produces natural-sounding avatars using enhanced deep learning networks. This provides a new channel for content creation. Whether you are a teacher, marketer, or someone in between, Synthesia is simple to use for making films. Synthesia is an advanced form of an Artificial Intelligence platform that converts text into a real-looking video with virtual characters. This technology uses improved deep learning networks to develop natural-sounding avatars by reading the particular text type. This opens a new way of creating content. Synthesia is easy to use to create videos, no matter who you are, whether you are a marketer, teacher, or anyone in between [29]. A creative technology that has transformed the way we produce and consume media is Synthesia. Assume with only a few clicks would suffice to transform ordinary words into appealing, photorealistic videos, with the help of Synthesia's advanced artificial intelligence technology. We can create realistic avatars that clearly and effectively convey your message while also saving money and time. Thus, Synthesia brings in a new era of dynamic, customized video production, regardless of our field whether it is in marketing, education or corporate training.

2.6. Voice Synthesis

2.6.1. Amazon Polly

Amazon Polly is a cloud service that converts text into real, human-like speech [30]. By using Amazon Polly, one can generate applications that improve accessibility and engagement. Several languages can be supported by Amazon Polly, which also has a variety of convincing voices. speech-enabled apps that function in many places and speak the voice that users choose can also be created with the help of Amazon Polly. There are numerous voice alternatives offered by Amazon Polly, such as traditional text-to-speech (TTS), generative, long-form and neural. These voices provide the most realistic and human-like text-to-speech voices available by employing modern machine learning technologies to produce significant developments in speech quality. Typical uses for Amazon Polly include eLearning platforms, games, newsreaders, accessibility apps for the blind and the Internet of Things (IoT) market [31]. The Payment Card Industry Data Security Standard (PCI DSS) and HIPAA (the Health Insurance Portability and Accountability Act of 1996) have approved Amazon Polly for utilisation with regulated workloads.

2.7. Design and Art

2.7.1. Canva

Canva is a graphic design application aimed to make digital design simpler. It is a well-known web-based graphic design tool that facilitates the creation of superior images and materials. Creating an account is simple and everything functions, whether you are using an iOS or Android app or a web browser. As a result, millions of people create digital invites, presentations, posters, social media graphics and printed products like business cards and brochures, using Canva [32]. One of the more successful cases of a digital design platform that balances the needs of both professional resources and user-friendly learning systems is Canva. As a result, it is an awesome chance to start teaching students how to best use design tools and the possibility of employing them in their careers later. In addition to being perfect for art and design, Canva can be utilized for assignments involving technology, geography, history, English, and other subjects. Additionally, students can learn a particular subject while learning how to use this technology at the same time. With the help of this application, which is packed with useful instructions and templates, teachers can make posters for their classes or construct charts, photos, and much more. This platform's incorporation of AI makes it more potent and practical than before, and it also qualifies as a truly excellent method of teaching generative AI [33]. With its easy-to-use drag-and-drop interface, Canva enables image editing and project-based learning, especially among younger pupils. It has several potential uses in the classroom, covering everything from group brainstorming to individual project development. Because Canva is optimized for Chromebooks, even the most demanding image-based projects can be completed with seamless interaction on most machines. Because of its simple to operate interface, Canva offers a lower barrier to access than more powerful products. Canva's broad range of templates is its greatest practical feature [34]. There are thousands of templates in more than 100 design types, even with a free membership. From a personal CV to an Instagram post for your band's upcoming live performance, there are templates for almost every purpose you can imagine. Vectors and graphics, stock photos, colour palettes, font groups, and page layouts are all included in most templates. These are extra components, including shapes, stickers, frames, or occasionally animated icons, that are used to give a template personality. Some stock photos can be obtained straight from Canva's collection. One has the option to replace them with their own photos or keep these. Most templates adhere to a particular colour scheme for all their different components in order to maintain a unified look. The designers at Canva have chosen some font pairings. This is particularly true for multi-page layouts like brochures and presentation decks. Like Google Slides or PowerPoint, each page will usually have multiple layout possibilities [35].

2.7.2. Adobe Firefly

Adobe Inc has been adding AI-driven capabilities for its eCommerce, multimedia content creation tools and other product suites at a brisk pace recently. With the launch of Firefly, it has attempted into the generative AI segment [36]. The beta version of Adobe Firefly is currently available for public use. A variety of generative AI capabilities are available in Adobe Firefly for tasks ranging from photo editing and vector creation to text-to-image conversion. In simple terms, Firefly is an artificial intelligence mode or rather, an ensemble of AI models—created by Adobe, the massive software company that makes programs like Photoshop and Illustrator [37]. Because the model was trained on hundreds of images and text descriptions to teach it to create images from text prompts, it is similar to the finest AI art generators. However, Adobe has used the idea in a few ways. In addition to being a stand-alone browser application, it powers features in Adobe's current software, such as Photoshop and Premiere Pro. The features of Adobe Firefly, for now, is its ability to deliver desired results by understanding text-based instructions [38].

2.8. Education and Learning

2.8.1. Grammarly

Grammarly is a well-known online writing assistant that has been available since 2009. It is used by job seekers, writers and other professionals to proofread and edit their documents [39]. It is mainly cloud-based and basically enhances the vocabulary by checking for spelling, grammar and punctuation errors and corrects it. Grammarly can identify spelling mistakes and jumbled phrases. Every sentence is analysed by the Grammarly AI system, which looks for suitable replacements for any mistakes it finds. In certain cases, the algorithm suggests particular word options to choose from. However, the user is responsible for making any particular modifications. A list of alternate spellings is provided along with a list of spelling errors. Users can choose alternative phrases and avoid repetition by using the synonym checker. Along with details on the kind of error you made, Grammarly also offers explanations for the suggested corrections.[40].

3. Applications of Democratized Generative AI across Various Industries

3.1. Media and Entertainment

In the media and entertainment industry, the infusion of Artificial Intelligence has set the stage for a remarkable change. It has emerged as a remarkable force in the realms of advertising, in the development of online games, production of movies and in advertising [41]. AI has become a medium to satisfy the ever-growing requirement in the media and entertainment sector, which has sparking strategic investments and anchoring a determined pursuit. We have robots and augmented intelligence who are now the planners of amazing, next-generation consumer experiences in this creative age. Various leading companies in the fields of media, entertainment, and technology sectors have collected their knowledge to develop, introduce and improve a wide range of AI-driven innovations, improving the sector.

The creation of content is one of the primary fields in which AI influences media and entertainment. AI is also being used to produce new kinds of content, such computer-generated musicians and virtual influencers. Basically, AI is also being used to enhance the customers experience in the entertainment industry, by voice recognition technology which is being used to enable consumers to manage their entertainment. In order to answer frequently asked questions and provide efficient customer care, Chatbots are being employed more and more by entertainment firms.

Google Assistant and Amazon's Alexa, let users control their entertainment experience with voice commands, which is an entertainment system that integrates AI-powered personal assistants. This AI-driven animation and character modelling has improved the realism of 3D models in video games and films [42]. Composers are creating imaginative soundtracks more easily with AI-powered music creation tools. In addition to this AI expedites the content creation process thereby causing lower costs and higher productivity. Finally, the influence of AI is crucial for engagement of audience and marketing. Here it makes it possible to target ads exactly to the customer guaranteeing that the proper people see the information. Social media analysis also assists businesses to enhance their plans through recognition of patterns. More precise measurement of their online influence can be seen by these tools. By improving efficiency, innovation, and customization, AI has a revolutionary effect on the media and entertainment industry [43].

3.2. Healthcare and Life Sciences

Data of millions of patients are collected on a day-to-day basis from various sources. The purpose is to help improve everyone's health by safely, securely and ethically extracting the insights contained in this enormous amount of data. The identifying patterns at a scale that is impossible for humans to achieve can be achieved only through the AI algorithms. However, the challenge is to handle the sensitive health data carefully and under strict regulation [44].

To tackle global issues like climate change and emerging diseases, numerous innovative scientific applications are present which are results from the recent rapid advancements in AI. Among all the applications of AI, increasing scientific output is the most beneficial to society and the economy and this has better equipped the OECD nations [45].

The data indicates that pharmaceutical firms are the most benefited from AI in healthcare. By speeding up their drug discovery process and automating target identification, AI has helped in eliminating time-consuming data monitoring methods.

3.3. Education and E-Learning

Application of democratized AI in Education and E-learning A significant role in a society's development is played by education. Over the period it has undergone several significant adjustments in order to reflect the most contemporary issues like development in technology or climate change and global warming. Educational systems that use AI and data analytics to customize how students learn are referred to as adaptive learning technologies. Based on every student's performance, their style of learning and their preferences, all these technologies are modified dynamically and the course material is presented [46]. By constantly assessing data on student interactions and offering customized support, focused feedback, and enhanced learning pathways is developed and this results in Adaptive learning systems. In general, the Information technologies and artificial intelligence (AI), are revolutionizing modern education. Nowadays learning management and training systems rely heavily on AI algorithms and educational robots to support a variety of AI in education (AIED) teaching and learning activities [47].

The four main categories can be classified as Adaptive learning and personalized tutoring, intelligent assessment and management, profiling and prediction, and emerging products. Among these adaptive learning and personalized tutoring have received the most research. The most popular research topics range from impact of AIED, system design and implementation, adoption and use and its challenges. Out of these theories the most active theories that guide the research design are constructivist learning theory, learning style theory, cognitive theories of learning and item response theory. The studies say that critical, up-to-date overview of the evolving research landscape, incorporating the latest articles are considering the recent trend of a substantial surge in AIED research articles and the review works on specific AIED domains. The valuable insights provided by the research lend useful assistance in shaping the development of the AIED research field. These include the integration of new AI technologies, the enhancement of scientific rigor through theory-guided research design and the elevation of theoretical contributions in research [48].

3.4. Retail and E-Commerce

Ecommerce businesses have implemented AI across various business functions and will continue to find new and innovative applications for AI in ecommerce as adoption increases and the technology advances. One of the main areas of the use of AI are Personalized product recommendations where data from past customer behaviour, browsing history, and purchase history to suggest products are used. The AI can understand their customers' language and images and match them with the desired products [49]. Suggestions based on size, colour, shape, fabric, and brand are made available with features like "People also purchased" or "Customers also viewed" and the details of the last purchases we made. Secondly the chatbots and virtual assistants help field customer queries and facilitate online shopping by providing tips, which act as customer service representatives for our ecommerce business. These applications can handle simple transactions, process orders, and provide personalized offers to customers, making it easier to field a large volume of requests across various points-of-sales. AI can also collect customer data with respect to sizing and the reasons for inquiry, which can help inform product development and improve customer service.

Online businesses can also integrate a chatbot into the checkout page so customers can easily ask about product details, quantities for highly sought-after items, and shipping information, without leaving their cart. These also provide 24/7 customer service. Chatbots and virtual assistants can provide prompt responses 24/7, allowing your live support agents to address more complex customer service issues [50]. AI can help you reduce customer service costs by automatically resolving disputes and processing refunds. Further, AI can assist in fraud detection and prevention of the same by analysing data, detecting anomalies and monitoring transactions. This technology can spot unusual transactions, such as high-value transfers, multiple transactions within a short time frame or from unfamiliar locations and flag them for further investigation. Another area where AI can help is to manage inventory by analysing historical sales data and predicting future demand. AI-enabled inventory management can automate the inventory replenishment processes by integrating with suppliers to ensure timely restocking. AI is also used to forecast transit times and shipment delays and communicate these updates with all stakeholders. One of the most important areas where AI has helped is in dynamic pricing that allows one to adjust the prices and offerings based on real-time user behaviour, global supply & demand and competitors. With the power of AI, you can anticipate optimal discounting opportunities and dynamically determine the minimum discount required to drive a successful sale. Further, AI allows ecommerce businesses to understand customers better and identify new trends. It can analyse customer engagements across POS channels and offer insights for optimization as more consumer data becomes available. Lastly, Generative AI is an artificial intelligence system that generates text, images, or other media based on prompts. Popular generative tools include ChatGPT and DALL-E. Ecommerce businesses are using generative AI to scale the production of their marketing collateral and tailor it to different audiences [51]. Language and images and matches them with the desired products [49]. Suggestion based on size, colour, shape, fabric, and brand are made available with features like "People also purchased" or "Customers also viewed" and also the details of the last purchases we made. Secondly the chatbots and virtual assistants help field customer queries and facilitating online shopping by providing tips, which act as customer service representatives for our ecommerce business. These applications can handle simple transactions, process orders, and provide personalized offers to customers, making it easier to field a large volume of requests across various points-of-sales . AI can also collect customer data with respect to sizing and the reasons for inquiry, which can help inform product development and improve customer service. While online businesses can also integrate a chatbot into the checkout page so customers can easily ask about product details, quantities for highly sought-after items, and shipping information, without leaving their cart. These also provide 24/7 customer service. Chatbots and virtual assistants can provide prompt responses 24/7, allowing your live support agents to address more complex customer service issues [50]. AI can help you reduce customer service costs by automatically resolving disputes and processing refunds.

Further, AI can assist in fraud detection and prevention of the same by analyzing data, detecting anomalies and monitoring transactions. This technology can spot unusual transactions, such as high-value transfers, multiple transactions within a short time frame or from unfamiliar locations and flag them for further investigation. Another area where AI can help is to manage inventory by analysing historical sales data and predicting future demand. AI-enabled inventory management can automate the inventory replenishment processes by integrating with suppliers to ensure timely restocking. AI is also used to forecast transit times and shipment delays and communicate these updates with all stakeholders. One of the most important areas where AI has helped is in dynamic pricing that allows one to adjust the prices and offerings based on real-time user behaviour, global supply & demand and competitors. With the power of AI, you can anticipate optimal discounting opportunities and dynamically determine the minimum discount required to drive a successful sale. Further, AI allows ecommerce businesses to understand customers better and identify new trends. It can analyze customer engagements across POS channels and offer insights for optimization as more consumer data becomes available. Lastly, Generative AI is an artificial intelligence system that generates text, images, or other media based on prompts. Popular generative tools include ChatGPT and DALL-E.

Ecommerce businesses are using generative AI to scale the production of their marketing collateral and tailor it to different audiences [51].

3.5. Manufacturing and Engineering

The engineering terrain has revolutionised the thrusting industry into a period of supreme innovation and efficiency. Two of the most important areas being intelligent design and simulation in engineering where AI has made an enormous effect. Engineers can identify defects and enhance product designs before creating a physical model by utilizing machine learning algorithms. Hence, engineers can conserve time and money by carrying out virtual checks with AI-powered simulations. They can also examine a variety of design options which in turn helps in producing more creative and reliable solutions [52]. AI- driven intelligent design and simulation techniques are also helping in improving product designs while stimulating engineering innovation. By simulating intricate situations and iterating through numerous options for design, engineers are able to find new solutions and options for design. This predictive maintenance backed by AI has completely transformed the way businesses maintain their machinery and equipment, AI systems have the ability to forecast the equipment faults and offer maintenance regimens, by analysing real-time sensor data. With this proactive strategy the maintenance expenses are largely lowered. Further, by avoiding expensive malfunctions and unscheduled downtime the predictive maintenance goes beyond just foreseeing breakdowns in equipment. These days, AI-powered systems are able to schedule repairs, order replacement parts, and propose specific fixes. Autonomous systems, like drones and self-driving automobiles, are prime examples of AI's scientific potential. For navigational and making choices in everyday situations, these systems rely on complex AI algorithms and deep models of learning. Self-driving cars have the chance to transform transportation through boosting safety, reducing accident rates, and raising overall efficiency in the auto industry. The use of autonomous systems has expanded rapidly beyond self-driving cars and drones to domains which includes manufacturing, logistics, and agriculture. AI-powered machinery and robots eliminate hazardous and routine tasks, improving operational efficiency and security for employees [53]. Another field where AI is used is NLP which is a subfield of machine learning which investigates how computers and human language interact. NLP has grown increasingly popular in engineering because of its willingness to handle and fully understand enormous volumes of technical documentation. Engineers are able to use NLP-powered tools to extract valuable data from research papers, patents, and manuals in order to encourage innovation and speed down knowledge sharing. NLP's impact on engineering goes way beyond its ability to extract information from technical papers. Chatbots and virtual assistants with linguistic processing (NLP) capabilities are helping the engineers to collaborate and communicate through the ability to real-time sharing of knowledge and problem-solving. This improves customer happiness which is the most important aspect of any business and brand reputation. By significantly reducing product recalls and solving problems. Predictive analytics is another component of AI's contribution to the industrial quality control area which aids in businesses in predicting any flaws and setting preventative measures in place. By optimizing processes through the examination of data from different stages of production, AI algorithms can continuously improve the quality of goods [54].

3.6. Finance and Banking

AI is currently displacing the banking industry in a number of ways when banks already have a reputation for implementing computers and offering internet-based financial services. While they have long been at the forefront in technological breakthroughs, the development of AI has brought in a new era of development. These technologies comprise chatbots for customer service and tools to help prevent complex frauds in the sector. Compared to traditional approaches, these innovations have allowed banks to offer tailored solutions, function more effectively and reduce risks more effectively [55]. As a result, the application of AI in banking keeps growing, opening new possibilities, and changing the financial services industry. AI has found its way into banking systems driven by the significant cost savings, efficiency gains, and security enhancements that it comes with. AI is picking up pace in the banking sector mainly because it enhances customer service delivery, reduces fraudulent activities, simplifies credit scoring processes, and enhances risk management mechanisms. One significant factor for the increased usage of AI in banks is improving customer service quality.

AI chatbots or power virtual assistants enable 24-hour seven days support which handles routine questions as well as transactions quickly and efficiently. It not only reduces waiting periods but also involves personal interactions for better customer satisfaction. Fraud detection is also essential for AI to enter the area of banking. This has become a significant issue with modern cyberattacks becoming more sophisticated by the day such that financial fraud stands out as one major concern among many others especially in the context of AI in banking. It is here that AI algorithms using real-time transaction data analysis on a huge scale can identify any irregularities and raise alerts on possible fraud activities. The major applications in banking are pertaining to customer service, Fraud detection and prevention, Credit Scoring and Loan Approvals, Risk Management, Process Automation, Investment and Wealth Management, Customer Insights and Marketing [56].

3.7. Marketing and Advertising

The use of generative AI in the marketing and advertising industry promotes innovative ideas and designs that could increase conversions. Businesses can discover innovative solutions that solve their problems and help them to acquire valuable data to guide them across all consumer interactions. It is proven to be efficient in terms of time and money as it can cut down on the amount of time spent on creating projects and technologies, allow businesses the freedom to computerise basic marketing strategies and can produce content in less than a minute. It aids in content creation by creating new content like blog posts, emails and social media posts, designing advertisement copies and product descriptions and writing scripts for video advertisements and product demos. Tools like DALL-E, Runway and Midjourney make use of generative adversarial networks (GANs) that help them generate images and videos from textual prompts. This helps them to create exceptional product demos, video advertisements and graphics, make innovative brand resources, such as logos and create pictures for posts on social media. Marketers can use generative AI to create customized advertising strategies that focus on the customer which increases their preference towards the product [57].

3.8. Legal and Compliance

Legal professionals are increasing their use of generative AI to automate repetitive processes legal research, contract review and investigation. This gives practitioners more time to concentrate on delicate legal matters and client strategies which leads to increase in productivity and efficiency. Generative AI is increasingly being used in tasks like legal writing, assisting negotiation and even for basic legal reasoning making it more accessible and reasonably priced for a wider range of people and companies [58]. Large volumes of legal data can be analysed using generative AI to find potential risks and gaps, producing more precise and reliable legal documents. With the help of data that is input by humans and preset templates, AI can generate drafts of legal documents like wills, pleadings, etc. This gives lawyers more time to concentrate on modifying the document according to the case. Attorneys could save hours of writing and research by using generative AI to analyse case laws and generate summaries that contain important information to support the evidence. AI can also identify grammatical errors, inconsistent legal citations and suggestions for improving the clarity and meaning of legal texts. AI can quickly scan vast amounts of electronic records, finding appropriate keywords and highlighting potentially sensitive content. To answer common client questions, schedule appointments and offer basic legal information, law firms can use chatbots driven by generative AI. This lessens administrative burdens and increases the availability of assistance for customers. AI can create customized legal documents for clients, including standard conditions of service or non-disclosure agreements, according to their requirements and industry regulations. Generative AI can examine huge amounts of data obtained from the previous cases and court rulings. AI can also examine contracts to find hidden terms and possible risks, thereby, assisting organisations in making sensible decisions during negotiations [59].

3.9. Real Estate and Construction

The creation of AI-powered project monitoring systems has significantly enhanced efficiency and increased productivity. These tools track the status of projects and revenue in real time. In the real estate agency, automating recurring tasks, such as creating preliminary property descriptions or generating data-driven reports, can be simplified by using generative AI services. This gives more time to devote to more effective strategies and personalised client interactions analysing user preferences and successful advertising campaigns. It can assist in introducing fresh concepts for advertising materials and property presentations. Gen AI is excellent at analysing complex data sets, discovering hidden patterns and spotting potential possibilities. This enables them to target the appropriate audience, improve the advertisements and close sales more quickly by using data to fuel the decisions. Crucial information from lease agreements such as maintenance responsibilities, rent escalations and lease terms can be automatically extracted and analysed using generative AI which can save countless hours and reduce the possibility of human error. Generative AI systems have the capacity to automatically generate descriptions that highlight a property's prominent features, such as hardwood floors, latest appliances or breathtaking views. In addition to ensuring consistent and interesting property descriptions across advertisements, this saves the brokers' valuable time. Generative AI also examines photos of the real estate and produces appropriate phrases that precisely capture the unique features of the property for an attractive advertisement [60].

3.10. Transportation and Logistics

The transportation sector has been steadily evolving over the years. Artificial intelligence in the transportation industry marks the next stage of its evolution. AI algorithms have been used in transportation for decades. The technology was silently transforming the industry, largely unnoticed by the public because the first smart systems were tested and refined in laboratories and academic circles. Now, transportation has become smart. If we zoom out and look at the big picture of the initial uses of AI in transportation and logistics, we could see that it was penetrating the industry through numerous solutions [61]. Some of the earliest applications are Self-driving cars, Route Planning and Optimization, Traffic management. Today, smart technology is behind cutting-edge logistics and transportation solutions: smart city infrastructures, supply chain management, traffic incident detection, and more. Critical developments in machine learning, data analytics, and sensor technology during the last two decades have supercharged AI in all its forms. Owing to these advancements, transportation systems not only became smarter but also more adaptive to changing road conditions. AI in transportation got an upgrade and can now instantly respond to congestion, detect accidents as soon as they happen, or prioritize pedestrians over vehicles near school zones during peak hours. With its improved predictive capabilities, artificial intelligence also became an indispensable tool for more accurate traffic forecasting. AI in transportation has grown to the extent that it's impossible not to notice its impact. The technology makes the industry more user-oriented and automated. The few best examples of AI in transportation and how they are remodelling the sector are in the areas of Autonomous Vehicles, Traffic Flow Optimization, Road Condition Monitoring, Traffic Incident Detection, Pedestrian Detection, Driver Monitoring, Smart Parking Management, AI in

Logistics and Supply Chain Management, Automated License Plate Recognition, Ridesharing and Mobility as a Service (MaaS). The volume of data currently available is so much underutilized that there's massive potential for machine learning. With massive advancements in intelligent technologies being announced almost every few months, the future of AI in transportation is bright and full of opportunities [62].

3.11. Government and Public Sector

AI offers to governments and the private sector in similar areas. These offerings can be broadly classified into three categories viz., savings due to operational efficiency, new and improved services and data-driven decision making. The state and local officials surveyed had excessive paperwork burdens that impacted their ability to get work done, this can be resolved by the application of AI. Citizen-facing applications like self-driving shuttles and personalized education improve the quality of services governments deliver to its citizens [63]. Governments are collecting an abundant amount of data every day. Yet, without an accurate analysis, data is not adequate for actionable insights. Better decision making has the potential to both improve services and save costs. Other social welfare and healthcare AI applications in government are Identifying fraudulent benefits claims Tracking disease spreads, triaging patients and handling citizens health related queries. The Domestic security related AI applications are useful for Predicting a crime and recommending optimal police presence, surveillance. The use of autonomous military drones is also referred to as Unmanned combat aerial vehicles (UCAV), are military weapons that carry combat payloads like missiles are usually under real-time human control, with varying levels of autonomy. With respect to Transportation, autonomous shuttles are a flexible solution to move people and monitor social media to identify incidents, which needs to be monitored by the Government [64].

Further in the field of personalised Education and marking exam papers, the role of AI is prevalent in Government establishments. Government agencies also need to classify emergency calls based on their urgency wherein voice recognition technologies and ML algorithms can help governments automate emergency call lines by understanding and categorizing queries and in case of fire predictions ML & DL map the dryness of forests to predict wildfire better. Public relations services like usage of chatbots and checking on social media posts for citizen feedback purposes are quite frequently used to improve their services. Major uses of AI are in the file of document automation which includes extraction and inputting of invoices, architectural drawings, certificates, charts, drawings, forms, legal documents and letters. Other uses are in Drafting documents & announcements and in Translation. Some best practices of AI transformation are that they Involve people more, enhance technology infrastructure, improve data quality & collection, Involve the experts, Reduce bias in AI [65].

4. Impact on Society and Economy

In order to be a leader in your field of business we need to act today and adopt the new wave of generative AI systems as it has the potential to transform the whole industry. The AI models can perform tasks that are monotonous and by a sophisticated conversation with users they also generate original contents. This has revolutionised our lives in terms of business, daily interactions and healthcare. Its ability to make independent decisions has reshaped the Finance and Biopharma industries to a great extent [66]. The impact of AI has just begun to tap into its full capabilities. Meetings are being scheduled and reports on data from spreadsheets are being generated and presentations are made easily by people in all walks of life using AI. This has significantly increased efficiency and the employees get enough time to focus on tasks of more value and interest. This means that the individuals need no technical knowledge to make the best use of AI, and they have a chance to focus. They are good with a lot of time for their hobbies and passions while they can quickly complete their tasks which they get the income from. The routine tasks in business can be performed with increased efficiency and zero human error [67]. This also helps in reducing business costs. AI technology is changing the way software has been developed by giving the tools and resources to create applications by simply giving their proposal. The architects can generate 3D models of their proposed constructions and make necessary changes easily after taking inputs from their customers. This can help in innovative thinking and quicker decision making by the customers. The game developers can design characters, the filmmakers can understand the target audience and create virtual environments.

The democratization of Generative AI is more than just a technological trend which signifies a primary change in how we use technology. Since it increasingly gets into various areas of our lives, the opportunities for innovation, productivity, and revolution are unlimited. Making GenAI technology available to everyone in healthcare, is likely to transform how illnesses and disorders are detected and how they can be cured after treatment. Gen AI technology quickly assesses the patient information, history of the disease and it can create possible diagnoses. Instantly recommending treatment options ensures improved tailored healthcare, enabling care providers to attend more patients within a given time. We can imagine production and manufacturing units operated by smart GenAI systems, smoothly generating unique products using prior information and trends in the present market. The advantages are manifold like less or human intervention, increase in productivity and efficiency and the capability to immediately adapt to changing consumer needs. Education is also on the verge of facing disruption. The democratization of GenAI could tailor educational resources for every student by adjusting to their unique learning preferences to enhance personalized learning [68].

4.1. Challenges in Adoption of Democratized Generative AI

In the coming years, AI will advance to be multimodal and further surrounded in our day-to-day routines, improving human skills and easing innovative ways of communication. This also means the challenges or risk of the individuals misusing or misinterpreting the data. It cannot be denied that there are risks like data loss, misuse of information and copyright concerns. However, it is impossible to ignore the immense advantages AI could offer us [69]. Along with the technological advancements, there is a pressing need to focus on ethical principles and laws to ensure the responsible use of AI. Not only the concerns about data security and privacy in GenAI systems will loom, but there will also be serious concern to job displacement. Further as democratized GenAI becomes more dominant, there will be a change in the need for skills. Jobs will be related to or focused on developing, supervising, and upkeeping AI programs. Subsequently, human guidance to ensure responsible use of AI will be required. Among the various challenges, slow decision-making process, poor quality data, misaligned incentives and hesitancy to touch complex ERP applications needs to be faced. Since Generative AI is easily accessible to one and all, it allows to create contents which could be misleading and send persuasive emails and messages and also create such websites. This could result in tactics of luring the victims, phishing attacks and malware that imitate genuine communication and interfaces, thereby trapping the innocent users. Therefore, it makes it very difficult for individuals as well as administrators to differentiate between real and fake or dangerous communications, thereby raising the hackers' skills to take advantage of the user's weaknesses. This leads to higher efficiency in their attacks. The cyber threats are dynamically changing on a day-to-today basis and this calls for quick adaptation in recognising the new threats [70]. This dynamic daily challenge needs human intervention which means efficiency of these systems will have an impact. The main concerns are creation of realistic deepfakes and illegal manipulation of sensitive data and high chance of creation of deceptive information. The need for implementing high security measures to check the evolution of potential vulnerabilities is on rise due to the extensive availability of Gen AI. Web - based learning entails consecutive training as data becomes available to everyone, whereas in conventional approach the steps involved are pre-observing data, creating a dataset, and training the model with the dataset. Nevertheless, to say, this method may result in inaccurate forecasts, which could have a negative impact on results and thereby its network functions. Keeping in view the need to reduce the risks connected with the democratization of generative AI and to encourage responsible use across various domains, it is imperative to strike a balance between security and accessibility. Secure learning presents another challenge, especially when online learning techniques like Reinforcement Learning (RL) and Active Learning (AL) are used in training discriminative models in real time. This lack of ingenuousness possesses several difficulties. To begin with, the users may find it difficult to understand and interpret the output and may also have issues identifying the possible errors in the output. Further, if the interpretation and evaluation of the output are not available then the users might find it difficult to trust the system and its answers or suggestions. Furthermore, from a legal and regulatory perspective, it becomes difficult for the controlling agencies to assess whether the generative AI system is principally biased or unfair. Excessive dependence on Gen AI may hamper the growth of critical thinking abilities in humans. This discourages the growth of human judgment capacity and the in-built creativity in individuals. This over-dependability, especially in critical areas like content creation and decision-making, can lead to consequences that are unpredicted which could cause moral dilemmas and a disappearing sense of accountability, if we thoughtlessly rely on programmed systems [71].

Balancing individual independence and organizational control is always a difficult task. In the end, this is the sole method we will succeed in utilizing the potential of Generative AI. We find ourselves at a point where we must decide as the future of AI needs to advance with a smooth-edged conception of its significance. As we utilize this powerful tool, we should do it with a sense of responsibility and loyalty to the welfare of the society. It is our duty to ensure that AI is developed and controlled intelligently. Despite riding the wave of revolution, all individuals across the globe must unite to create responsible governance and ethical use of AI. Regulations in creative sectors should promote originality and protect intellectual assets. It should also avoid deteriorating current inequalities or introducing new types of corruption. In this GenAI era, these abilities distinguish us and make us not only employable but also priceless. Nevertheless, they necessitate ongoing improvement and development, highlighting the significance of lifelong learning. Our greatest strength in the face of the AI revolution will be our capacity for adaptation and skill acquisition. Overpowering the hindrances, improving AI-enhanced digital prototyping, fortifying encryption and authentication techniques and cultivating interdisciplinary insights for societal impact should be the main goals of future directions for democratizing generative AI. The future of democratized Gen AI promises to change enterprise productivity in a responsible and inclusive way by addressing barriers and placing a strong emphasis on accessibility and education. Realizing the full potential of democratized generative AI in enterprise productivity requires striking a balance between opportunities and responsible implementation. Even though AI is capable of automating tasks, human-specific abilities like creativity, critical thinking, and emotional intelligence become even more important. A skill that AI cannot duplicate is critical thinking, which entails evaluating, challenging, and drawing connections between disparate pieces of information. Both emotional intelligence—the capacity to recognize, understand, and react to the emotions of others—and creativity—the capacity to envision and create—are uniquely human [72].

Conclusion

GenAI has the capacity to change the way people in general and professionals in particular work. This has enabled the businesses to grow and thrive more rapidly. Generative AI's democratization of knowledge and ability to access the required information signifies a paradigm shift in the way we operate it as well. In future when GenAI contributes to greater productivity, efficiency and innovation across a variety of company operations, it will be made possible by companies navigating this revolutionary path to be carefully evaluating the risks and benefits and taking decisive action led by IT executives. This means that while developing guidelines and policies for minimizing risks and effective uses of AI, the administrative agencies and IT professionals need to recognize the transformative potential of GenAI. Finally, embracing the possibilities of democratized generative AI reflects an evolutionary step towards a more inclusive society and a responsible use of the AI.

References

[1] Winston, P. H. (1992). *Artificial intelligence.* Addison-Wesley Longman Publishing Co., Inc.

[2] Hunt, E. B. (2014). *Artificial intelligence.* Academic Press.

[3] Ertel, W. (2024). *Introduction to artificial intelligence.* Springer Nature.

[4] Strelkova, O. (2017). *Three types of artificial intelligence.*

[5] Khanzode, K. C. A., & Sarode, R. D. (2020). Advantages and disadvantages of artificial intelligence and machine learning: A literature review. *International Journal of Library & Information Science (IJLIS),* 9(1), 3.

[6] Banh, L., & Strobel, G. (2023). Generative artificial intelligence. *Electronic Markets,* 33(1), 63.

[7] van der Zant, T., Kouw, M., & Schomaker, L. (2013). *Generative artificial intelligence.* Springer Berlin Heidelberg.

[8] Wang, K., Gou, C., Duan, Y., Lin, Y., Zheng, X., & Wang, F. Y. (2017). Generative adversarial networks: Introduction and outlook. *IEEE/CAA Journal of Automatica Sinica,* 4(4), 588–598.

[9] Singh, C., Khajuria, H., & Nayak, B. P. A Comprehensive IoT Security Framework Using Edge Computing: Approaches and Challenges. *Network Optimization in Intelligent Internet of Things Applications*, 274-297.

[10] Kılınç, H. K., & Keçecioğlu, Ö. F. Generative artificial intelligence: A historical and future perspective. *Academic Platform Journal of Engineering and Smart Systems,* 12(2), 47–58.

[11] Ooi, K. B., Tan, G. W. H., Al-Emran, M., Al-Sharafi, M. A., Capatina, A., Chakraborty, A., & Dwivedi, Y. K. (2023). The potential of generative artificial intelligence across disciplines: Perspectives and future directions. *Journal of Computer Information Systems,* 1–32.

[12] Bak Herrie, M., Maleve, N. R., Philipsen, L., & Staunæs, A. B. (2024). Democratization and generative AI image creation: Aesthetics, citizenship, and practices. *AI & SOCIETY,* 1–13.

[13] Costa, C. J., Aparicio, M., Aparicio, S., & Aparicio, J. T. (2024). The democratization of artificial intelligence: Theoretical framework. *Applied Sciences,* 14(18), 8236.

[14] An, J., Ding, W., & Lin, C. (2023). ChatGPT: Tackling the growing carbon footprint of generative AI. *IEEE Transactions on Systems, Man, and Cybernetics: Systems,* 615, 586.

[15] Wu, T., He, S., Liu, J., Sun, S., Liu, K., Han, Q. L., & Tang, Y. (2023). A brief overview of ChatGPT: The history, status quo, and potential future development. *IEEE/CAA Journal of Automatica Sinica,* 10(5), 1122–1136.

[16] Lo, C. K. (2023). What is the impact of ChatGPT on education? A rapid review of the literature. *Education Sciences,* 13(4), 410.

[17] Azaria, A. (2022). ChatGPT usage and limitations.

[18] Iorliam, A., & Ingio, J. A. (2024). A comparative analysis of generative artificial intelligence tools for natural language processing. *Journal of Computing Theories and Applications,* 9104.

[19] Banasik, A., & Pikiewicz, P. (2023). Application of AI in crisis management. Scientific Papers of Silesian University of Technology. *Organization & Management,* 186.

[20] Vu, D. (2024). *Impact of artificial intelligence on employees in digital marketing.*

[21] Singh, G., Deng, F., & Ahn, S. (2021). *Illiterate DALL-E learns to compose.* arXiv preprint.

[22] Zhou, K. Q., & Nabus, H. (2023). The ethical implications of DALL-E: Opportunities and challenges. *Mesopotamian Journal of Computer Science,* 16–21.

[23] Wermelinger, M. (2023). Using GitHub Copilot to solve simple programming problems. In *Proceedings of the 54th ACM Technical Symposium on Computer Science Education* V. 1 (pp. 172–178).

[24] Dakhel, A. M., Majdinasab, V., Nikanjam, A., Khomh, F., Desmarais, M. C., & Jiang, Z. M. J. (2023). GitHub Copilot AI pair programmer: Asset or liability? *Journal of Systems and Software,* 203, 111734.

[25] Singh, C., Khajuria, H., & Nayak, B. P. (2023, March). A Study of Implementing a Blockchain-Based Forensic Model Integration (BBFMI) for IoT Devices in Digital Forensics. In *International Conference on Computer Science, Engineering and Education Applications* (pp. 318-327). Cham: Springer Nature Switzerland.

[26] Roohparvar, K. (2023). A novel approach to extending music using latent diffusion. Master's thesis, California Polytechnic State University.

[27] Li, S., Dong, W., Zhang, Y., Tang, F., Ma, C., Deussen, O., Lee, T. Y., & Xu, C. (2024). Dance-to-music generation with encoder-based textual inversion of diffusion models. arXiv preprint.

[28] Battini, P., Chung, K., Dontuboyina, N., Ozkaya, S., & Rentachintala, K. (2024). *Bridging the gap in generative AI for audio generation.*

[29] Joseph, J. (2023). Assessing the potential of laboratory instructional tool through Synthesia AI: A case study on student learning outcome. *International Journal of e-Learning and Higher Education (IJELHE),* 18(2), 5–16.

[30] Sierszen, A., & Drabek, D. (2024). Learning artificial intelligence/machine learning technologies based on Amazon Web Services solutions. In *INTED2024 Proceedings* (pp. 6798–6805).

[31] Fernández-Peña, A. C. R. (2023). AI is great, isn't it? Tone direction and illocutionary force delivery of tag questions in Amazon's AI NTTS Polly. *Journal of Experimental Phonetics,* 32, 227–242.

[32] Klug, B., & Williams, U. (2016). Canva. *The Charleston Advisor,* 17(4), 13–16.

[33] Fauziyah, N. L., Widodo, J. P., & Yappi, S. N. (2022). The use of 'Canva for Education' and the students' perceptions of its effectiveness in the writing procedure text. *Budapest International Research and Critics Institute-Journal (BIRCI-Journal),* 5(1), 289–296.

[34] Singh, C., & Das, A. K. (2024). Transforming digitization in supply chain management using artificial intelligence and machine learning. In *Supply Chain Management* (pp. 119-139). CRC Press.

[35] Vargas, I. M., Garcia Cabrera, C. I., Achata Cortez, C. A., Acero Apaza, I. M., & Díaz Reátegui, M. (2022). The Canva platform and meaningful learning in regular basic education. *International Journal of Health Sciences,* 6(S7), 643–658.

[36] Angelova, N. (2024). The capabilities of the art-oriented artificial intelligence Adobe Firefly and its visual advantages and disadvantages. *Journal "Fundamental Sciences and Applications,* 30(1), 1–10.

[37] Huang, J. (2024). The Art of AI: A human-centered AI (HCAI) user study of integrating image-generative tools in visual art workflows: The case of Adobe Firefly. *Proceedings of the IEEE Conference on Human-Centered AI.*

[38] Nair, S. S. (2024). Redefining creativity in design: Exploring the impact of AI-generated imagery on design professionals and amateurs. In *11th International Conference on Computing for Sustainable Global Development (INDIACom),* 1723–1728.

[39] Ghufron, M. A., & Rosyida, F. (2018). The role of Grammarly in assessing English as a Foreign Language (EFL) writing. *Lingua Cultura,* 12(4), 395–403.

[40] Karyuatry, L. (2018). Grammarly as a tool to improve students' writing quality: Free online proofreader across the boundaries. *JSSH (Journal Sains Sosial dan Humaniora),* 2(1), 83–89.

[41] Arguedas, A. R., & Simon, F. M. (2023). Automating democracy: Generative AI, journalism, and the future of democracy. AI & Society.

[42] Schatten, M. (2024). AI and the future of entertainment technology. *Proceedings of the International Symposium on Future Technologies.*

[43] Archer, G. (2024). The good, the bad, the ugly… and the gray uses of generative AI in the media and entertainment industry, disinformation, and offensive content. Newhouse Impact, 9.

[44] Sai, S., Gaur, A., Sai, R., Chamola, V., Guizani, M., & Rodrigues, J. J. P. C. (2024). Generative AI for transformative healthcare: A comprehensive study of emerging models, applications, case studies, and limitations. IEEE Access.

[45] Singh, C., Khajuria, H., & Nayak, B. P. (2024). Rapid Advancement and Trends of Big Data Analytics and Cyber-Physical System Embedded in Healthcare and Industry 4.0. In *Intelligent Security Solutions for Cyber-Physical Systems* (pp. 216-233). Chapman and Hall/CRC.

[46] Tolety, V. B. P., & Evani, V. P. (2023). Enhancing adaptive e-learning with generative AI: Expanding the horizon beyond recommendation systems. International Conference on Computing and Communication Networks, 755–767.

[47] Singh, C., Khajuria, H., & Nayak, B. P. (2024). Sustainable transformation of biomass into diverse high-value materials using biorefineries in the circular economy. In *Advances in Energy from Waste* (pp. 343-369). Woodhead Publishing.

[48] Kanont, K., Pingmuang, P., Simasathien, T., Wisnuwong, S., Wiwatsiripong, B., Poonpirome, K., Songkram, N., & Khlaisang, J. (2024). Generative AI as a learning assistant? Factors influencing higher-ed students' technology acceptance. *Electronic Journal of e-Learning,* 22(6), 18–33.

[49] Kshetri, N. (2024). Generative artificial intelligence and e-commerce. *Computer,* 57(2), 125–128.

[50] Li, R., & Zhong, Q. (2024). On the application of generative artificial intelligence ChatGPT in digital trade. *Procedia Computer Science,* 247, 112–120.

[51] Shaikh, N. (2023). Generative AI use cases for e-commerce. *International Journal of Computer Science and Mobile Computing,* 12, 10–14.

[52] Haridasan, P. K., & Jawale, H. (2024). Generative AI in manufacturing: A review of innovations, challenges, and future prospects. *Journal of Artificial Intelligence, Machine Learning & Data Science,* 2(2), 1418–1424.

[53] Rane, N., Choudhary, S., & Rane, J. (2024). Intelligent manufacturing through generative artificial intelligence, such as ChatGPT or Bard. *Proceedings of the International Conference on AI and Industrial Systems.*

[54] Plathottam, S. J., Rzonca, A., Lakhnori, R., & Iloeje, C. O. (2023). A review of artificial intelligence applications in manufacturing operations. *Journal of Advanced Manufacturing and Processing,* 5(3), e10159.

[55] Desai, A. P., Mallya, G. S., Luqman, M., Ravi, T., Kota, N., & Yadav, P. (2024). *Opportunities and challenges of generative AI in finance.* arXiv preprint arXiv:2410.15653.

[56] Lee, D. K. C., Guan, C., Yu, Y., & Ding, Q. (2024). A comprehensive review of generative AI in finance. *FinTech,* 3(3), 460–478.

[57] Kshetri, N., Dwivedi, Y. K., Davenport, T. H., & Panteli, N. (2024). Generative artificial intelligence in marketing: Applications, opportunities, challenges, and research agenda. *International Journal of Information Management,* 75, 102716.

[58] Terzidou, K. (2023). Generative AI for the legal profession: Facing the implications of the use of ChatGPT through an intradisciplinary approach. MediaLaws.

[59] Hacker, P., Engel, A., & Mauer, M. (2023). Regulating ChatGPT and other large generative AI models. *Proceedings of the ACM Conference on Fairness, Accountability, and Transparency,* 1112–1123.

[60] Ma, J., & Huang, K. (2023). ChatGPT in real estate. In Beyond AI: ChatGPT, Web3, and the Business Landscape of Tomorrow, 219–242.

[61] Patil, D., Rane, N. L., Rane, J., & Paramesha, M. (2024). Artificial intelligence and generative AI, such as ChatGPT, in transportation: Applications, technologies, challenges, and ethical considerations. *Proceedings of the International Conference on AI in Transportation.*

[62] Singh, A., Jia, T., Nalagatla, V., Cunningham, B., & Siwani, T. (2024). Application of generative AI to derive insight from supply chain and logistics contracts. *Abu Dhabi International Petroleum Exhibition and Conference,* D031S101R004.

[63] Aryfiyanto, H., & Alamsyah, A. (2024). Public service with generative AI: Exploring features and applications. In *7th International Conference of Computer and Informatics Engineering (IC2IE),* 1–7.

[64] Beltran, M. A., Ruiz Mondragon, M. I., & Han, S. H. (2024). Comparative analysis of generative AI risks in the public sector. *Proceedings of the 25th Annual International Conference on Digital Government Research,* 610–617.

[65] Bright, J., Enock, F. E., Esnaashari, S., Francis, J., Hashem, Y., & Morgan, D. (2024). *Generative AI is already widespread in the public sector.* arXiv preprint arXiv:2401.01291.

[66] Mannuru, N. R., Shahriar, S., Teel, Z. A., Wang, T., Lund, B. D., Tijani, S., & Pohboon, C. O. (2023). Artificial intelligence in developing countries: The impact of generative artificial intelligence (AI) technologies for development. *Information Development.*

[67] Solaiman, I., Talat, Z., Agnew, W., Ahmad, L., Baker, D., Blodgett, S. L., & Chen, C. (2023). *Evaluating the social impact of generative AI systems in systems and society.* arXiv preprint arXiv:2306.05949.

[68] Orchard, T., & Tasiemski, L. (2023). The rise of generative AI and possible effects on the economy. *Economics and Business Review,* 9(2), 9–26.

[69] Kreps, S., & Kriner, D. (2023). How AI threatens democracy. *Journal of Democracy,* 34(4), 122–131.

[70] Singh, C., Khajuria, H., & Nayak, B. P. (2023, March). A Study of Implementing a Blockchain-Based Forensic Model Integration (BBFMI) for IoT Devices in Digital Forensics. In *International Conference on Computer Science, Engineering and Education Applications* (pp. 318-327). Cham: Springer Nature Switzerland.

[71] Cantens, T. (2024). How will the state think with ChatGPT? The challenges of generative artificial intelligence for public administrations. AI & Society.

[72] Subhadra Sarngadharan, A., Narasimhamurthy, R., Sankaramoorthy, B., Singh, S. P., & Singh, C. (2022). Hybrid optimization model for design and optimization of microstrip patch antenna. *Transactions on Emerging Telecommunications Technologies*, *33*(12), e4640.

Chapter 7

Unleashing the Power of Democratized Machine Learning Models

A. Ashwini[1,*]
D. Menaka[2]
S. Balasubramaniam[3,†]
and Seifedine Kadry[4]

[1]Department of Electronics and Communication Engineering,
Vel Tech Rangarajan Dr. Sagunthala R&D Institute of Science and Technology,
Avadi, Chennai, Tamil Nadu, India
[2]Department of Electronics and Instrumentation Engineering,
Noorul Islam Centre for Higher Education, Kumaracoil, Tamil Nadu, India
[3]School of Computer Science and Engineering, Kerala University of Digital Sciences,
Innovation and Technology, Digital University Kerala, Thiruvananthapuram,
Kerala, India
[4]Department of Computer Science and Mathematics, Lebanese American University,
Beirut, Lebanon

Abstract

Machine learning (ML) Democratization is fundamentally changing technology with access to sophisticated algorithms and tools for everyone. The Democratization of machine learning (ML) is a technological transition that has empowered people and businesses to tap into high-powered algorithms. It also helps foster a new wave of Innovation in domains by creating a wide and varied response. This chapter will discuss these advancements and how they have enabled

* Corresponding Author's Email: a.aswiniur@gmail.com
† Corresponding Author's Email: baluttn@gmail.com

In: Democratized Generative AI: Principles, Challenges and Applications
Editors: S. Balasubramaniam and Seifedine Kadry
ISBN: 979-8-89530-684-0

people and companies, both startups and corporations, to access machine learning capabilities without being an expert in the field. Like easy-to-use platforms, open-source tools and no-code solutions within a short period brought machine learning out of data science. It has placed it in the hands of business users by enabling potentially more users to innovate at a large scale. It also features some use cases of democratized ML and its large-scale impact. This chapter dives into leveraging these affordable replicated technologies, from healthcare advancements to sustainability solutions, more innovative business, and retail management. The Democratization of ML leads to creative problem-solving techniques, improved decision-making, and an acute level of participation in the digital economy. The chapter finally considers the challenges and risks of universal access, covering fairness, transparency, and data security. However, these ML techniques come with some consequences. The issues about ethics, regulation, and security that follow the Democratization of ML are also highlighted. Another set of concerns relates closer to social challenges that need to be met to continually advance the continued effectiveness of these technologies, including fairness issues, avoiding Bias, and data privacy concerns. Finally, the chapter dwells on future work, learning, and global competitiveness due to the Democratization of ML and the further opening of new innovative prospects for industries.

Keywords: democratization, digital economy, healthcare advancement, industries, democratized machine learning, sustainable solutions

1. Introduction to Democratized Machine Learning

Democratized machine learning means applying the ability and results of machine learning (ML) for a nonspecific audience. Earlier, machine learning was made possible only to expert researchers or organizations with vast resources due to the processes' intricate nature and demands on computational capacities. However, with the developments in machine learning and a cloud environment, models, friendly interfaces, and open libraries, machine learning is becoming more available to non-specialists [1]. Such a shift means a broader class, from developers to business analysts, who can apply ML to their professional domains. The Democratization of machine learning is fueled partly by easier access to tools that make model creation easier. Low code and no code interfaces for ML include Google's TensorFlow, Microsoft's Azure ML, and the ability to build models without much coding involved. Moreover, models can be retrieved directly from repositories like Hugging Face or

Google Cloud AutoML, which makes it even easier to avoid developing them in-house. With this, users can fine-tune these models for particular tasks irrespective of their understanding of these algorithms' fundamentals.

Furthermore, the Democratization of machine learning is a significant concept regarding Innovation and non-discrimination. When more and more people, including individuals and small organizations, can expand their portfolio with ML and experiment with it within fields, it creates an opportunity for Innovation. Business sectors like health, the financial industry, and even education or small startups can now accurately reap the benefits of machine learning solutions. While this Democratization comes with its advantages, it also poses certain disadvantages, including the question of how to exercise proper use, maintain data privacy, and prevent Bias in AI; therefore, the need for education and governance is part of the developing area.

2. Overview of Machine Learning Accessibility

The concept of accessibility in the providence of the ML entails the interaction with the technologies without the necessity for technical skills, funds, or processing power. That is why, with the progression of ML, the attempts to make it available for broader usage have also increased due to the necessity of opening it to various fields of work and industries. Open sources include scikit-learn, Google's TensorFlow, and PyTorch. These frameworks enable the creation, training, and deployment of ML models with little or no knowledge of carefully chosen mathematical computations. In addition, Google Cloud AI, AWS SageMaker, and Microsoft Azure, for instance, provide swift, prescription-ready environments to apply and use ML capabilities, all without having to own or rent costly equipment. Figure 1 shows the positive and negative impact of ML on democracy.

Low-code and no-code are also used to improve Machine Learning accessibility. It makes it easy for business majors, teachers, and even inexperienced users to integrate machine-learning methods into their work. These developments make ML more broadly applicable, with fundamental questions of how users are informed about the ethical implications, potential model bias, and data privacy issues vital to the appropriate technology employment [2].

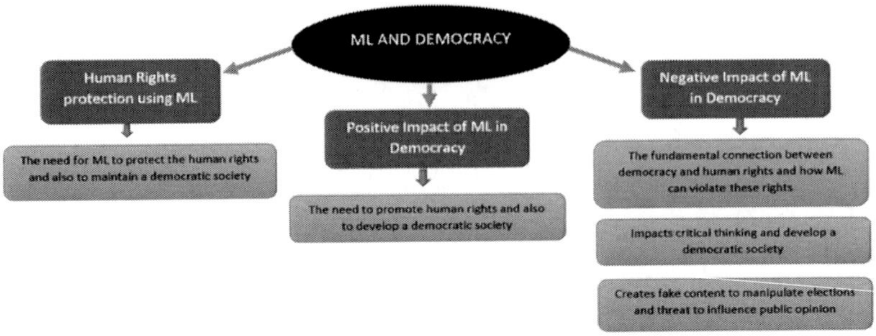

Figure 1. Positive and negative impact of ML on democracy.

3. Open-Source Machine Learning Framework

A democratized open-source machine learning (OS ML) framework is defined as a type of ML platform that involves a series of tools for machine learning model development and training and its deployment. These frameworks are intended to make machine learning more accessible to ordinary people who don't have to be programmers to interact with machine learning applications [3]. These tools are also free to use and easy to acquire and learn, thereby allowing their usage to seep into every facet of business and operation, regardless of their intricate algorithm or profound mathematical foundation. Figure 2 shows the key features of open source machine learning framework.

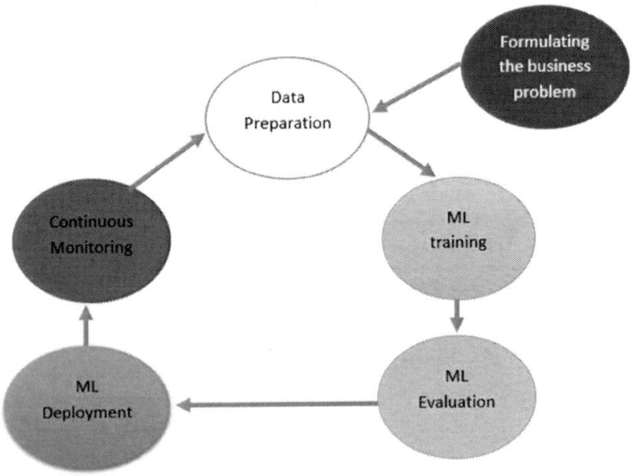

Figure 2. Key features of open source machine learning framework.

3.1. Key Features of Such Frameworks

3.1.1. Ease of Use

Currently, fully open-source platforms make the reach of democratized ML as easy as using drag and drop, low-code, or no-code environment models [4]. They are meant to simplify the utilization of machine learning for data scientists or anyone with a computer programming background, such as a business analyst, teacher, or student.

3.1.2. Scalability

Many democratized frameworks allow users to scale experiments from small to large datasets and computations using cloud resources. Cloud platforms such as Google's AutoML or Azure ML offer simplified interfaces for building machine learning models without the need for advanced algorithm knowledge or extensive computational power [5].

3.1.3. Pre-Trained Models

Another democratizing feature is the availability of pre-trained models and APIs that users can leverage directly. Frameworks like Hugging Face's Transformers, Flow Hub, Google's Tensor, and Fast.ai provide access to models that have already been trained on vast datasets. Users can fine-tune these models for specific applications without requiring extensive technical expertise in model architecture or training.

3.2. Examples of Open-Source Democratized Machine Learning Frameworks

3.2.1. Hugging Face Transformers

One of the natural language processing techniques is hugging face, which offers pre-trained models for tasks like text file classification and transient sentiment analysis. This enables a new user-friendly interface that makes the community active, helping to handle real-world tasks with the reduced setup function [6].

3.2.2. AutoML

AutoML from the Google Cloud is an automated machine learning system that helps users use ML based on customized models without any expertise in the mentioned field. It uses neural techniques to automatically search for the optimum models and reduce the hyper-parameter manual tuning using deep algorithms. Figure 3 shows the AutoML flow diagram.

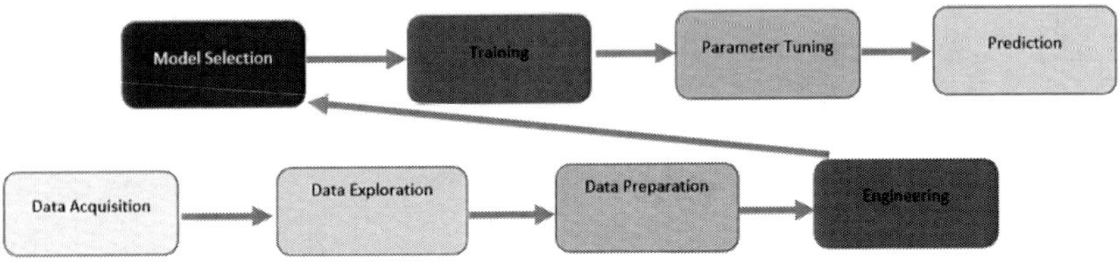

Figure 3. AutoML flow diagram.

3.2.3. Fast.ai

Fast.ai is a library developed on top of PyTorch for fast implementation of elements that often require very complex computations and the provision of high-level functionalities. It can be used to build the most advanced models in the field with just a few lines of code. The Fast.ai course is famous for popularizing machine learning for the audience, including those without experience with it.

3.2.4. H2O.ai

Yet another open-source platform, H2O.ai, works to make AI and machine learning technologies available to everybody with tools. These are frameworks for a general upswing aimed at a large-scale introduction of machine learning [7]. However, this Democratization of machine learning ensures proper usage of these models, accuracy in the models that cannot be biased, and proper disclosure of machine learning.

4. No Code Democratized Machine Learning Platforms

Democratized no-code machine learning is a platform that allows users to build, train, and deploy a machine learning model without having to write a single line of code. These platforms creatively enable individuals with little or no programming knowledge to use ML to enhance their work, academics, or business needs. These platforms are beneficial because they make the process of machine learning more accessible to developers through their mostly graphical user interfaces and by trying to handle most of the complex processes behind the scenes. Figure 4 shows various no-code democratized machine learning platforms.

4.1. Google Cloud AutoML

Google's AutoML is machine learning that enables users to develop highly accurate models. The users upload data, and AutoML then runs training on various models and launches the best model [8]. It is used to address issues such as image identification and natural language processing. Even though ordinary users can build reliable models, Google has developed a rather sophisticated AI-related platform.

4.2. Microsoft Azure ML Studio

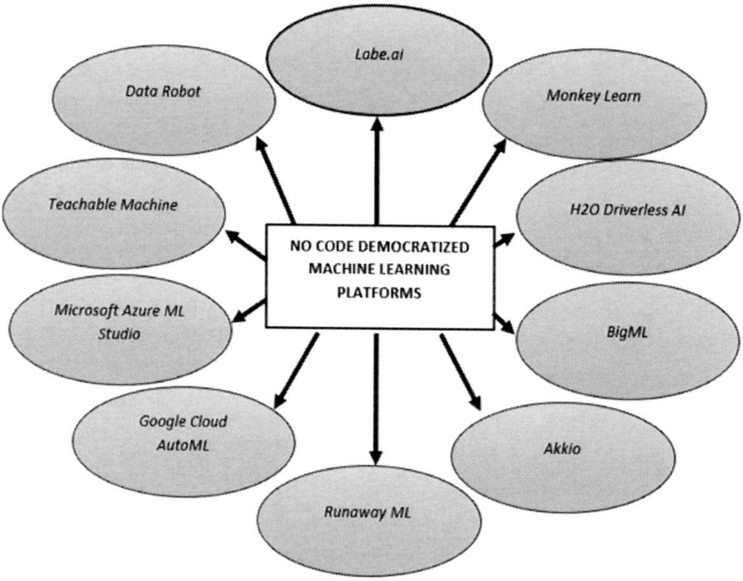

Figure 4. Various no-code democratized machine learning platforms.

Azure Machine Learning Studio is a cloud-based environment for machine learning where users can effortlessly build, train, and deploy models by simply dragging and dropping. With such no-code tools, users can design whole ML workflows from the platform's comfort. Azure ML also works with other Microsoft services, such as Power BI, and allows businesses to develop machine learning solutions that easily blend with existing structures. Additional features such as brought-in algorithms and automatic machine learning (AutoML) make developing a model easier.

4.3. Teachable Machine

Teachable Machine is another new tool created by Google that was designed as a no-code platform. It is as simple as a beginner can get. With data that the user feeds into the system, machine learning models can be trained for tasks such as image recognition, audio classification, and much more. It is also noteworthy that models trained using Hugging Face can be served either on a web application or downloaded offline, making it ubiquitous in real-world applications [9].

4.4. DataRobot

DataRobot is a no-code AI/ML platform that intends to provide solutions for automating the entire data science workflow. Users can upload datasets to the system, and the system will identify which algorithms to apply, train the models, and offer reasons for the results. DataRobot also has deployment templates for various business initiatives so that users can quickly build and deploy models for forecasting, anomalies, etc. It mainly targets firms that heavily use enterprise applications and different AI tools, which makes ML more transparent to business professionals and analysts [10].

4.5. Lobe.ai

Lobe.ai, a no-code platform from Microsoft, lets users build their machine-learning models despite encoding. Lobe is incredibly friendly for those with no prior coding experience or anyone wanting to embark on a basic introduction to the world of machine learning, and it is particularly suitable for scenarios involving images. It allows users to upload, tag, and drag and drop pictures into Lobe's GUI to train a model to recognize those images. Users can also export the platform models for applications, which are helpful in various system development.

4.6. MonkeyLearn

MonkeyLearn is a no-code NLP business. It includes features for text analytics, such as the ability to analyze sentiment, extract keywords, and classify topics. It is very user-friendly to such an extent that an average user can train machine learning models using simple text sample labeling [11]. MonkeyLearn is used for business purposes, such as learning from customer feedback and analyzing social media.

4.7. H2O Driverless AI

Driverless AI by H2O.ai is a no-code ML platform with many components of ML workflow managed at the enterprise level. It is a tool intended for business users who require deploying machine learning solutions. This makes some visualization and model explainability components accessible to users, which is crucial for AI's explicability and societal impact.

4.8. BigML

BigML is an intuitive no-code machine learning platform available strictly through web browsers. However, using BigML, models from datasets can be built by simply drag-and-drop using its set of automated tools and APIs that let users integrate its models into applications [12]. It also provides visual tool panels for comprehensive model assessment and application release.

4.9. Akkio

Akkio is a no-code AI developed for plain business users. By using Akkio, the users can upload their datasets, and the intelligent algorithms of the platform generate models for the predictive tasks and train themselves. Furthermore, Akkio works well with tools such as Google Sheets and CRM to help users draw in data, rating predictions, and obtain valuable insights. The layout of the service provided is relatively easy to use in a way that would allow business professionals to directly manage the tool using artificial intelligence without technical support from computer science experts.

4.10. RunwayML

RunwayML is a no-code application designed to align machine learning with artistic practice, where users are primarily creators. It offers an option to use ready-made models for image and video editing and generation, object detection, and text generation. It is crucial to note that RunwayML adopted a graphic user interface, meaning that anyone who has even a hint of using computers can turn around and create something fascinating using these machine learning tools in video editing, 3D modeling, and interactive media applications.

4.11. Key Features of No-Code Democratized ML Platforms

These no-code ML platforms have contributed significantly to democratizing machine learning. Therefore, anyone with little programming knowledge can use artificial intelligence [13]. Still, these platforms hide the complexity of building ML models from the users, which means that these users have to think about issues such as data quality, model bias, ethical implications, etc.

4.11.1. Drag-and-Drop Interfaces

Visual workflows do not require programming, making ML implementable on anyone's part.

4.11.2. Automated Machine Learning (AutoML)

Most integrate AutoML features, selecting models, training them, and optimizing them independently.

4.11.3. Pre-built Models

An additional advantage of deep learning is that for most problems, users can build upon pre-existing models rather than start from scratch.

4.11.4. Integration with Existing Tools

Compared to other platforms, most of them integrate with business tools such as spreadsheets, CRMs, or databases to apply the modeling to the organizational workflow.

5. Performance Prediction Models and Platforms

Performance predicting analysis in democratized machine learning are methods that anticipate the performance or behavior of systems making use of past data information. These models can be employed in several contexts and settings, such as forecasting sales, customer attrition, inventory management, or potential and existing employee performance [14]. Due to advances in ML technology, these performance prediction models are easily accessible by way of automated web user interfaces where non-technical personnel can build, train, and deploy models without deep technical knowledge.

5.1. Key Components of Performance Prediction Models

5.1.1. Historical Data

Performance prediction models are developed based on historical performance data and aim to describe performance characteristics. This data can include financial data, relationships between customers and firms, firm performance data, etc.

5.1.2. Feature Engineering

Some of the features of the data are chosen for constructing the model. Certain democratized platforms embedded within them create the steps of feature extraction as well as feature selection.

5.1.3. Algorithms

Some familiar machine learning algorithms for performance prediction include regression, decision trees, random forest, gradient boosting, and artificial neural networks. Mainstream ML platforms select the best-fitting algorithm themselves.

5.1.4. Evaluation Metrics

In most cases, these models are assessed based on their efficiency for prediction via qualitative measures, including accuracy, mean absolute error (MAE), the root mean square error (RMSE), or F1 scores, based on the nature of the prediction task, that is, regression or classification.

5.2. Use Cases of Performance Prediction Models in Democratized ML

5.2.1. Business Forecasting

Performance prediction models may also be utilized to anticipate future sales, revenues, or operational costs [15]. Most of these models aim to provide historical performance so businesses can use them in planning and budgeting.

5.2.2. Customer Churn Prediction

Predicting customer churn is an important step in customer retention. ML models can categorize customers and predict those who are in danger of churning so that appropriate action can be taken.

5.2.3. Predictive Maintenance

In industries that utilize equipment that requires infrastructure, these performance prediction models assist in estimating equipment failure and also help in avoiding frequent breakdowns that are likely to reduce productivity.

5.2.4. Financial Risk Management

Business organizations rely on predictive models to establish credit risk or equity prices and identify market trends. A professional assistant can use these models to make the right investment and minimize the risks involved.

5.2.5. Employee Performance

In human resources, performance prediction models are also helpful for predicting employee productivity, high performers, or those potential performers who can cause concern regarding poor productivity.

The increased availability of democratized machine learning platforms has advanced performance prediction modeling. A predictive model's easy generation, validation, and implementation allow organizational and individual decisions for forecasting risk, customers, and operations [16]. Nevertheless, the following pitfalls are critical and user-friendly when designing and implementing these models: Data quality, inconsistent model bias, and ethical ramifications.

6. Real-World Applications

It is essential to describe numerous examples of utilizing democratized machine learning in various fields and companies to emphasize the potential and usefulness of using AI and data for people who are not specialists. Here are some key applications:

6.1. Healthcare

Thanks to recent advancements in democratized ML models, medical practitioners can diagnose various diseases and forecast patient development and tailored regimens. Low-code or no-code facilities help hospitals and clinics anticipate patient readmissions, analyze medical images, and provide solutions to the population at risk without requiring professional programming knowledge.

6.2. Retail and E-commerce

Businesses employ ML to make sales predictions, set the right prices, and decide which products to stock. Retailers are informed of the sales to expect, the overall cost of inventory, and even the nature of the customer using democratized databases that strongly consider purchase histories and customer behavior.

6.3. Finance

Banking and other financial institutions use ML in credit scoring, fraud detection, and risk evaluation. Due to available end-to-end ML tools, even small financial institutions can create models for loan risk, credit score, or fraud detection [17].

6.4. Marketing

Some of the most common applications of ML in marketers include advertising campaign management, customer churn prediction, and audience segmentation. These democratized ML platforms help marketing teams analyze customers' data, estimate campaigns' efficacy, and use AI-driven solutions to send more effective recommendations, which enhances the overall ROI in the marketing sector.

6.5. Manufacturing

Operational use cases include leveraging machine learning to support predictive maintenance, which can enhance the durability of manufacturing equipment. With the Democratization of ML tools, corporations can develop models for identifying equipment malfunctions, improving flow in production lines, and ensuring quality.

6.6. Education

In education, the application is used to identify learners' performance, manage learning processes, and make administrative decisions [18]. Educators can now utilize democratized ML tools to predict who might require affirmative intervention in class or examine a pattern of underachievement.

6.7. Human Resources

Organizations deploy ML to augment existing HR Management in primary areas such as recruitment, talent management, and employee performance prediction. In democratized platforms, specific models can be created for attributes like turnover prediction, improving recruitment or selection processes, or the identification of star performers.

These applications show that the increased availability of machine learning is providing working professionals of all fields the capability to use data and achieve better performance and results. However, they may not possess explicit knowledge of AI or machine learning [19].

7. Balancing Innovation of Democratized AI and Ml with Ethical Usage

One of the significant challenges is advancing democratized AI with other important aspects and ethical usage. This points to the recurrent issue of ensuring that AI and machine learning are used responsibly as the tool becomes available to the average, non-specialist user. Thus, the conflict is in advancing mass-scale Innovation and, simultaneously, avoiding the potentially harmful ethical implications of this process, like discrimination, violation of the customer's privacy rights, and relatively low levels of transparency.

7.1. Ensuring Fairness and Reducing Bias

Another significant concern with the Democratization of AI and ML is the problem of Bias. However, as democratized platforms allow even people without machine learning experience to create models, it is possible to be mistaken in selecting data to train them. It can provide discrimination in employment, credit, or even in criminal justice systems [20]. The platform needs to include ways of detecting and eliminating such biases, including requiring data to be used to train the models to be diverse. Furthermore, increasing awareness of Bias and fairness is important, even for ordinary users.

7.2. Data Privacy and Security

Persons and bodies operating AI/ML will likely infringe on the privacy rights of others. The democratized platforms make it simple to upload personal data for calibrating models. Stronger measures to protect data, such as encryption, anonymization, and following regulations like GDPR, must be added. At the same time, Innovation in Artificial Intelligence has to imply the creation of new methodologies like differential privacy and federated learning to enable data sharing without infringing on user's privacy.

7.3. Transparency and Explainability

In democratized AI, where users employ the tools, opacity reduces trust and results in adverse effects. This includes giving tools for model interpretation and creating explainable by-nature versions of interpretations [21]. At the same time, the arrival of new ideas to solve existing problems must be legitimate, open, and easy to trace back.

7.4. Ethical Guidelines and Education

Promising based on the Democratization of AI, there is a question of ethical guidelines and schemes and their voicing across the community AI models. Preparing simple ethical guidelines and essential training handouts is also vital for people to learn about responsible AI. It involves creating awareness regarding informed consent in using personal data and the risks of implementing algorithms and other automation. Sustaining the pace of Innovation in artificial intelligence demands the integration of these principles into AI platforms to encourage responsible use across the improved platforms.

7.5. Avoiding Harmful Applications

The democratized AI platforms can be exploited for adverse effects without any ill intentions, or vice versa. For example, a person can develop models to make fake news, violate privacy, or even make decisions damaging to people or groups of people [22]. The platforms must develop measures including ethical review, usage policies, and monitoring mechanisms to prevent it. Innovation is good but should not be put at the peril of the public and a potentially broken trust.

7.6. Accountability and Oversight

AI technology should be democratized, but companies should accept the responsibility of ensuring ethical uses, methods of identifying biased models, and policies used to enhance ethical purposes. However, the organizations that apply these models need to take full responsibility for implementing the AI solutions, particularly discussing areas like healthcare, education, or finance. Policies for controlling and regularly monitoring new technologies can prevent the client from overlooking unethical behavior while allowing the firm to continue its innovative practices. It is crucial to outline the key approaches to mediating the innovational democraticization of AI and ML and its ethical use [23]. These are eliminating prejudice, guaranteeing data confidentiality, demonstrating clarity, raising awareness, excluding negative uses, and establishing responsibilities. It is possible to impart ethical considerations into the design and implementation of AI solutions and continue strengthening the overall availability of AI and wrapping up potential hazards of AI.

8. Impact on Market Competition and Innovation

Making ML accessible to the broad public in recent years has affected competition and Innovation in the market significantly in terms of how entrepreneurs and individuals apply AI. Digitalization of ML through no-code/low-code platforms and AutoML opens the barriers to the traditional exclusive use of ML tools.

8.1. Lowering Barriers to Entry

Democratization of Machine Learning means that technical and financial thresholds for organizations and persons interested in utilizing ML are significantly reduced. Historically, the need for machine learning involved significant specialization and significant IT, capital funds, and data science skills commitments. In the present age, ranging from newly established enterprises, small and medium scale enterprises (SMEs) have the opportunity to apply surface ML platforms such as Google Cloud AutoML, DataRobot, or Microsoft Azure ML to create predictive models, carry out data analysis, and implement decision-making processes [24]. This has led to uniformity between small-scale players to fight efficiently with large corporations and advance Innovation in various industries by allowing newcomers to use AI with minimal capital.

8.2. Accelerating Innovation

Through the Democratization of ML, more people will find themselves asking the right questions and getting access to the tools to compute with more experimentation and faster iteration. Agility means organizations can easily use AI insights to prototype ideas, products, or services. This has shifted the pace at which organizations adopt artificial intelligence solutions in healthcare, finance, retail, and manufacturing industries. Platforms have also empowered some professionals to create custom ML models without coding their industry [25]. Therefore, Innovation is not limited to the technological sector or applied in research organizations but by specialists in different spheres with the help of AI applications.

8.3. Increased Market Competition

This ML Democratization is increasing rivalry in the market since many organizations are applying and incorporating elements of artificial intelligence into their processes. Startups can optimize operations and improve gain using ML-powered recommendation systems, which can deploy AI-driven customer segmentation models.

8.4. Enabling Customization and Personalization

ML is now accessible to those who can employ it for better efficiency management, customer satisfaction, and bargains meant for great technology-savvy large corporations. For instance, small e-commerce sellers will use an ML-based recommended system that can deploy a customer segmentation model [26]. This has increased competition among large organizations to avoid being outcompeted by the market.

8.5. Fostering Collaboration between Industries

In the existing economy, consumers anticipate high customization that firms can fulfill. Small firms can now offer levels of service that match large companies by deploying out-of-the-box on their precise requirements. The complexity of products and services today has led to this area seeking ways to increase their appeals to their targeted markets.

8.6. Empowering AI Startup and New Business Models

Democratized ML fosters the exchange of information and experience among the parties. Due to advancements in the availability of the means for practicing machine learning, more disciplines and professionals originating from non-information technology backgrounds are partnering with artificial intelligence experts to create new forms. This idea is fuelling advancement in fields such as diagnoses, prognosis, nutrition advice, and manufacturing and investment advice systems [27]. Also, no-code AI startups act as software enablers for businesses that provide no-code platform solutions that work in correlation with various industries, promoting AI use in different sectors and thus generating new market segments. Consequently, the ecosystem for AI startups is now healthy, and new applications of AI are being developed.

8.7. Faster Time-to-Market

Democratized platforms let businesses implement ML models faster, increasing the time to implement AI products and services. Organizations can generate new ideas and concepts far more quickly, release new products and services, and adapt to market requirements and consumers' needs more efficiently. This faster development cycle pressures a dynamic competitive environment that can renew itself quicker and in a better position. As of today, the requirement for quick adaptation plays a crucial role in industries such as fintech, and democratized ML allows various businesses to meet customers' and technologies' demands when needed.

8.8. Challenging Traditional Tech Giants

Democratization of ML also affects the competitive environment due to the disruption of the monopoly of classical IT players. While big players such as Google, Amazon, and Microsoft remain dominant in the AI infrastructure market, the overall cloud services market has created opportunities for other companies to add value through unique applications or unique AI-related solutions [28]. This has led to spreading AI capacities and expertise from the few dominating tech giants.

8.9. Ethical and Regulatory Considerations

The constantly accelerating rate of Innovation due to the Democratization of AI demands better rules on competition and adherence to ethical standards. Those organizations focused on creating AI in compliance with the established ethical norms and standards can succeed in their market. Knowledge dissemination frees startup companies and individual merchants, making the market competitive [29]. Nevertheless, democratized ML arrives with problems such as ethical issues and calls to legal and regulatory frameworks that will also help determine market competition in AI in the future.

9. The Rise of Automl in Democratization

AutoML is why it has been easier for regular users to get a taste of what machine learning is all about and use artificial intelligence in their projects without having to learn how it works as a technology. With AutoML functionality applied to acquire, build, and optimize the ML models, the accessibility of creating the predictive and prescriptive tools rises significantly for businesses, professionals, and individuals without deep data experience [30]. This trend is modifying industries and fostering Innovation on a large scale. Table 1 shows the performance comparisons of various models in Democratization.

Table 1. Comparison of various ML models in democratization

Model	Precision	F1 score	Depletion Time	Accuracy	Recall
Microsoft Azure ML	86.5	86.1	11	89.1	85.3
DataRobot	91.2	90.6	14	92.5	90.7
Google AutoML	92.5	90.7	12	91.4	89.7
BigML	86.1	84.7	3	84.9	82.5
DataRobot	91.8	91.3	10	91.8	90.4

9.1. Simplifying the ML Pipeline

Historically, data preparation, feature extraction or engineering, model selection, model parameters optimization, and model assessment have been done to build a machine learning model. Each of these steps requires expert knowledge regarding a particular subject, which can take much time. AutoML fully automates all these tasks. It does feature selection, algorithm selection, hyper-parameter optimization, and sometimes even model evaluation. AutoML has a feature that optimizes the ML pipeline so that people with little to no programming knowledge can create and launch models on the web. This automation helps businesses to address their main issues and decisions rather than enter into details of developing ML. It dramatically accelerates the time to value so organizations can deploy solutions based on AI without the need to hire data scientists or invest in machine learning capabilities.

9.2. Expanding AI Accessibility

AutoML is a critical driver of democratizing ML since it extends the practice of machine learning to everyone. In the past, machine learning was exclusive to experts who understood statistics, computational capacity, and data well. AutoML has brought a significant transformation in the world of analytics, and now, even business analysts, marketers, product managers, domain experts, etc. Web applications like Google Cloud AutoML, Microsoft Azure AutoML, DataRobot, and H2O Driverless AI allow for data uploading, setting parameters through simple interfaces, and creating powerful ML models in an instant [31]. These tools offer a basic framework, linear and straightforward operations, and the process is documented, making ML development's technical aspect less complicated.

9.3. Fostering Innovation Across Industries

AutoML in healthcare lets medical practitioners develop models for outcomes, diagnosis, and treatment without coding knowledge. Sometimes, in retail and e-commerce, AutoML is applied in demand forecasting, inventory management, and recommendation systems. Likewise, manufacturing industries use AutoML to detect equipment failure early, enhance production rate, and manage the supply chain [32]. AutoML makes these processes efficient, allowing organizations to make effective decisions and innovate at a much higher rate faster than before.

9.4. Reducing the Skills Gap

Highly qualified data scientists are in very low supply, and, as the industry publications suggest, the demand for such professionals is relatively high. AutoML makes machine learning accessible for non-technical users, which assists in filling this gap. AutoML seeks to provide machine learning models and applications on an easy platform to develop viable models, thereby democratizing artificial intelligence. This helps advance AI speed and scale and encourages more diverse groups of people to contribute intelligent technologies.

9.5. Balancing Automation and Human Expertise

AutoML has brought a significant transformation in the world of analytics. Even business analysts, marketers, product managers, domain experts, and others can create predictive models and insights from data without knowing the algorithms.

9.6. Challenges and Future Directions

Web applications like Google Cloud AutoML, Microsoft Azure AutoML, DataRobot, and H2O Driverless AI allow for data uploading, setting parameters through simple interfaces, and creating powerful ML models in an instant [33]. AutoML in healthcare lets medical practitioners develop models for outcomes, diagnosis, and treatment without coding knowledge. Sometimes, in retail and e-commerce, AutoML is applied in demand forecasting, inventory management, and recommendation systems. Likewise, manufacturing industries use AutoML to detect equipment failure early, enhance production rate, and manage the supply chain. AutoML makes these processes efficient to allow organizations to make effective decisions and innovate at a much higher rate faster than before.

The primary challenge to using AI has been accessing data science personnel. Highly qualified data scientists are in very low supply, and, as the industry publications suggest, the demand for such professionals is relatively high. AutoML makes machine learning accessible for non-technical users, which assists in filling this gap. While there are still challenges to address, such as interpretability and data quality, the impact of AutoML on democratizing machine learning is undeniable. It is driving Innovation, reducing the skills gap, and enabling organizations of all sizes to leverage the power of AI to solve real-world problems [34].

Conclusion

In conclusion, the Democratization of machine learning, significantly propelled by the rise of Automated Machine Learning (AutoML), is reshaping the technological landscape by making powerful AI tools accessible to a broader audience. This shift not only lowers the barriers to entry for individuals and businesses without extensive technical expertise but also fosters Innovation across various industries. By simplifying the ML pipeline and automating complex processes, AutoML empowers non-experts to build, deploy, and utilize machine learning models efficiently, enabling them to derive valuable insights and make data-driven decisions. This Democratization fosters a culture of experimentation and collaboration, leading to novel applications of AI and spurring growth in emerging sectors. It is essential to address the ethical challenges accompanying it, such as Bias, transparency, and data privacy, to ensure responsible usage of AI technologies. By prioritizing education, ethical guidelines, and robust data practices, the potential of democratized ML while mitigating the risks is ensured. Ultimately, the Democratization of machine learning holds the promise of creating a more inclusive and innovative AI ecosystem where diverse voices and perspectives can contribute to advancing technology for the benefit of society.

References

[1] Chen, W., Zhao, L., Kang, Q., & Di, F. (2020). Systematizing heterogeneous expert knowledge, scenarios and goals via a goal-reasoning artificial intelligence agent for democratic urban land use planning. *Cities*, *101*, 102703.

[2] Rubeis, G., Dubbala, K., & Metzler, I. (2022). "Democratizing" artificial intelligence in medicine and healthcare: Mapping the uses of an elusive term. *Frontiers in Genetics*, *13*, 902542.

[3] Badillo, S., Banfai, B., Birzele, F., Davydov, I. I., Hutchinson, L., Kam-Thong, T. & Zhang, J. D. (2020). An introduction to machine learning. *Clinical pharmacology & therapeutics*, *107*(4), 871-885.

[4] Reddi, V. J., Plancher, B., Kennedy, S., Moroney, L., Warden, P., Agarwal, A. & Tingley, D. (2021). Widening access to applied machine learning with tinyml. *arXiv preprint arXiv:2106.04008*.

[5] Yuksel, B. F., Kim, S. J., Jin, S. J., Lee, J. J., Fazli, P., Mathur, U., & Miele, J. A. (2020, April). Increasing video accessibility for visually impaired users with human-in-the-loop machine learning. In *Extended abstracts of the 2020 CHI conference on human factors in computing systems* (pp. 1-9).

[6] Van De Schoot, R., De Bruin, J., Schram, R., Zahedi, P., De Boer, J., Weijdema, F. & Oberski, D. L. (2021). An open source machine learning framework for efficient and transparent systematic reviews. *Nature machine intelligence*, *3*(2), 125-133.

[7] Nguyen, G., Dlugolinsky, S., Bobák, M., Tran, V., López García, Heredia, I. & Hluchý, L. (2019). Machine learning and deep learning frameworks and libraries for large-scale data mining: a survey. *Artificial Intelligence Review*, *52*, 77-124.

[8] Kholod, I., Yanaki, E., Fomichev, D., Shalugin, E., Novikova, E., Filippov, E., & Nordlund, M. (2020). Open-source federated learning frameworks for IoT: A comparative review and analysis. *Sensors*, *21*(1), 167.

[9] Tokui, S., Oono, K., Hido, S., & Clayton, J. (2015, December). Chainer: a next-generation open source framework for deep learning. In *Proceedings of workshop on machine learning systems (LearningSys) in the twenty-ninth annual conference on neural information processing systems (NIPS)* (Vol. 5, pp. 1-6).

[10] Sundberg, L., & Holmström, J. (2024). Teaching Tip: Using No-Code AI to Teach Machine Learning in Higher Education. *Journal of Information Systems Education*, *35*(1), 56-66.

[11] Ilame, N. (2024). Machine Learning-Powered Programming: Exploring the Fusion of AI and Coding. *Innovative Computer Sciences Journal*, *10*(1), 1-11.

[12] Masood, A., Hashmi, A., Masood, A., & Hashmi, A. (2019). Democratization of AI Using Cognitive Services. *Cognitive Computing Recipes: Artificial Intelligence Solutions Using Microsoft Cognitive Services and TensorFlow*, 1-17.

[13] Balasubramaniam, S., Sumina, S., Kumar, K. S., & Prasanth, A. (2024). Machine learning based models for implementing digital twins in healthcare industry. In *Metaverse Technologies in Healthcare* (pp. 135-162). Academic Press.

[14] Kross, S., Peng, R. D., Caffo, B. S., Gooding, I., & Leek, J. T. (2020). The Democratization of data science education. *The American Statistician*, *74*(1), 1-7.

[15] Zhang, R., He, J., Luo, X., Niyato, D., Kang, J., Xiong, Z. & Sikdar, B. (2024). Toward Democratized Generative AI in Next-Generation Mobile Edge Networks. *arXiv preprint arXiv:2411.09148*.

[16] Samaras, G., Mertiri, M., Xezonaki, M. E., Theodorou, V., Chartsias, P. K., & Bozios, T. (2024, June). Democratizing Predictive Analytics with Generative Artificial Intelligence towards AI-Native Networks. In *2024 IEEE Symposium on Computers and Communications (ISCC)* (pp. 1-6). IEEE.

[17] Nam, S. (2024). Who Gets Paid (for) What? The Cultural Political Economy of News Content in Generative AI. *Emerging Media*, *2*(3), 397-421.

[18] Burkhardt, S., & Rieder, B. (2024). Foundation models are platform models: Prompting and the political economy of AI. *Big Data & Society*, *11*(2), 20539517241247839.

[19] Bak Herrie, M., Maleve, N. R., Philipsen, L., & Staunæs, A. B. (2024). Democratization and generative AI image creation: aesthetics, citizenship, and practices. *AI & SOCIETY*, 1-13.

[20] Ashwini, A., Kavitha, V., & Balasubramaniam, S. (2024). 2 Early Roots of Generative AI Models and LLM: A Diverse Landscape. *Generative AI and LLMs: Natural Language Processing and Generative Adversarial Networks*, 23.

[21] Berson, I. R., & Berson, M. J. (2023). The Democratization of AI and its transformative potential in social studies education. *Social Education*, *87*(2), 114-118.

[22] Rane, N. (2023). ChatGPT and Similar Generative Artificial Intelligence (AI) for Smart Industry: role, challenges and opportunities for industry 4.0, industry 5.0 and society 5.0. *Challenges and Opportunities for Industry*, *4*.

[23] Wang, X., & Wu, Y. C. (2024). Balancing Innovation and Regulation in the age of geneRative artificial intelligence. *Journal of Information Policy*, *14*.

[24] Costa, C. J., Aparicio, M., Aparicio, S., & Aparicio, J. T. (2024). The Democratization of Artificial Intelligence: Theoretical Framework. *Applied Sciences*, *14*(18), 8236.

[25] Ovadya, A. (2023). Reimagining democracy for ai. *Journal of Democracy*, *34*(4), 162-170.

[26] Baskara, F. X. R., Vasudevan, A., & Sain, Z. H. (2024). Redefining educational paradigms: Integrating generative AI into society 5.0 for sustainable learning outcomes. *Journal of Infrastructure, Policy and Development*, *8*(12), 6385.

[27] De Bettignies, J. E., Liu, H. F., Robinson, D. T., & Gainullin, B. (2023). Competition and Innovation in markets for technology. *Management Science*, *69*(8), 4753-4773.

[28] Gilbert, R. J. (2006). Competition and Innovation. *Journal of Industrial Organization Education*, *1*(1), 1-23.

[29] Chen, T., Kenneth Cheng, H., Jin, Y., Li, S., & Qiu, L. (2021). Impact of competition on Innovations of IT industry: An empirical investigation. *Journal of management information systems*, *38*(3), 647-666.

[30] Feurer, M., Eggensperger, K., Falkner, S., Lindauer, M., & Hutter, F. (2022). Auto-sklearn 2.0: Hands-free automl via meta-learning. *Journal of Machine Learning Research*, *23*(261), 1-61.

[31] Levitsky, S., & Way, L. A. (2006). Linkage versus leverage. Rethinking the international dimension of regime change. *Comparative politics*, 379-400.

[32] Fish, M. S. (2001). The Inner Asian anomaly: Mongolia's Democratization in comparative perspective. *Communist and post-communist studies*, *34*(3), 323-338.

[33] Muthumeenakshi, R., SINGH, C., SAPKALE, P. V., & MUKHEDKAR, M. M. (2022). An Efficient and Secure Authentication Approach in VANET using Location and Signature-Based Services. *Adhoc & Sensor Wireless Networks*, *53*.

Chapter 8

Edge AI Revolution: Democratizing Machine Learning for Resource-Constrained Devices

B. Abisha[1,*]
V. Sheeja Kumari[2]
V. Suresh Kumar[3]
and N. R. Wilfred Blessing[4]
[1]Department of Computational Intelligence, Saveetha School of Engineering, SIMATS University, Chennai, India
[2]Department of Computational Intelligence, Saveetha School of Engineering, SIMATS University, Chennai, India
[3]Department of Computer Science and Engineering, Saveetha School of Engineering, Saveetha Institute of Medical and Technical Sciences, Thandalam, Chennai
[4]College of Computing and Information Sciences, University of Technology and Applied Sciences-Ibri, Sultanate of Oman

Abstract

The Edge AI revolution is a game-changing paradigm in deploying AI and ML technologies in resource-constrained environments. When the demand for processing data in real-time and making intelligent decisions is rising daily, it becomes essential to equip devices with lower computational capacity and energy with sophisticated ML capabilities. This chapter focuses on how edge computing can facilitate machine learning by making it interoperable across various domains such as health, agriculture, manufacturing, and smart cities. However, there are inherent challenges as traditional cloud-based AI solutions face latency, bandwidth limitations, and privacy concerns. Edge AI decentralizes data

[*] Corresponding Author's Email: abishab9070.sse@saveetha.com

In: Democratized Generative AI: Principles, Challenges and Applications
Editors: S. Balasubramaniam and Seifedine Kadry
ISBN: 979-8-89530-684-0

processing, enabling real-time data analysis and action on the device and creating a better experience for the user. We explore breakthrough approaches allowing resource-constrained devices, emphasizing techniques like model-compression methods (including pruning and distillation), quantization for low-precision arithmetic, and federated learning for distributed model training while maintaining user-data security. In addition, we provide a general perspective on their incorporation with the prototyping of Edge AI on legacy layers to deploy lightweight algorithms for specific applications. Successful implementations that have resulted in improved efficiency, reduced operating costs, and improved service delivery are documented in case studies. The chapter also highlights the ethical issues and challenges related to the uptake of Edge AI, like the need for significant security and fair access to technology. Edge AI helps advance technology and enhances IT literacy by enabling developers and end-users to tap into machine learning on their devices. Finally, we imagine a world in which intelligent systems help make things more innovative and connected worldwide, thus benefitting all.

Keywords: edge AI, resource-constrained devices, model compression, localized computation, AI democratization, cloud computing alternatives

1. Introduction

Edge AI is a rapidly developing technology that directly extends machine learning (ML) capabilities to devices that operate at the "edge" of networks, including embedded systems, smartphones, Internet of Things devices, and sensors. AI models may be executed in real-time on the device itself, unlike traditional cloud-based AI, which depends on centralized servers for data processing and decision-making [1].

The cloud moves precious intelligence to the Edge, nearer to latency, which enhances privacy and ensures continuity and operation in conditions with recurrent or complete absence of internet accessibility. Say Edge is an increasingly chief building block in the environment of the modern technology ecosystem -iles such segments that require real-time decisions, really low latency, and high data security. Applications that use edge computing for quicker, real-time decision-making delays or vulnerabilities of cloud transmission range from health to autonomous transport and even to smart cities. In everyday life, where the number of IoT devices keeps increasing, efficient, safe, and responsive AI is in demand; hence, Edge AI becomes crucial for future technological development.

It means making such advanced machine learning capabilities available to a more extensive section. Deploying AI models on edge devices empowers industries. It enables individuals and communities in remote or resource-limited areas to leverage AI without dependence on high-cost infrastructure or constant internet access [2]. It also democratizes AI technologies to make them more accessible to everyone, allowing the accruing benefits to be disseminated more equitably to other regions and populations, contributing toward reducing the digital divide and propelling innovation at the global scale.

2. Evolution of Machine Learning from Cloud to Edge

2.1. Traditional Cloud-Based Machine Learning

Cloud was a necessity for the early phases of ML and AI: model deployment, training, and operation. In cloud-based machine learning, the training and inference operations are done via centralized high-performance servers. The cloud platforms receive big datasets processed by specialty hardware and powerful GPUs [3]. As enabled by cloud computing, large-scale parallelization allows the training of complex models, such as deep neural networks, on large volumes of data. This infrastructure's availability was instrumental in accelerating the pace of AI research and applications, especially for industries that have to deal with enormous volumes of data, such as banking, e-commerce, and healthcare.

Once these models are trained, their deployment often relies on the cloud. Devices such as smartphones, IoT sensors, or other connected devices send their data to cloud servers for inference, with results then transmitted back to the devices. This centralized model places significant demands on network infrastructure, creating bottlenecks that can impede seamless AI use in practical scenarios, mainly where constant connectivity is unavailable or impractical

2.2. Challenges of Cloud-Based AI

Although cloud-based ML provides benefits like scalability and access to powerful computing resources, it faces notable challenges, particularly for applications demanding low-latency performance or stringent privacy measures.

1) *Latency Issues:* One of the significant challenges associated with cloud-based AI involves latency. The time used to transfer data from edge devices to cloud servers and vice versa introduces unacceptable delays in many time-sensitive applications. Applications such as autonomous vehicles, drones, or real-time medical diagnostics require immediate decisions, and any delay in data processing could lead to disastrous results.
2) *Data Privacy and Security:* Cloud-based AI systems need to send possibly sensitive data continuously over the internet. This presents a lot of privacy risk, especially in sectors like healthcare or finance, where leakage or interception of personal data could lead to regulatory and legal challenges. Centralizing data also increases the attack surface for malicious actors, making cloud-based AI more vulnerable to breaches.
3) *Cost and Resource Intensity:* Cloud infrastructure maintenance for ML is expensive and resource-intensive. Most AI workloads necessitate a high-performance computer that is expensive and power-hungry. For many organizations, such as small businesses or those in resource-poor environments, the associated financial cost of cloud-based AI is quite inhibitive. Furthermore, this cost is added to the requirement of maintaining network connectivity at constant and high speeds.
4) *Dependence on Connectivity:* Cloud-based AI systems require stable and fast internet connections. This model performs inconsistently in places with low or no connectivity. Even in the best-connected regions, congestion or outages of networks disrupt AI services and result in unsatisfactory user experiences or critical failures in vital systems.

2.3. Shift Toward Edge Computing

Due to the constraints of cloud-based AI, edge computing—where data is processed closer to its source on the originating devices—is increasingly being adopted [4]. Furthermore, edge AI enhances this approach by deploying machine learning models directly on devices such as IoT sensors, autonomous vehicles, smart home appliances, and smartphones. Recent advancements have facilitated a shift from cloud-heavy AI architectures to more distributed and lightweight AI systems.

1. *Advancements in Hardware:* Generally, edge devices have become more powerful, especially with the newer generations of processors and GPUs and powerful dedicated AI hardware like TPUs and NPUs, which enable edge devices to perform most of the ML processes. These optimizations make possible the reallocation of models that before demanded cloud computing to execute on more compact gadgets.
2. *Optimization Techniques:* To reduce the size and processing requirements of the machine learning models, knowledge distillation, pruning quantization, and model compression techniques have been a problem solved. Whereas quantization allows the model to operate with less accurate computations, helping to cut on memory and computing power, compression minimizes the model's size. Reducing enables the model to be practiced more efficiently on edge devices, reducing the superfluous components. These techniques ensure that even deep learning models can efficiently run on resource-limited edge hardware.
3. *Energy Efficiency:* This makes Edge AI significantly reduce the extent to which it demands the concentricity of constant communication with the cloud, which in turn savages energy. Mass data exchange between the gadgets is no longer required, making AI solutions more environmentally friendly and sustainable, especially for IoT networks with limited energy capacities.
4. *Real-Time Processing:* On the same note, edge computing cuts down latency as computation is performed where data is obtained, enabling instantaneous decision-making. This is more relevant to areas where quick decisions can mean the difference between getting a good return on investment or saving lives, for instance, in the case of driverless cars, the automation industry, diagnosis of diseases, and smart city technologies.
5. *Privacy and Security:* Since computations are performed at the network's edge, edge AI increases privacy and security since less data is transferred across networks. Despite this fact, this localized form of AI reduces the potential threats posed by data theft. It ensures that personally identifying or corporate information is processed more

confidentially, making Edge AI most appropriate for use in verticals such as healthcare and finance.

2.4. The Future of Machine Learning: Cloud and Edge Synergy

Even while edge computing solves many issues with cloud-based AI, a hybrid approach is probably what machine learning will look like in the future. Cloud and edge AI might operate together through federated learning, which enables models to be trained across several decentralized devices while maintaining local data. This methodology enhances the privacy and scalability of AI systems since the devices involved in the training can interact without sharing their data in the cloud [5]. Some of the features that cloud computing will progress include the capacity to source and assemble massive amounts of data, train models on giant data sets, and recalibrate models that may subsequently be installed on edge devices. Figure 1 shows the comparison between cloud and Edge AI.

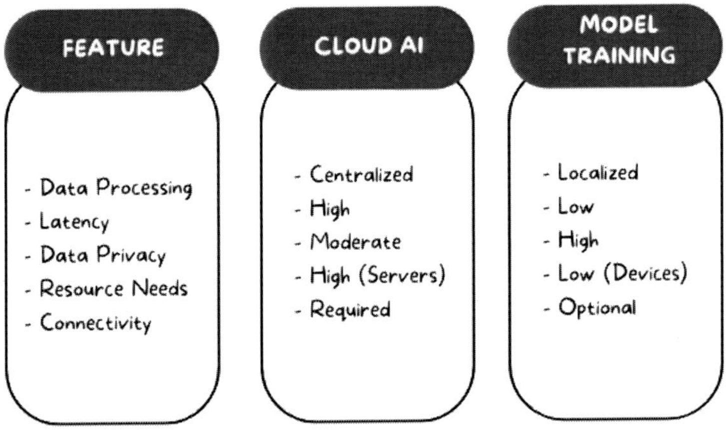

Figure 1. Comparison of Cloud vs. Edge AI.

Finally, another essential paradigm shift is the general transition from using Cloud ML in deploying AI systems to the Edge AI concept. This transition is necessary due to the need for Apps to process in real-time for privacy and accessibility in various environments. It is for this reason that Edge AI will simplify Artificial Intelligence across the globe as popular, sturdy, and flexible across many domains in the future.

3. Technological Innovations Enabling Edge AI

The birth of Edge AI is mainly attributed to various integrated advanced technologies that have allowed various machine learning (ML) models to work on low-processing systems such as sensors, smartphones, and Internet of Things devices [6]. These technologies are mainly used to form new hardware, fine-tune software, and improve energy efficiency, which is all necessary for AI processing at the edge.

3.1. Compact AI Models

One of the key challenges in deploying AI on edge devices is the constrained computational power, memory, and storage capacity. Traditional machine learning models, intense learning models, are resource-intensive and require significant processing power and memory, which are typically available only in data centers or on cloud platforms. To overcome this, the development of compact AI models has been crucial.

- *TensorFlow Lite:* It is a light version of Google's TensorFlow designed to be used only on mobiles and edges. It provides installation, optimization, and conversion tools designed to ensure that the models run efficiently on comparatively less computational power. TensorFlow Lite offers a set of techniques, such as quantization, which reduces the number of bits processed by a given model to a minimal degree that will not affect its performance noticeably while at the same time also reducing the number of calculations a machine needs to perform and resulting in less required memory.
- Open Neural Network Exchange, or ONNX, is an open-source framework that enables AI models to work across many runtimes and platforms, including edge devices. It makes optimizing models across various hardware backends easier and guarantees efficiency and compatibility when used on limited devices.
- *TinyML:* This is a relatively new application area aimed at driving machine learning algorithms with exceptionally low-power MCUs. These microcontrollers have a tiny memory footprint – measuring in kilobytes – but can accurately perform very advanced ML operations

because of the progress in model compounds and execution engines in minimal forms. TinyML, however, finds great applicability in IoT devices often deployed in large quantities, where energy consumption and costs are of utmost importance.

These small models allow for scaling full AI capabilities down and loading them onto edge devices without impacting Aspen. Modeling methods such as pruning, quantization, and knowledge distillation provide opportunities to make complex models less complex without a critical loss of efficiency.

3.2. Hardware Advancements

While software optimizations have played a large part in enabling edge AI, progress in the hardware technologies that underpin the on-device computation of ML models has been essential [7].

- *GPUs (Graphics Processing Units):* Typically created for Displays and Video, GPUs became the key to AI, especially for parallel computing. Some device peripherals on different edge devices, particularly economically influential smartphones, have integrated GPUs required for managing the parallelism of machine learning processes and internal enrichment of AI models.
- *NPUs (Neural Processing Units):* NPUs are said to be created to be focused on calculating mathematical operations used in neural network models. These are designed to carry out operations such as matrix multiplications and convolutions, which are the key functionalities of deep learning. NPUs, therefore, provide a much more significant performance upgrade whilst using less power than traditional CPUs or GPUs and are well-suited to mobile devices such as smartphones, drones, and autonomous systems.
- *TPUs (Tensor Processing Units):* Google developed TPUs, which are machine learning hardware accelerators meant for TensorFlow but can be used for other machine learning frameworks as well. Although TPUs are primarily used in cloud settings, the concept of smaller and energy-efficient TPUs is making its way into devices used at the edge to perform powerful AI computations without relying on the cloud.

- *FPGAs (Field-Programmable Gate Arrays):* FPGAs are hardware platforms that may be configured to perform particular machine learning operations. They are well suited to efficiency for specific AI applications, making them ideal for edge devices where highly tuned prowess between power provision and AI requirements is required.

These hardware developments have been pivotal in helping enhance the deployment of ML models on edge devices. Underwater target recognition through AI computation for determining objects and distances from videos can be done by offloading computation to processing units like GPUs and TPUs, which enable devices to process more sophisticated models in real time without significantly consuming much power and memory resources.

3.3. Energy Efficiency and Battery Life

Of all the limitations that edge devices, especially mobiles and IoT sensors, have, power consumption is a common issue. Most of these devices are portable and powered by batteries; activities such as running ML models consume battery power rapidly. Consequently, energy efficiency is a key driver to the effectiveness of Edge AI solutions [8].

Several innovations have helped address these challenges:

- *Low-Power Hardware:* Today's edge nodes are increasingly armed with these low-power NPUs and other energy-efficient FPGAs that are well suited to support AI processing without high power consumption. Some of these hardware elements can perform tasks, such as speech recognition, computer vision, or anomaly detection, while using as little power as possible, making them perfect for always-on applications like smart home assistants, wearable health monitoring devices, and security cameras.
- *Dynamic Voltage and Frequency Scaling (DVFS):* DVFS is a power management method implemented in most present-day processors to control the power and speed of the implementation according to the implemented computation. In the case of AI tasks, the processor can cut down the amount of power it draws at any one time and power up only under certain conditions. This task assists in saving energy as famous edge devices that require extended AI processing continuously drain batteries.

- *Event-Driven Processing:* Most edge devices are designed to spend most of their time in low-power modes while waiting for an event that will require AI processing. For instance, out of all the functionalities in a smart camera, image recognition is only turned on when there is motion. Such modes of operation in event-driven devices can be power-saving since devices only use computational resources when performing events.
- *Federated Learning:* At times, edge devices are employed to provide decentralized machine learning through federated learning. This approach enables devices to learn models locally and send updates to a central server rather than the actual data. Here, federated learning increases efficiency in that it mainly trains on-device, thus reducing energy consumption associated with data communication while at the same time achieving better privacy.
- *Adaptive Inference:* Adaptive inference refers to an AI model's capability to decide how much computing is needed to perform a given task. For instance, a device might have a simple model that is light to load and use during everyday operations but a more complicated version that is used when special circumstances arise. This selective computation strips down power consumption to the bare minimum required while being ready to deliver when asked.

This condition makes it possible for devices to have longer operational lives even though they incorporate burdensome machine learning procedures in Edge AI with the inclusion of these energy-efficient techniques. This is mainly useful when used in hard-to-reach areas or where replacing batteries or recharging is a major problem.

4. Key Platforms and Frameworks Driving Edge AI

The movement to Edge AI is due to the improvement of platforms and frameworks for AI that can enhance ML models for embedded devices [9]. These tools assist developers in creating, enhancing, and deploying such models for edge devices such as smartphones, IoT sensors, and microcontrollers. Some of the main platforms and frameworks that are at the helm of the Edge AI revolution are as follows.

4.1. TensorFlow Lite

Of the fielded adaptations of Google's TensorFlow deep machine learning platform, TensorFlow Lite is light and designed expressly for the mobile and embedded markets. This is suitable for many edge devices such as smartphones, IoT devices, and even embedded systems because it provides tools for running machine learning models with low roaming capability, low energy usage, and moderate memory usage.

- *Key Features:* It includes techniques like quantization, which brings model precision to the range of numbers from -128 to 127, and pruning, which, as you guessed, removes some weights from the model without a strong impact on accuracy. Linux version-wise, it also offers interpreter APIs for Android and iOS and allows a developer to deploy it on multiple platforms.
- *Use Cases:* TensorFlow Lite's application includes machine intelligence operations such as voice recognition, object identification, and augmented reality, which are in real time and ideal for mobile Android devices.

With inherent convenience and low latency, TensorFlow Lite is widely used in AI model deployment at the end-device level; the seamless connectivity to Google's ML environment offers incredible solutions surrounding the training, optimization, and, ultimately, the delivery of the models.

4.2. PyTorch Mobile

PyTorch Mobile uses the well-known PyTorch framework and applies it to mobile and edge computing. While PyTorch is one of the most flexible open-source platforms for machine learning and AI research, known for its modularity and simplicity employed in R&D, the platform introduced mobile support to let developers build applications for Android or iOS [10]. This brings PyTorch's dynamic computational graph and great debugger to mobile ML apps.

- *Key Features:* Quantization and pruning work on PyTorch Mobile is appropriate for decreasing memory consumption and enhancing the inference rate on mobile architectures. Developers can also utilize pre-trained models, which results in high-level transfer learning and quick app development.

- *Use Cases:* PyTorch Mobile is especially suitable for workloads that involve on-the-fly decision-making, such as computer vision language processing or edge AI, including mobile robots.

In their current state, developers can export their existing models for mobile environments without writing large parts of their code again while maintaining the flexibility that PyTorch is renowned for translating into production code.

4.3. Edge Impulse and TinyML

Edge Impulse and *TinyML* make it easier for developers to deploy machine-learning models for microcontrollers and similar devices. These tools enable developers, whether amateurs or professionals, hobbyists or industry players, to introduce AI spades to the edge without needing a powerful CPU, high RAM, or broad storage area.

- *Edge Impulse:* This environment assists developers in creating, training, and deploying machine learning models directly to microcontrollers and other CCGs [11]. Edge Impulse claimed further to solve the problem of teaching the small devices to make decisions. It turned AI into a platform for people without deep knowledge of Machine Learning algorithms.
    - *Key Features:* The Edge Impulse's user interface provides easy data acquisition, model building, and instantiation features. It is also integrated with TinyML, which popularises and optimally implements tiny models that run on microcontrollers with negligible memory, as low as a few kilobytes.
    - *Use Cases:* Some of Edge Impulse's common uses include health monitoring devices such as wearables, industrial Internet of Things applications, home automation gadgets, and climate monitoring.
- *TinyML:* This is actually part of a larger push within the machine learning community to put AI models on tiny, low-power microcontrollers (MCUs) and the like. TinyML frameworks are

combined with ultra-low power consumption principles so that AI-based devices can last for months, or even years, on small batteries.

- *Key Features:* Such frameworks allow deploying models using as little computational power and memory as possible, so it is possible, for example, to apply machine learning algorithms, such as identifying audio or visual patterns or anomaly detection, on IoT devices.
- *Use Cases:* Today, TinyML is applied in smart sensors, environmental monitoring systems, and ever-wake speech recognition devices.

As tools like Edge Impulse and TinyML bring the notion of AI and edges to millions of embedded hardware, developers and hobbyists are finding ways to create intelligent and battery-friendly solutions.

4.4. AutoML for Edge Devices

AutoML systems, including Microsoft Azure AutoML and Google Cloud AutoML, provide tools for anyone to execute, create, train, and deploy new and original machine learning models. These platforms are especially valuable for solving the problems of optimizing and deploying models for further use on the edges, contributing to the democratization of AI.

- *Google Cloud AutoML:* This set of machine learning libraries helps beginners develop and fine-tune superior-quality models.
  - *Key Features:* Google Cloud AutoML allows users to train and deploy models in an end-to-end fashion by masking the underlying programming from the users. It also supports TensorFlow Lite, which enhances the compatibility of the models it produces with the mobile and embedded platforms.
  - *Use Cases:* AutoML is applied in areas such as image categorization, object recognition, and natural language processing on smart devices, IoT sensors, cameras, and wearable gadgets.
- *Microsoft Azure AutoML:* Like Google's AutoML, Microsoft allows the generation of finely tuned models for deployment on different

hardware, including the edge. Azure's platform allows model export to ONNX, which facilitates using it with low resource availability.

- *Key Features:* Azure AutoML also makes it easy to manage model performance and memory consumption to maximize utilization across low-power devices. It supports a range of hardware accelerators to ensure the model being deployed is optimized properly for the device it will be deployed on.
- *Use Cases:* AutoML, as used by Microsoft, is extensively used in edge processes such as predictive maintenance in IIoT and sentiment analysis from mobiles, to name but a few.

By making it easier to debut machine learning models on edge devices, these AutoML technologies allow ordinary software developers or large enterprises that might not know much about ML to fully unlock the power of AI at the edge. Automating the training and optimization of models negates the time, efficiency, and inclusiveness hurdles associated with applying Artificial Intelligence. Figure 2 shows the benefit of Edge AI.

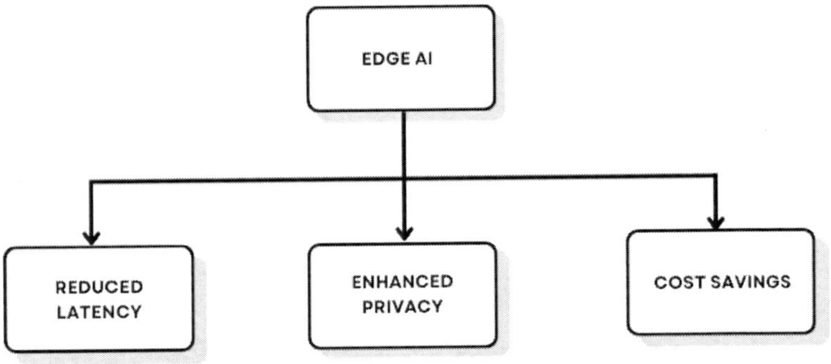

Figure 2. Benefits of Edge AI.

5. Applications of Edge AI

Edge AI's application spans different industries, changing how devices make decisions in real-time and giving a wide range of intelligent, responsive solutions in different settings. Below are key areas where Edge AI is making a significant impact:

5.1. Smartphones and Personal Devices

Edge AI enables various sophisticated features on smartphones and personal devices, facilitating real-time, on-device processing that enhances user experience and overall functionality.

- *Personal Assistant Apps:* Virtual assistants such as Google Assistant, Siri, and Alexa leverage Edge AI to handle voice commands locally, ensuring quicker responses and better privacy. These applications can carry out tasks like setting reminders, making calls, or managing smart home devices without requiring continuous cloud connectivity.
- *Real-Time Translation:* Language translation apps utilize Edge AI to process speech and text in real time, even when offline. For example, Google Translate can interpret spoken words or text through on-device processing, which is particularly beneficial in regions with limited internet connectivity.
- *Camera Enhancements:* Modern smartphones leverage Edge AI to enhance photos and videos. Capabilities such as object recognition, scene detection, and portrait mode optimize camera performance by making real-time adjustments to improve image quality without uploading data to the cloud.

Edge AI in smartphones improves user interaction, strengthens privacy, and enables faster, more efficient task processing.

5.2. IoT and Smart Cities

Edge AI serves as a fundamental element of the Internet of Things (IoT) ecosystem, facilitating smart city infrastructure's more effective function by utilizing real-time data analytics and decision-making directly at the edge.

- *Traffic Management:* Edge AI analyzes traffic patterns and adjusts traffic lights in real-time to reduce congestion. For example, intelligent cameras equipped with AI can detect vehicle movements and adapt signals accordingly, improving overall traffic efficiency without relying on centralized cloud systems.
- *Energy Optimization:* Smart grids and energy systems leverage Edge AI to optimize energy consumption. These systems can forecast

energy demand, enhance distribution, and minimize waste in real-time by processing data locally.

- *Public Safety:* Machine vision in edge AI is applied in live movement detection found in security cameras and sensors for monitoring public areas. These systems can detect abnormalities and threats and generate an alert immediately, improving people's safety as compared to incident response time.

Smart cities also use Edge AI to optimize infrastructures, optimize costs, and, most importantly, upgrade the standard living conditions in cities.

5.3. Healthcare and Wearables

In healthcare, Edge AI is instead changing the delivery of smart medical objects such as life-saving devices and wearable technology gadgets that offer real-time information on the client's health status.

- *Wearable Devices:* Fitness trackers and health monitors, such as *Fitbit, Apple Watch,* and other medical-grade devices, use Edge AI to track vital signs like heart rate, blood oxygen levels, and sleep patterns [12]. These wearables analyze data locally and provide users instant feedback, helping them monitor their health in real time.
- *Medical Devices:* Edge AI is integrated into portable medical devices for real-time diagnostics. Devices like portable ECG monitors, glucose monitors, and smart inhalers use AI to analyze health data on the device, enabling timely intervention without relying on cloud servers. This study ensures greater privacy and reduces latency in life-critical situations.
- *Remote Health Monitoring:* Edge AI in a telemedicine framework includes remote patient monitoring, particularly in areas with poor connectivity. They can also process health information and exchange only the latest information with doctors instead of overloading centralized systems.

Mobile AI in healthcare improves the way that people monitor their health, the ability to diagnose patients, and, hence, the way that different decisions are made in emergency healthcare situations.

5.4. Agriculture and Remote Monitoring

Edge AI is transforming agriculture in a way that seemed impossible before, mainly when the internet connection is poor and ML decisions must be made instantly.

- *Precision Agriculture:* Applications of Edge AI are seen in drones, tractors, and self-driving farming equipment used to survey fields and manage farming processes. Such devices can monitor possible conditions and dangerous plants and pests or crops, thus offering farmers useful information for precise farming. This results in efficient water consumption, fertilizers, and pesticides, which can be used sparingly but achieve more yields.
- *Predictive Analytics:* Edge AI-based sensors used on the device can anticipate weather conditions, monitor plant growth, and control irrigation systems to provide plants with this kind of environment. This means farmers can use it even in areas with weak networks, making it a better solution for farming.
- *Remote Monitoring:* Edge AI also allows a farmer to monitor livestock's health status and field conditions and identify disease or water scarcity before it occurs. With the help of alerts and data, Edge AI requires less human intervention or monitoring than more traditional methods of farm management.

In agriculture, the use of Edge AI helps farmers make sensible decisions faster, thereby improving the efficacy of the farming process while saving money.

5.5. Autonomous Vehicles and Drones

Self-flying cars and drones also use Edge AI to make decisions on the go and control their movement. These devices require tremendous signal processing capacity and frequently need to answer for considerable portions of data within brief periods of time. The unpredictability of the environment may be dangerous if these devices do not operate immediately.

- *Self-Driving Cars:* Self-driving cars apply Edge AI to operate data received from cameras, radar, LiDAR, and other data-driven sensors to make driving decisions. Edge AI helps the car identify barriers, signs, and behavior of pedestrians and other vehicles in a split second without relying on the cloud.

- *Drones:* Edge AI-integrated drones can be used for some functionality, like surveillance, making maps, and delivering goods. Edge AI empowers drones to perform image analysis initially, including object avoidance, path following, and environment updates, in real-time.

The use of Edge AI in self-driving cars and drones enhances timely and secure determinations, limiting the reliance on cloud operations for sensitive operations.

6. Democratization through Edge AI

It is the process of bringing innovations to other populations, especially other people from less developed and poor communities. Edge AI is a central enabler of this change because it provides access to ML solutions in various fields and contributes to the innovation process. Below are key areas illustrating how Edge AI is democratizing access to AI technologies:

6.1. Accessibility to Low-Income Regions

Since edge AI allows for the processing of data locally, it has the chance of significantly enlarging the gap in access to AI technologies where there is still poor infrastructure, such as in remote and low-income communities [13]. With Edge AI, the problem of unpredictable connections and high cloud computing costs is solved by processing information on the device itself rather than in a cloud.

- *Remote Healthcare:* In underprivileged areas, Edge AI helps to offer distributed healthcare applications that support accurate remote medicine. The AI devices can often perform the analysis on the collection of health data as they are mobile enough to take intervention near the patient without the need for a strong internet connection. For instance, mobile health diagnostic devices help monitor patient status and give instant results if no stations or clinics are available.

- *Environmental Monitoring:* Edge AI also advances environmental management by using sensors capable of functioning offline. These sensors can record ecological information, including air quality, availability and use of water resources, and weather conditions, which will benefit communities and local authorities. Through observation in real time, communities can effectively react to pro-environmental problems, hence enhancing their contribution to sustainable development at large.

6.2. Reducing Costs for Businesses and Startups

Edge AI has emerged as one of the critical benefits since it reduces the overall operational and computational costs that enable newcomer startups and small businesses to adopt new forms of AI technologies for which they might not be able to afford substantial cloud frameworks.

- *Lower Infrastructure Investment:* Traditional cloud-based AI demands considerable investment in servers, storage, and operational expenses [14]. On the other hand, Edge AI enables organizations to run lightweight models on existing hardware, eliminating the need for many expensive cloud services. It is a misconception that startups cannot afford to incorporate AI solutions, as edge hardware and frameworks can be obtained at a relatively low cost.
- *Scalability:* When it comes to organizational growth, Edge AI makes it easier for firms to do so to a greater degree. They can easily use multiple edge devices in different areas without problems of central data processing. This flexibility is particularly useful for small companies with aspirations of expansion while keeping operating costs low.
- *Real-Time Analytics:* Edge AI allows small businesses to collect and analyze data in real-time, which enhances their up-to-date decision-making and, thus, organizational effectiveness. This competence is vital for companies wishing to compete actively in rapidly changing markets but do not have the privilege of large teams and loose purse strings.

6.3. Empowering Developers and Hobbyists

Edge AI has thus been able to enhance the capability for developers, enthusiasts, and hobbyists, providing everyday users with user-friendly tools and affordable gear that might help them carry out tests and possibly learn at the Edge.

- *Developer-Friendly Platforms:* Some such tools include TensorFlow Lite, PyTorch Mobile, and Edge Impulse, which have been developed to be as easy for developers of all kinds [15]. These tools help to reduce the entry threshold into the creation, training, and usage of machine learning models for edge devices, which will allow more people to understand how AI works and what it can do even though they do not have knowledge in pertinent fields such as data science.
- *Inexpensive Hardware:* Inexpensive edge hardware such as Raspberry Pi, Arduino, and different microcontrollers are now commonly available, allowing enthusiasts, individual inventors, and small groups to test and experiment with AI applications. These tools offer a relatively cheap method of research, development, and even idea creativity. These technologies are increasingly applied in central spaces, national organizations, and institutions to foster creativity and gain against AI.
- *Community and Collaboration:* Whereas the Edge AI community is rapidly developing, collaboration and knowledge sharing are welcome among its members. Online communities such as forums, Wiki-based projects, and maker fairs offer channels where developers who engage in such projects and hobbyists can exchange their experiences and work on new innovative ideas. Easier, the community-driven approach increases the learning rate and development of theories, making it easier for people in the field to make meaningful contributions.

7. Challenges of Edge AI and Overcoming Barriers

Despite the myriad advantages of Edge AI including improved efficiency, reduced latency, enhanced privacy, the former also faces several barriers which if addressed, can yield the full potential of Edge AI. The subsequent outlines principal difficulties associated with Edge AI in addition to approaches to overcome these issues. Figure 3 shows the challenges and solutions in Edge AI.

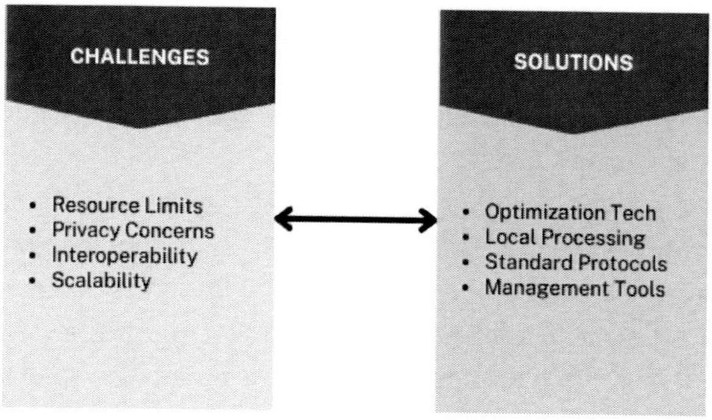

Figure 3. Challenges and Solutions in Edge AI.

7.1. Resource Limitations

7.1.1. Challenges

As mentioned before, edge devices are typically characterized by restricted computational and communicational capabilities [16]. Some of the IoT devices and mobile application have diminished computation power of regular cloud systems, hence cannot support the typical machine learning solutions.

- *Processing Power:* In general, edge devices can lag, or they are not capable of handling complex work loads or running complex models of ML which in turn limits them.
- *Memory Limitations:* Most edge devices are characterized by their limited RAM and storage space, which becomes a challenge while trying to store and execute enlarged data solutions.
- *Energy Consumption:* Energy consumption in battery operated devices must be kept to the lowest level to maximize operation time of the battery which in many cases may present a challenge in feeding the power requirements of the AI algorithms.

7.1.2. Overcoming Barriers

- *Model Optimization Techniques:* Advancements over the past few years have increasingly made it possible to optimize the models by enhancing model quantization, pruning, and distillation, all of which help minimize the dimension and complexity of the models. Techniques of this kind allow for using simplified versions of the models on devices with low memory consumption while the loss of accuracy is minimal.
- *Edge-Specific Architectures:* Building a specialised architectures, like MobileNet or SqueezeNet, that is optimized to be used in environments where there are restricted resources makes computation to be efficient. These architectures allow optimization of performance with the usage of resources and make it possible to run intricate tasks on edge devices.
- *Energy-Efficient Hardware:* Chips like Neural Processing Units (NPUs) and Tensor Processing Units (TPUs) bring a new type of energy efficiency to the processing power available. This hardware is designed to execute AI related works and thus it is fit to be deployed at the edge.

7.2. Data Privacy and Security

7.2.1. Challenges

Experience with Edge AI, that moves computation to the source of data to improve privacy as the information is analyzed locally, raise new security concerns [17]. Privacy and security of the data that is stored and processed on the edge devices might be even more of an issue because such systems are often far more exposed to the potential attacks than any centralized systems.

- *Local Data Processing:* The storage and processing of data within the district help to overcome the concern related to privacy; yet, to solve the problem, an effective protection method must be developed to prevent data from being used by unauthorized people or leaked.
- *Device Vulnerability:* Edge devices are less likely to be updated or patched, which can expose them to security threats during large implementations.

7.2.2. Overcoming Barriers

- *Enhanced Security Protocols:* Thus, integration into edge devices should include such measures as encryption of data at rest, secure boot mechanisms, and secure configurations in order to safeguard information, which is involved in active usage at the edge devices. This way even though the device is infected other data on the system is safe.
- *Regular Updates and Monitoring:* Regularity of monitors and updates also prevents compromise of device integrity through remote monitoring. This could be through OTAs to make certain that devices get the correct security fixes,firmware upgrades in the right time.
- *Data Anonymization:* Since collecting user data may be a concern, data anonymization should be used in order to analyze the collected data while still helping to protect the privacy of the users. This solution will help organizations avoid the risk of profiling individual users by working with aggregated data.

7.3. Interoperability

7.3.1. Challenges

Different hardware and software used in edge devices bring in compatibility issues. It is important for devices with dissimilar platforms to work well and interconnect to optimize the integration of machine learning models into the Edge AI concept.

- *Hardware Variability:* The characteristics of edge devices can differ radically with regard to computing power, memory, and interface, which creates challenges with regard to model replication.
- *Software Fragmentation:* Fluctuating operating systems, libraries, and frameworks can make integration challenging; only homogenous hardware should be used when deploying cohesive AI solutions across a network of devices.

7.3.2. Overcoming Barriers

- *Standardization:* Establishing normative reference models for system connection and application communication can help in addressing questions of compatibility among the devices. Integration is facilitated by standardization initiatives that are being carried out by OpenAI Initiative and organizations of like nature.

- *Cross-Platform Frameworks:* The ability to develop models with TensorFlow Lite and ONNX guarantees the creation of applications that can function on different platforms. These frameworks do deprive some of the underlying complexities and make the integration a relatively easier process.
- *Middleware Solutions:* Middleware can also be used as a message middle to increase compatibility between different devices. Middleware solutions used for Dataset integration and Model Deployment help heterogeneous edge environments.

7.4. Edge AI at Scale

7.4.1. Challenges

This is especially the case when considering the deployment of Edge AI across a large number of devices, in extensive networks [18]. Ensuring model updates, security update, and device coordination has to be done at the correct time in real time to maintain the security of Edge AI.

- *Model Updates:* This becomes a huge problem when it comes to timely updating of machine learning models across all of the edge devices, especially if one is managing large numbers of devices distributed in different geographical locations.
- *Coordination and Monitoring:* Operations coordination in many edge devices need the support of a strong framework to facilitate the overall performance and status tracking of the device. This is because lack of visibility may make the troubleshooting and maintenance of such components very hard.

7.4.2. Overcoming Barriers

- *Cloud-Edge Hybrid Models:* Managing scalability is possible with hybrid architectures of cloud service and edge services. Although edge devices do real-time processing, the cloud can take up non-real-time processing duties such as training of models and new updates.
- *Decentralized Management Platforms:* Organizational structures for decentralized management of distributed applications that incorporate

real-time acknowledging and controlling of edge devices are efficient. They can support remote update and checking of statuses, analysis of performance that enhance the overall operations.

- *Containerization and Orchestration:* Containerization technology, for example Docker when used in conjunction with orchestration software, for instance Kubernetes, facilitates the deployment of applications at the edge devices. It also makes scaling easy to implement as well as guaranteeing that the application is going to perform just as it is expected in the next scale.

8. Ethical Considerations and Impact on Society

Below are some remarkable ethical implication and Societal issues concern with Edge AI as it innovative and develops further in different sectors: Such factors are important for making sure that deployment of Edge AI will be of benefit to society and at the same time control any negative impacts that may arise.

8.1. Reducing the Digital Divide

8.1.1. Impact

There is also much promise in edge AI to narrow the digital divide, supplying intelligence-enhanced technologies to locations that lack robust connectivity. Since Edge AI empowers local computation and decision-making, it can be useful to bring appropriate services and information, hence improving the standard of living in such areas.

- *Accessibility:* Edge AI makes it possible to apply several uses like remote healthcare, education and support of agriculture in the areas which are not very connected. For example, the acquisition of the diagnostic tools by rural health clinics can feed into the Edge AI to deliver on the spot health assessments thereby enhancing access to health services without the need for the high-speed internet.
- *Inclusion:* Promoting AI to be deployed through edge AI will benefit the underprivileged groups within the society, the less privileged, get

an opportunity to be part of the digital economy hence gain a better socio economic status.

8.1.2. Challenges

However, successful implementation of these potentials requires that further precaution is made to avoid worsening the existing digital divide by denying marginalized communities the necessary resources and capacity to make optimum use of Edge AI.

8.2. Potential for Job Creation and Skill Development

8.2.1. Impact

The development of Edge AI will result to job creation and new skills will be developed especially in engineering, data science and equipment manufacturing [19]. This is especially true in emergent economy where employment generation can greatly boost periphery economy.

- *New Job Roles:* In the future, when businesses integration Edge AI technologies, there would be a need for AI model developers and managers whose function would be to develop, deploy and maintain the AI applications. Specific employment opportunities like Edge AI engineers, data scientist, and system integrators employments will gradually be valuable.
- *Skill Building:* This need for guru's in Edge AI will compel learning institutions to design courses and curricula in AI technologies. Such measures could enable communities at the grassroots level to get skills required in the emerging economic environment dominated by artificial intelligence.

8.2.2. Challenges

For job creation to have the greatest impact, it is important that those from disadvantaged backgrounds are able to access training and resources in order to enter this new working field.

8.3. Environmental Impact

8.3.1. Impact

It becomes easier to achieve sustainability if systems for Edge AI are in place since they eliminate high carbon utilization as compared to cloud computing.

- *Energy Efficiency:* Edge AI happens on peripheral devices so as to reduce the amount of data that needs to be sent to centralized cloud computing systems. This localized computational paradigm helps to address the issues of energy consumption that are associated with the transfer of data and the widespread data centers and thus leads to the conservation of total energy use.
- *Sustainable Solutions:* Smart applications like smart agriculture that utilize Edge AI can explore the need for resources such as water and fertilizers and make wise use of them to conserve.

8.3.2. Challenges

Although Edge AI may help reduce environmental impacts when implemented, it is important that hope of sustainability should also embrace the manufacturing and disposal of the edge devices that are used in implementing Edge AI to avoid problems of e waste and the likes.

8.4. Bias and Fairness

8.4.1. Ethical Considerations

The usage of AI models on edge devices is the deployment of particular and advanced forms of AI with critical ethical consequences, including algorithmic bias and fairness.

- *Algorithmic Bias:* AI solutions deployed at the edge when trained on a biased dataset will, therefore, continue to deepen the inequity given the field's highly sensitive nature in sectors such as healthcare and public safety. If the algorithms are not controlled properly and tuned properly, they could lead to discriminating results, and this would mean that a diagnosis made by the algorithm could be wrong or that a specific defined segment of the population could be surveilled.

- *Transparency and Accountability:* Since AI algorithms are complex, they hinder transparency and therefore, the users cannot easily understand the approaches used in decision making. Holding Edge AI systems responsible for the action performed is crucial as to their roles across various sectors that have substantial impacts on human life.

8.4.2. Challenges

However, to ensure non defStyleAttrinstitutional and overly prejudice is not inherent into the Edge AI systems in making decisions, the organizations must pay attention to ethical considerations in the practice. These are; consciously performing bias checks, using diverse data in AI and involving a range of stakeholders with different backgrounds in the AI making process.

9. The Future of Edge AI

They are the future of Edge AI now providing revolutionary innovations and a new level of advancement, and powered by the following: the next-generation hardware, connectivity, applications, and partnerships that work together to democratize the access. Therefore, highlighting some of the trends and development that should define the future world of Edge AI is important. Figure 4 shows the architecture of Edge AI.

Figure 4. Architecture of Edge AI.

9.1. Next-Generation Hardware

9.1.1. Advancements

The ongoing advancement in the hardware technology will determine the future of Edge AI devices [20]. New innovations, for instance, quantum processors and advanced TPUs for edge computing has the capability to change the edge computing capabilities of companies.

- *Quantum Processors:* One of the greatest potential benefits of quantum computing is enhanced computing capacity, which can enhance the ability of machines to learn on edge devices. This capability would enable real-time data analysis and decisionism, expanding new fronts for users who need fast processing of huge amounts of data.
- *Enhanced TPUs and AI Accelerators:* Subsequent generations of TPUs and other types of AI accelerators will yield increasingly higher computational rates and even higher unified, energy-related efficiency. Such advancements will make it possible to deploy more complex models on the limited-power edge devices to let the scope to cover even further.

9.2. 5G and Edge AI Synergy

9.2.1. Impact of 5G

The deployment of 5G networks is anticipated to enhance the Edge AI empowering dramatically due to high speed and low latency.

- *Accelerated Data Processing:* 5G technology has emerged and propels the ability of Edge devices to transmit or receive data at a high speed, owing to analytical processes and interaction. This advance will be particularly beneficial for uses that require quick actions, such as self-driving cars, smart factories, and telemedicine.
- *Richer Applications:* The increase in bandwidth in 5G will pave the way for more complex applications in areas such as augmented reality (AR) and virtual reality (VR) simply because 5G will allow for the streaming and processing of data at the network's edge. This synergy will then give end users new horizons and solutions across several different industries.

9.3. AI-Driven Innovation in Edge Computing

9.3.1. Future Innovations

The evolution of Edge AI is expected to drive several innovations that reshape industries and enhance human experiences.

- *Self-Sustaining Smart Ecosystems:* Future Edge AI systems could facilitate self-sustaining smart ecosystems that autonomously manage resources, optimize energy consumption, and enhance environmental sustainability [21]. For example, smart cities could leverage Edge AI for integrated traffic management, energy distribution, and waste management, creating efficient urban environments.
- *Autonomous Systems:* Edge AI will be pivotal in the development of autonomous systems, such as drones and robots, which will rely on real-time data processing and machine learning to navigate and interact with their environments. This capability will extend to various sectors, including agriculture, logistics, and disaster response.
- *Enhanced Human-Machine Interaction:* When Edge AI technologies develop, people will be able to behave naturally with the machines. It has innovative uses of interactive features such as NLP, Gesture, and Emotion sensors to enhance smooth interaction between the users and automation to make them more friendly to the end users [22].

9.4. Expanding Access

9.4.1. Collaborative Efforts

Therefore, to popularize the Edge AI to the whole world, more cooperation between governments, industries, and various institutions of learning will be crucial.

- *Policy and Infrastructure Development:* Governments can therefore encourage the utilisation of Edge AI through provision of infrastructure, and through development of framework for innovation. This includes, funding for research, setting standard guidelines for the responsible creation of these intelligence systems, and policy that guarantees everyone an equal chance at using it.
- *Industry Partnerships:* Market appeal for hi-tech equipment as well as the relations between private companies and local communities may foster programs designed to extend various Edge AI applications to target districts. Through partnerships, the organisations' can coordinate and utilise their assets, skills, and experience to strengthen the stock of knowledge and animate the economic growth.

- *Educational Initiatives:* The skills of computer learning and other programs required in Edge AI can also be developed in educational institutions. Through training, workshops, and certifications, they are in an ideal place to help people from any background prepare for dealing with AI. Efforts to introduce technical education, especially in the areas of science, technology, engineering, and mathematics (STEM), especially for the needy, will go a long way in shaping the manpower needed to address the shortage [23]. Figure 5 shows the use cases of Edge AI.

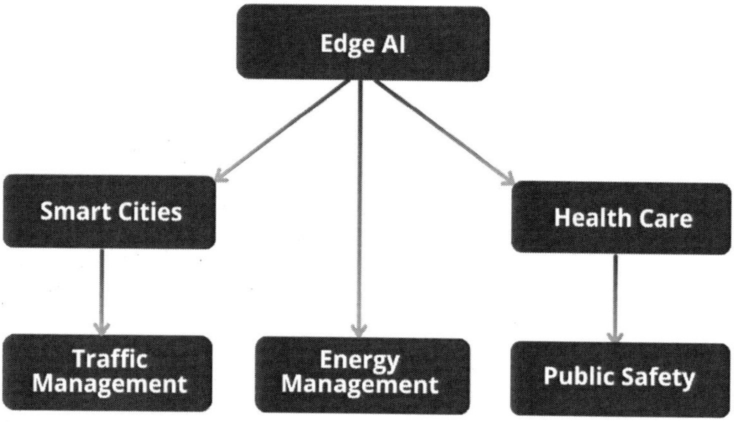

Figure 5. Use Cases of Edge AI.

10. Results and Discussion

This section shall provide an overview of what has been discovered in the analysis of the Edge AI technologies and their deployment, then a focused discussion on the implications, limitations, and outlook for Edge AI.

10.1. Key Findings

- *Performance of ML Models on Resource-Constrained Devices:* The application of various optimization models, including pruning, quantization, and knowledge distillation, makes ML models act effectively in low-memory and processing capability devices. The execution of these techniques helps to maintain small levels of performance degradation in return for smaller model size and energy demand.

- Example: Smartphone models for voice assistants demonstrate almost identical effectiveness as the full-precision models, yet they use considerably less power.

- *Impact of Hardware Accelerators:* Advanced hardwares such as TPUs, NPUs, FPGAs boost the computational ali, enabling real time artificial intelligent processing on the edges of the devices. Most of these hardware accelerators are in the process of being integrated into Internet of Things (IoT) frameworks, wearable devices and gadgets and robotics and more.
- *Industry Adoption:*
    - *Healthcare:* Real-time monitoring in wearable health devices entails fewer cloud connections and keeps users' information safe by processing it through Edge AI.
    - *Smart Cities:* Micro cameras and sensors placed at the edge make it possible to control traffic and monitor the climate without much cloud computing assistance.
    - *Autonomous Systems:* Automated drones, self-driving cars, and robotics find Real-time decisions on the edge to be effective for safety and response.

10.2. Challenges in Deploying Edge AI

- *Model Optimization Trade-offs:* Although algorithms that manage to minimize computational demand have been developed, they diminish the accuracy level. The process of balancing the size of the model and the achieved predictive capabilities is still an unsolved problem.
- *Limited Power and Memory:* Edge devices, especially battery-powered ones, must balance energy efficiency with computational demands, requiring innovations in both hardware and software.
- *Fragmentation of Hardware Ecosystems:* The diversity of hardware platforms and processors (e.g., ARM, RISC-V, and custom accelerators) complicates model deployment and optimization.

- *Security Concerns:* Although Edge AI improves privacy by localizing data processing, securing devices against physical attacks and firmware vulnerabilities is still a concern.

10.3. Opportunities and Future Directions

- *Federated Learning:* Future study can be extended on applying federated learning that lets all the edge devices train the models cooperatively while not disclosing raw data.
- *Energy-Aware Algorithms:* They also propose further works on the development of reconfigurable and low power energy efficient algorithms and adaptive AI models for Edge AI implementation in ultra low power devices.
- *Standardization Efforts:* More integration work is expected by different key players in a similar field in the future, so the standardization of the software frameworks and the hardware interfaces (TensorFlow Lite, ONNX, etc.) is crucial.
- *AI at the Edge for Sustainability:* Since Edge AI helps avoid the extensive use of cloud referencing, it can be considered as safe and environmentally friendly by saving energy consumption and the Earth's resources used for data centers.

Conclusion

Edge AI is one of the most critical developments in the field of machine learning and AI that can bring several disruptive opportunities for different industries. It expounds on Edge AIs, where computational resources are located near the data sources to enable real-time decisions, reduce latency, and ensure data privacy. Its importance lies not only in its technical features but also in the ability to bring technology to everyone and make AI tools accessible to many different communities and sectors. The challenge of democratizing Edge AI has profound implications for individuals, businesses, and communities. Edge AI allows access to intelligent systems in regions without strong infrastructure, meaning users can utilize machine learning for healthcare, agriculture, smart city projects, and more. This availability not only encourages innovation but drives economic development, social equity, and environmental sustainability. However, realizing the totality of what Edge AI can offer is going to require a renewed commitment to innovation, ethical practices, and global cooperation. With various players—from government and academia to industry—sitting at a table together, we must ensure that we continue to be inclusive and address the needs of marginalized and underserved communities. Thus, it ensures that the benefits of Edge AI are equitably shared, paving the way for a future in which intelligent systems enrich the quality of life for all. Including all of these ideas into practice will require continued investment in research, education, and ethical guidelines, ensuring that Edge AI makes a positive impact and advances behavior in a technology-driven world.

References

[1] Chan, Y. Z. and S. C. Y. Chan, “Democratizing Artificial Intelligence through Edge Computing,” *Journal of Computer Networks and Communications*, vol. 2021, Article ID 5577394, 2021.

[2] ABI Research, “Edge AI: Democratizing AI for the Future,” 2022. [Online]. Available: https://www.abiresearch.com.

[3] Varma, “TinyML: Machine Learning for IoT Devices,” in *Proceedings of the IEEE International Conference on Computer Vision and Pattern Recognition Workshops (CVPRW)*, 2020, pp. 167-173.

[4] Berger, S., M. Schwarzkopf, and O. Mutlu, "A Case for Resource-Constrained Inference in Cloud and Edge Systems," *IEEE Transactions on Parallel and Distributed Systems*, vol. 33, no. 3, pp. 662-676, Mar. 2022. doi: 10.1109/TPDS.2021.3077310.

[5] Gartner, “Predicts 2022: AI Will Be a Major Driver of Innovation,” 2022. [Online]. Available: https://www.gartner.com.

[6] Google Cloud, “A Beginner’s Guide to TensorFlow Lite and Edge AI,” [Online]. Available: https://cloud.google.com/blog/topics/developers-practitioners/a-beginners-guide-to-tensorflow-lite-and-edge-ai.

[7] Li, H., K. Ota, and M. Dong, "Learning IoT in Edge: Deep Learning for the Internet of Things with Edge Computing," *IEEE Network*, vol. 32, no. 1, pp. 96-101, Jan. 2018. doi: 10.1109/MNET.2018.1700202.

[8] Yu, H., Z. Qin, Z. Pang, and G. Fortino, "A Survey on Internet of Things From Industrial Market Perspective," *IEEE Access*, vol. 8, pp. 69200-69216, 2020. doi: 10.1109/ACCESS.2020.2983001.

[9] Lee, I., K. Lee, and Y. Lee, "Blockchain-Based Secure Firmware Update for Embedded Devices in an Edge AI System," *IEEE Access*, vol. 8, pp. 63445-63453, 2020. doi: 10.1109/ACCESS.2020.2984727.

[10] International Telecommunication Union (ITU), "AI for Good: How Artificial Intelligence is Helping the World," 2020. [Online]. Available: https://www.itu.int/en/ITU-T/AI/Pages/default.aspx.

[11] Lin, J., W. Yu, N. Zhang, X. Yang, H. Zhang, and W. Zhao, "A Survey on Internet of Things: Architecture, Enabling Technologies, Security and Privacy, and Applications," *IEEE Internet of Things Journal*, vol. 4, no. 5, pp. 1125–1142, Oct. 2017. doi: 10.1109/JIOT.2017.2683200.

[12] Deng, L., "Deep Learning: From Speech Recognition to Language and Multimodal Processing," *IEEE Signal Processing Magazine*, vol. 29, no. 6, pp. 82-97, Nov. 2012. doi: 10.1109/MSP.2012.2205597.

[13] Zhang, L., Z. Liu, and K. Wang, "Edge AI: A Comprehensive Survey on Challenges and Opportunities," *IEEE Internet of Things Journal*, vol. 8, no. 12, pp. 9673-9694, 2021.

[14] Faruque, M. O., et al., "Machine Learning at the Edge: A Survey of Recent Advances," *IEEE Access*, vol. 9, pp. 80394-80414, 2021.

[15] McKinsey & Company, "The Future of AI: A New Era of Innovation," 2021. [Online]. Available: https://www.mckinsey.com.

[16] NVIDIA, "What is Edge AI?" [Online]. Available: https://www.nvidia.com/en-us/deep-learning-ai/solutions/edge-ai/.

[17] Girshick, R., "Fast R-CNN," *Proceedings of the IEEE International Conference on Computer Vision (ICCV)*, Santiago, Chile, 2015, pp. 1440-1448. doi: 10.1109/ICCV.2015.169.

[18] Zhou, S., Z. Liu, J. Xu, and Y. Wu, "Edge Intelligence: Paving the Last Mile of Artificial Intelligence with Edge Computing," *Proceedings of the IEEE*, vol. 107, no. 8, pp. 1738-1762, Aug. 2019. doi: 10.1109/JPROC.2019.2918951.

[19] Schmidt, T. L., D. Hubaux, and S. E. Sarma, "Autonomous and Decentralized Management of Digital Identities," *Proceedings of the IEEE*, vol. 108, no. 6, pp. 1054-1068, Jun. 2020. doi: 10.1109/JPROC.2020.2978632.

[20] U.S. National Institute of Standards and Technology (NIST), "AI Risk Management Framework," 2023. [Online]. Available: https://www.nist.gov/itl/applied-cybersecurity/nist-cybersecurity-center-excellence/ai-risk-management-framework.

[21] Shi, W., J. Cao, Q. Zhang, Y. Li, and L. Xu, "Edge Computing: Vision and Challenges," *IEEE Internet of Things Journal*, vol. 3, no. 5, pp. 637-646, Oct. 2016. doi: 10.1109/JIOT.2016.2579198.

[22] Gollagi, S. G., & Balasubramaniam, S. (2023). Hybrid model with optimization tactics for software defect prediction. *International Journal of Modeling, Simulation, and Scientific Computing*, *14*(02), 2350031.

[23] Balasubramaniam, S., Prasanth, A., Kumar, K. S., & Kavitha, V. (2024). Medical Image Analysis Based on Deep Learning Approach for Early Diagnosis of Diseases. In *Deep Learning for Smart Healthcare* (pp. 54-75). Auerbach Publications.

Chapter 9

Unlocking the Democratized Generative Artificial Intelligence in Small and Medium-Sized Enterprises (SMEs)

Wasswa Shafik*

Dig Connectivity Research Laboratory (DCRLab), Kampala, Uganda

Abstract

Generative Artificial Intelligence (GAI) is changing how we do business. As more advanced and democratized AI services emerge in the market, the deployment of AI is no longer restricted to industry giants. Instead, small and medium-sized enterprises (SMEs) now have an opportunity to use AI to revolutionize business operations and explore innovative business models. In the journey towards digital transformation, SMES must use state-of-the-art AI approaches. It is playing an increasing role in finding new solutions, driving innovation more autonomously, and supporting decision-makers who steer their organizations in the desired direction. The innovative power inherent in the ever-expanding field of GAI can provide key success drivers for that subset of enterprises in the European Union (EU), which characterize the long tail of its economic landscape, namely SMEs that have some minor reach when it comes to capital investments. This chapter will establish an understanding of how generative GAI works and discuss its potential to unlock the innovative power of enterprises, small and large, but with a focus on SMEs. Moreover, insights regarding the practical implementation of a generative tool will be presented and discussed based on participatory action research conducted over two and a half years in academic and real-

* Corresponding Author's Email: wasswashafik@ieee.org

In: Democratized Generative AI: Principles, Challenges and Applications
Editors: S. Balasubramaniam and Seifedine Kadry
ISBN: 979-8-89530-684-0

life settings. The reflection draws on insights gained from the recent understanding of human-GAI interaction. It provides a model of how the respective capacities could complement one another in their problem-solving and innovation processes. Finally, the benefits and risks of the possible transfer of new knowledge derived from generative GAI tools into patent-worthy intellectual property are discussed based on a proposed new concept for the hierarchical classification of knowledge.

Keywords: generative GAI, small and medium-sized enterprises, business innovation, automation, cost efficiency, product development, GAI-powered solutions, digital transformation

1. Introduction

In the age we live in, generative artificial intelligence (GAI) is rapidly becoming accessible to smaller companies, whether it is access control solutions that can cope with changing real-world conditions, dialog agents that can efficiently communicate with customers, or prediction algorithms that can anticipate future market trends to find an opening for a product launch [1]. Although the latter is mainly seen as a mere extension of existing machine learning methods with an added social aspect, it cannot be denied that its underlying logic is fundamentally different, and its potential impact on business operations and the economy can be just as profoundly influential as large-scale machine learning. This advancement has enabled SMEs to leverage their smaller size, lower technological commitment, and greater employee flexibility to enhance their strategic operations and compete effectively with much larger corporations. These companies can also engage in significant mergers [2]. Initially, some proprietary accesses powered by generative AI models could be offered at a much lower cost than would typically be, thereby unleashing some of the dark economic models' network effects for the company's clientele. Second, by using them in conjunction with other services or products, companies can obtain substantial cost savings within their internal value chain, which can be transferred to end consumers through lower costs. In addition to merely using them, insightful data within the company can be unlocked, which can become potent competitive weapons when dynamically supplemented by domain expert knowledge or used as the only element of an AI [3]. Our point is that generative innovation today not only presents a tool for SMEs to work more competitively and effectively, but it can also unlock novel business workflows and strategic procedures.

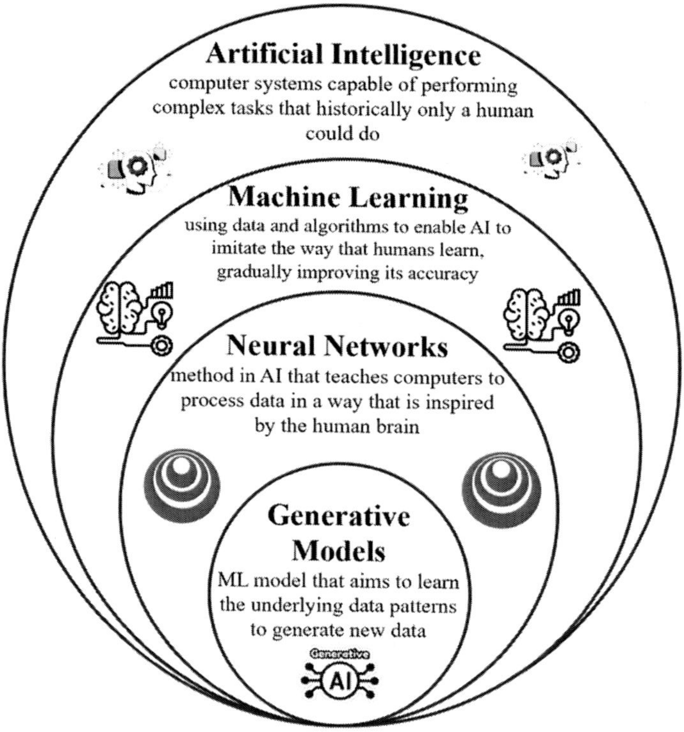

Figure 1. Significant types of Expert systems.

The idea of a 'creative' computer has existed since at least the 1960s, proven through technologies like automated theorem proving. It was over the next twenty years that, for the first time, systems could learn from patterns of data, such as checkers and other simple games, through simple modeling of the human brain's neurons. This development represented a significant moment in the history of AI and played a critical role in shaping deep learning. The next breakthrough was the introduction of the backpropagation algorithm in the 1980s, which was found to significantly speed up the training of neural networks, a precursor of today's AI [4]. Deep learning is built on this: the algorithms that allow computers to look at images, understand human speech, drive cars, and beat humans in certain games. What has changed is that these methods have become more powerful and have become commoditized. This is known as generative AI. Because deep learning is based on a collection of algorithms known as 'neural networks', which are inspired by the structure and function of the brain, it has become far easier to build far more widely suited models than before. The improvements in ability have come by joining up AI with other technologies; cloud computing has made it easier to store vast amounts of data [5]. Now, data resources have grown, and statisticians can map how data points are connected accurately. Further, improvements in computer processing power have made repeatedly crunching the numbers into a complete model far more efficient. These enhancements have allowed for a boom in artificial intelligence capabilities, making the technology more accessible to a broader audience, particularly with the rise of SMEs looking to apply these techniques, though challenged differently [6]. Understanding the background of generative AI is vital for understanding the benefits for an SME of using a deep learning approach as Figure 1 presents the critical aspects of expert systems that entail GAI.

1.1. Background and Rationale

Growing interest and attention on AI, especially deep or large-scale learning, has produced innovations, including disproportionate performance increases, across a range of business applications. Many companies in developed economies have started leveraging the power of AI to improve efficiency, agility, and competitiveness. However, SMEs generally have limited access to expert knowledge and resources for AI development. In particular, few of those SMEs considering the use of generative AI technologies to expand their range of products and services can utilize disentangled, semantic, or multimodal latent representations to understand AI's internal structure [7]. They may then need help from professional staff with sufficient expertise in image recognition, text processing, and generative model training to explore using novel techniques and models. The shift towards democratized or democratically available generative AI technology is the future. We hope that software engineers, entrepreneurs, and enterprises that focus on democratizing generative AI will increase availability and utilization among currently underserved end-users. With proper user accessibility and re-implementation, we can achieve faster democratization and cheaper operation of generative AI in our increasingly digital society. Software templates or third-party services will help reduce the depth and time requirements for user system understanding and coding development [8]. After reaching a critical mass of both developers and users, SMEs and entrepreneurs from all walks of life should not only improve their self-sufficiency and time-to-market in generative AI usage and development but also open up entirely new usage scenarios.

1.2. Research Objectives

Firms have been swift to introduce AI, emphasizing the competitive rationale that such AI technologies can open up and highlight the potential they carry. As if on cue, a flurry of policies has emerged proclaiming the economic and social benefits that will result from these technologies. However, recognizing its potential is not the same as investing in it. Currently, only 4% of firms have adopted AI, while a mere 32% are exploring or experimenting with these data-intensive AI technologies, a situation that can lead to a splintering of markets that is of particular concern for SMEs [9]. This research seeks to fill a significant gap by taking an SME-centered view and asking:

1) What are the forces at play when it comes to implementing AI technologies in SMEs?
2) What does AI technology mean for human workers in SMEs and
3) What can be done to facilitate AI adoption in SMEs?

At the core of the research is democratizing access to the broader business benefits of next-stage AI technology. In doing so, we critique the usual voiceless worker lens and assume a deeper SME understanding with a granular demarcation that emphasizes constructive and purposeful conversation founded on a tenable acceptance of mutual respect: workers accept AI technologies, and the AI technologies accept workers [10].

1.3. Scope and Delimitations

This study is set within four specific areas: GAI that democratizes AI technology, SMEs as the target organization, the broad technological scope from management information systems as well as management systems and management studies perspectives to sustain SMEs' market position, and the surrogate management perspective of generative AI for the specific model. Thus, the problem areas of generative AI and SMEs, usually treated distinctly, were combined. This combination is non-trivial as the technology is usually primarily discussed in its own right, mainly dealing with its future implications for society and humanity. At this time, the second subject is extensively treated in incumbent literature. Going further, our treatment is based on reducing the specific management functions processed in SMEs, as those organizations do not have most of the comprehensive management functions [11].

The corresponding limitations are clear: this study is not positioned within either AI research, technology-system research, or management/systems studies that deal with these two independent issues in more detail. However, the focus was placed on strengthening situated theory-aware systems, SMEs dependent on the market situation, among specialized management information systems. This general problem area was customized to build a typical foundation of situated AI—SMEs and to develop a model of the technology, specifically considering the business functional dependency of managers in SMEs. Support for the population is the judgment-realistic need driven by the model, which somewhat pinpoints the specific technology offered to the market [12]. To whatever extent a high-performance training of the surrogate model is possible, we believe we have marked a new direction in the link between AI, especially addressing SMEs and the business of those companies.

2. Understanding Generative Artificial Intelligence

GAI is a field within AI that investigates models that can generate new examples statistically similar to their training data. G-AIs in their generative models are approximately the inverse of their discriminative counterparts that take an image or text and classify or recognize the image as cats or dogs and natural language when fed a sentence. At the core of any generative model is a joint probabilistic model. GAIs will also allow other progress from data science to be used with GAIs to transform data, use deep learning visualization techniques, and explainability to increase the model's transparency and accuracy [13]. This research helps the managers of SMEs to build G-AIs in their organizations systematically. GAIs can create real value for organizations by unlocking the democratization of deep learning in their quest to delineate the limitless applications of generative models in standard economics, help address scalability challenges, and conceptualize practical and ethical cyberspace security issues. Many existing AI applications in practice are classified into wave one and two shares of trends among other conceptual frameworks. The deep learning-specific tools have recently conquered the top phase of unsupervised GAN and Natural Language Processing (NLP) functions of large data repositories [14]. They are designed to provide valuable services for managers and organizational researchers, helping them identify simple, theoretical, and technical tools that leverage the capabilities of GAI to generate business benefits. Empirical evidence, particularly from linguistic data, suggests that GAIs, including transformers, are extremely powerful and continuously improving in handling sequential data.

To avoid locking in data or rigid conceptual frameworks, efforts should focus on developing adaptive GAI systems capable of evolving alongside rapidly advancing research fields [15].

2.1. Definition and Concepts

Artificial intelligence and machine learning systems once belonged mainly to big companies but are becoming increasingly accessible to SMEs. AI and machine learning (ML) technologies, such as generative AI, which supports innovative designs and content, are emerging as a democratized form, which increases the diversity of innovation contexts. Through democratization, this study considers that small companies can also benefit from cutting-edge innovation. First, disruptive innovation benefits smaller firms to a greater degree because these firms are more likely to develop 'game-changing' innovations based on fundamentally new knowledge and are less constrained by organizational conservatism, incentives, and previous product choices. In the second mechanism, larger firms are constrained by internal structure, rigid communication, bounded rationality, formalized procedures, and expensive validation demands [16]. However, SMEs, in particular, can make fast decisions, utilize decentralized incentives and fast learning, and select innovation as a significant strategy. GAI is the next category of AI technology, often referred to as providing capabilities that allow the production of semi-creative, human-interesting material that was previously thought to be impossible, whereas human beings might produce it. Its application areas include music, short stories, greenhouse design, and digital assistive art. This AI was co-developed by an organization that has business ties with SMEs. By comparing the range of application areas, both within and between sizeable firms and SMEs, using generative AI may increase the diversity of innovative activities in small companies, which can contribute to a positive impact [17].

2.2. Types of Generative AI

There are various types of generative AI, which the varying nature of the input data can distinguish. Image-to-image models: Such models convert the input data into an image. The model accepts one image and generates a related picture to match the input. Engaging with this type of model is possible with a high level of confidence as the model first uses the pixel-to-pixel mapping technique. Next, the model gains data on the matched relations between input and output pictures and makes use of GAN to generate the desired output picture in the second phase. An easy example of this could be an image colorizer model that converts grayscale photos into colored ones in a single click [18]. Text-to-image generative models: These models allow for context synthesis of the scene perception before image creation. They typically use text-based descriptions of the required output images to accomplish this perception. There is a major obstacle with text-to-image models. Unlike other generative models, they do not have immediate access to the sizeable centralized repository of raw data. This means that sampling output from basic processing is much less particular. Furthermore, most existing models in this category do not have a clear quantitative understanding of the input text from the output [19].

2.3. Applications in SMEs

Following the current trends, SMEs have started integrating and embracing AI technologies into their business activities. Today, the number of firms leveraging AI is soaring, with small companies taking the largest share of AI implementations. They primarily use AI in their finance or sales and marketing functions, with nearly four in ten implementing AI to automate processes in these areas. Having facilitated faster and more considerate business decisions and streamlined business processes, the AI-driven solutions have resulted in various benefits, including substantial labor cost reductions, error minimization, faster service delivery, and heightened data management capabilities. Some companies are already using AI tools, ranging from various categories, from BI platforms using AI to the use of various algorithms for customer service. There seems to be significant potential for AI-based solutions for all economic sectors, and this potential is exceptionally high for AI-based applications yet to be implemented. Small companies will soon recognize this potential for the implementation of AI. The hype and fear about AI are replaced by business impact and demand. There are still sufficient reasons to hesitate to implement AI, as there is significant uncertainty about business benefits, direct financial costs, and daunting technological obstacles [20]. However, AI investments take off from the early adopters' limited partnerships, and this growth should eventually spread to a broad base of small companies, taking into account the apparent progression and the availability of affordable and easy-to-use AI applications optimized for small companies.

3. The Democratization of Artificial Intelligence

AI democratization is a movement to make artificial intelligence and its resources available to the public. The concept is based on the idea that artificial intelligence and machine learning capabilities used to be specialized technologies that required coding, licensing, complex maintenance, and complicated setup.

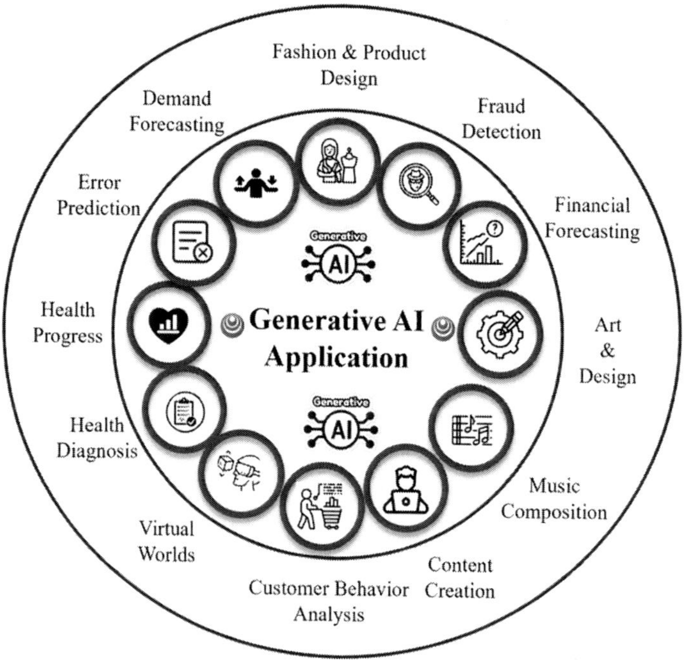

Figure 2. Generative artificial intelligence application in SMEs.

AI democratization allows the general public to use artificial intelligence and machine learning resources without too much tech savviness or for free through resources available in the form of code libraries, services, data, and APIs. Democratized AI will allow customers to self-service customer support, sales, product recommendations, and further personalization. AI democratization is an effort to reduce the division between AI technology and the general public. Individuals, companies, and governments can influence the broader adoption of AI given the required actions and necessary political and investment measures. For SMEs, unlocking the power of AI is about enabling small teams to innovate with emerging technologies rapidly [21]. These emerging technologies include artificial intelligence, where teams require access to resources and services for developing new AI solutions without necessarily having comprehensive data science and machine learning capabilities in their skills repertoire; sampled applications of GAI in SMEs are presented in Figure 2.

3.1. Historical Context

The Industry 4.0 era, characterized by the highly advanced modularization, miniaturization, and democratization of information and communication technology, is changing the paradigm of information processing by pushing artificial intelligence to the edge. As the penetration of the fourth industrial revolution is extended, AI methods have evolved from decision-making automation for simple and repetitive functions, descriptive and predictive analysis for complex and multidomain functions, to perception intelligence for multimodal real-time signal processing. Shortly, various AI services will be democratized and stacked to form an AI service ecosystem. The rich AI service ecosystem combines many individual AI services to work harmoniously, seamlessly supporting and augmenting our day-to-day activities in enterprise or SME workplaces to accomplish our information processing mission. The advent of such a democratized generative artificial intelligence era will have a profound impact on SMEs [22]. However, in today's global economy, democratized or commoditized intelligence services can be delivered very differently to this type of enterprise. While sizeable companies have the resources, both human and financial, to gather raw data and AI services from providers, SMEs typically lack these sorts of resources. Without access to these resources, it is difficult for SMEs to accurately and honestly evaluate or use the advantages of AI, which can generate business value from the gathered raw data in a short time. Accordingly, this paper advocates that the generative AI method, rather than the data-hungry AI method, is appropriate for SMEs and many areas in the current enterprise workplaces. It also provides advice for moving toward this vision before articulating some of the significant opportunities of generative AI in the SME value chain. It argues that developing next-generation SMEs will usually require partnerships with other stakeholders across all industries.

3.2. Benefits and Challenges

Benefits Generative AI opens new opportunities by helping companies introduce or modernize a wide range of automation in their processes and products. Such companies will achieve a competitive edge in the classification and generation of data types, patterns, and intelligence. Applications can be automated, resources directed, and time to market reduced. Many companies require different steps to engage, realize value, and apply generative AI, primarily because the benefits are related to the number and potency of training material, modeling needs, and use case specifications. The key involves understanding the inherent nature and constraints of generative AI and then applying them to case-dependent methods. The democratization of generative AI also drives the rewriting of conventionally created business models within and across sectors. Challenges Several functions must be completed in practice, and the number of functions increases with a higher development and application complexity of the model. Achieving success with generative AI within companies is not easy, and most operating generative AI enterprises are venture companies, as the ability to bring new services to the market is highly tied to different resource limitations of traditional companies, including time and expertise, development models, functionality, and investment and cost of goods. The risk of generative firms failing to accomplish certain cases is crucial to consider, as are the costs associated with such scenarios [23]. Due to unpredictable and latent factors, this process is comparable to exploring uncharted chemical domains in search of new discoveries.

3.2.1. Technical Challenges

This section revolves around solving the technical issues of generative artificial intelligence in SMEs. Technical issues refer to obstacles to the usage or non-usage of generative AI technologies. The first set of obstacles is linked to various technical issues that must be addressed or overcome. A common situation for SMEs is that they have only limited processing capabilities to work on increasingly complex data. To be successful, generative AI heavily relies on having trustworthy suppliers and process capability. Generative AI heavily relies on top-quality data. Yet many SMEs do not have it today, or if they have it, they cannot often access and use it for generative AI purposes. Nearly all AI models require a significant preprocessing step to clean and transform the input data into a format that the AI model can use; this is often a sizeable portion of the work in an AI project [24].

Another main obstacle to adopting AI that respondents mentioned is that their systems are highly customized and integrated with other third-party software or are home-grown. Changing these to integrate AI requires highly skilled developers and is high risk. Modeling with generative AI today requires advanced technical and analytical expertise. Without a strong understanding of both the artificial ('AI') and intelligence ('I') aspects, there is a risk of inefficient resource allocation. All generative AI projects require some form of initial training to function effectively.This may be formal training, or it may involve using outside experts or consultancy services to kick-start the initiative. When one supplier suggests training as a solution, the other half of suppliers reject training as an obstacle. They argue that this is mainly due to a lack of knowledge of AI methods and potential ROI in AI projects within SMEs. Financial issues and risk aspects are highlighted in supplier responses as further reasons for their clients' aversion to taking AI training. From the technical viewpoint, these are the most critical challenges that our studies identified as relevant for SMEs: data quality, data processing capabilities, and IT system integration. There are many ways to solve these issues, such as outsourcing or integrating new know-how, machine learning services, and infrastructure for AI generation, which also address the lack of specialized workforce in AI [25]. We advise SMEs to examine such solutions formally. Decision-makers should act with a clear outlook. Correcting the SME's business challenge may involve outsourcing, buying, and integrating rather than doing everything in-house with one's operators, team, or partners.

3.2.2. Ethical and Legal Considerations

As AI gains more generalizability, the potential for AI to produce substantially creative works is gaining importance. The most critical question is whether using AI tools to create is fair. Generative models use authentic data to train, thus enabling them to create realistic-looking or sounding samples. Most importantly, firms integrating AI into art activities must represent an ethical viewpoint involving the deployment of AI. Similar to the artistic domain, there are numerous concerns, mainly because the generated content is derived from someone else's data. A participant comments on the possibility of "slapping an image representing the brand's anti-bias ethos on merchandise when, in reality, the company's leadership team has not changed." This echoes the findings that "the AI HLEG consensus statement demands the availability of an AI creator self-identity system' to be deployed in 'creative sectors.' Despite the widespread use of classifying features, face recognition tools, and speech synthesis in creative sectors, this is not what people want." In addition, some informants' input implied concern that generated texts might hinder the development of writers' effective storytelling skills. Others have brought to our attention that AI tools and products, in general, can demonstrate inaccuracy or possess the ability to propagate misinformation, misrepresentation, and a propensity for bias if not managed with utmost care [26]. For some industry participants, the words "representing the brand's anti-bias ethos" and "intent that is just not there" point to the necessity for a conversation about the potential link between intellectual property and individual identity.

4. Integration of Generative Artificial Intelligence in SMEs

Several factors determine the rate at which technology such as GAI is adopted in organizations, and preparation for such a transformation through GAI has proven to be complex and difficult when addressing societal issues since we must integrate the democratization of work ethic to reach stable social equity. One is that cultures change skills. It's knowing what's in use tied to whatever develops under the organism. Thus, we propose leadership in the manners to adapt leadership, methods, and strategy utilizing self-reflection and educational service within societal citizenry in partnerships and servant leadership theories affecting performance in wet. As SMEs typically specialize in relatively smaller markets, they generally can be more accustomed and better suited to grasp local requirements and solve societal challenges. However, these capabilities become larger hurdles when stepping into the role of developer of more advanced solutions with advanced technology such as GAI. To overcome this bottleneck, these SMEs are challenged to double the digitalization of their internal functions by quickly learning to integrate advanced services with acquired GAI in their processes either as a direct development or as an add-on to current recurring services. They need professional partners that grow their capability. Fundamentally, sizeable investments are no longer required as new, yet mature services are accessible and cloud-based without high upfront costs [27]. This makes advanced technology a feasible option for them to improve and grow their services towards higher sophistication without sizeable investments, tedious learning, and extra work. They focus and leave the rest to the chosen professional partners using GAI, such as ChatGPT, as illustrated in Figure 2.

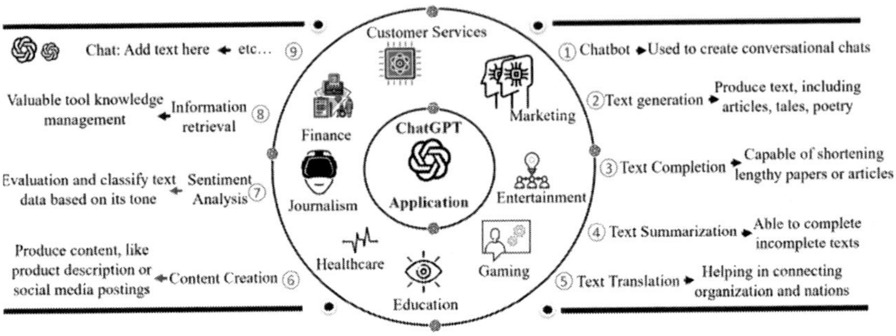

Figure 3. ChatGPT application in developing SMEs.

4.1. Pre-Implementation Considerations

The journey to democratize GAI in SMEs begins with a clear articulation of the business issues to be addressed. The issues can be aspirations yet to be realized, issues yet to be solved, fundamental changes being considered, or questions about why things are the way they are. SME owners, management, employees, customers, suppliers, or partners can contribute to this process. The contributions may be made through movement workshops, surveys, interviews, or other means. Articulations, restatements, reframes, or re-expressions of the business issues should not be compromised due to concerns of insurmountable complexity or findings pointing to ill-formulated objectives. The purpose is to reorient the owner, executives, management, or team members from where they initially assumed they were heading, discovering the need to head or the desire to head. Championing authentic innovation might be risky. There is often no precedent to place you in a comfortable frame of reference, guideposts on what to trust, or instruction manuals providing the criteria of confidence. Occasionally, re-evaluating the decision seems more feasible and less daunting than living with the consequences. Is exploring a GAI solution worth pursuing if the target business issues are not solved? Is the process guiding how to train and apply the GAI solution feasible? Can the risk strategies be extended for your company? The team members may have articulated, stated, or asked for generative AI. However, if the elucidations were based upon naivety, unparalleled hyped expectations, prototype demonstrations, unrealistic assessments, or unchallenged promises, authentic innovation would not be realized or bought into [28]. SMEs face an avalanche of emerging hopefuls contending to assist in their continual learning journey. The SME must pre-judge the intention to make the transition path clear and smooth. Figure 3 shows the ChatGPT application in developing SMEs.

4.2. Implementation Strategies

Developing the capacity of SMEs to deploy the latest AI tools internally would represent a strategic investment from the perspective of national economies seeking to stay ahead of the competition in AI. Specific support measures to help SMEs unlock the many benefits that artificial intelligence applications present would be essential, in particular, to help small and medium-sized companies on the pathway already. This section discusses the key actions that would be needed to help SMEs derive benefits from AI at an early stage. One critical aspect of AI policy related to supporting SMEs is context-specific differentiations for various policy measures. When it comes to AI support, SMEs in developing countries have different needs than those in expanded economies. For the former, access to AI technologies, data, digital infrastructure, and developed capabilities is more critical than for the latter. Country-led AI support policies that future SMEs in developing countries will be able to range from access to publicly funded data to open AI collaborative programs. Providing an AI education program across the entire supply chain would likely have different plans tailored by the level of operations [29]. Helping SMEs establish basic data practices, exceptionally by linking them with AI technologies for data governance and management, could facilitate this.

4.2.1. Building Internal Capabilities

Building internal capabilities is key, as employees within SMEs already have the needed insight and creativity about how generative AI technologies can be used. Internal capabilities can be built through various initiatives, including in-house development programs, workshops, or by providing access to external offerings. Senior employees can also contribute by sharing their knowledge and offering mentorship opportunities. Experimental cultures are known for generating innovative ideas on integrating new technologies in novel ways; hence, this is something to encourage, as entrepreneurship training and competencies are likely to help SMEs in the long run [30]. At the start-up phase, three key qualities are required by SMEs that would need to be cultivated among their employees:

1) AI competence – for understanding how generative AI methods work;
2) creativity – to come up with new and creative ways to help develop new ideas or concepts; and
3) a high level of sectoral knowledge – to situate the AI-generated output into the in-depth understanding of the broader practice or sector.

In the majority of cases, existing employees will need to be retrained, the costs of which it would be beneficial for SMEs to meet fully. This would, in turn, increase employee loyalty. Third-party service providers can offer the training or can be sourced from the internal network of the enterprise. In terms of how much should be aimed for in terms of investment, it was suggested that at least 20% of SME expenditure linked to the adoption of generative AI technologies should be dedicated to the training of internal employees who do not have access to core AI-focused programs. Given the exponential pace at which new technologies are developing and the imperative for one of the key advantages of AI to be its adaptability, it is likely that the development of internal AI-focused competence will contribute to sustained competitive advantages in the future, by focusing on the development of internal expertise when the next technological revolution occurs, as it inevitably will, continued success can be ensured. SMEs, in particular, are recommended to build in-house competencies and capabilities to adapt to new and changing environments as necessary without needing to depend on other actors [30].

4.2.2. Collaborations and Partnerships

In some cases, building collaborations and partnerships can reduce the complexity and effort of deploying these democratized generative AI solutions. Engaging with established generative AI partners can enable SMEs to tap into existing expertise and resources and to benefit from economies of scale. By aggregating market demand, SMEs can reduce the cost of custom technology solutions significantly. Such partners include tech companies that have generative AI as part of their core business, research institutions that have tested novel generative AI concepts, and newer SME- or industry-focused organizations like industry consortiums, where goals are specifically aligned with and operations guided by the participating industry. Currently, many

SMEs do not have on-site generative AI expertise and will only have limited experience working with academic researchers. By engaging in these partnership models, SMEs can benefit from developing new, transferable knowledge that can support cutting-edge technologies, research and development support, and upskilling. This is due to physical and virtual networking through a mechanism to help them gain skills, develop competence, and enhance knowledge sharing with a view to innovation in their firms. The collaborative approach is expected to be a critical strategic outcome related to the area of work concerning generative AI as well. The literature highlights this area of work as a collaborative approach to researching the capabilities of AI models in decision support. Information exchange between partners will be key in using generative AI to create 3D visual simulations of new engineering designs, particularly to explore the implications of different design choices [31]. Pre-trading, these services provide valuable performance feedback to designers who can use this information to pressure test new design ideas. We discuss four different types of partnerships or collaborations SMEs might establish to obtain these benefits.

5. Ethical and Legal Implications

The growing accessibility of AI technologies has spurred discussion on the framework needed to assess the ethical, economic, and social implications of democratized GAI. To ensure the responsible deployment of GAI, the bilateral relationship that creates alignment between GAI and SMEs must consider industry-specific ethical, legal, and moral dilemmas arising from the employment of narrow AI and must explore the balance and responsibility in value capture for the formidable transformation in the global workforce made possible by GAI, either replacing, augmenting, or assisting in the performance of their current work. Information, insurance, and market regulatory policies should motivate GAI-induced changes in economic behavior that serve society, as providing social legitimacy for GAI may require segments or the totality of value produced by GAI to be converted into goods and services of perceived value to the standard of living of a broad spectrum of market participants. Resonating with the ethical, technical, economic, social, and societal focus of the EU's founding ambition and its sustainable market economy competencies, a comprehensive set of forward-looking collaborations between government and SMEs should seek to foster designs for a future with GAI [32].

5.1. Privacy and Data Protection

Privacy and data protection are likely to be two of the more critical legal challenges for AI, stemming from the significant quantities of personalized data necessary for training, making data protection a critical focal point not only for producers, developers, and deployers but also for the entire ecosystem. Accordingly, data protection regulations are understood as the most encompassing legal framework currently to protect individuals when AI is enabled. Additionally, many other regional or corporate platforms are already based on similar principles. Nevertheless, Europe is positioning itself as a global reference in the field, with the upcoming Data Act aiming to unlock the broad potential of data. If, on the one hand, the mentioned legislation constitutes an enormous competitive advantage in the global economy, on the other, many non-European initiatives have ethical guidelines contributing to responsible AI. Besides complying with the regulation, companies can use specialized systems to pose queries and enact such policies in a privacy-by-design way, avoiding training AI models on sensitive and controversial topics. Additionally, combining homomorphic encryption with AI helps improve cybersecurity, enabling authorized agents to receive insights without accessing the data. This privacy-protective method of AI has become a traditional challenge in the data-sharing research community since blockchain and AI are complementary technologies, and research shows that both evolve at a speed that is one of the fastest in the technological era. Furthermore, these methods also require a broader involvement of people in the design and use of AI since people are the best solution to vulnerabilities, making bias and regulation easy to understand and avoid [33]. Towards reducing impact, people also help set AI accountability and explainability while increasing the benefits provided by AI.

5.2. Bias and Fairness

The democratized real-world integration of bias and fairness tools is crucial for SMEs, potentially constraining the debut of generative AI. Small companies rely on their generalist knowledge more than on specific ethics technologies to drive the moralization of their generative AI. Efforts to develop explainable AI are one area where industry representatives feel advances in the technology could help SMEs by giving them a better understanding and confidence in how the algorithms that sit at the heart of many commercialized tools and platforms produce their results. The debate over whether a democratized AI that performs with high precision and recall and provides secure data hosting will inherently democratize or anti-democratize innovation, jobs, and wealth creation is a legitimate one, not withdrawn or rooted in ideology. Groups of stakeholders should be expected to position themselves on either side of the debate, which should not be ignored within public decision bodies. For small companies entering the AI market, the incorporation of fair signals is also significant in that it supports the organization's response to their broader political and societal environment. In contrast to discussions among lawmakers about AI technologies, the moral contexts of which are, to a large extent, derived from within the respective societies, AI technologies are increasingly developed in or purchased from sprawling global ecosystems [34]. Such markets consequently force societies to acknowledge that a broader political and societal reflection on AI developments includes those imported and operated across borders, as is the case with tools and platforms that underpin the domestic operations of many SMEs, given the often-heated debate in which ethical AI is now discussed and the significant amount of such discussion taking place.

5.3. Regulatory Compliance

Regulatory compliance is an essential process in any business, thereby organizing ways to ensure compliance with the innumerable legal requirements of existing and potential markets. The use of artificial intelligence raises specific challenges, both to its legal and regulatory status when the machine is put forward as the maker of a decision and to the intrusion of artificial intelligence into areas defined by law. However, it is critical to weigh the tension between efficiency and compliance in the use of technology. A decision made using an AI-based system will raise legal concerns and requirements for the company. Additionally, challenging the use and output of the AI system, in particular, requires a more robust technical response. The difficulty of keeping artificial intelligence systems under control is exacerbated when machine learning techniques are used, as the decision-making process is invisible if the models are not interpretable or if the system remains manipulable. This potential lack of transparency makes it complex to control the system and problematic if it is used to break the law or to flout the rules, whatever these rules may be. Indeed, artificial intelligence makes it possible to conceive more complex models with which we reach new thresholds of effectiveness, thereby modulating efficiency and allowing processes to be optimized, increasing customer satisfaction, improving the management of third-party risks, and offering tailored products and services [35].

6. Future Trends and Innovations

Governments, companies, and society as a whole shift through the three great stages in the development of AI: consumer AI, business AI, and democratizing AI. In consumer AI, companies have invested in developing and programming technologies to recognize, understand, and respond to customer demands. While democratized AI has opened the door to creating new knowledge and opportunities, enterprises can use machine learning results to optimize their operational efficiency, develop and deliver the best customer experience, and improve and create new services. To open the door to greater profitability, the democratized model does not require a big investment. Many platforms operate in different market niches that provide these services through connections. These platforms provide the infrastructure, accumulation, cloud-scale AI, and high-performance computing capacity. Companies can focus on integrating these services to develop new use cases and more agile and innovative business strategies [36].

In the last stage of the AI revolution, AI democratization accelerates widespread adoption. We define it as the facilitation of effective access to AI arts and sciences for broader groups and objectives than the existing domain professionals, such as research AI professionals or experimental AI professionals, in addition to the different needs of all types of users. The release of most of the capabilities of AI and the addition of numerous parts of artificial intelligence to markets outside the traditional simulation. SMEs have significant potential to unlock the democratized power of generative AI. Neither large amounts of training data nor substantial investments in computational hardware are needed. They may be able to use the large number of model weights and architectures published by researchers on various platforms. Small-scale applications may share weights and structures, starting points for custom training with a differentiating approach, and respond specifically to the genotype or niche of individual companies. They will benefit from fast and affordable developments [37].

6.1. Advancements in Generative Artificial Intelligence

The advancements in deep learning models and affinity for learning algorithms in capturing complex data distributions and predicting future events have gradually opened new horizons associated with generative AI, having the ability to create new forms of data. It can synthesize more natural images, realistic voice models, and personas and convert texts into language-consistent representations between languages while not having labels. The transferability of these language characteristics certainly helps translate across languages, recognizing different voices and speakers in line with natural language processing, natural sound processing, and the computer animation industry. Mostly, small-sized enterprises with limited resources operating in various sectors, including managing storage, are significant for society (health, transportation, city management, ,and local companies). Innovative services generated with inter-generative algorithms can enhance value-added services with the leverage offered by this democratization process. For innovative services powered by generative AI, from these tools and algorithms' point of view, with sufficient accuracy, special requirements, and modules have emerged within a variety of different domains. Particularly in its domain of data, GANs are getting specialized, such as pharmacy data retrieval, vanished person image creation, entrepreneurial awareness based on monthly income class, and many others [38].

6.2. Emerging Technologies

GAI capabilities have the potential to be extended with other emerging technologies, thus enabling a wide range of possibilities and applications. In the following, we briefly introduce these emerging technologies and their potential for democratization. Augmented Reality (AR) makes digital objects appear as if in the physical world. Whereas Virtual Reality (VR) is gaining momentum in gaming or training, AR increasingly supports SMEs in creating immersive and integrative customer experiences and brings more interactive interfaces. NLP is the basis for most conversational AI offerings and can automate sizeable parts of customer communication and marketing processes. But it also makes chatbots, voice assistants, or AI-supported content creation with rich insights possible that enhance customer experience. Automation, i.e., replacing routine functions, is not a novel technology. Nonetheless, recent developments in robotic process automation and IoT bring automation capabilities to processes that were previously seen as too complex [39].

These technologies have value beyond traditional automation and can assist complex decision-making. Real-time analytics include capabilities that collect and analyze data in real-time to make decisions immediately. Technologies such as computer vision allow events to be identified and analyzed live, thus enhancing production and customer management processes. Machine Learning (ML) and AI. These capabilities help SMEs deal with customer interaction or create specific customer offerings based on underlying processes and generated or analyzed data. The interplay of these capabilities with other fast-growing technologies presents an enablement for SMEs. These complementary capabilities offer new possible points of entry to generative AI and show application possibilities where new tools can be exploited. SMEs need to remain open and often proactive in adopting novel tools, services, and emerging technologies, as the onset of novelty will most likely disrupt their industry. Frontier technologies hold the promise to drive industries up the innovation ladder. SMEs need to be aware of these novel technologies regardless of technology adoption, as they could shape the future landscape of the industry. In the following, we discuss two additional capabilities that could be bolted onto other technologies, either extending or easing the scope of the existing marketplace for generative AI capabilities [40].

6.3. Potential Impact on SMEs

SMEs are the backbone of the economy. There are 19 million small companies in the U.S. However, most companies fail during their initial or growth stages. Thus, it is critical to build innovations and digital strategies into SMEs early and often. This generative AI can be valuable to companies for innovation, creativity, and context-based task-solving. SMEs can use that to communicate with internal and external stakeholders effectively and efficiently. This research will attempt to close the SMEs' competitive disadvantage gap with Big Tech [40].

7. Key Findings and Recommendations

Within this section, identified insights and recommendations are presented.

7.1. Key Findings

Our key findings regarding GAI, in general, are: sagacity, requiring theoretical and humanities knowledge, and problem-solving skills appear to be both prerequisites for effective and reflective use and direct outcomes from the use; using the developed creativity and new value proposition of GAIs by SMEs inside the firm and marketing extensions are the most direct outcomes; and GAI is democratized, and it is increasingly easy-going, automizing, and affordable, empowering self-learning. There are many valuable use cases generated. SMEs gained new core competencies, massively transforming their strategy into a design-based, value-based approach. This attracted some skilled freelance creative workers and developed long-lasting network relationships, resulting in external entrepreneurship. The democratized GAI allows SMEs to directly design, develop, and learn as they drive multicultural ecosystems characterized by synergy, inclusion, and mutual respect. However, our literature review shows that the most valuable literature stream is just beginning to grow, presenting few theoretical knowledge and tools, mostly focusing on in-depth case studies and participant testimonials, some books and newsletters, and much popular literature [41].

Currently, most efforts addressing the lack of rigorous, scientific appraisal of the effects and sustainability of the use of democratized GAI can be retrospectively classified into two main categories—instruments aiming to profile the current use and appraisal of future humanity and expose quick benefits. However, though there is an awareness of the great transformative potential of democratized GAI, this potential is still invisible, elusive, and distorted. We cannot overstate how complex, sensitive, and pivotal economic, social, and political relationships among stakeholders are to improve. The sunset scenario of the increase of the digital divide, the concentration of power, the destruction of social and working relations, and the robust liability risks are perceived to be real. This is why, in our prescriptive proposal, we leverage the Value Sensitive Design approach, characterized by a dedicated and extensive effort oriented to knowledge and information sharing and to implementation suggestions for the improvement of the usage efficacy and efficiency of democratized GAIs [42]. In many use cases, our proposal is found to be comprehensive. Key insights are briefly illustrated below.

1) Generative AI has enormous potential to transform processes and drive innovation in and for companies across customer experience

and service, internal operations, IT systems design, and data understanding.

2) Adopters in SMEs, and
3) external consultants and providers identify the key challenges lying in the technical aspects of generative AI and the ethical dimensions of its application.
4) Conceptual barriers to adoption are also identified, concerning, for example, the skills needed to engage technical partners and the internal staff to implement and embed AI-assisted solutions. Adopter SMEs and external providers also highlight the potential for internal staff to understand and scope challenges that can potentially be addressed through generative AI adoption.
5) The ability of these people, and capacity and capabilities within the business more broadly, to learn and remain updated—either via internal training or by learning from external partners —is seen as particularly critical.
6) Generative AI has the potential to enable a range of innovations and improvements in the efficiency and effectiveness of SMEs. While these business model innovations are more complex to pin down in advance, the findings suggest that easier-to-envisage benefits extend to efficiency improvements structured around better operational, internal management, and customer-focused activities.
7) Looking forward, the successful implementation of generative AI will lead to tangible improvements to the SME, typically through improved operational efficiency, enhanced communications with existing customers or accessing new markets, and the identification of trends and growth area.
8) Such a proactive approach, developing AI frameworks and applications, allows adopter companies to increase competitiveness and ensures our region remains at the cutting edge of technology rather than just parachuting in. Core to the ability to implement generative AI and these efficiencies is a good understanding of the evolving digital landscape.
9) Identifying trends 'towards AI' helps to inform future investments in readying companies for deploying generative AI and what external support organizations must know to support SMEs in the journey.

7.2. Practical Recommendations for SMEs

We provide some practical advice approximately sorted from the most fundamental, such as the technology of increasing importance, which under the right circumstances may result in applying more advanced technology and optimization of operations in a generation and research organization to increase output and reduce time and other costs. We first consider some obstacles to AI adoption, determining the currently recommended specific measures for SMEs. Skilled AI developers are expensive, and demand across all industries is high [43]. It is difficult for SMEs to have the opportunity to recruit experienced AI developers, and it is appropriate to respond by incorporating AI experience into the existing team or making adequate use of external services. Furthermore, collaboration between departments and stakeholders is critical. It is based on various appraisal methods for which the requirements can be met most easily and quickly. SMEs are encouraged to 'start anyway' in development careers, building some systems for many applications. This may mean that small companies cannot recruit and develop a whole team of developers [44]. Besides, this can be delivered through courses or self-study methods.

Conclusion

In conclusion, this chapter argued that integrating democratized GAI solutions into existing operations would unlock enormous opportunities for SMEs, including accelerating innovation, increasing customer engagement, improving process efficiency, and reducing costs. With access to seamless and affordable AI capabilities, business model innovation and enterprise transformation are enabled to address unprecedented practical opportunities. In developing this argument, the paper advanced the notion of democratized generative artificial intelligence as a nascent technical breakthrough, leveraging recent advancements in deep learning, and also demonstrated the potential in four applications in retail, finance, healthcare, and humans-in-the-loop software. The aim was to call for a more vibrant conversation on generative AI and nudge the start of community building towards developing new capabilities, which include democratized generative AI-based start-ups serving small and medium-sized business customers. The vision is to develop an ecosystem with these innovative capabilities that can ease the adoption of this powerful technology for the global SME community. At the time of writing, the significant advance in democratized generative AI is rooted in the technical capacities of AI benchmarks, APIs, and frameworks built by big-name enterprises. After laying out the promise, the questions to address are: What should SMEs do? What organizational capabilities should SMEs consider? In terms of organizing, we suggest SMEs should align generative AI strategy with other organizational goals around customer experience, operational excellence, service innovation, and business model innovation. On learning, because of the predominantly non-AI core companies of commercially found SMEs, we advocate that internalization of generative AI expert commoditization be as low as possible, both internally and from a money investment perspective. Business managers increasingly must focus on leveraging experiments and models developed in mature scientific areas and less on funding extensive proprietary AI research. In terms of distributing, complementary assets would be non-AI operations and other analytical tools enabling decisions, thus encouraging SME management to invest more in process simplification and data management. Furthermore, we suggest incremental use and implement automation where possible through ML decision-support tools. Finally, in terms of monitoring, we advance the notion of investing in IoT and context-specific supervision in the areas of real-time processing. On the managerial front, we advocate for delegating tactical AI decisions to domain experts in risk identification and decision-making. Our work indicates where the organizational changes should be while putting the democratization of generative AI at the disposal of SMEs on the management calendar of objectives [45, 46].

References

[1] Abrokwah-Larbi, K. (2023). The role of generative artificial intelligence (GAI) in customer personalisation (CP) development in SMEs: a theoretical framework and research propositions. *Industrial Artificial Intelligence*, *1*(1). https://doi.org/10.1007/s44244-023-00012-4.

[2] Beerbaum Dr., D. O. (2023). Generative Artificial Intelligence (GAI) Ethics Taxonomy- Applying Chat GPT for Robotic Process Automation (GAI-RPA) as Business Case. *SSRN Electronic Journal*. https://doi.org/10.2139/ssrn.4385025.

[3] Brown, O., Davison, R. M., Decker, S., Ellis, D. A., Faulconbridge, J., Gore, J., Greenwood, M., Islam, G., Lubinski, C., MacKenzie, N. G., Meyer, R., Muzio, D., Quattrone, P., Ravishankar, M. N., Zilber, T., Ren, S., Sarala, R. M., & Hibbert, P. (2024). Theory-Driven Perspectives on Generative Artificial Intelligence in Business and Management. *British Journal of Management*, *35*(1). https://doi.org/10.1111/1467-8551.12788.

[4] Budhwar, P., Chowdhury, S., Wood, G., Aguinis, H., Bamber, G. J., Beltran, J. R., Boselie, P., Lee Cooke, F., Decker, S., DeNisi, A., Dey, P. K., Guest, D., Knoblich, A. J., Malik, A., Paauwe, J., Papagiannidis, S., Patel, C., Pereira, V., Ren, S., … Varma, A. (2023). Human resource management in the age of generative artificial intelligence: Perspectives and research directions on ChatGPT. In *Human Resource Management Journal* (Vol. 33, Issue 3). https://doi.org/10.1111/1748-8583.12524.

[5] Chuma, E. L., & De Oliveira, G. G. (2023). Generative AI for Business Decision-Making: A Case of ChatGPT. *Management Science and Business Decisions*, *3*(1). https://doi.org/10.52812/msbd.63.

[6] Horak, J., Kolencik, J., Văduva, C., & Woodward, B. (2023). Generative Artificial Intelligence and 3D Virtual Simulation Technologies, Ambient Scene Detection and Automated Employment Decision Tools, and Visual Data Mining and Immersive Remote Collaboration Systems in Decentralized Autonomous Organizations. *Analysis and Metaphysics*, *22*. https://doi.org/10.22381/am2220237.

[7] Humphreys, D., Koay, A., Desmond, D., & Mealy, E. (2024). AI hype as a cyber security risk: the moral responsibility of implementing generative AI in business. *AI and Ethics*, *4*(3). https://doi.org/10.1007/s43681-024-00443-4.

[8] Hussain, M. (2023). When, Where, and Which?: Navigating the Intersection of Computer Vision and Generative AI for Strategic Business Integration. *IEEE Access*, *11*. https://doi.org/10.1109/ACCESS.2023.3332468.

[9] Kanbach, D. K., Heiduk, L., Blueher, G., Schreiter, M., & Lahmann, A. (2024). The GenAI is out of the bottle: generative artificial intelligence from a business model innovation perspective. In *Review of Managerial Science* (Vol. 18, Issue 4). https://doi.org/10.1007/s11846-023-00696-z.

[10] Kim, J., & Choi, G. (2024). Assessing the Impact of Generative Artificial Intelligence on Customer Engagement in Business-to-Customer Scenarios. *Asia-Pacific Journal of Convergent Research Interchange*, *10*(2). https://doi.org/10.47116/apjcri.2024.02.09.

[11] Korzynski, P., Mazurek, G., Altmann, A., Ejdys, J., Kazlauskaite, R., Paliszkiewicz, J., Wach, K., & Ziemba, E. (2023). Generative artificial intelligence as a new context for management theories: analysis of ChatGPT. *Central European Management Journal*, *31*(1). https://doi.org/10.1108/CEMJ-02-2023-0091.

[12] Mondal, S., Das, S., & Vrana, V. G. (2023). How to Bell the Cat? A Theoretical Review of Generative Artificial Intelligence towards Digital Disruption in All Walks of Life. In *Technologies* (Vol. 11, Issue 2). https://doi.org/10.3390/technologies11020044.

[13] Peres, R., Schreier, M., Schweidel, D., & Sorescu, A. (2023). Editorial: On ChatGPT and beyond: How generative artificial intelligence may affect research, teaching, and practice. *International Journal of Research in Marketing*, *40*(2). https://doi.org/10.1016/j.ijresmar.2023.03.001.

[14] Peruchini, M., da Silva, G. M., & Teixeira, J. M. (2024). Between artificial intelligence and customer experience: a literature review on the intersection. *Discover Artificial Intelligence*, *4*(1). https://doi.org/10.1007/s44163-024-00105-8.

[15] Shafik, W. (2024). Generative AI for Social Good and Sustainable Development. In *Generative AI: Current Trends and Applications* (pp. 185-217). Singapore: Springer Nature Singapore. https://doi.org/10.1007/978-981-97-8460-8_10.

[16] Rane, N., Choudhary, S., & Rane, J. (2024). Gemini or ChatGPT? Capability, Performance, and Selection of Cutting-Edge Generative Artificial Intelligence (AI) in Business Management. *SSRN Electronic Journal.* https://doi.org/10.2139/ssrn.4731281.

[17] Shafik, W. (2023). Introduction to ChatGPT. In *Advanced Applications of Generative AI and Natural Language Processing Models*. https://doi.org/10.4018/9798369305027.ch001.

[18] Shafik, W. (2024). Factors Affecting Green Purchase Behaviors for Small and Medium Enterprises (SMEs) in Uganda. In *Entrepreneurial Strategies for the Internationalization and Digitalization of SMEs* (pp. 198–224). IGI Global. https://doi.org/10.4018/979-8-3693-3518-5.ch009.

[19] Shafik, W. (2024). Navigating Emerging Challenges in Robotics and Artificial Intelligence in Africa. In *Examining the rapid advance of digital technology in Africa* (pp. 126–146). IGI Global. https://doi.org/10.4018/978-1-6684-9962-7.ch007.

[20] Shafik, W. (2024). Shaping the Next Generation Smart City Ecosystem: An Investigation on the Requirements, Applications, Architecture, Security and Privacy, and Open Research Questions. In *Smart Cities: Innovations, Challenges and Future Perspectives* (pp. 3–52). Springer. https://doi.org/10.1007/978-3-031-59846-3_1.

[21] Wu, S. (2024). Artificial Intelligence-Enhanced Learning: A New Paradigm in the "Business Data Analysis and Application" Course. *Journal of Contemporary Educational Research*, *8*(2). https://doi.org/10.26689/jcer.v8i2.6081.

[22] Yahaya, M., Umagba, A., Obeta, S., & Maruyama, T. (2023). Critical Evaluation of the Future Role of Artificial Intelligence in Business and Society. *Journal of Artificial Intelligence, Machine Learning and Data Science*, *1*(1). https://doi.org/10.51219/jaimld/moshood-yahaya/03.

[23] Shafik, W. (2023). Artificial intelligence and Blockchain technology enabling cybersecurity in telehealth systems. https://doi.org/10.1049/PBHE061E_ch11.

[24] Kovšca, V., Vincek, Z. L., & Murić, D. (2024). Contemporary Forms of Financing for Small and Medium-sized Enterprise: Country Case Study of Croatia. *TEM Journal*, *13*(1). https://www.ceeol.com/search/article-detail?id=1223193.

[25] Cruz, Y. J., Villalonga, A., Castaño, F., Rivas, M., & Haber, R. E. (2024). Automated Machine Learning Methodology for Optimizing Production Processes in Small and Medium-sized Enterprises. *Operations Research Perspectives*, 100308. https://doi.org/10.1016/j.orp.2024.100308.

[26] Shafik, W. (2024). The Role of Generative Artificial Intelligence in E-Commerce Fraud Detection and Prevention. In *Strategies for E-Commerce Data Security: Cloud, Blockchain, AI, and Machine Learning* (pp. 430-469). IGI Global. https://doi.org/10.4018/979-8-3693-6557-1.ch018.

[27] Yordanova, D., Dana, L. P., Manolova, T. S., & Pergelova, A. (2024). Digital Technologies and the Internationalization of Small and Medium-Sized Enterprises. *Sustainability*, *16*(7), 2660. https://doi.org/10.3390/su16072660.

[28] O'Connor, P. (2024). The democratization of tourism distribution: a Horizon 2050 paper. *Tourism Review*. https://doi.org/10.1108/TR-12-2023-0852.

[29] Shafik, W. (2024). Cyber Attacker Profiling and Cyberbullying Overview. In *Cyber Space and Outer Space Security* (pp. 125-149). River Publishers. https://doi.org/10.1201/9781003558118-5.

[30] Pham, H. V., & Moore, P. (2024). Applied Hedge Algebra Approach with Multilingual Large Language Models to Extract Hidden Rules in Datasets for Improvement of Generative AI Applications. *Information*, *15*(7), 381. https://doi.org/10.3390/info15070381.

[31] Shafik, W. (2024). Data Privacy and Security Safeguarding Customer Information in ChatGPT Systems. In *Revolutionizing the Service Industry with OpenAI Models* (pp. 52-86). IGI Global. https://doi.org/10.4018/979-8-3693-1239-1.ch003.

[32] Shafik, W. (2025). Quantum Computing and Generative Adversarial Networks (GANs): Ethics, Privacy, and Security. In *Quantum AI and its Applications in Blockchain Technology* (pp. 111-156). IGI Global Scientific Publishing. https://doi.org/10.4018/979-8-3373-1657-4.ch007.

[33] Suneeth, S. N., Yashwant, S. N., Dharmendar, P., & Plugmann, P. Future Trends in Predictive Analytics and Generative AI for Marketing. In *Predictive Analytics and Generative AI for Data-Driven Marketing Strategies* (pp. 25-32). Chapman and Hall/CRC. https://doi.org/10.1201/9781003472544-3.

[34] Potthoff, L., Naussedat, R., & Gunnemann, L. (2024). Exploring Generative AI's Role in Manual Assembly: Application Potentials and Use Concepts. *Procedia CIRP*, *130*, 194-199. https://doi.org/10.1016/j.procir.2024.10.075.

[35] Shafik, W. (2025). Human-Computer Interaction (HCI) Technologies in Socially-Enabled Artificial Intelligence. In *Future of Digital Technology and AI in Social Sectors* (pp. 121-150). IGI Global. https://doi.org/10.4018/979-8-3693-5533-6.ch005.

[36] Wörsdörfer, M. (2024). Mitigating the adverse effects of AI with the European Union's artificial intelligence act: Hype or hope?. *Global Business and Organizational Excellence*, *43*(3), 106-126. https://doi.org/10.1002/joe.22238.

[37] Shafik, W. (2024). Deep Learning Ipacts in the Field of Artificial Intelligence. In *Deep Learning Concepts in Operations Research* (pp. 9-26). Auerbach Publications. https://doi.org/10.1201/9781003433309-2.

[38] Tuan, N. T., Moore, P., Thanh, D. H. V., & Pham, H. V. (2024). A Generative Artificial Intelligence Using Multilingual Large Language Models for ChatGPT Applications. *Applied Sciences*, *14*(7), 3036. https://doi.org/10.3390/app14073036.

[39] Jayadatta, S., & Majeed, M. (2024). An insight into the consequences of digitalization and digital technologies for small and medium enterprises (SMEs) in Africa. *Digital Transformation in African SMEs: Emerging Issues and Trends, 2*, 73. https://doi.org/10.2174/9789815223347124020007.

[40] Kim, J. S., & Seo, D. (2023). Foresight and strategic decision-making framework from artificial intelligence technology development to utilization activities in small-

and-medium-sized enterprises. *foresight*, *25*(6), 769-787. https://doi.org/10.1108/FS-06-2022-0069.

[41] Rather, I. H., Kumar, S., & Gandomi, A. H. (2024). Breaking the data barrier: a review of deep learning techniques for democratizing AI with small datasets. *Artificial Intelligence Review*, *57*(9), 226. https://doi.org/10.1007/s10462-024-10859-3.

[42] Veiga, J. P. C., & Martin, S. B. (2024). Artificial Intelligence: Latin America's Contested Norms. In *South American Policy Regionalism* (pp. 267-292). Routledge. https://doi.org/10.4324/9781003519577-16.

[43] Hibban, M. (2024). Innovation management among the Indian small and medium-sized enterprises focusing on artificial intelligence: Opportunities and the way forward. *Indian Journal of Commerce and Management Studies*, *15*(2), 10-17. https://www.ijcms.in/index.php/ijcms/article/view/667.

[44] Rajaram, K., & Tinguely, P. N. (2024). Generative artificial intelligence in small and medium enterprises: Navigating its promises and challenges. *Business Horizons*. https://doi.org/10.1016/j.bushor.2024.05.008.

[45] Kadry, S., Dhanaraj, R. K., K, S. K., & Manthiramoorthy, C. (2024). Res-Unet based blood vessel segmentation and cardio vascular disease prediction using chronological chef-based optimization algorithm based deep residual network from retinal fundus images. *Multimedia Tools and Applications*, 1-30.

[46] Balasubramaniam, S., Arishma, M., & Dhanaraj, R. K. (2024). A Comprehensive Exploration of Artificial Intelligence Methods for COVID-19 Diagnosis. *EAI Endorsed Transactions on Pervasive Health and Technology*, *10*.

Chapter 10

Empowering Innovation: Open-Source Platforms and the Democratisation of Generative AI

J. Alphonsa[1,*]
Sheeja Kumari[2]
V. Suresh Kumar[3]
and N. R. Wilfred Blessing[4]
[1]Department of Computer Science and Engineering, SIMATS Engineering, Saveetha Institute of Medical and Technical Sciences, Thandalam, Chennai
[2]Department of Computer Science and Engineering, SIMATS Engineering, Saveetha Institute of Medical and Technical Sciences, Thandalam, Chennai
[3]Department of Computer Science and Engineering, SIMATS Engineering, Saveetha Institute of Medical and Technical Sciences, Thandalam, Chennai
[4]College of Computing and Information Sciences, University of Technology and Applied Sciences - Ibri, Sultanate of Oman

Abstract

In this chapter, open source is assumed to be the process through which open platforms can affect this transformative influence on the democratization of generative AI. The problem with accessible artificial intelligence: as these AI startups become more powerful across industries, the opportunities to access these advanced AI tools grow more crucially. Open-source platforms are emerging as the number one player since complex AI models and development frameworks are being put in the public domain for an irreversibly expanding global audience. It has

---

* Corresponding Author's Email: alphonsaj9063.sse@saveetha.com

In: Democratized Generative AI: Principles, Challenges and Applications
Editors: S. Balasubramaniam and Seifedine Kadry
ISBN: 979-8-89530-684-0

enabled a diverse range of individuals—including young developers, researchers, parents, day traders, and large corporate entities—to collaborate in building, improving, and deploying AI technologies for a common cause.

This chapter explores open-source initiatives and their impact on software development practices. It also examines how these principles shape the AI community. We briefly review major open-source platforms, including TensorFlow, PyTorch, and the more recent Hugging Face, which has simplified AI development. Furthermore, the chapter highlights how open-source generative AI models, such as GPT and Stable Diffusion, have fostered innovation in art, language processing systems, and scientific research. Despite providing good benefits coverage, the chapter also looks at the challenges of open-source AI, including security, ethical usage, and misuse. It discusses the benefits and perils of the open-sourcing of Artificial Intelligence technology and puts forward that community-governed frameworks must continually balance the application of AI to address relevant global challenges and the potential risks that stem from AI technology. Finally, it proposes a long-term evaluation of democratized AI, focusing on its impact on education, the emergence of new entrepreneurs, and social contributions. It argues that democratization is not only accelerating AI advancements but also reshaping the technological landscape into one that is more diverse and, ultimately, more equitable.

This chapter emphasizes the relationship between open source standing and generative AI while also understanding how cooperation at the ecosystem level guarantees open access to intricate AI technologies, moving us towards a more transparent, open, and accountable future of AI.

Keywords: open-source platforms, democratization, AI technologies, hugging face, PyTorch, stable diffusion, social contribution

2. Introduction

Now that TA generative AI has caught on, industries have been defined, and how machines perceive, and reason with people has shifted. The principal element contributing to this change is open-source platforms, which have provided equal opportunity to access the best AI tools, frameworks, and information offered. For instance, TensorFlow [1, 2] has contributed to popularizing Dev and Research around the world with the help of toolkits provided free of charge rather than free software proprietary software.

Thankfully, open-source projects are needed to level the playing field for people and organizations alike to take AI out of the particular treatment paradigm and allow a broad cross-section of the population to assist in creating these technologies.

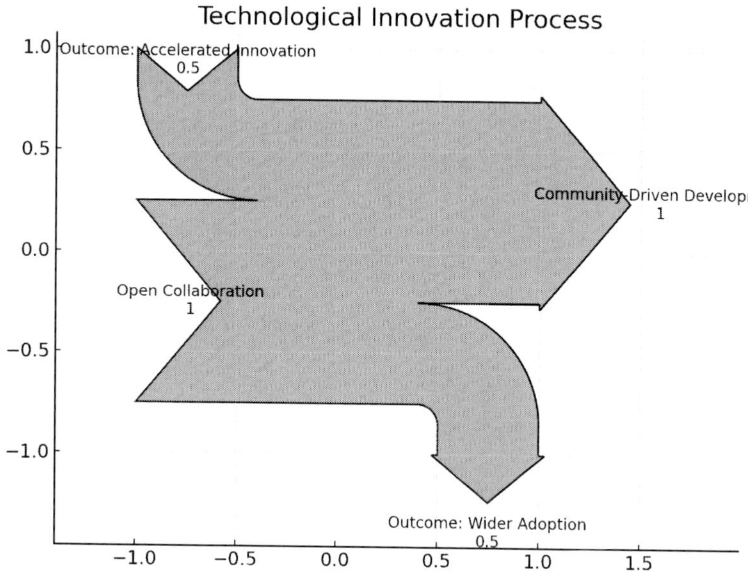

Figure 1. Technological Innovation Process.

Of course, the availability of AI has given way to waves of generative AIs and the relative ease and increasing ease of getting to the Internet for collaboration and using open-source platforms. Moreover, these platforms have made it possible for language models like OpenAI GPT 3 [3] to emerge from nowhere with the capability of producing text from human creative consciousness for Hugging Face's Transformers, an Open-source library for NLP. These efforts to lower the adoption bar of AI technology release complex AI models and algorithms to small businesses, researchers, and even enthusiastic amateurs who can solve complex problems with their help.

Although the technical implementations will keep increasing, these open-source platforms are the genesis for breeding opportunities where sharing ideas is doable across borders, open and AI ecosystems, which is growing on someone else's information. Various researchers contribute to enhancing the resiliency and flexibility of AI models. For instance, some studies focus on evolving model architectures [4], while others concentrate on improving language modeling and zero-shot learning capabilities [5].. This study proves that generative AI will not reach the next level if open-source solutions that allow for fast prototyping are not provided and provide low-cost – high-benefit solutions across all industries. Figure 1 depicts the technological innovation process.

However, democratizing the existing closed-end applications on open-source platforms is difficult. Some challenges include Security threats, questions on ethical use, and misuse of the powerful generative models. However, as these sophisticated modes of AI continue to develop, the aspects of being open also assume great significance, as does responsibility. Moreover, studies by [6] and [7] highlight that ensuring credible and reliable deployment of artificial intelligence relies significantly on the governance frameworks overseeing AI innovation. Such governance frameworks should consistently uphold ethical principles.

3. Related Work

Open-source paradigms have actively promoted transparency concerning the basis of contemporary artificial intelligence (AI). TensorFlow and PyTorch are the two most popular platforms that have raised AI accessibility, and any individual can contribute to the further development of AI. In particular, using generative AI artificial intelligence models, including GPT-3 and transformers by Hugging Face, demonstrated that open-source tools can enhance natural language processing. Their failures facilitated the emergence of innovative applications and created ethical issues as strong AI models are effortless to implement and can be prejudiced, misused, or contain security issues. Solving them requires cautious stewardship compatible with the call for AI to be advanced responsibly, as researchers who prefer developing community-based solutions believe.

3.1. A Large-Scale Development of Open-Source Platforms

One can keep insisting that open-source systems are crucial in the development of AI. TensorFlow is one of the most used open-source libraries for machine learning, and it was introduced [8]. The four essential aspects noted include ease of use, scalability, and flexibility, which, in one way or another, saw developers and researchers from various fields using the platform. In the same vein, PyTorch is an open-source deep learning framework that has dominated academia and the industrial uses of AI [9]. However, the technological barriers to entries, which were previously enforcing the set high standards of developing with AI in those platforms, made it easier for a diversified population to come on board and co-develop AI with other developers, enhancing the most recent promotion of cutting-edge abilities in the field of machine learning and generative AI. Such contributions have democratized AI, and more and more players from academia, industrial endorsements, and individual developers are working together.

3.2. On Generative AI and Open-Source Contributions

Note that open-source platforms have had significant applications in generating generative AI models, especially in natural language processing. Similarly, OpenAI's GPT-3, a state-of-the-art language model made public and available through its API, has advanced text generation, content creation, and solving problems in various ways [10]. Hugging Face extended this work by releasing its transformer models under an open-source license, making it easier to develop and customize generative models for any language or topic. They are examples of how the freely available and open-source AI frameworks can use poetry to stimulate large-scale experimentation and iteration to generate new kinds of generative AI.

3.3. The Democratization of AI

This idea can be democratized because other variants of the platforms with powerful technologies exist for the rest of the public. However, it is possible to do this within available small datasets and with simple architectural designs using components for zero-shot text-to-image generation, meaning that small organizations and independent developers can train and use AI models that major technology players are only starting to apply [11]. Similarly, the features discussed provide clarity regarding the contributions of the AI tool Paddle. Paddle significantly expanded AI accessibility in China and globally, in addition to supporting applications in natural language processing and computer vision [12]. Without these platforms, there will be much smaller contributions of non-computing science/something similar specialists; in other words, people will not be 'creating' AI.

3.4. Artificial Intelligence Development Cooperative Systems

However, organic development approaches fit best; for AI, these approaches fit large communities rather than small ones. For the same reason, the authors also acknowledge that the current approach to artificial intelligence creation has to be trustworthy and explainable with cooperation. The researchers introduce community-power AI, which can be applied to address the ethical and security issues that come with the complete openness of the applied AI models. PyTorch and TensorFlow reduce collaboration culture by allowing the creator to create, contribute, and test ideas with a global group of developers. Innovation is made unlimited and evolutionary; on the one hand, AI technology progresses rapidly concurrently; on the other, Innovation is turned into a community-level process instead of a few large-scale companies.

3.5. Ethical Topics in Democratizing AI

It still makes ethical issues the new imperative as open-source paradigms emancipate AI. In this respect, concrete issues present in the paper are presented as general problems in AI safety [13]. They mention such threats as bias, injury by AI, and exploitation of the generative model. This content is especially pertinent when we have these compelling generative AI models that get leaked to the public, and one starts to ask how one even begins to regulate said stuff. In their study, mechanisms are suggested to support verifiable AI claims and help prevent the misuse of open-source AI [14]. The issue here is to protect their openness with guardrails against malicious use of AI.

4. Proposed Model

The illustrated model in Figure 2 incorporates three dimensions into a unified structure that explains open-source platform and generative AI relationships. The following section outlines the complete aspects of the model:

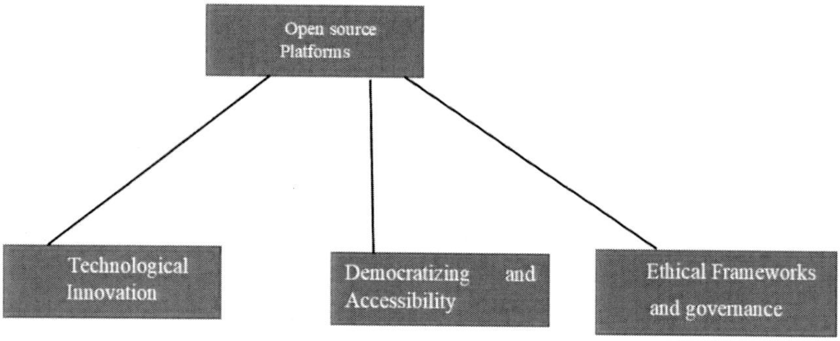

Figure 2. Open-Source Platforms.

4.1. Technological Innovation

4.1.1. Open-Source AI Frameworks

The model is based on interfaces like TensorFlow, initially described by, and PyTorch, initially described as the foundational third-party platforms where millions of developers worldwide experiment, code, and explore possible solutions to come up with new sources of interaction [15]. Generative AI Models: Recent upgrades to generative models like GPT 3 and Hugging Face Transformers have brought in new creativity and approaches to using AI across many industries [16]. Open Collaboration: The case with open-source platforms is that the worldwide innovation process sets these; many individuals from various backgrounds enhance the main models, which leads to the refinement of frameworks and further advances the ability of AI generation. Community-Driven Development: They are open platforms, and as such, they have the potential to get better rapidly at an incredible rate. Many algorithms, tools, and techniques found within the developer world will improve from periods of peer review and overall development. Accelerated Innovation: Thus, they work on the most advanced AI models and can develop generative AI solutions within the minimum period and with the minimum resources possible. Wider Adoption: The availability of these platforms implies that the entry is not controlled, thereby allowing a more diverse set of innovators to come and fine-tune generative AI models for their particular uses.

4.2. Democratizing and Accessibility

Accessibility of AI Tools: With open-source frameworks like Paddle, members and small organizations can develop AI models that are usually built using minimal resources [17].

Low-Cost Development: AI research and development can be performed in proofs; hence, no expensive software licenses are needed, which allows more people, researchers, startups, and hobbyists to participate.

Global Reach: Such platforms are inherently open and decentralized, democratizing AI to anyone from any country – of geographic and economic prohibitive restraints from accessing the same tools and free wares they have at top-tier research institutions and tech conglomerates.

Customization and Flexibility: These generative AI models are developed under the open-source model, as developers are responsible for fine-tuning them to meet specific niche requirements. Owing to the variance in problems, the implementation of these models differs from country to country.

Broader Participation: Open-source platforms make AI far more equitable, and those who otherwise would not be able to take advantage of it get to do so.

Decentralization of AI Power: The concept of open source decentralizes AI development by distributing people who construct AI infrastructures and diverting them away from the large key players in the field.

So, let us dive deep into Ethical Frameworks and governance.

Ethical AI Development: Besides the exciting discussion of the business and technical impact of generative AI, ethical problems connected with deepfakes, bias, and misinformation must also be discussed.

Governance and Regulation: Open-source platforms must include measures to ensure the proper use of AI.

Trustworthy AI Initiatives: Ethical frameworks ensure that the open-source community creates transparent, easily understandable algorithms resistant to negative influences, enabling the establishment of AI models with ideal and practical human values.

Collaborative Governance: The open-source governance model has enabled contributors to provide the standard and norm on responsible AI through community-led governance initiatives.

Ethical AI Deployment: Open governance models engulf developers who deliver work and hold to account for the moral outcome of the work created. AI can only be developed in a way that keeps it from doing harm or achieving societal goals if the community participates, that is, participating in the resolution of various problems such as prejudice, which fears are legitimate, and others.

Regulation Integration: Regulations and standards piloted through open-source solutions can serve as a foundation for governments and intergovernmental organizations to develop their own frameworks.

5. Overall Model Outcome

First, they increase the rate at which AI tech is developed; second, they ensure that the development of this technology is carried out inclusively and responsibly. The model also elucidates the two-way relationship between democratization and Innovation: more open AI tools facilitate improved technological development and are associated with the best possible ethical protection. The visual representation of open platforms depicted in Figure 3.

5.1. Model Architecture

5.1.1. Central Node: Open-Source Platforms

- *Description:* This is the model's core, representing the open-source platforms (e.g., TensorFlow, PyTorch, Hugging Face) that provide the necessary tools and frameworks for AI development.
- *Components:*
  - *Frameworks:* TensorFlow, PyTorch, Paddle
  - *Community Contributions:* GitHub repositories, forums, tutorials

5.1.2. Pillars Supporting the Central Node

These pillars interact with the central node and each other, forming a dynamic ecosystem.

5.1.2.1. Technological Innovation

- Subcomponents:
  - Development of AI Models: Generative models like GPT-3, DALL-E
  - Research Collaborations: Joint projects among academic institutions, researchers, and industry.

- Rapid Prototyping: Tools for developers to quickly test and deploy new ideas.

5.1.2.2. Democratization and Accessibility

- Subcomponents:
  - Wider Access to Tools: Availability of libraries and frameworks for anyone.
  - Educational Resources: Online courses, workshops, and documentation.
  - Global Community: Diverse participation from different regions and backgrounds.

5.1.2.3. Ethical Frameworks and Governance

- Subcomponents:
  - Trustworthy AI Initiatives: Development of guidelines and best practices.
  - Community Oversight: The Role of Peer Review, Ethical Boards, and Discussions
  - Regulatory Collaboration: How Engagement with Policymakers Shapes Regulations.

5.1.2.4. Interaction and Feedback Loops

- *Bidirectional Arrows:* Indicate the interactions and feedback between the components.
- *Technological Innovation ↔ Democratization:* Innovations increase accessibility, while broader access fosters further Innovation.
- *Democratization ↔ Ethical Frameworks:* Increased access raises ethical concerns, necessitating the development of robust frameworks.
- *Technological Innovation ↔ Ethical Frameworks:* Innovative tools must be evaluated within ethical contexts, ensuring responsible development.

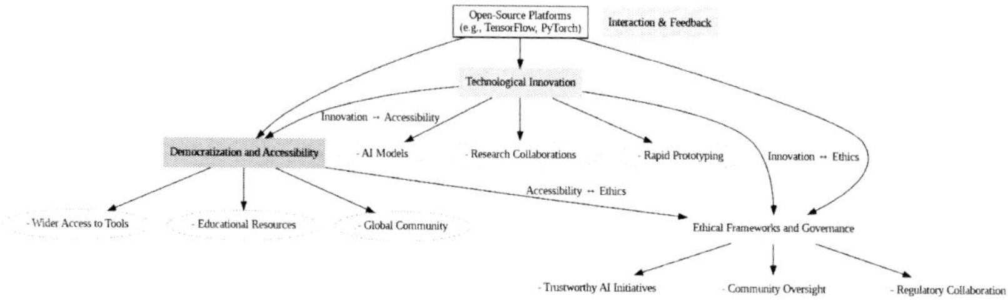

Figure 3. Visual Representation of Open Platforms.

6. Case Studies of Open-Source Platforms

6.1. Case Study 1: Hugging Face

Hugging Face has emerged as a leading platform in natural language processing (NLP) and generative AI. Their open-source library, Transformers, allows developers to easily access and implement state-of-the-art models for tasks like text generation, translation, and summarization. Figure 4 depicts the key contributions of the Hugging Face platform.

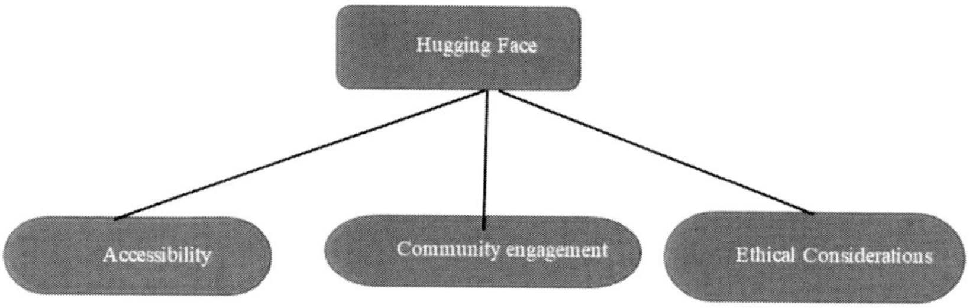

Figure 4. Case Study Hugging Face.

6.1.1. Key Contributions

- *Accessibility:* Hugging Face provides pre-trained models and a simple user interface that allows individuals from diploma level to those with technical knowledge in natural language processing to access these sophisticated technologies.
- *Community Engagement:* The development and expansion of the model occur through collective work done by developers and researchers who belong to a common professional community. This engagement results in sustainable development and Innovation.

- *Ethical Considerations:* However, at Hugging Face, ethical issues are not ignored; the organization takes the time to outline explicit responsible AI usage and ensure that users report model performance and drawbacks. Through its incremental and accessible approach, Hugging Face has made state-of-the-art NLP technologies much more available to the user community, including educators, researchers, entrepreneurs, and developers who do not have theoretical backgrounds and experience using the newest generative AI solutions.

6.2. Case Study 2: OpenAI's GPT-2 Model

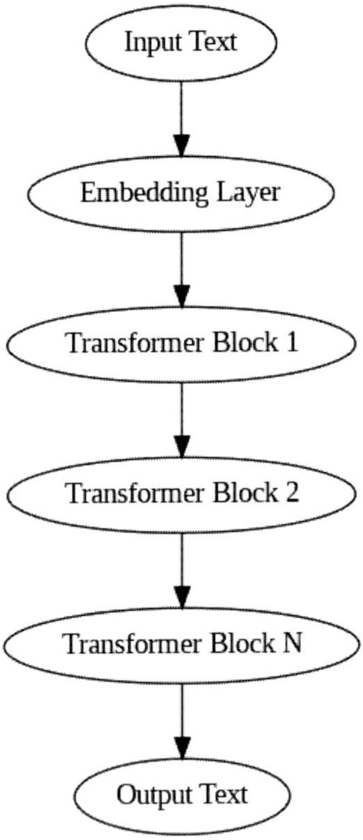

Figure 5. Chat GPT -2 model block diagram.

GPT -2 is a large-scale, publicly available, unsupervised model developed by OpenAI. The decision to launch the model is to contribute to developing research on the topic for providing proper usage of AI technologies. Chat GPT 2 model block diagram shown in Figure 5.

6.2.1. Key Contributions

- *Research Facilitation:* By releasing GPT-2 as open source, OpenAI endowed researchers with a valuable instrument for probing the field of generative language modeling, which led to numerous works and developments.
- *Community Contributions:* Since GPT-2 was also open-sourced, there were follow-up releases and fine-tuned versions, along with its libraries of applications such as chatbots, content generation, and creative writing.
- *Ethics and Safety:* For its part, OpenAI approached the question of ethics from a proactive standpoint, performing a study on how the model can be abused and setting clear rules for its safe utilization. Since the release of GPT-2, we have seen a positive shift in the generative AI model's expansion as multiple researchers continue to join the mission by working together to advance the field and focus on the appropriate considerations for building AI systems.

6.3. Case Study 3: TensorFlow and TensorFlow Hub

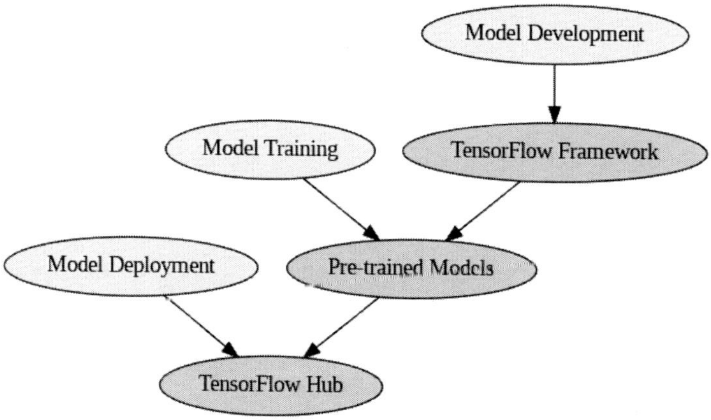

Figure 6. Tensor Flow and Tensor Flow Hub block diagram.

TensorFlow, created by Google, is one of the most popular open-source machine learning software for several vital reasons in the AI community. TensorFlow Hub is a collection of modules that can be effortlessly deployed into applications. Figure 6 represents tensor flow and tensor flow hub diagram.

6.3.1. Key Contributions

- *Broad Accessibility:* This function is essential in AI because TensorFlow is open source, making it easy for researchers and developers to design constructively and share modified models with the rest of the community.
- *Modularity and Reusability:* TensorFlow Hub allows users to share pre-trained models with others who intend to speed up their work based on others' results, which can also help create a moderately low entry barrier for new users.
- *Educational Resources:* The TensorFlow community has been quite spirited in creating tutorials and documentation that can teach users how to apply generative AI models. For many people, TensorFlow has become the starting point for their AI experiences. This tool has allowed many application levels and experimentation, from first-time users to advanced developers, to incorporate generative AI into their industries.

6.4. Case Study 4: Runway ML

Runway serves as an open-source platform which gives designers and artists the means to develop ML tools through its interface. This platform serves as an easy-to-use solution for people who wish to include sophisticated artificial intelligence models in their inventions.

6.4.1. Key Contributions

- *Creative Accessibility:* Runway ML is an essential tool for artists to reduce the entry of complex models into the artistic world, as it requires no code to run.
- *Collaboration and Community:* The platform draws together artists, technologists, and researchers to create an environment for burgeoning AI creative works.

- *Ethical AI Use:* Effective AI cannot be accomplished without focusing on sustainability – that is why Runway ML encourages people to create ethical projects, and AI-generated content shares this information with the public. Runway ML is unique in that it seeks to apply a creative lens to the use of generative AI tools, as well as offering a diverse set of users a means to interpret the technical aspects of these technologies with relevance specifically to art and design, making the positive applications toward a broader and more diverse population possible by featuring determining ML applications for creative endeavors according to their approach.

6.5. Case Study 5: The Creative AI Lab

This pilot Creative AI Lab, located at various institutions, seeks to bring together artists, AI researchers, and humanists to investigate the creative possibilities of generative AI technologies in artistic practices. The lab interacts with open-source tools to collaborate on research and build projects that apply AI to artistry. It is depicted in Figure 7.

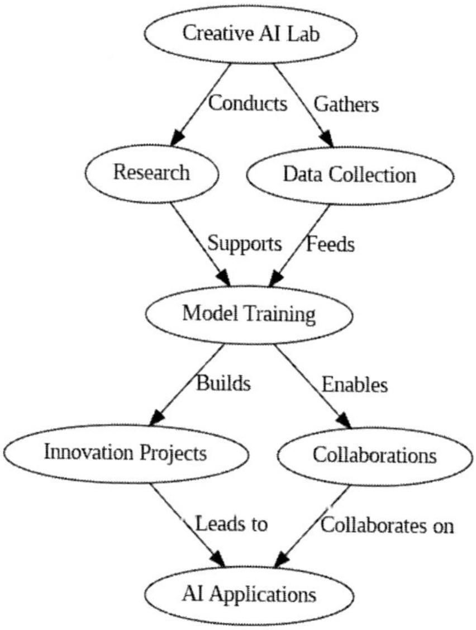

Figure 7. The Creative AI Lab Block Diagram.

Table 1. Comparative study of open-source platforms in the democratization of generative AI

Criteria	Hugging Face	OpenAI GPT-2	TensorFlow	Runway ML	Creative AI Lab
Overview	A hub for NLP models and tools, fostering community collaboration.	A Powerful Open-Source Language Model	A Widely Used Machine Learning Framework with Extensive Libraries	AI-Powered Creativity Platform for Artists	Interdisciplinary Lab for Generative AI in the Arts
Core Features	Transformers library, model sharing, community forum.	Pre-trained Models and Research Publications in AI	TensorFlow Hub: Extensive Model Library and Educational Resources	User-Friendly Interface and Creative Tools for Artists	Open-source projects, collaboration among artists and researchers.
Accessibility	Highly accessible with intuitive APIs for users of all skill levels.	Accessible to researchers but less user-friendly for non-experts.	Requires some technical knowledge, but extensive resources are available.	Designed for artists, requiring minimal coding knowledge.	It focuses on academic and artistic communities, requiring some expertise.
Community Engagement	Strong community support with active contributions and discussions.	Limited community engagement; primarily research-focused.	Large and active community contributing to resources and model development.	A Collaborative Hub for Artists and Technologists	Encourages collaboration across disciplines, fostering creativity.
Ethical Considerations	Actively addresses ethical issues and promotes transparency in models.	Developed ethical guidelines for responsible use but limited public interaction.	Guidelines for Responsible AI Use and Bias Awareness	Emphasizes ethical AI use and transparency in creative processes.	Critical Discourse on AI's Impact on Creativity
Strengths	Extensive library, active community, and intense focus on NLP.	A Robust Language Model Fueling Groundbreaking Research	A robust framework for various AI tasks and excellent documentation.	Focus on creativity and user-friendly tools for non-experts.	Interdisciplinary Approach to Fostering Innovation
Weaknesses	Primarily focused on NLP, which may limit broader applications.	Limited user-friendliness for non-experts; mainly research-oriented.	The steeper learning curve for beginners requires technical knowledge.	Limited to creative applications, which may not appeal to all users.	Focus on academia may restrict broader community engagement.

Criteria	Hugging Face	OpenAI GPT-2	TensorFlow	Runway ML	Creative AI Lab
Impact on Democratization	Democratizing NLP: Empowering	Diverse Users Advancing Generative Language Models and Their Applications	Enabled widespread use of AI tools across industries, promoting Innovation.	Empowering Artists and Designers to Explore AI-Driven Artistic Expression	Encouraged exploration of AI in the arts, promoting interdisciplinary dialogue.

6.5.1. Key Contributions

- *Interdisciplinary Collaboration:* The lab fosters working relationships among artists, computer scientists, and humanists to develop projects that unravel AI's role in human creativity.
- *Open-Source Projects:* The lab provides examples and code as free AI designs and prototypes for people to tinker with generative AI in art.
- *Research Publications:* While the output type is primarily research, the lab generates papers analyzing the prospects of generative AI in creative fields and its contributions to the scholarly conversation about AI and creativity. Creative AI Lab demonstrates how open-source platforms can be used in multidisciplinary synergy, aid in research on generative AI and creativity, and build a community of practice around these artifacts.
- A comparative study can generate valuable information on the efficacy and penetration of different open-source tools in decentralizing generative AI. The following is a structured comparative study that compares several noteworthy platforms and their features, strengths, weaknesses, and contributions to the field.

Table 1 shows the Comparative analysis of open source platforms in the democratization of Generative AI.

7. Insight Analysis

7.1. Hugging Face

Hugging Face represents this panorama with a friendly interface and less accessible APIs toward which users refer, hence different levels and types of expertise. On the contrary, it leaves something to be desired compared to other platforms, such as OpenAI GPT -2, which will probably work magic under user-technical conditions. Similarly, Runway ML specializes in tool provisioning targeted toward the artists and their creations; coding competencies are thus reduced. Moreover, in contrast, TensorFlow offers a large cadre of resource material and an even more extensive library of tools but is otherwise best suited to users at the high end of the programming spectrum.

7.2. Community Building

Platforms like Hugging Face and TensorFlow have vibrant, active communities, providing ample space for model development and sharing valuable information, particularly for novice users. In contrast, OpenAI GPT -2, with its focused research approach, attracts a highly specialized user group, but its community outreach efforts are limited. Runway ML is a powerful tool that bridges the gap between artists and technologists, making it a top choice for the creative community. Here, this lab is aimed mainly at interdisciplinary collaborations, which will produce the most needed innovations to close the gap between technology and the arts.

7.3. Ethical Considerations

Even though all these parties raised ethical concerns, each party's methodological differences are distinct. Hugging Face and Runway ML become increasingly proactive in promoting transparency and responsible use of AI through their platforms and community initiatives. However, OpenAI GPT-2 emphasizes studying the research implications of this initiative, as one might expect to match with its academic orientation. Then, this wing of Creative AI Lab plays an innovative role in the ethical discourse by revealing the perspective of AI by scrutinizing its effect on creativity and thus fostering an intellectual discourse on the ensuing socio-cultural impact resulting from the introduction of AI in the arts.

7.4. Democratization Effect

Every platform democratizes AI in its way. Hugging Face opens doors to users in the thin air of natural language processing, making advanced NLP tools available. However, TensorFlow is for developers and organizations, enabling them with tools that would primarily be beneficial when AI technologies have become more widely adopted. Not to mention, Runway ML, which converts creative professionals into experimenters with generative AI, facilitates access to sophisticated technology for persons without technical knowledge. OpenAI GPT-2 predominantly catalyzes avant-garde research; it is limited to academic and specialized communities. The Creative AI Laboratory seems to bridge research between technology and the arts, enriching the democratization of AI and perhaps creating additional opportunities in creative areas.

This study compares and contrasts the different ways open-source platforms democratize generative AI and examines features, community involvement, ethical issues, and democratization impact—each contributing directly to democratization in the field. The findings from the study bring to the forefront the necessity of accessibility, community involvement, and ethics in making inclusive a conscious AI environment.

7.4.1. Open-Source Platform Development

First, formative development will define crisp objectives and requirements for an open-source platform in generative AI. The stage here is how to identify the goals of this platform - democratizing access to better and more sophisticated technologies in AI, facilitating collaboration between researcher and developer, and the third relates to embedding ethical standards just after this use of the platform. One of the most critical things is the understanding between educators, students, or industry professionals and tailoring functionalities to their needs. This clarity of purpose guides the later stages of development and thrusts the platform forward in executing its primary purpose.

7.4.2. Choose a Technology Stack

What matters in choosing the technology stack during the implementation of such a platform is that Python for AI development is the preferred language as it has a wide variety of libraries and lots of support in terms of community. Deploying generative models involves propagating the TensorFlow and PyTorch frameworks, building user-friendly interfaces by leveraging Flask and Django, and even picking an excellent hosting service like AWS or Google Cloud for scaling and performance.

7.4.3. Design Architecture

The functionality of the platform is based on the architectural design of the platform. Such high-level architecture should include a notable component, such as a model repository and a UI that supports API integration with community engagement features. A modular design ensures that individual components can be updated and maintained easily, irrespective of how the system works. A good architecture allows us to collaborate and bring those new features in with the constant improvement of democratizing generative AI.

7.4.4. Core Features Development

All open-source platforms have some core features. One of the significant features would be the complete repository for all generative AI works, a single center for uploading, downloading, and sharing different works of an individual from generating AI work in a single hub. Accessibility is therefore increased as a simple interface becomes benevolent to the average user and non-expert in using sophisticated AI technology. The APIs connect these models to a third-party developer who can now use these models to create new applications. We will grow and innovate by exploring such core features on this platform to satisfy different user requirements.

7.4.5. Community Features Enablement

The hallmark of a successful open-source platform depends on its involvement of community members. A discussion platform and forum need to exist for users to exchange their work solutions with one another and contribute to problem-solving initiatives. Users need documentation and tutorials which serve as essential tools to learn the platform as well as master generative AI tools effectively. The platform will thus create an environment through which knowledge will flow freely, optimizing its success in generating collective advancements in generative AI by creating a sense of community and collaboration.

7.4.6. Establish Ethical Guidelines

Emerging with ever-increasing capabilities, generative AI necessitates the development of the most acute ethical frameworks. Transparency, accountability, and responsible use should form the core of such guidelines, with all related terms such as training datasets, interaction rules, outputs, and metrics to measure success. There should be a reporting mechanism through which users may report misuse or biases when using the AI model. The platform continues to support past ethical guidelines through this approach. Early ethical concern resolution establishes user trust and leads to proper advances in the development of generative AI technology.

7.4.7. Testing and Validation

Rigorous testing and validation are essential to ensure the platform's reliability and effectiveness. This phase involves conducting unit, Integration, and user acceptance tests to identify and rectify any issues before deployment. Additionally, validating models for bias and accuracy is crucial for maintaining ethical standards. By prioritizing thorough testing, the platform can provide users with high-quality, reliable, generative AI tools they can trust in their applications.

7.4.8. Deployment and Maintenance

Deploying the platform is a critical moment in the development journey. Hereafter, it is the concern of selecting and setting up a host infrastructure that will deliver effective service within the user traffic and model processing demands. Developers set up systems to monitor their performance metrics on user engagement, thereby fixing issues before they appear. Generative AI should be democratized, and it is to that extent that we keep making our users happy to stay relevant and valuable while updating features continuously through user feedback and technology advancement.

7.4.9. Iterative Development

The conclusion of the establishment process underlines the significance of iteration in the development process. The adaptable culture is cultivated by continuously collecting users' feedback and platform updates. An approach that helps pre-release reviews improves the assessment of the platform's effect on generative AI democratization. Maintaining the iterative approach will allow the platform to develop in response to the users' needs and industry trends, leading to its success and relevance in the fast-changing face of AI technology.

7.4.10. Democracy Score Calculation

The democratizing mission is the generation of AI within open-source platform policies. We have prepared a mathematical model to evaluate its effectiveness, including the most critical dimensions, such as accessibility, user engagement, resources, community contribution, and technical simplicity.

For instance, consider a hypothetical platform with the following scores:

- Accessibility (A): 0.8
- Engagement (E): 0.7
- Resources (R): 0.9
- Community Contributions (C): 0.6
- Technical Complexity (T): 0.4
- After computing D will be $D=2.06/1.4 \approx 1.47$

This result suggests that the platform does an excellent job of facilitating access to generative AI technologies by decreasing barriers for users. With a democratization score of 1.479, the platform offers advanced tools, a supportive community, and plenty of resources. Therefore, this is an excellent example of democratization in this field.

This calculation highlights the importance of open source in unlocking inclusive and innovative generative AI experiences and supporting a diverse user base. Notes for Integration This proves how easily the platform is making access to generative AI technologies by lowering barriers to users. With a democratization score of 1.479, the platform is granted access to advanced tools, a community of support, and numerous assets, an excellent specimen of democratization in AI. This calculation emphasizes the contribution of open-source contributions in providing democratized revolutionary generative AI experience/toolkits to a wide-ranging recipient. The argument must be framed in context, with its introduction at the beginning of the text, right before the chapter, to make the point truly relevant; with a brief outline of why democratization measuring is essential, it serves the reader better. Use appropriate transitional phrases for full integration from part to part without stopping to keep the logical flow of ideas intact. Formatting the mathematical equations like the rest of the chapter makes all the difference in clarity and professionalism and thus contributes more to readability. Grasping the democratization of generative artificial intelligence technology is very important for such innovations to benefit a wide variety of users. Introducing a democratization score can help quantify how platforms effectively break barriers and enhance accessibility. This chapter explains why they level democratization against an underscore and what implications result from discussing that democratization on a figured score.

8. Results

The democratization score computed for a fictitious portal comes to around 1.47. This calculation denotes that it is a highly accessible and usable portal. This score exceeds that of regular scales as the platform's capabilities exceed and exceed user requirements. The compelling trend shows the importance of open-source platforms in providing access to generative AI technologies. A high accessibility score implies that users utilize advanced generative AI tools without deep technical expertise. An example of such a platform is Hugging Face, where users build their NLP solutions quickly through user-friendly interfaces and extensive documentation. Platforms such as Runway ML are living proof of the spirit of active user communities. Knowledge and collaborative projects result in faster innovation, which is how they build the collective expertise that accelerates advancements. Such platforms can also ensure the high involvement of users like TensorFlow by continuously offering educational media, tutorials, and forums that maximize their understanding and applicability of generative AI technologies. All features will be well advanced, but consideration must be given to ease-of-use platforms. Simplified interfaces must be built within the platform. It is inferred that the facts relating to the structure or construction of the building will support its handling of the dangers of earthquakes. However, these do not make buildings earthquake-proof because earthquakes can only cause physical destruction to infrastructure. As much as the architecture appears concrete-based, it may not be so in generic terms. As it relates to earthquakes, it alone does not make the building earthquake-proof.

9. Discussion

The open-source platform democratizes generative AI mainly to empower non-technical users (say, from the fields of art and design) and widen the scope for contributors, creators, and applications across diverse fields. With their collaborative structure, open-source platforms improve innovation acceleration; for example, Hugging Face and Runway ML allow their expert users to contribute models, tutorials, and insights to add value to their commercial and academic undertakings. The more available generative AIs become, the more urgent concerns about ethicality will be. Platforms like Creative AI Lab are wagging their talons to lead discussions on responsible AI practice and are gearing towards ethical applications within communities. Open-source platforms are the most flexible and scalable regarding user contribution adjustments. The research tracks resource levels to match them against modifications in community demands. The process guarantees ongoing democratization combined with ongoing progress. Developing interfaces for users takes priority in design and research activities which focus on building innovative and friendly interfaces for multiple user groups. Further action will focus on interpretation research and practice in design improvements. A place where the user groups would have well-resourced and multilingual platform localized resources would be aimed at selling platforms to non-English-speaking communities. The introduction and enforcement of clear ethical frameworks for generative AI would mitigate risks and benefit responsible innovation as much as possible. Future research projects should consider the partnerships between technologists and professionals from various disciplines, including the arts, education, and social sciences, to promote interdisciplinary applications. Impact studies- using democratization efforts would offer significant revelations in user engagement, community development, and technological advancement. Developing comprehensive metrics to assess democratization programs' satisfaction, community contribution, and ethics adherence would be extremely important for measuring success.

Conclusion

The open-source paradigm makes eminent advances toward democratizing the generative AI environment; it opens access to an impressive range of modern tools and encourages people's participation and interaction. It empowers all types of use- from the researcher to the developer and the artist to the educator by reducing technical barriers and innovations in what can be achieved. There is then the validity of the democratization arguments, with algebras of technical challenges and ethics now demanding an active stakeholders' engagement in promoting responsible practices. Forward movement must occur on better user designs, improved worldwide access, consideration of ethical principles, and interdisciplinary cooperation. Open-source platforms facilitate democratization as they can use generative AI to bring responsible and inclusive innovation to the hands of individuals and communities. Developers, teachers, researchers, and policymakers must work together to harness this technology entirely for the benefit of all society.

References

[1] Abadi, M., Barham, P., Chen, J., et al. (2016). TensorFlow: A System for Large-Scale Machine Learning. *Proceedings of the 12th USENIX Symposium on Operating Systems Design and Implementation (OSDI 16)*.

[2] Vaswani, A., Shazeer, N., Parmar, N., et al. (2017). Attention is All You Need. *Advances in Neural Information Processing Systems (NeurIPS)*, *30*, 5998–6008.

[3] Brown, T. B., Mann, B., Ryder, N., et al. (2020). Language Models are Few-Shot Learners. *Advances in Neural Information Processing Systems (NeurIPS)*, *33*, 1877–1901.

[4] OpenAI. (2020). GPT-3: An Autoregressive Language Model. *GitHub Repository.*

[5] Hugging Face. (2020). *Transformers: State-of-the-Art Natural Language Processing. GitHub Repository.*

[6] Baidu Research. (2021). PaddlePaddle: A Deep Learning Platform Based on Open-Source Community Contributions. *Baidu Research.*

[7] Ramesh, A., Pavlov, M., Goh, G., et al. (2021). Zero-Shot Text-to-Image Generation. *Proceedings of the 38th International Conference on Machine Learning (ICML)*, 3779–3789.

[8] McMahan, H. B., Moore, E., Ramage, D., et al. (2017). Communication-Efficient Learning of Deep Networks from Decentralized Data. *Proceedings of the 20th International Conference on Artificial Intelligence and Statistics (AISTATS).*

[9] Paszke, A., Gross, S., Massa, F., et al. (2019). PyTorch: An Imperative Style, High-Performance Deep Learning Library. *Advances in Neural Information Processing Systems (NeurIPS).*

[10] Radford, A., Wu, J., Child, R., et al. (2019). Language Models are Unsupervised Multitask Learners. *OpenAI Blog.*

[11] Brundage, M., Avin, S., Clark, J., et al. (2020). Toward Trustworthy AI Development: Mechanisms for Supporting Verifiable Claims.

[12] Amodei, D., Olah, C., Steinhardt, J., et al. (2016). Concrete Problems in AI Safety. *arXiv Preprint.*

[13] Ruder, S. (2019). Neural Networks for NLP. *Sebastian Ruder Blog.*

[14] He, K., Zhang, X., Ren, S., & Sun, J. (2016). Deep Residual Learning for Image Recognition. *Proceedings of the IEEE Conference on Computer Vision and Pattern Recognition (CVPR)*, 770–778.

[15] Balog, M., Gaunt, A. L., Brockschmidt, M., et al. (2017). DeepCoder: Learning to Write Programs. *Proceedings of the 5th International Conference on Learning Representations (ICLR).*

[16] Balasubramaniam, S., Nelson, S. G., Arishma, M., & Rajan, A. S. (2024). Machine Learning based Disease and Pest Detection in Agricultural Crops. *EAI Endorsed Transactions on Internet of Things, 10.*

Chapter 11

Democratizing Generative AI for Inclusive Education: Legal and Ethical Considerations for Children with Disabilities

Navonita Mallick[1]
Shashwata Sahu[2,*]
and Imran Hossain[3]
[1,2]School of Law, KIIT-DU, Bhubaneswar, KIIT-DU, Bhubaneswar, India
[3]Political Science Department, Varendra University, Bangladesh

Abstract

The concept of Generative AI is ground-breaking for both the depth and breadth it adds to inclusive education, specifically those about disabled children. The democratization of AI can significantly alter the educational landscape, particularly for disenfranchised populations. However, these heightened access and data protection risks have brought significant legal challenges in compliance and ethics. This paper delves into the implications of how democratized AI might converge with the rights and needs of children with disabilities. This study endeavors to assess how the existing law governing AI in education catering to disabled children faring, gaps missing from legislation which might impede the protection of the rights of such kids, laying down a roadmap for ensuring responsible implementation by constructing ethical and legal guidelines underpinning working with Artificial Intelligence, exploring possibility could play pivotal role enabling personalized implementations as well making learning experiences responsive. It is a doctrinal research

[*] Corresponding Author's Email: contactshashwata@gmail.com

In: Democratized Generative AI: Principles, Challenges and Applications
Editors: S. Balasubramaniam and Seifedine Kadry
ISBN: 979-8-89530-684-0

paper reviewing relevant legal frameworks, including the UNCRPD and ethical guidelines on consent and data privacy issues. Using broader experiences demonstrates that democratized AI is an ally of increased access, moving toward inclusion, and at odds with existing inequalities through debacles such as algorithmic bias and privacy. The testimony of everyday Americans indicates that many laws are obsolete and unable to keep up with new technologies. The paper goes on to say that for AI-enabled technology to be leveraged while protecting children's rights, policymakers need statutory legal frameworks that are spacious and forward-thinking, i.e., compelling the newly lurking threat vectors of this capability landscape.

Keywords: democratized AI, inclusive education, disable children, legal frameworks, ethical considerations

1. Introduction

> "Education is the most powerful weapon you can use to change the world."
>
> - Nelson Mandela

As with other fields, generative AI is revolutionizing education. Machine learning and AI have come a long way in the past century, now generating anything from text to images or simulations, opening up new mediums for teaching and learning. AI-powered systems can use vast amounts of data to create a custom learning profile for every student, focused on the sources that appeal to and work best with them. [1]. Use cases are wide-ranging, from automating mundane administration to creating interactive educational content. From the very beginning, AI gave a chance to children with disabilities to overcome obstacles that were inherent in their inability for much of history. Generative AI makes learning more inclusive by using adaptability to help students with physical, sensory, and cognitive disabilities receive the educational materials they need in an accessible format. [2]. For example, text-to-speech technology and AI-generated visuals can help students with visual or auditory disabilities. Similarly, for children who may find it difficult due to learning disabilities like dyslexia or autism, AI can be used to develop personalized, powerful modules that would deliver the content at their 'comfort' pace and style of understanding [3]. Yet, for all the exciting progress possible because of integration in education, doing so also poses challenges that must be overcome most acutely, such as equitable access and responsible use.

Inclusive education is a human right and the core of several international documents ratified throughout various countries, such as part of the "United Nations Convention on the Rights of Persons with Disabilities (UNCRPD)." This, in turn, hopes to create a school where all children, irrespective of their abilities, can gain equal schooling opportunities [4]. For children with disabilities, inclusive education means more than mere access to schooling: a learning environment must be in place that recognizes and caters to their different educational needs. This is a reality-based problem that traditional educational systems are poorly equipped to deal with, as we have historically seen how some of the most marginalized students can get less than ideal support and not thrive in learning. Part of them will be evened out by AI in education, giving everyone a user-specific lesson on demand [5]. Generative AI improved engagement in content personalization through automation. It dramatically enhances children with disability' learning outcomes by automating content customization. It also provides continuous feedback to track each student's performance in real-time, allowing educators to adapt their teaching methods accordingly. Moving to inclusive education is not merely a matter of justice but also the foundation for creating a fairer society where every child, regardless of disability status, can grow and flourish.

In other words, democratizing AI makes these technologies available to anyone with any degree of technical expertise or class. This means creating AI tools that schools can readily apply and get used to, especially in historically underserved or marginalized areas. Democratized AI can potentially empower all children, including those with disabilities, by providing personal learning tools that typically require specialized and expensive resources [6]. This way, by using AI in future education, we can bring technology to even those who are less privileged or disabled and allow them access to tools that were previously available only for a few chosen. AI democratization will make these benefits possible in varied educational settings, not just in wealthy schools or urban epicenters but also in rural and under-resourced areas. If AI tools were distributed equitably, disparities in educational outcomes would be vastly decreased, and we could have a more inclusive system where kids with disabilities can learn right alongside their peers [7]. Although the promise of Generative AI is enormous to benefit educational outcomes for children with disabilities, its deployment must be carefully managed so as not to worsen already-existing inequalities. Legal frameworks and ethical guidelines should thus be put in place to govern the responsible use of AI tools while upholding children's rights. Despite their promise, these systems have significant limitations and dangers; data privacy vulnerabilities and algorithmic biases are some ethical issues that must be addressed to prevent social damage [8]. For example, using AI systems with children's data demands strong safeguards to counter potential abuse. In addition, safeguards should be established to prevent AI tools from reinforcing biases through imperfect or corrupted information as well as biased algorithmic decision-making for the most vulnerable populations, such as children with disabilities.

2. Research Objectives

This study aims to:

1) Research existing legal frameworks related to AI-driven education tools for children with disabilities.
2) Highlight areas and problems in existing laws that fall short of protecting the rights of these children using AI technology for education.
3) Suggest appropriate legal and ethical solutions so that the misuse of Generative AI will not happen in Inclusive Education.
4) Discover how Generative AI technology can organically empower learning capabilities, making it more accessible and equitable for all kids.

3. Research Methodology

The methodology used in this paper is a doctrinal method, and the advantage of using it is we would be able to analyze it from national & international legal frameworks such as UNCRPD. It also refers to case laws, statutes, policy reviews, and legislative measures where AI has been applied in educational practices. This is followed by a review of ethical standards related to the use of AI in children's education, consent, data privacy, and protection against bias.

4. The Potential of Democratized AI for Inclusive Education

New opportunities in education generative AI have opened up all sorts of possibilities for enriching education and are specially designed to give something more advanced than any non-specialized student. The democratization of AI technologies with the evolution of how much AI software we can use opens up a more inclusive schooling environment. Democratized AI means enabling everybody, with or without technical expertise or resources, to leverage sophisticated advanced technologies, allowing disadvantaged students who otherwise could not [9]. Democratized AI can be used for personalized learning experiences, adaptive teaching textiles, and to provide tools & resources specially made to the requirements of students with disabilities since it is inclusive. AI is also integral in providing immediate responses and adapting teaching methodologies for those with disabilities to ensure they meet all curricular requirements. Yet, realizing the complete value of AI in ed relies on delivering these tools more equitably across educational spaces. Everyone should get access to these AI-driven tools, from rural schools to urban centers, and they can support them as per their learning needs. It would make for us [10]. Further, democratized AI can serve as a crucial dismantling force of educational inequity by collapsing the artificial divides created through systemic injustices. AI can deliver affordable automation of truly individualized education, untethered from specialized resources and educators, so that learning is possible and beneficial for everyone, even those historically disenfranchised or neglected by the system. Figure 1 shows the key ways in which AI can be used for Inclusive Education.

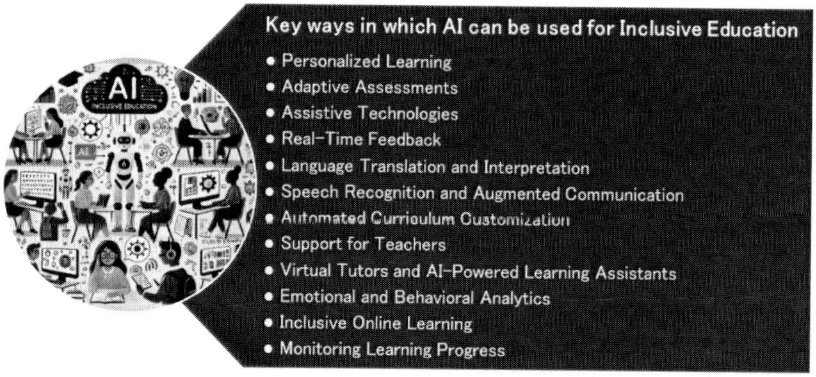

Figure 1. Key ways in which AI can be used for Inclusive Education.

4.1. Democratization of AI: Accessibility and Personalization

AI Democratization, at its core, is about tearing down barriers that have historically restricted access to cutting-edge tech. This makes the process transformative in education, especially for children with disabilities, who have a hard time finding equally enriching learning tools due to systemic challenges. Democratized AI allows the spread of cutting-edge educational tools so it is possible for students concerned with their learning and from different backgrounds, including those with disabilities, to have personalized and specific experiences. All can access the benefits of democratized AI [11]. A core benefit to democratizing AI is that everyone gets access. Many AI-based educational platforms, if not all, are built to be very user-friendly and do not require heavy tech expertise, for instance, for educators and schools that do not have the resources or know-how to work with intricate systems. Enabling educators to use AI tools easily allows them to concentrate on teaching and less on managing technology, which is very important in inclusive settings where individual needs must be carefully considered [12]. Artificial intelligence, for instance, can be leveraged to create automatic lesson plans that modify themselves according to a learner's learning speed and personal style; this way, children with special needs are not excluded just because they don't fit the traditional curriculum.

If democratized, AI is to deliver on other critical features, such as personalization. Conventional education systems frequently stick to a one-size-fits-all standard, which means pupils with disabilities often get left out. AI democratization makes it easy to create individual learning paths for each student [13]. For instance, applications with AI capabilities can adjust the complexity of lessons relevant to student proficiency levels, offer visual assistance for students with a hearing impairment, or prima facia convert in-text content into voice-over text, providing significant aid to visually impaired students. By allowing educational content to adapt dynamically, AI helps fill a void often seen in traditional classroom settings that can leave special-needs children behind. Also, it helps provide continuous feedback, which allows the teacher to change the pattern if necessary [14]. Rather than needing the formal assessment at regular intervals to tell us that a student has fallen through gaps, AI could keep pace in real time so we can address issues long before summative assessments. It's beneficial for students with disabilities, where a real-time adaptation might be needed multiple times per day. Decentralizing AI is thus a potent weapon to democratize education and make it more inclusive, flexible, and personalized.

4.2. Implications for Educational Equity

The most important implication of a democratized AI is its capability to level the playing field in education. Through the lens of equity, much harm is done to children during school years who have various physical and cognitive challenges because they are not receiving appropriate support. These challenges are worse for under-resourced or remote areas, where schools may not have the tools, e.g., educational funding or people power, i.e., trained staff, to support inclusive education [15]. When AI is democratized, it levels the playing field by ensuring that quality education tailored for each student can be provided universally regardless of location or socio-economic background. AIs can also automate a great deal of work that was once done by highly trained specialists, like creating "Individualized Education Plans (IEPs) for students with disabilities." AI can Assist schools in implementing personalized learning strategies at scale and a reasonable price so that even resource-constrained institutions are also able to cater to customized educational experiences [16]. This is particularly important for marginalized students who might have difficulty accessing specialized staff or expensive materials in communities with low socio-economic status.

In addition, AI can overcome some challenges associated with the digital divide. Although AI-powered educational platforms help bridge this disparity at a learning level to the extent possible due to the restricted use of technology in any geographic area, availability can be relatively higher only when available [17]. AI can democratize education in a way that traditional methods are never able to by offering low-cost or even free tools such as those adapting to the needs of disabled students. This paradigm shift is critical to increasing educational equity and ensuring that all students achieve academic success, regardless of their background. Yet, for AI to help with educational equity, it needs to be used in a way that considers the unique experiences and backgrounds of varied student communities [18]. This will require eliminating bias in AI algorithms and ensuring the data these systems learn from represents all students, especially disadvantaged groups. Without proper governance, AI can worsen rather than ameliorate societal disparities.

4.3. AI-Driven Support for Disabled Children

Paradoxically, this creates a fantastic opportunity for children with a disability but simultaneously requires more resources to accommodate them everywhere within traditional education. This is where AI-driven educational tools come into the picture to offer students customizable learning material that can make it easier and more useful [19]. Through leveraging AI, educators can design a learning setting that offers more flexibility to students but is intelligent and responsive to individual students' needs.

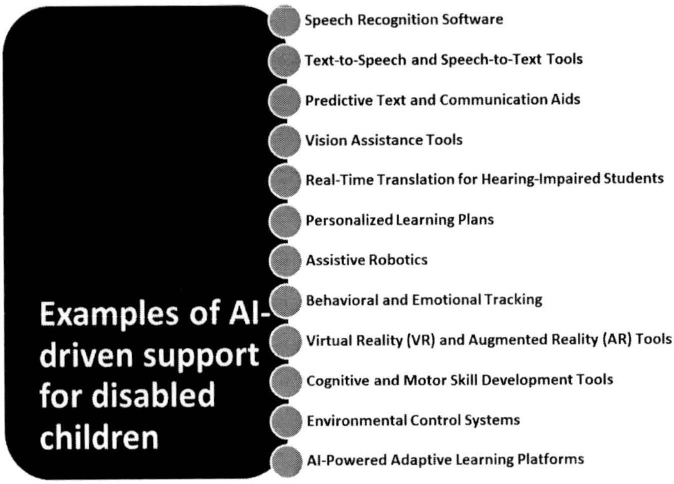

Figure 2. Examples of AI-driven support for disabled children.

Figure 2 show the examples of AI driven support for disabled children. They contribute significantly to improving the lives of people with disabilities in terms of learning, communication, and independence. Speech recognition, text-to-speech, and predictive text systems support students with speech or manual dexterity impairments; vision assistance tools and real-time sign language detection assist deaf or hard-of-hearing learners to engage fully. Tools such as personalized learning plans and adaptive learning platforms are tailored to an individual's cognitive or physical needs [20]. However, there is also equipment from assistive robotics that provides physical support for motor impairment. AI also detects social and emotional deficits in autistic kids, and VR/AR instruments put forward interactive learning for cognitive impairments. These are all solutions to a more inclusive and accessible collegiate experience. One example is that AI systems can support children with physical disabilities and convert interactions into forms that are alternative to traditional interface mechanisms transmitted via typing actions by their hands [21]. For example, students who cannot type or write can participate in classroom activities using speech recognition software.

Likewise, AI can also assist children with cognitive difficulties by studying complex tasks in smaller steps or through visual and auditory cues to ensure that learning takes place. It would enrich learning and equip our younger generation to come out and take charge of their education. Another advantage of AI-based support is that it offers you real-time feedback and assessments [22]. For students with disabilities, who may need changes to their learning plans made more frequently than traditional norms allow for, which typically requires periodic testing, holding fast to this model can be a source of enormous distress. In contrast, AI systems can continuously support students and give teachers near-immediate feedback so they can adjust their teaching in real-time. For students with disabilities, this may be very useful to prevent them from losing pace.

5. Legal and Ethical Risks of AI Implementation in Education

As AI is pushed into educational systems, we have the opportunity for exciting things to happen and many challenges. Although the possibilities for AI revolutionizing and improving education, especially from a disability standpoint, if applied correctly to young children, one with great caution due to risks [23]. One of the main issues is whether AI works or turns out otherwise; it could make educational gaps worse than they already are due to a lack of responsible production. There are many critical issues, such as unequal access to AI tools, privacy violations, algorithmic bias, and ethical dilemmas in decision-making processes. Figure 3 shows the legal and ethical risks of AI implementation in Education.

Legal and ethical risks of AI implementation in education	Data Privacy Concerns
	Informed Consent
	Algorithmic Bias
	Lack of Transparency and Accountability
	Inequitable Access
	Over-reliance on AI
	Misuse of Data
	Impact on Employment
	Intellectual Property Issues
	Ethical Dilemmas in Decision-Making

Figure 3. Legal and ethical risks of AI implementation in education.

Table 1. Legal and ethical challenges of generative AI in inclusive education disabled children

Legal and Ethical Challenges	Description	Potential Solutions
Data Privacy Concerns	AI systems require large amounts of sensitive data from students, especially children with disabilities, raising the risk of data misuse.	Stronger data protection laws, encryption, anonymization, and limited data collection.
Informed Consent	Children and their guardians may not fully understand the implications of sharing personal data with AI systems.	Continuous informed consent, clear communication with parents/guardians, and transparency in data usage.
Algorithmic Bias	AI systems may produce biased outcomes if trained on unrepresentative data, leading to discrimination against disabled students.	Use diverse, inclusive datasets for training AI and regular audits of AI systems for bias detection.
Lack of Transparency	Many AI systems operate as “black boxes,” making it difficult for educators and students to understand how decisions are made.	Mandate transparency in AI systems, ensuring that decision-making processes are explainable.
Inequitable Access	Students in under-resourced areas may not have access to AI-driven tools, exacerbating educational inequalities.	Public-private partnerships to ensure equitable access and government funding for AI in underserved schools.
Over-reliance on AI	There is a risk of replacing human educators with AI, particularly in special education, which may harm students requiring personal care and attention.	Define the role of AI as a supplement to human educators rather than a replacement, and promote balanced use of AI tools.

What is at stake here, especially for kids with disabilities? While AI can provide more tailored support, it can violate privacy rights and perpetuate discrimination if not well-regulated. Furthermore, AI-powered educational tools might necessitate resources like stable internet connections, hardware, or particular software that are not universally present, especially in impoverished communities and rural populations. This has raised questions about a lack of access for many and the capacity for this technology to exacerbate, rather than ameliorate, the digital divide. The most significant question mark when applying AI in education is privacy-related [24]. Children, in particular those with disabilities, are a vulnerable population, and the rich data obtained by AI systems for personalized learning experiences needs to be safeguarded so that not only can children learn but also their privacy is protected. Another problem is transparency in AI algorithms. In the absence of sufficient checks and balances, such systems can reinforce existing biases and potentially disadvantage students with disabilities. These challenges underscore the importance of robust legal and ethical frameworks for responsible AI use in education. Table 1 shows the various legal and ethical challenges of Generative AI in Inclusive Education for the disabled childrens.

5.1. Unequal Resource Distribution and Access Gaps

One of the core concerns with implementing AI into education is also connected to insufficient resource distribution, which can lead directly to a lack of overall accessibility for disabled students. AI seems to have great potential for personalizing education, but sadly, a lot could depend on access provided by infrastructure and connectivity like high-speed internet, advanced hardware tools known as devices like tablets or computers with browser-based versions of software installed somewhat similar to cloud computing model-based system, etc., along with well-trained educators [25]. This, in turn, further deepens the digital divide between schools that have resources versus those from low-income or rural areas. This uneven apportionment of resources can compound inequalities in learning that already exist. Since states allocate education funds based on the number of students they serve, a formula that may not change even with greater use of AI in schools, the students likely to end up worst off are those whose districts can afford extras. This digital divide is an even bigger issue for students with disabilities, as many require specialized technology to participate in school [26]. These students may encounter even more challenges in pursuing their educational goals without equal access to AI tools. For instance, an AI helps a child who has poor eyesight use text-to-speech software to participate fully in class. The disadvantage is that the child's learning experience is significantly compromised due to limited technology.

In addition, no AI tools mean only the right to exploit AI potential. Not only does this compound the existing inequity in education, but it also serves to introduce new dimensions of disadvantage where some groups, particularly students with disabilities in low-socioeconomic status areas, become even more marginalized. However, the equitable promise of AI in education to address variability cannot be accomplished if all schools, regardless of socioeconomic status, do not have access to resources [27]. Policymakers must recognize the significant availability constraints. Some answers may lie in government initiatives to equip schools with the necessary technology and training and public-private partnerships to make AI tools cheaper and more available [28]. In the absence of such coproduced measures, democratizing AI in education will continue to sit on ground zero, and students most disadvantaged– including those with disabilities still up against a wall.

5.2. Privacy Concerns for Disabled Children

With its pervasive role in education, the inclusion of AI has raised worrying questions about data privacy, especially since often voice-related information is being leveraged and personal to particularly vulnerable segments like children with disabilities. Personalized learning is one of the primary goals of an AI-powered tool, but to achieve that, these tools generally collect and analyze a lot of personal information [29]. This data can contain sensitive information about the health, cognitive functioning, and learning behaviors of children with disabilities. On the one hand, while collecting data can help AI generate personalized learning pathways, it presents enormous risks if improperly dealt with. Backup concerns are over the use of personal data. Without strong legal frameworks, AI systems collecting sensitive information could be open to access from advertisers or even potentially malicious actors. It would open the door to a litany of potential harms, from marketing designed for kids with disabilities to more extreme forms of exploitation [30]. Moreover, suppose there is no correct data governance. In that case, it can open the doors for misuse of this standardized record, such as commercial use, which does not have any way or means to leverage something on education. Informed consent is another primary source of concern. For this reason, children are not yet allowed to share their data with AI-driven platforms as they may reveal information about persons needing care. Even when parents or guardians consent, there must be greater transparency about data collection and use [31]. AI systems should be engineered in a privacy-first method to collect only the data needed and apply strong encryption standards for sensitive information.

Additionally, there are ethical implications of storing personal information over time and what people might do with their data later. For instance, might the data amassed while a person is growing up be utilized to make decisions about jobs and healthcare automatically? The lack of legal boundaries for data management, retention, and usage still raises fears about future abuses. The answer is that we need to have robust data privacy laws and regulations. Policies and frameworks to protect children with disabilities will need to be broader-based, recognizing the unique challenges AI presents in learning scenarios as well [32]. This may entail regulations stipulating that AI systems are subject to regular privacy audits and outlining when data must be retained.

5.3. Algorithmic Bias and Its Impact on Learning Outcomes

One of the most dangerous risks in education is the algorithmic bias associated with AI. This is especially critical for children who have disabilities. AI systems are not inherently biased but merely a mirror of the input data used in training. Those algorithms could make biased decisions if that training data reflects societal biases or has excluded certain marginalized groups regarding concepts or representation [33]. This is worrying, especially in the case of education, where biased algorithms can affect students' learning outcomes and opportunities. This hazardous process, particularly its consequences, can be severe for children with disabilities. For example, suppose an AI system is not trained on data that accurately represents the diversity of students with disabilities. In that case, it may falsely believe certain things about these children are correctly general truths [34]. For example, it suggests that a child be placed in an alternative class or should not receive the accommodations needed. Further, algorithmic bias has the potential to support inherently flawed stereotypes that students with disabilities are not as able as their non-disabled peers. Ensuring that AI systems have been trained using appropriate data is a key driver in addressing algorithmic bias [35]. However, the developers are responsible for ensuring this data includes a wide diversity of young people, especially if marginalized. So we are not perpetuating harmful inequalities. In addition, AI systems should be assessed for bias regularly, with processes in place to remedy any clear imbalances that have been discovered.

5.4. Ethical Dilemmas in AI Usage in Education

AI in educational practice is also associated with many ethical challenges, especially respecting the rights and welfare of students with disabilities. One of the significant ethical questions is whether or not AI will be able to replace human teachers in some regions of education. It can assist and be very helpful, but it does not replace teachers' empathy or understanding [36]. For students of all types, particularly those with a disability, who rely on this personalized, focused attention from their educators, moving too far in the opposite direction into AI has penalties that may well outweigh its benefits for empowerment. It is another ghastly conundrum of ethics which breeds grounds for questioning fairness. If AI systems are not kept in check, they could help deepen educational gaps [37]. Specifically, if AI tools are more available in affluent schools, students in poorer areas could be left behind. Creating an inclusive educational environment requires using AI in a way that is aligned with fairness and equity.

6. Legal Oversight and Ethical Guidelines for AI in Education

AI is a term that will soon be intertwined with our educational system, but in doing so, laws and some ethical guidelines need to be moderated. Not only in the aspects of learning, but it has also evolved into an innovation that serves inclusivity needs and provides effective outreach programs for students with disabilities [23]. Yet, AI can also create problems for students if not adequately regulated, including privacy breaches, algorithmic bias, and inequity of access to educational resources. As a result, they need legal and ethical frameworks that guarantee the application of AI technologies to be fair and transparent and to protect student rights. The legal oversight for AI in education comprises several key areas. The first step is that it should not violate students' rights, especially in terms of privacy and data security, through the use of AI [38]. Since AI systems often need to gather vast amounts of personal information to offer personalized learning, they must also comply with data protection acts currently in books. At the same time, AI systems must operate under clear ethical guidelines that ensure they are not inadvertently helping perpetuate discrimination or bias [39]. This is particularly important for students with disabilities, who are a population that might be disproportionately harmed by any algorithm biases detecting their needs or abilities inaccurately.

Ultimately, legal frameworks need mechanisms that ensure AI tools are available & accessible to students of all backgrounds. AI implementation in schools, therefore, could potentially widen the educational disparities because institutions of those types may not have the resources required to implement AI if practices are allowed without regulations [40]. To meet these reasons, policymakers must join hands with educators and technologists and consider ethicists to make suitable comprehensive legal and ethical guidelines that invite us to discuss how AI should be used responsibly within education. Table

2 depicts the comparative overview of legal frameworks governing AI in education for children with disabilities.

Table 2. Comparative overview of legal frameworks governing AI in education for children with disabilities

Jurisdiction	Relevant Law/Framework	Key Provisions Related to AI and Education for Children with Disabilities	Gaps/Challenges
United States	Individuals with Disabilities Education Act (IDEA)	Ensures access to special education and services for children with disabilities. It does not explicitly address AI in education but mandates assistive technologies.	Lacks provisions on how AI can be integrated into IEPs and oversight on AI-driven tools.
European Union	General Data Protection Regulation (GDPR)	It provides strict regulations on data privacy, including those for AI systems used in education. Requires consent for data processing and enforces data security measures.	Does not explicitly address educational AI's ethical challenges, such as algorithmic bias and transparency in decision-making.
United Kingdom	Equality Act 2010	Protects individuals with disabilities from discrimination, including in education. The act covers the use of technology in making education accessible.	There are no clear guidelines on AI use in education for children with disabilities; it does not address AI transparency or biases in decision-making.
India	Rights of Persons with Disabilities Act (RPwD), 2016	It provides inclusive education for children with disabilities, mandating assistive technologies.	There are no specific provisions for AI use in education. Lacks robust privacy protection and ethical guidelines for AI-driven tools.
Australia	Disability Discrimination Act (DDA), 1992	Mandates reasonable educational adjustments for children with disabilities, including using technology to facilitate learning.	There are no specific regulations for the use of AI in educational settings. Lacks legal oversight for AI-driven decision-making in education.
Canada	Accessible Canada Act, 2019	Focuses on improving accessibility, including in education, for persons with disabilities. Encourages the use of innovative technologies.	There is no specific focus on AI use in education. Does not address issues of AI transparency, privacy, and algorithmic bias.

The table below shows some of the primary legal frameworks that affect AI in education for children with disabilities across international jurisdictions, including the United States, the European Union, the United Kingdom, India, Australia, and Canada. All jurisdictions have laws concerning equal access and use of assistive technologies in the education of children with disabilities and challenges to the regulations on how AI may be used.

6.1. Need for Stronger Regulatory Mechanisms

One of the first problems is that rapid progress in deploying AI technologies for educational purposes has moved faster than the mechanisms needed to regulate and control their use. Data Protection laws like the General Data Protection Regulation GDPR in Europe also allow for some supervision. However, the regulation was not designed to accommodate all issues caused by AI actors operating within educational settings. These AI systems are analyzing a massive amount of learning data [41]. Further, they make decisions that affect students' subject outcomes in one way or provoke questions about accountability, transparency, and fairness. Source Complexity is one of the key drivers for more excellent governance systems, owing to AI-centric determination processes against it. In many cases, AI systems function as black boxes, even to developers who may not understand why an AI made a particular decision. Lack of transparency is particularly disconcerting in education, where AI now powers student performance assessments and prescriptive algorithms for identifying at-risk students [42]. Without robust regulatory guidance, there is a risk of these AI systems arriving at discriminatory and unfair decisions with potentially devastating consequences for students with disabilities.

Likewise, the burgeoning use of AI in schools poses novel privacy concerns. Artificial intelligence has often been depicted as an almost omnipotent force that can solve any problem with few limits on its capabilities, but in practice, AI systems require personal information essential for their operation. Insights into students' health conditions and ability levels are vital to understanding how materials should be presented so that they are accessible to all students regardless of background or learning differences [43]. While data protection regulations such as the EU GDPR aim to provide some safeguards, these rules are not explicitly designed to protect privacy risks caused by AI-powered personalized learning. This situation highlights the requirement for regulatory frameworks that extend beyond traditional data protection rules and encompass norms relating to algorithmic transparency, accountability, and ethical AI in education [44]. Regulators also need to address other vital concerns related to AI, such as the availability of AI technologies. It's hoped that AI might help to level the playing field by giving individualized support to students with disabilities if all of these learners have access. Most schools do not have the capacity, particularly in low-income or rural areas where resources are spread thin and teachers are busy [45]. In the absence of regulatory controls to guarantee equal access, AI has the potential to reduce disparities in education and increase them. Policymakers should work to require access to AI technologies in schools through regulation and funds for their deployment into the less served areas.

6.2. Legal Frameworks: Current Policies and Gaps

Although some legal frameworks apply to certain domain areas of the use of AI in education, such as data protection laws or anti-discrimination laws, none are sufficient to address all issues raised by the application of AI. The GDPR, for example, creates a regulatory environment governing data privacy; it mandates that organizations must secure explicit permission to acquire information and ensure the protection and processing of said specific details [46]. However, the GDPR does not cover robots or AI in education systems, where continuous data collection is processed, such as the effective use of a personalized learning program to tailor specific tasks for an individual student.

The most crucial loophole of current legal frameworks is the absence of rules on algorithmic accountability. AI systems are increasingly used to see decisions affecting students' educational futures, from deciding which learning paths to identifying who may need extra help. However, this shadow court system is kept wholly confidential from the public or any overseeing organization, which might ensure these decisions are made and applied relatively [47]. Such lack of accountability is most worrisome for students with disabilities, who stand to be more affected by racially biased algorithms that may discriminatorily impact their educational placements. The helplessness of students who have been negatively affected by the results or scores that AI-derived decisions serve makes it issue a considerable amount in society due to the absence of current legal frameworks routine requiring AI developers to disclose how their systems make decisions and under what standards they operate, along with mechanisms for challenging those arbitrary black-box explanations [48]. Thus, one of the deficiencies in current legal frameworks is that they do not contain explicit provisions regarding AI use in education. While several countries published a national AI strategy with ethical guidelines on using AI, these strategies are primarily generic and do not focus on specific challenges for educators or students. The United States is a case in point, with proposed national legislation such as the AI in Education Act of 2020 emphasizing but not detailing requirements for student well-being and equitable access to AI technologies by students with disabilities [49]. In addition, balanced IA solutions to facilitate its equitable distribution in schools require legal bases. People in low-income or rural areas who do not have access to an AI-driven tool will continue without knowing they may be making a mistake. Should such legal requirements not be in place even then, AI is likely to exacerbate educational inequities [50]. Policymakers should fill this gap by crafting rules that mandate schools to offer access for all pupils and providing finance to support the machine learning-powered educational tools that might be introduced there.

6.3. Safeguarding Children's Rights in AI-Driven Education

One of the biggest worries when it comes to using AI for educational purposes is the safeguarding of Children's Rights. This has understandably spawned both ethical and legal concerns due to the population at stake being children, some of which are disabled. Personalized learning systems driven by AI often rely on sensitive personal data such as students' cognitive abilities, learning preferences, and even health conditions [51]. Although these systems promise to improve learning outcomes by tailoring support, they threaten our children's privacy and agency. In the case of AI-driven education, we need to frame laws prioritizing privacy and transparent & fair use of their data. A central part of these frameworks should be strong privacy policies that focus on the usage of AI in education [52]. Although laws such as GDPR are a good starting block for data privacy, new standalone regulations need to be implemented governing the creation of AI and machine learning-driven educational tools. For example, some options could include enforcing that AI developers use privacy-preserving techniques such as data anonymization or requiring affirmative consent before guardians share sensitive information.

Another essential part of protecting children's rights is understanding how automated processes have made all these decisions. AI systems can be used for education when they clearly explain why a given decision is taken concerning the output. And it's mandatory if outcomes are linked directly to the student's confidence [53]. This is a particular issue with students with disabilities, as biased algorithms may harm them more. Legislation should mandate that AI developers explain how their systems arrive at decisions and manifest ways for those decisions to be contested in the event of unfair or discriminatory results. Finally, legal frameworks should guarantee universal access to AI-driven educational tools for students with learning disabilities or from different backgrounds [54]. That includes expanded AI access in schools and being thoughtful about how students with disabilities might need AI systems to accommodate their needs. Artificial intelligence-based personalized learning tools should, for instance, be interoperable with screen readers or speech recognition software to make specific innovations inclusive and allow all students to take a whole part of their education [55]. Policy-makers should also fund the deployment of AI-driven tools in low-resourced areas to ensure equal access and opportunity for all students.

7. Ethical Standards and Recommendations

7.1. Gaps in Current Legal Frameworks for AI in Inclusive Education

As AI usage in education grows, meaningful holes in current legal structures don't establish the requirements for this type of technology. Most of the concern is identifying non-discrimination in learning and teaching AI for disabled children. While there are some guidelines and laws regarding data privacy, as well as protections for the rights of an educational entity to access those models, they are not specific enough given that both interplay with how AI systems function, like making decisions or dealing with injections by its very nature, highly personal information [56]. This is even more alarming in the times of inclusive education. Meanwhile, AI has the potential to completely transform how children with disabilities engage in learning experiences that are personalized for them specifically. Yet, if not properly monitored, it could reinforce biases and do more harm than good [57]. For example, AI systems that are based on biased data can result in unfair consequences for minority students. Ensuring AI does not guide these powerful new technologies in education environments and what can be done with the technology is challenging [58]. Hence, they genuinely support all students regardless of their accessibility or disabilities. In an era of AI, evolving legal frameworks must carry the burden of safeguarding vulnerable populations, including some in education.

7.2. Outdated Policies and Legislation for Disabled Children

The laws and practices that are there to protect children from disabilities in education cannot adequately meet the challenges when it comes to 21st-century AI technologies. A large number of inclusive education laws preceded the development of AI in a learning environment and, thus, do not consider some of the risks specific to using an AI-powered tool for educational purposes [59]. This is reflected in legislation such as The Individuals with Disabilities Education Act (IDEA), which exists primarily to ensure that children who have disabilities access special education services. However, this legislation does not fully capture the expanding array of diverse ways AI can also contribute to or detract from efforts toward inclusive education. There are no established rules for incorporating AI systems in IEPs and monitoring methods to verify the absence of discriminatory behavior [60]. Moreover, most current policies do not directly protect from this misuse at educational institutions, including data piracy and other harmful practices. In the context of AI, it is crucial to update these laws to protect the rights of children with disabilities.

7.3. Ethical Standards: Informed Consent, Data Protection, and Bias

Using AI responsibly within education, particularly with children with disabilities, means taking practices around informed consent, data protection, and bias mitigation incredibly seriously. The absence of these ethical standards would pose an existential threat to the proper use and application without causing harm or infringing on students' rights.

- *Informed Consent:* A child cannot be expected to understand the ethical implications of sharing their data with AI systems in educational settings. Parents or guardians must give informed consent to their children, but there needs to be honest-to-goodness notice of the process. Institutions need to address, if not explicitly, how AI systems process student data and the risks and benefits of such [61]. Instead, consent must be an ongoing process that allows guardians to reverse their decision and withdraw permission should they feel uncomfortable about how data-related processing is affecting or willing to affect the conduct of the minor.

- *Data Protection:* The information gathered by NLP in education has been sensitive personal data, especially when we talk about children with disabilities, and the types of questions asked to them might be related to health-related info, learning abilities & cognitive challenges, etc. It is crucial that schools and AI developers put in place strong data protection mechanisms to secure this information. Among these are encryption use, data anonymization where possible, and collecting only what the project requires [8]. AI systems should also adhere to data protection laws like the European General Data Protection Regulation (GDPR), which obliges organizations to protect the personal data they are correctly processing by design.
- Bias Mitigation: AI systems can be biased, especially if the data that goes into training these systems does not include various needs among students with disabilities. In other words, an AI model trained on mostly non-disabled student data might predict a lot of the disability-aimed educational methods incorrectly [62]. AI developers must use diverse and inclusive datasets to train their systems. Still, it is not enough-routing human biases whilst developing a machine learning model will never lead us away from instances like the Tay Tweets [63]. Schools and parents must also be able to see how such systems make decisions so that they can challenge them in situations where the outcomes are either unfair or biased.

8. Recommendations for Comprehensive Legal and Ethical Frameworks

The rapid inclusion of AI within inclusive education means tremendous potential to increase educational outcomes for students with identification labels. Yet, the application of AI in this field comes with some significant risks and challenges that it has to overcome. A holistic legal and ethical framework is needed to ensure AI will be deployed responsibly and moderately in education. This framework should be implemented at the federal level to protect children's rights while encouraging innovation and leveraging AI benefits for enriching learning experiences [64]. The immediate point to be addressed in creating educational policies that apply AI is the development of AI-specific education privacy. This selling of inclusive education fits well with the current legislative context, which has been described in the Individuals with Disabilities Education Act (IDEA) and was initially passed without disability used as a qualifier. This legislation must now be softened into guidelines for how AI systems can support learning environments. This should include changing the legal standards we already have in place to make way for incorporating AI into our special education system [65]. Policies should also detail how AI-powered tools may be used to assist in generating and reviewing Individualized Education Programs (IEPs) for students with disabilities. In this way, educators can be confident that these tools are utilized most effectively and appropriately for each student. And second, there needs to be accountability mechanisms for AI systems being used in education. So, having more accountability will help reduce the risks of bias and discrimination in AI applications [66]. Policymakers also could require AI developers to be transparent about how their systems reach decisions, even requiring them, in some cases, to outline the data sets and algorithms they use. We must go even further and require schools to regularly audit their AI systems to ensure that the language used in these technologies does not promote any form of bias or discrimination. These audits would also work to expose and fix any adverse side effects for an overall better, more equitable education system.

The other crucial part of the framework is resilient data protection controls. AI-powered educational tools require large amounts of data, which could be problematic for the privacy needs of children with disabilities. Strict data protection regulations should accompany this to ensure that all information collection is encrypted and, where possible, anonymized, only obtained as necessary. Schools also must offer parents and guardians easy access to information about their data collection activities and the ability for guardians to opt-out at any time [67]. This will help gain the trust of students and protect their privacy rights. It is also essential that these AI technologies are made available to all so as not to perpetuate any existing educational disparities. AI can be the great equalizer in educational access provided all students, regardless of socio-economic status and home location, have access to it. Governments should make funds and other resources available to assist schools in low-income or rural areas get AI-driven tools [68]. These technologies could be made affordable if public-private partnerships are used to help, so a push should be directed at providing the infrastructure necessary for AI integration in schools—and, finally, the creation of ethical standards for AI in education. While legal frameworks establish the rules within such boundaries, ethical guidelines restrict control-enablement in deep learning approaches. Guidelines should promote avoiding bias, working openly, protecting future autonomy and dignity, and providing decent treatment to students, including those with disabilities [69]. Some might think we do not need human education because Data uses AI. Still, the opposite is true to integrating these tools across all classrooms and schools sustainably, where appropriate educators will require professional learning around responsible AI practice, ensuring diversity, equity & belonging for each child. Hence, more AI in education requires a mixed approach to ensure that the benefits are realized while respect for the rights and well-being of students is maintained. Developing such policies along with mechanisms for accountability, securing privacy through data protection measures, as well as facilitating equitable access and providing ethical guidance to applicable stakeholders, can indeed lead to an education system where the adoption of AI further enriches and reinforces learning for all students, including students with disabilities.

Conclusion

"The measure of a society is how it treats its most vulnerable members."
- Mahatma Gandhi.

Generative AI in education is a double-edged sword, especially for children with special needs. Contextualization AI offers substantial benefits to personalize learning and foster inclusivity. However, it comes with its associated legal and ethical challenges. This includes balancing innovation and accountability to ensure AI-driven tools are used responsibly [70]. Scrutiny is essential to protect students and shield personal information, for Lyon says regulatory oversight would build in checks on everything from bias against it, making things worse likely the less remarked-on part of AI could otherwise have severe negative impacts and close off the sound effects we want [71]. Finally, Policymakers have a crucial role in regulating the use of AI in education. Robust policies need to be crafted to safeguard the rights of vulnerable groups, including children with disabilities, including that take into account data privacy, algorithmic transparency, and access & affordability of AI technologies [72]. Policymakers should collaborate with educators, technologists, and ethicists to lay down mechanisms that govern AI as a technology and make its usage accessible, feasible & equitable [73].

Therefore, regulations must be dynamic to respond to technological advancement and updated technology to ensure fairness while holding platforms accountable for their content. There is considerable hope for the democratized AI future in education, especially as it pertains to making our schools more inclusive and accessible, with one of them being children suffering from a disability [74]. Maximizing this potential, however, must be through responsible deployment that ensures fairness and governance. This deploys the power of technology to create inclusive educational environments by putting in place holistic frameworks that ensure responsible and fair use of AI. With the ongoing evolution of AI, we must ensure its development aligns with our values for fairness, access to content, and respect for every learner's rights [75].

References

[1] Lee, D., Arnold, M., Srivastava, A., Plastow, K., Strelan, P., Ploeckl, F., Lekkas, D., & Palmer, E. (2024). The impact of generative AI on higher education learning and teaching: A study of educators' perspectives. *Computers and Education: Artificial Intelligence*, *6*, 100221. https://doi.org/10.1016/j.caeai.2024.100221.

[2] *Challenges and Opportunities of Generative AI for Higher Education as Explained by ChatGPT*. (n.d.). Retrieved October 26, 2024, from https://www.mdpi.com/2227-7102/13/9/856.

[3] *Analysing Disability Descriptions and Student Suggestions as a Foundation to Overcome Barriers to Learning | Journal of Interactive Media in Education*. (n.d.). Retrieved October 26, 2024, from https://jime.open.ac.uk/articles/ 10.5334/jime.836.

[4] *Inclusive education and accountability mechanisms—UNESCO Digital Library*. (n.d.). Retrieved October 26, 2024, from https://unesdoc.unesco.org/ ark:/48223/pf0000259577.

[5] *The right of children with disabilities to education: A rights-based approach to Inclusive Education*. (n.d.). Retrieved October 26, 2024, from https://www.unicef.org/media/126506/file/UNICEF-Right-to-Education-Children-Disabilities-ENG.pdf.

[6] Capraro, V., Lentsch, A., Acemoglu, D., Akgun, S., Akhmedova, A., Bilancini, E., Bonnefon, J.-F., Brañas-Garza, P., Butera, L., Douglas, K. M., Everett, J. A. C., Gigerenzer, G., Greenhow, C., Hashimoto, D. A., Holt-Lunstad, J., Jetten, J., Johnson, S., Kunz, W. H., Longoni, C., … Viale, R. (2024). The impact of generative artificial intelligence on socioeconomic inequalities and policy making. *PNAS Nexus*, *3*(6), pgae191. https://doi.org/10.1093/pnasnexus/pgae191.

[7] *Applying Artificial Intelligence in Physical Education and Future Perspectives*. (n.d.). Retrieved October 26, 2024, from https://www.mdpi.com/2071-1050/13/1/351.

[8] *The effects of artificial intelligence applications in educational settings: Challenges and strategies—ScienceDirect*. (n.d.). Retrieved October 26, 2024, from https://www.sciencedirect.com/science/article/pii/S0040162523007618.

[9] *The application and challenges of ChatGPT in educational transformation: New demands for teachers' roles—ScienceDirect*. (n.d.). Retrieved October 26, 2024, from https://www.sciencedirect.com/science/article/pii/S2405844024003207.

[10] Bhutoria, A. (2022). Personalized education and Artificial Intelligence in the United States, China, and India: *A systematic review using a Human-In-The-Loop model. Computers and Education: Artificial Intelligence*, *3*, 100068. https://doi.org/10.1016/j.caeai.2022.100068.

[11] *Artificial Intelligence Alone Will Not Democratise Education: On Educational Inequality, Techno-Solutionism and Inclusive Tools*. (n.d.). Retrieved October 26, 2024, from https://www.mdpi.com/2071-1050/16/2/781.

[12] *Democratizing artificial intelligence: How no-code AI can leverage machine learning operations—ScienceDirect*. (n.d.). Retrieved October 26, 2024, from https://www.sciencedirect.com/science/article/pii/S0007681323000502.

[13] *Out of the laboratory and into the classroom: The future of artificial intelligence in education | AI & SOCIETY*. (n.d.). Retrieved October 26, 2024, from https://link.springer.com/article/10.1007/s00146-020-01033-8.

[14] Chan, C. K. Y., & Hu, W. (2023). Students' voices on generative AI: Perceptions, benefits, and challenges in higher education. *International Journal of Educational Technology in Higher Education*, *20*(1), 43. https://doi.org/10.1186/s41239-023-00411-8.

[15] *Generative AI and the future of education: Ragnarök or reformation? A paradoxical perspective from management educators—ScienceDirect*. (n.d.). Retrieved October 26, 2024, from https://www.sciencedirect.com/science/article/pii/S1472811723000289.

[16] *Artificial Intelligence and the Sustainable Development Goals: An Exploratory Study in the Context of the Society Domain*. (n.d.). Retrieved October 26, 2024, from https://www.scirp.org/journal/paperinformation?paperid=124905.

[17] *The digital divide in action: How experiences of digital technology shape future relationships with artificial intelligence | AI and Ethics*. (n.d.). Retrieved October 26, 2024, from https://link.springer.com/article/10.1007/s43681-024-00452-3.

[18] Scientist, S. A., Data. (2024, April 11). How AI is transforming Education: Potential Benefits and Challenges Ahead. *Medium*. https://medium.com/@sahin.samia/how-ai-is-transforming-education-potential-benefits-and-challenges-ahead-0ad827575b93.

[19] *Challenges and opportunities of AI in inclusive education: A case study of data-enhanced active reading in Japan | Smart Learning Environments | Full Text*. (n.d.). Retrieved October 26, 2024, from https://slejournal.springeropen.com/articles/10.1186/s40561-023-00286-2.

[20] *A Conceptual Model for Inclusive Technology: Advancing Disability Inclusion through Artificial Intelligence – ScienceOpen*. (n.d.). Retrieved October 26, 2024, from https://www.scienceopen.com/hosted-document?doi=10.57197/JDR-2023-0060.

[21] *Virtual Reality Technology as an Educational and Intervention Tool for Children with Autism Spectrum Disorder: Current Perspectives and Future Directions*. (n.d.). Retrieved October 26, 2024, from https://www.mdpi.com/2076-328X/12/5/138.

[22] *Artificial Intelligence Enabled Personalised Assistive Tools to Enhance Education of Children with Neurodevelopmental Disorders—A Review*. (n.d.). Retrieved October 26, 2024, from https://www.mdpi.com/1660-4601/19/3/1192.

[23] *Exploring the Potential Impact of Artificial Intelligence (AI) on International Students in Higher Education: Generative AI, Chatbots, Analytics, and International Student Success*. (n.d.). Retrieved October 26, 2024, from https://www.mdpi.com/2076-3417/13/11/6716.

[24] *Technology Use for Teacher Professional Development in Low- and Middle-Income Countries: A systematic review—ScienceDirect*. (n.d.). Retrieved October 26, 2024, from https://www.sciencedirect.com/science/article/pii/S2666557322000088.

[25] Almusaed, A., Almssad, A., Yitmen, I., & Homod, R. Z. (2023). Enhancing Student Engagement: Harnessing "AIED"'s Power in Hybrid Education—A Review Analysis. *Education Sciences*, *13*(7), Article 7. https://doi.org/10.3390/educsci13070632.

[26] *The digital divide in online education: Inequality in digital readiness of students and schools—PMC*. (n.d.). Retrieved October 26, 2024, from https://pmc.ncbi.nlm.nih.gov/articles/PMC9435462/.

[27] Holstein, K., & Doroudi, S. (2021). *Equity and Artificial Intelligence in Education: Will "AIEd" Amplify or Alleviate Inequities in Education?* (No. arXiv:2104.12920). arXiv. http://arxiv.org/abs/2104.12920.

[28] European Parliament. Directorate General for Parliamentary Research Services. (2020). *The ethics of artificial intelligence: Issues and initiatives*. Publications Office. https://data.europa.eu/doi/10.2861/6644.

[29] *Unveiling the shadows: Beyond the hype of AI in education—ScienceDirect*. (n.d.). Retrieved October 26, 2024, from https://www.sciencedirect.com/science/article/pii/S2405844024067276.

[30] *Humanizing the Digital Economy: Connecting Religious Humanism with Platforms for a Collaborative Society | SpringerLink*. (n.d.). Retrieved October 26, 2024, from https://link.springer.com/book/10.1007/978-3-031-37507-1.

[31] Viljoen, S. (2021). A Relational Theory of Data Governance. *The Yale Law Journal*.

[32] *The right to encryption: Privacy as preventing unlawful access—ScienceDirect*. (n.d.). Retrieved October 26, 2024, from https://www.sciencedirect.com/science/article/pii/S0267364923000146.

[33] *Artificial intelligence in education: Addressing ethical challenges in K-12 settings—PMC*. (n.d.). Retrieved October 26, 2024, from https://pmc.ncbi.nlm.nih.gov/articles/PMC8455229/.

[34] Timmons, A. C., Duong, J. B., Fiallo, N. S., Lee, T., Vo, H. P. Q., Ahle, M. W., Comer, J. S., Brewer, L. C., Frazier, S. L., & Chaspari, T. (2022). A Call to Action on Assessing and Mitigating Bias in Artificial Intelligence Applications for Mental Health. *Perspectives on Psychological Science : A Journal of the Association for Psychological Science*, *18*(5), 1062. https://doi.org/10.1177/17456916221134490.

[35] *View of Encoding normative ethics: On algorithmic bias and disability | First Monday*. (n.d.). Retrieved October 26, 2024, from https://firstmonday.org/ojs/index.php/fm/article/view/12905/10788.

[36] *Ethical principles for artificial intelligence in education | Education and Information Technologies*. (n.d.). Retrieved October 26, 2024, from https://link.springer.com/article/10.1007/s10639-022-11316-w.

[37] *(PDF) Impact of AI-Based Special Education on Educators and Students*. (n.d.). Retrieved October 26, 2024, from https://www.researchgate.net/publication/374409074_Impact_of_AI-Based_Special_Education_on_Educators_and_Students.

[38] Nguyen, A., Ngo, H. N., Hong, Y., Dang, B., & Nguyen, B.-P. T. (2023). Ethical principles for artificial intelligence in education. *Education and Information Technologies*, *28*(4), 4221–4241. https://doi.org/10.1007/s10639-022-11316-w.

[39] *Preserving data privacy in machine learning systems—ScienceDirect*. (n.d.). Retrieved October 26, 2024, from https://www.sciencedirect.com/science/article/pii/S0167404823005151.

[40] *Systematic review of research on artificial intelligence applications in higher education – where are the educators? | International Journal of Educational Technology in Higher Education | Full Text*. (n.d.). Retrieved October 26, 2024, from https://educationaltechnologyjournal.springeropen.com/articles/10.1186/s41239-019-0171-0.

[41] Timan, T., & Mann, Z. (2021). Data Protection in the Era of Artificial Intelligence: Trends, Existing Solutions and Recommendations for Privacy-Preserving Technologies. In E. Curry, A. Metzger, S. Zillner, J.-C. Pazzaglia, & A. García Robles (Eds.), *The Elements of Big Data Value: Foundations of the Research and Innovation Ecosystem* (pp. 153–175). Springer International Publishing. https://doi.org/10.1007/978-3-030-68176-0_7.

[42] Khosravi, H., Shum, S. B., Chen, G., Conati, C., Tsai, Y.-S., Kay, J., Knight, S., Martinez-Maldonado, R., Sadiq, S., & Gašević, D. (2022). Explainable Artificial Intelligence in education. *Computers and Education: Artificial Intelligence*, *3*, 100074. https://doi.org/10.1016/j.caeai.2022.100074.

[43] Seo, K., Tang, J., Roll, I., Fels, S., & Yoon, D. (2021). The impact of artificial intelligence on learner–instructor interaction in online learning. *International Journal of Educational Technology in Higher Education*, *18*(1), 54. https://doi.org/10.1186/s41239-021-00292-9.

[44] Ye, X., Yan, Y., Li, J., & Jiang, B. (2024). Privacy and personal data risk governance for generative artificial intelligence: A Chinese perspective. *Telecommunications Policy*, 102851. https://doi.org/10.1016/j.telpol.2024.102851

[45] *AI-enabled adaptive learning systems: A systematic mapping of the literature—ScienceDirect*. (n.d.). Retrieved October 26, 2024, from https://www.sciencedirect.com/science/article/pii/S2666920X21000114.

[46] Ruschemeier, H. (2023). AI as a challenge for legal regulation – the scope of application of the Artificial Intelligence Act proposal. *ERA Forum*, *23*(3), 361–376. https://doi.org/10.1007/s12027-022-00725-6.

[47] Kaminski, M. E., & Urban, J. M. (2021). The Right to Contest Ai. *Columbia Law Review*, *121*(7), 1957–2048. https://www.jstor.org/stable/27083420.

[48] *Accountable Artificial Intelligence: Holding Algorithms to Account—PMC*. (n.d.). Retrieved October 26, 2024, from https://pmc.ncbi.nlm.nih.gov/articles/PMC8518786/.

[49] Fu, Y., & Weng, Z. (2024). Navigating the ethical terrain of AI in education: A systematic review on framing responsible human-centered AI practices. *Computers and Education: Artificial Intelligence*, *7*, 100306. https://doi.org/10.1016/j.caeai.2024.100306.

[50] Rainie, J. A. and L. (2018, December 10). 3. Improvements ahead: How humans and AI might evolve together in the next decade. *Pew Research Center*. https://www.pewresearch.org/internet/2018/12/10/improvements-ahead-how-humans-and-ai-might-evolve-together-in-the-next-decade/.

[51] UNICEF (Ed.). (2017). *Children in a digital world*. UNICEF.

[52] *Full article: The promise and challenges of generative AI in education*. (n.d.). Retrieved October 26, 2024, from https://www.tandfonline.com/doi/full/10.1080/0144929X.2024.2394886.

[53] Adams, C., Pente, P., Lemermeyer, G., & Rockwell, G. (2023). Ethical principles for artificial intelligence in K-12 education. *Computers and Education: Artificial Intelligence*, *4*, 100131. https://doi.org/10.1016/j.caeai.2023.100131.

[54] Fedele, A., Punzi, C., & Tramacere, S. (2024). The ALTAI checklist is a tool to assess ethical and legal implications for trustworthy AI development in education. *Computer Law & Security Review*, *53*, 105986. https://doi.org/10.1016/j.clsr.2024.105986.

[55] Javaid, M., Haleem, A., Singh, R. P., Khan, S., & Khan, I. H. (2023). Unlocking the opportunities through ChatGPT Tool towards ameliorating the education system. *BenchCouncil Transactions on Benchmarks, Standards and Evaluations*, *3*(2), 100115. https://doi.org/10.1016/j.tbench.2023.100115.

[56] Chan, C. K. Y. (2023). A comprehensive AI policy education framework for university teaching and learning. *International Journal of Educational Technology in Higher Education*, *20*(1), 38. https://doi.org/10.1186/s41239-023-00408-3.

[57] Gabriel, J. (2024). How Artificial Intelligence (AI) impacts inclusive education. *Educational Research and Reviews*, *19*(6), 95–103. https://doi.org/10.5897/ERR2024.4404.

[58] *Ethics and discrimination in artificial intelligence-enabled recruitment practices | Humanities and Social Sciences Communications*. (n.d.). Retrieved October 26, 2024, from https://www.nature.com/articles/s41599-023-02079-x.

[59] MacKenzie, A., Owaineh, M., Bower, C., & Özkaya, C. (2023). Barriers to inclusive education under occupation: An evaluative approach using Nussbaum's capabilities approach. *International Journal of Educational Research Open*, *5*, 100299. https://doi.org/10.1016/j.ijedro.2023.100299.

[60] *The Individuals With Disabilities Education Act (IDEA) for Children With Special Educational Needs—PubMed*. (n.d.). Retrieved October 26, 2024, from https://pubmed.ncbi.nlm.nih.gov/26620061/.

[61] Aitken, M., & Briggs, M. (n.d.). *Engaging children with AI ethics*.

[62] *Trained AI models exhibit learned disability bias, IST researchers say | Penn State University*. (n.d.). Retrieved October 26, 2024, from https://www.psu.edu/news/information-sciences-and-technology/story/trained-ai-models-exhibit-learned-disability-bias-ist.

[63] Niazi, S. K. (2023). The Coming of Age of AI/ML in Drug Discovery, Development, Clinical Testing, and Manufacturing: The FDA Perspectives. *Drug Design, Development and Therapy*, *17*, 2691. https://doi.org/10.2147/DDDT.S424991.

[64] Abulibdeh, A., Zaidan, E., & Abulibdeh, R. (2024). Navigating the confluence of artificial intelligence and education for sustainable development in the era of industry 4.0: Challenges, opportunities, and ethical dimensions. *Journal of Cleaner Production*, *437*, 140527. https://doi.org/10.1016/j.jclepro.2023.140527.

[65] Chauncey, S. A., & McKenna, H. P. (2023). A framework and exemplars for ethical and responsible use of AI Chatbot technology to support teaching and learning. *Computers and Education: Artificial Intelligence*, *5*, 100182. https://doi.org/10.1016/j.caeai.2023.100182.

[66] *Application and theory gaps during the rise of Artificial Intelligence in Education—ScienceDirect*. (n.d.). Retrieved October 26, 2024, from https://www.sciencedirect.com/science/article/pii/S2666920X20300023.

[67] *AI and Data Privacy in Schools. Artificial intelligence (AI) is rapidly… | by Niall McNulty | Medium*. (n.d.). Retrieved October 26, 2024, from https://medium.com/@niall.mcnulty/ai-and-data-privacy-in-schools-safeguarding-student-information-a0e8436a5f5e.

[68] *(PDF) The AI Revolution & Higher Education: Why 21st Century Durable Skills Are Needed More Than Ever*. (n.d.). Retrieved October 26, 2024, from https://www.researchgate.net/publication/370637059_The_AI_Revolution_Higher_Education_Why_21st_Century_Durable_Skills_Are_Needed_More_Than_Ever.

[69] *Ethical approaches in designing autonomous and intelligent systems: A comprehensive survey towards responsible development | AI & SOCIETY*. (n.d.). Retrieved October 26, 2024, from https://link.springer.com/article/10.1007/s00146-024-02040-9.

[70] *Generative AI in Education: Technical Foundations, Applications, and Challenges | IntechOpen*. (n.d.). Retrieved October 26, 2024, from https://www.intechopen.com/chapters/1181569.

[71] *AI Regulation Is Coming*. (n.d.). Retrieved October 26, 2024, from https://hbr.org/2021/09/ai-regulation-is-coming.

[72] Kurian, N. (n.d.). 'No, Alexa, no!': Designing child-safe AI and protecting children from the risks of the 'empathy gap' in large language models. *Learning, Media and Technology*, *0*(0), 1–14. https://doi.org/10.1080/17439884.2024.2367052.

[73] Radanliev, P., & Santos, O. (2023). *Ethics and Responsible AI Deployment* (No. arXiv:2311.14705). arXiv. http://arxiv.org/abs/2311.14705.

[74] Walter, Y. (2024). Embracing the future of Artificial Intelligence in the classroom: The relevance of AI literacy, prompt engineering, and critical thinking in modern education. *International Journal of Educational Technology in Higher Education*, *21*(1), 15. https://doi.org/10.1186/s41239-024-00448-3.

[75] Abinaya, M., Vadivu, G., & Balasubramaniam, S. (2024). 4 Importance of Prompt Engineering in Generative AI Models. *Generative AI and LLMs: Natural Language Processing and Generative Adversarial Networks*, 69.

Chapter 12

Breaking Barriers Through Generative AI: Charting a Global Empowered Future

A. Joel Livin[1]
A. Ashwini[2,*]
and S. Balasubramaniam[3]

[1]Engineering Department, University of Technology and Applied Science, Sultanate of Oman
[2]Department of ECE, Vel Tech Rangarajan Dr. Sagunthala R&D Institute of Science and Technology, Chennai. Tamilnadu, India
[3]School of Computer Science and Engineering, Kerala University of Digital Sciences, Innovation and Technology, Digital University Kerala, Thiruvanathapuram, Kerala, India

Abstract

Generative AI is an emergence in the tech frontier that one day will revolutionize creative, industrial, and, indeed, societal realms. Thus, through the demonstrated capacity to create human-like content, solve problems, and improve decision-making, AI presents opportunities to flatten existing structures that have excluded many from accessing technology and resources. The ability of progressive generative AI to be made available for people and groups other than the traditional academic organizations, corporations, and governments will help to use democratic tools for empowering people around this world to innovate and to change the existing world, to give voices to the voices less heard from specific regions; to unite; and to help break the barriers between the haves and the have-nots. The general availability and distribution of generative AI to common people and organizations will create new populations of

[*] Corresponding Author's Email: a.aswiniur@gmail.com

In: Democratized Generative AI: Principles, Challenges and Applications
Editors: S. Balasubramaniam and Seifedine Kadry
ISBN: 979-8-89530-684-0

unique producers by empowering global citizens through innovations that cut across disparities between developed and developing nations. This movement is paramount for constructing the future in which AI not only belongs to large firms but can change the world for the better. Therefore, the most significant impact of applying generative AI is identified about generating the potential for revolutionizing education, health care, and start-ups. For example, the generative use case areas include creating individual courses and materials relevant to general and specialized fields of study, producing healthcare content in various languages, and providing small enterprises with an atypical marketing arsenal used by large companies. Thus, AI removes these barriers to enable people to solve localized issues with localized solutions, thus decentralizing innovation. Nevertheless, this empowerment may only be realized if access to new generative AI tools is provided through affordable infrastructure and open-source platforms and interfaces developed for a heterogenic populace, including the technically illiterate. However, the road to a globally empowered future with generative AI is not without its problems. There are questions about the ethical applications of democratized systems, privacy, and the idea of misuse, which require responsible regulation and shared international policies. Furthermore, it would be best if AI systems did not preach discrimination to the public, meaning that such generative artificial intelligence should not be developed with biases that will cause stereotyping and increase the inequalities of the people. If these problems are solved, generative AI can transcend not only technology but also social and cultural judgments to create a future that matches the vision of the human souls. souls.

Keywords: AI tools, bias, democratic governance, education, ethical balance, generative AI, privacy, technological advancement

1. The Path to Democratization Using Generative AI

AI for generation belongs to the next generation of opportunities in the digital period, which can change human life and provide equal opportunities in terms of possessing information, creativity, and technology for everyone. Traditionally, the sophisticated instruments in innovation and solution finding have remained inaccessible to the majority, through limited affordability or technical feasibility or via restrictions to access only. The current generative AI flips this script by offering accessible, large-scale interfaces for content, code, art, and more that do not require select authorities to produce [1]. These tools act in a way that minimizes technological restraints while maximizing creative potential in the markets and creating equal ground on which people from distinct socio-economic and cultural strata can compete for a share in the burgeoning digital economy. Figure 1 shows the AI Principles in the path of democratization to generative AI.

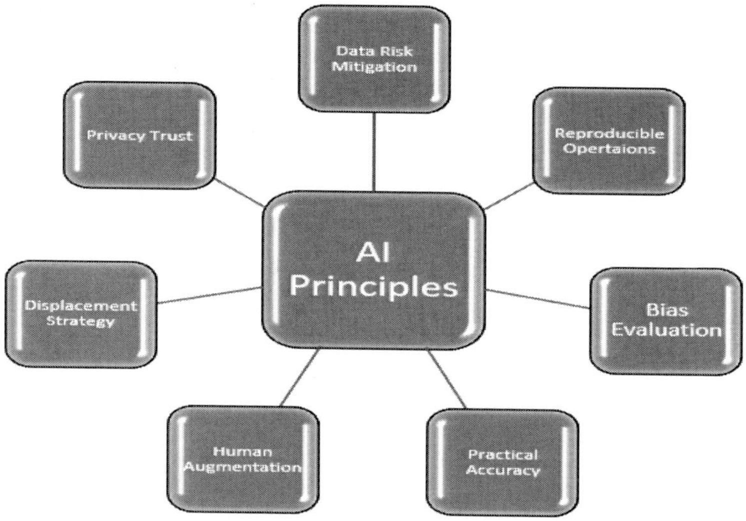

Figure 1. AI Principles in the path of Democratization to Generative AI.

Another potential area involves fostering democracy through the promotion of opportunities to learn and upgrade skills, which is addressed through the Utilization of generative AI. Platforms using AI-produced content allow learners across the world to have access to high-quality local language learning materials while minimizing barriers to teaching, such as the absence of appropriate teaching tools or geographical restrictions. For instance, AI can do the following: create lesson plans based on students' performance, create and model various learning environments, and even give feedback to students as it happens. This democratization of education makes it possible to educate the population in facing the challenges of the future world, the world based on digital technologies and artificial intelligence, and minimize the global gap in knowledge. When governments, industries, and communities engage in mutually beneficial affiliation and collaboration, generative AI has the potential to place the world on a path of an increased democratic, equitable, and empowered future. At this very juncture, it is incumbent upon us to emphasize the power of generative AI to breach unfavorable barriers to set the stage for technological growth, which will augment benefits to everyone and propagate worldwide unison across different nations.

Furthermore, using generative AI has created equal representation and highlights the voice of the minority. This empowers creatives who may not have access to formal equipment such as studio-quality or costly programs for films and other productions or writing, music, and the like. Also, generative AI tools enrich people by presenting various points of view and creativity in terms of cultures, languages, etc. For instance, major examples of how AI technologies are being harnessed to help endanger languages or to provide local content that is culturally sensitive and hence giving a voice to minorities. Elements of ethical concern include avoiding AI-generated outcomes from being utilized maliciously, maintaining the users' or consumers' right to understand the ways AI is used, and dealing with preconceptions or partiality in utilizing AI [2]. Finally, making generative AI accessible for low-income households also demands recognizing that those people might not always have access to the Internet, might not always be capable of reading complex text, and might not always be able to adhere to the principles of digital citizenship. Suppose policymakers, investors, and society establish the correct framework and investments. In that case, generative AI can not only disrupt industries but can be the enabler of equity and inclusion in a connected society.

2. Generative AI in Ethical and Social Implications

Generative AI is a revolutionary concept that holds a significant possibility of generating near-definition and unique values right from text, graphics, music, and videos. As promising as it is, it opens new ethical and social questions of controversies. Such implications have to be greatly scrutinized so that the appropriate application of this technology is observed and negative effects are prevented. It is estimated that one of the biggest ethical issues connected with generative AI is its possible application to the production of fake or malicious information. A backlash against AI is that it is relatively straightforward to create sophisticated deepfakes, fake news, and fake media that would endanger personal privacy, trustworthiness, and democracy. For instance, deepfake videos can be used to disseminate fake news or influence the opinions of the population, thus questioning the authenticity of content in media. This highlights the requirement for useful approaches to find AI-produced content and define its appropriate usage policies, as shown in Figure 2.

Figure 2. Implications of Generative AI in Democratization.

2.1. Establishing Clear Ethical Guidelines and Frameworks

The first of these is to identify the ethical concerns with tolerability. One of the main sets of ethical principles needs to be prescriptive for developers to gather more diverse datasets in the training of the generative models to nurture diversity instead of replicating the current existing social injustices. Reasoning is also important as it gives users an understanding of how these models make their decisions.

2.2. Promoting Transparency and Explainability

Since information is a valuable asset in generative AI, transparency and explainability are core components of the right use of generative AI. First of all, it is the responsibility of stakeholders to guarantee that the operation of these models is transparent, and they are, in fact, 'white boxes.' Explainability then becomes a critical requirement of the developers in that users and regulatory bodies will be able to follow the process through which a decision is arrived at, especially in sensitive areas that include health, finance, or legal jurisdictions [3]. For example, AI tools in the selection or creation of content and recommendation engines should provide why such results or recommendations were achieved. It is particularly important because people can question or change the result if there is a concern that a solution is unfair or could be prejudiced in some other way by using Explainable AI.

2.3. Ensuring Fairness and Mitigating Bias

Generative AI systems tend to amplify or even reinforce existing social biases. One of the decision-making methods is to integrate equal treatment concerning artificial intelligence design that is used to find and eliminate biases purposefully at the designing stage. Data professionals ought to earn a commitment to collecting and using data as diverse as society and regularly auditing the AI models to ensure that the output is not biased. Metrics, for example, in AI-produced media or job-injection tools, should be inclusive, and fairness checks should be applied to prevent the AI from leaning towards a particular minority or group based on the color, gender, or income level of the person in the picture. Ethical standards should require models to be revised cyclically to counter any bias or inequity in outputs [4].

2.4. Safeguarding Privacy and Data Security

One typical issue when using generative AI systems is the availability of big data sources, which may be a problem regarding data privacy. Perhaps it is necessary to strengthen the protection of personal data and guarantee that artificial intelligence does not take advantage of such data. Measures to ensure their privacy may involve data set anonymization and ensuring the users' permission to use the specified data, among other measures that enhance the use of strong encryption systems.

2.5. Addressing the Risks of Misuse

Anti-sybil filtering can be incorporated into generative AI to ensure the nonproduction of fake information, and deepfake detection systems can be incorporated into generative AI to stop the production of fake media. Besides, the creators of AI systems can design mechanisms to identify the usage of automatically generated content that violates the intended application purpose. This reveals that social and ethical guidelines must offer ways in which the exploitation by the wrong people will be checked so that responsible use of artificial intelligence will be allowed.

2.6. Public Awareness and Education

Another important area is to increase awareness regarding the opportunities and challenges that have to do with generative AI. This includes preventing future risks such as the spreading of wrong information, prejudices, and violation of privacy [5]. Creating so-called 'AI literacy,' which will allow people to be critical of content generated using AI and its impact, will be the primary outcome. Measures can entail learning and messaging activities together with schools and distinct organizations so that society can interact with generative AI safely. When AI applications are already widespread, a knowledgeable public can demand and oversee the actions of developers and institutions.

2.7. Continuous Monitoring and Regulation

Social and ethical concerns must emerge as deeper and more prominent concerns as generative AI technology develops. This can include state authorities, regulatory non-governmental organizations, and other bodies to oversee compliance with certain rules and to make sure that AI systems are not causing any negative impact on the population [6]. For instance, it is advocated for the incorporation of regulatory authorities to guarantee the application of AI in sensitive areas such as medicine and law enforcement is open, equitable, and constant with regard to time. There could be a need for the formulation of AI safety and ethics concerning international standards meeting away. Another issue is the risk of AI systems reproducing bias and inequalities about all sorts of attributes in the population. AI models beautify the data they were trained on, and therefore, if the data sets were biased, for example, in gender, race, or culture, the outputs would also be biased. For example, such generative AI programs recommend hiring discriminative employees, portraying stereotypical representations in art, or featuring or contributing material that discriminates against minority groups. From biasing the training data and developing algorithmic designs, it is very important that the fairness and inclusion principles as pillars of diversity are insisted upon to avoid the continuity of biased offers in service. In addition, generative AI has created social risks linked to creativity and ownership of material. With the advancement of AI in creating articles, there is going to be a big question mark as to who will be the article's author, the owner of the particular content, or who will get paid for creating that particular content. Moreover, there are concerns about the social impact on creative individuals due to concerns that AI-created art can lead to job losses for artists, writers, and designers.

3. The Impact of Collaborative Development on Accessibility

Current advancements in generative artificial intelligence have made a significant impact on the manner in which collaborative development affects accessibility. The capabilities of generative AI that create adaptive, personalized, efficient solutions, along with developers efforts, affected people, and finally general users, make a new age of accessibility [7]. Such synergy makes accessibility tools and services far more innovative and consequently more different-need responsive to break barriers for disabled people and other underprivileged communities.

3.1. Personalized Accessibility Solutions

AI means that generative AI allows creating unique and specific accessibility tools based on user preferences. In an environment where they work, developers can input the results of AI analysis on the overall functioning of the application, delivering features that change their behavior according to the needs of the target audience [8]. Computers are capable of text-to-speech conversion that can be trained with particular reference to the user's vocals, specific dialects, or intonation needed to help those who have speaking disabilities. Similarly, generative AI can develop content specifically for learners with cognitive impairment. This method of personalization means that accessibility tools will be even more helpful and enabling to different audiences.

3.2. Accelerating Assistive Technology Development

The availability of generative AI quickly enhances the process of creating new prototype assistive technologies. In this case, designing a product entails many time-consuming processes, which, when independently performed by the collaborative team, reduce design quality since the designers have to solely assess the user-centric features and give their input [9]. Organizations in a team developing sign language from AI can utilize generative AI models to create sign language videos and gestures to enhance real-time conversation for deaf people. This shortens the development cycle; it brings assistive technologies into the market much earlier and at a lesser cost.

3.3. Enhancing Accessibility in Content Creation

Generative consumer AI-based solutions transform how content is made available, especially in a cohesive, collaborative setting. AI can convert text into captions, audio descriptions, or simplified summaries where needed and thus make media and information more easily accessible [10]. This means that websites like YouTube or content makers who release their work in cooperation can use generative AI for the creation of captions for videos and descriptions for blind people for free, as it will be beneficial for people with hearing impairments. Such automation makes accessibility integral to the content production process rather than being an added extra.

3.4. Facilitating Global Collaboration through AI-Powered Translation

Generative AI breaks language barriers for people worldwide and encourages them to collaborate on accessibility projects. It enables developers, designers, and stakeholders from different linguistic and cultural backgrounds to work on a single project [11]. New ChatGPT or DeepL translates significant technical documents, feedback, and real-time project discussions to ensure equal and effective collaboration. This creates a broad and international approach to developing accessibility solutions that meet needs across different geographical locations and cultural backgrounds.

3.5. Democratizing Access to Development Tools

By integrating generative AI into product development, a complex process can be broken into easily understandable components, and the process becomes open for all sorts of people to contribute to a project regardless of their technical background. For instance, AI can support scripts and their layouts or even create prototypes for accessibility options for non-coders [12]. Generative AI interfaces can benefit patients with disabilities, as well as advocacy groups and organizations that can sketch plans for new assistive instruments that the actual technical teams can develop based on those notional concepts. This democratization makes it possible to obtain inputs relevant to the development process and from the key stakeholders, especially end users.

3.6. Continuous Feedback and Iteration

Feedback is the lifeblood of collaborative development, and generative AI can filter and analyze user input and generate practical suggestions for further improvement. The stored information in its current form facilitates the provision of prompt data and feedback to adjust the proposed accessibility measures progressively. It can also identify trends in a user's engagement with accessibility tools, potential problems with usability, or potential improvements the design could use [13]. This iterative approach keeps the longer-term focus on accessibility tools relevant and valuable. On the one hand, the utilization of generative AI in collaborative development has great potential; on the other hand, the concept also comes with issues. They found that such biases had the potential to lead to solutions that locked users with disabilities into a cycle of dependency and exclusion. These biases have to be managed by the collaborative teams, and part of that involves guaranteeing diverse training data. Generative AI and collaborative development are making it possible to envision a future where accessibility is a native component of technology and society. In this way, both the stakeholder competencies and the capacity of AI to transform and empower an approach that is realistic, scalable, and sustainable.

4. Bridging the Gap between Developed and Emerging Economics

As a result, it is a multi-dimensional approach involving technology, policy, and international cooperation in addressing the post-crisis gap between developed and emerging economies. These methods aim to support and create new economies through successful development, better infrastructure, better access to education and health care, and the sharing of knowledge and information.

4.1. Technology Transfer and Digital Inclusion

Technology transfer refers to transferring technologies—products, processes, knowledge, and other assets—from developed countries to developing economies. This can include automation of processes, energy such as through solar products, or information technology in the form of artificial intelligence (AI) and blockchain, among others. Digital access is especially relevant, as it will allow emerging economies to be part of the global digital system. The donor countries and the private companies can forge a long-term relationship to offer cheap technologies and connections to the Internet [14]. For example, broadband for some areas may be cheaper via satellite internet (Starlink). Technology opens new opportunities, increases efficiency, forms new sectors, and enables financial services such as mobile banking and digital payments to improve the economic development of emerging markets.

4.2. Foreign Direct Investment (FDI) and Infrastructure Development

They indicate that FDI is critical in filling the capital gap in emerging economies. Investment in constructing roads, bridges, ports, and the power sector is usually derived from FDI to improve trade and market destinations. Governments of developed states can motivate their corporations to invest in developing countries through desirable conditions, and multilateral agencies like the World Bank and IMF can grant credit for major structural development programs. The development of physical facilities has brought in more investors, enhanced communication, and escalated production, breaking the dependence on the foreign assistance cycle.

4.3. Education and Skill Development Initiatives

For developing nations to compete against global competition, the etiquette of a uniquely skilled workforce should be a significant concern. Education, vocational training, and digital literacy initiatives ensure a skills gap is closed and people are ready to fit into the modern economy [15]. Developed countries can support the skill development center and open scholarship opportunities for enhanced student learning in emerging economies. Also, universities like Coursera and edX can provide millions of people with quality education at a reasonable price. Education for people means efficient knowledge that is useful in creating new ideas, increasing work rates, and providing employment for the people, which propels the economy and erases the differences between the poor and the rich.

4.4. Trade Liberalization and Market Access

This prospect is facilitated by reducing barriers to trade between developed and emerging economies of the world. These economies get to sell goods and services in distant markets and, equally, get to source investments as well as obtain new technologies. Developed countries can bring down the tariffs, quantitative restrictions, and subsidies that lockout emerging economies' exports. Trade enhances export diversification and each country's GDP and helps new economies get the best advantage in global markets.

4.5. Sustainable Development Practices

Developing sustainability in the emerging economy guarantees sustainable future growth without compromising the environment [16]. This includes establishing a functional green economy through renewable resources, such as in the power sector, using green energy in agriculture, and green manufacturing. They can donate money, knowledge, and equipment to construct solar and wind power plants and climate change-adapted farming.

4.6. Knowledge Sharing and Capacity Building

Organizational development addresses local governments' and organizations' ability or capacity to manage resources efficiently and effectively. Activities like tech support, seminars, and policy sharing between countries assist the new economy in putting up sound structures in their governance and regulations. Policies lead to a more employed, stable, and productive economy, increasing investment and proper use of resources.

4.7. Social and Financial Inclusion Programs

Credit, health, and social protection services are some of the targeted services that social and financial inclusion seeks to bring for marginalized groups [17]. Microfinance, banking for the vulnerable, going mobile, and partnerships to bring financially exclusive services, including health services. These poverty reduction programs deal with poor economic participation and support the equal development of economic dignity, which dignifies society's socio-economic framework. These methods can be effectively applied sequentially and in combination with one another in a mutually linked way with the belief that the developed and the emerging economies can wish to create a fair world economy. They are all designed to cover different facets of development, including technology and governance, and let no country be left behind in pursuing development.

5. AI Driven Policy Insights

The democratized generative AI, the availability and utilization of AI to individuals, organizations, and government, can shorten the gap between developed and emerging economies. In respecting the opportunity that generative AI offers developing communities, bridging these countries to utilize advanced technologies without requiring massive capital investment, generative AI offers innovative economic development and equitable opportunities for growth in emerging economies.

5.1. Enhancing Digital Inclusion and Accessibility

Democratized generative AI helps emerging economy stakeholders innovate and solve problems as they seek entry-level competitive solutions in complex global markets. Marketing managers in emerging economy start-ups can use these applications to plan advertising campaigns, develop impressive graphics, or write persuasive texts without requiring costly tools or relevant skills. This makes the environment evenhanded, enabling SMEs in emerging economies to mayor with firms in developed nations and promote local economic progress.

5.2. Enabling Cost-Effective Innovation

Generative AI can cut out vast research, development, and innovation costs, as pointed out in [18]. It became apparent that these technologies can be democratized to encourage ingenuity in fresh economies instead of necessitating substantial capital investment in infrastructure and human capital. In the case of specific resource-limited businesses, AI tools can help to produce a prototype, improve the production line, or develop scientific approaches for hypothesis testing.

5.3. Transforming Education and Skill Development

Of all fields, education is one of the most significant beneficiaries of democratized generative AI. Technology-savvy platforms ensure that individuals within emerging economies get the correct training to fit the global market. Using generative AI in creating courses and ChatGPT also opens opportunities for a platform to deliver education in a natural language for students with localization and a personalized experience.

5.4. Evidence-Based Policy Recommendations

Realizing that generative AI can analyze large datasets and create clear policy recommendations informed by the data. The government's policy decision-making options are boosted with historical information and accurate and forecast data. The AI-driven platforms can estimate such approaches to analyze the effect of prior education reforms and outline evidence-based approaches to increase literacy levels where they are low in developed countries. This way, it is impossible to develop policies that are based on assumptions instead of improving the situation.

5.5. Scenario Modeling and Predictive Policy Design

In particular, such generative AI helps policymakers predict how different policy options will work and what result will be most favorable when implemented. Looking at outcomes, AI can simulate the consequences of specific actions on a particular economy, people's health, or the environment. Climate models using artificial intelligence capabilities can simulate the benefits and challenges of a carbon tax regime and inform policymakers to decide on a sustainable development strategy [19]. Scenario modeling applies to public policy processes since it minimizes risks and allows authorities to develop effective solutions before, during, and after an unexpected event.

5.6. Real-Time Policy Monitoring and Adaptive Frameworks

This makes it easier to oversee and place policies to effect through generative AI. By implementing AI, the performance of policies is evaluated constantly, and suggestions for changes corresponding to certain conditions could be provided. In urban planning, generative AI can diagnose traffic distribution and advise changes or additions to public transport policies to prevent new congestion problems. To this end, flexibility guarantees that policies are relevant in the fast-changing context.

5.7. Enhancing Inclusivity and Representation

It assists in developing policies, thus reflecting the needs of the different demographics [20]. It is possible to use AI in searching for the populations that need healthcare services and how best to approach the provision of the services to this population. This is pro-equality to all the groups, meaning none of the groups will be left out in policy formulation.

5.8. Automating Policy Drafting and Communication

Drafting policies, reports, and communication pieces can be time-consuming, but generative AI can complete this accurately. Presenting technical information in concise, easily digestible forms helps policies reach key contacts and the public more easily. Sophisticated systems, including ChatGPT, can create drafts of policies that include legal aspects, economic factors, and social context and save bureaucratic time [21].

5.9. Bridging Policy Gaps through Knowledge Sharing

Generative AI enhances global knowledge exchange by parsing and synthesizing policies from various zones, identifying the practical approaches that can be implemented locally [22]. Different poverty reduction programs conducted in one country can be examined by AI-powered platforms, and it will recommend ways to implement such programs in another country based on that country's socio-economic conditions. This promotes teamwork and also guarantees the implementation of suitable solutions in various countries.

5.10. Overcoming Resource Constraints in Emerging Economies

In the context of emerging markets, generative AI makes policy-making tools accessible because it does not require large amounts of human investment or financial capital. AI can offer information to resource-scarce governments that other wealthy nations with adequate analytic power can afford [23]. AI can help governments in low-income areas make informed choices on how much to spend on education, healthcare, or infrastructure while getting the most excellent value for the money they spend. This enables the new economy (mc) to develop sound policies for developing their country with limited resources.

Nevertheless, its application for generative AI policy-making prevents it from addressing the problems of bias, data privacy, and accountability [16]. This inaccuracy means that decisions based on such information are also prejudiced; the untimely use of artificial intelligence solutions reinforces social injustice. To meet these challenges, it becomes imperative for policymakers to embrace policy transparency and diversity in datasets and policy and form policy standards and guidelines for the use of AI. AI-generated policy recommendations are the most promising area of AI application in government, as they can enhance policy as an activity far beyond what anyone expected. Suppose governments take the right approach to this technology. In that case, some of the world's most pressing and complex problems can finally be solved, the confidence of societies can be gained, and political leadership that will guarantee sustainable development for generations to come can be promoted.

6. Innovations on Sustainable AI Systems

As much as these generative AI systems are revolutionary, they are burdensome regarding the resources needed to run them, especially power [24]. Large-scale models like GPT require huge data sets and extensive computation, a significant factor for a high carbon footprint. As environmental issues become apparent to people worldwide, advances aimed at optimizing the expenditure of generative AI systems become paramount. They are on the path to minimizing their environmental impact without losing efficiency—positive technological development. A new strain is energy-efficient AI architecture and algorithms. Various methods are used to obtain efficient models; the model pruning approach removes unnecessary parameters, and quantization and sparsity optimization reduces the number of computations. Applying these methods guarantees that the models are less tiresome in their consumption of resources but as effective.

They minimize the system's energy utilization by generative AI and enhance adoption possibilities for small entities. Another innovation concerns how these AI systems are powered—primarily through clean energy [25]. Businesses and scholars are now moving their AI systems to the data centers that operate on solar, wind, and hydroelectric power. Many of these renewable-powered systems are not only low carbon but also are strong evidence that, at scale, sustainable AI can indeed be achieved. Besides the support for renewable energy, cooling technology improvements now ensure energy efficiency in high-consumption data centers.

To help compare the costs and benefits of different AI training processes, tools such as Green AI benchmarks are being developed to report on their environmental costs and make efficiency an essential component of development. As mentioned, fully autonomous and centralized AI are not constant solutions that should be introduced to the population; on the other hand, decentralized and distributed AI systems are becoming sustainable. These approaches help lower the need for centralized and power-intensive data centers by processing data on the smartphone or IoT system. Such approaches, including federated learning, spread the computational load across clients and thus reduce power consumption while maintaining data confidentiality [26]. For example, generative AI solutions, such as content generation or health management applications, can be run from the user's device, reducing the reliance on cloud support. These innovations decrease energy consumption and help make generative AI more affordable for regions with low computational capabilities, thus fostering fairness in AI distribution in Figure 3.

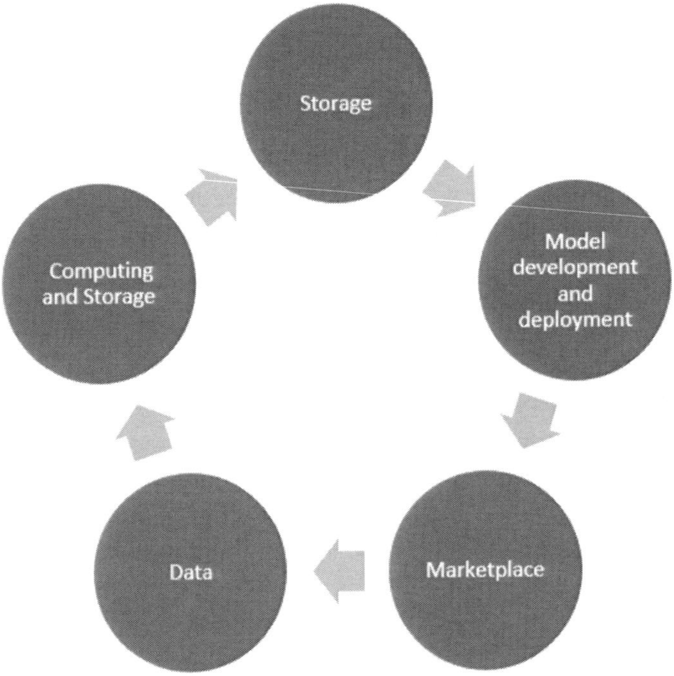

Figure 3. Sustainable AI Innovation Systems.

Advantages in intelligent design, energy sources, and distributed processing are creating prospects for generative AI systems. These concerns the environmental impacts of AI technologies and, thus, include a wider participation in AI development [27]. When these practices deepen, we will be presented with an entirely new and efficient way to advance technology while at the same time minimizing our impact on the environment.

7. Balancing Innovation, Ethics and Public Safety

Generative AI is a highly valuable technology that is revolutionizing industries; it presents advancements in solutions for healthcare or content generation and discovering new insights about the world [28]. This brings in its own set of ethical problems in certification, misuse, and safety concerns within the communities. The key challenge is to find the right balance and implement generative AI that creates added value while at the same time minimizing the associated risks that result from the potentially negative impact of the technology. The advancement in generative AI has led to innovations in the current markets, like drug discovery and learning and creative processes. For instance, generative models that are deep learning-focused can help generate new forms of molecules as medicines or generate individual forms of learning for students. Procuring such progress entails research efforts and development and, more importantly, promoting sharing between governments, private sectors, and academic institutions [29-31].

Ethical issues are core to the innovations of generative AI technology. One crucial issue is to prevent the release of unfair AI models about model accuracy. However, if taught with deficient information, which could be prejudiced, generative AI will reinforce or even deepen prejudicial differences, for instance, in employment, medical treatment, or judiciary systems [32]. An explanation of bias is yet another source where developers must put effort into applying techniques such as explainability and fairness audits, among others, to address such biases. In addition, ethical use covers ideas such as preventing AI from violating the existing authors' and other creators' intellectual property and stating plagiarism and copyright as problems for AI. Public safety is the third area of consideration, as most innovations offer enormous advantages and risks. Deepfakes, also known as synthetic media that AI creates, are often discussed with concerns about their possibilities of fraud, spreading fake news, or other unlawful actions. The rules for using and sharing generative AI platforms must be set to prevent public safety threats. For instance, the imposition of watermarks on texts generated with AI or the attempt to set higher standards for creating deep fake technologies can effectively reduce such excesses while allowing legitimate use [33].

At the same time, people can be targeted with unique campaigns to raise awareness of potential problems and ethical issues surrounding AI technologies so they can perform their actions responsibly. To morph generative AI into a viable and responsible technology in the future, there has to be a way to encourage continued advancement and innovation together with integrating humanity's checks and bounds and punishments for the technology when the latter is caused by the former. They have the potential to 'write code that writes code' for generative AI to foster cooperation, adopt the highest standards of the moral impact designs on the space, and set strong guardrails that allow the technology to progress and improve life for people without compromising trust [34-35].

Conclusion

The developed and emerging economies still have a considerable digital divide, and technology and infrastructure investments are needed for the latter to integrate into the AI economy. Nevertheless, the possibilities for developing democratized generative AI are tremendous and outlined below. From upgrading existing healthcare industries where the diagnostics are done by artificial intelligence to empowering small businesses in emerging markets to affect global markets, the technology is poised to deliver new possibilities and leave enduring good effects. As the field develops, it will be important to fine-tune the principles of uncontroversial use based on the objectives of transparency, fairness, and accountability to enhance the pros of generative AI while preventing the cons. Democratized generative AI is not simply a topic of conversation among technocrats. Still, it is a part of the complicated reality on which the future of humanity—the innovators, the problem solvers, and the consumers—will depend.

References

[1] Chen, A., Liu, L., & Zhu, T. (2024). Advancing the democratization of generative artificial intelligence in healthcare: A narrative review. *Journal of Hospital Management and Health Policy*, *8*.

[2] Elyoseph, Z., Gur, T., Haber, Y., Simon, T., Angert, T., Navon, Y. & Asman, O. (2024). An Ethical Perspective on the Democratization of Mental Health With Generative AI. *JMIR Mental Health*, *11*, e58011.

[3] Kreps, S., & Kriner, D. (2023). How AI threatens democracy. *Journal of Democracy*, *34*(4), 122-131.

[4] Allen, D., & Weyl, E. G. (2024). The real dangers of generative ai. *Journal of Democracy*, *35*(1), 147-162.

[5] Gupta, A., Pranathy, R. S., Binny, M., Chellasamy, A., Nagarathinam, A., Pachiyappan, S., & Bhagat, S. (2024). Voices of the Future: Generation Z's Views on AI's Ethical and Social Impact. In *Technology-Driven Business Innovation: Unleashing the Digital Advantage, Volume 1* (pp. 367-386). Cham: Springer Nature Switzerland.

[6] Partadiredja, R. A., Serrano, C. E., & Ljubenkov, D. (2020, November). AI or human: the socio-ethical implications of AI-generated media content. In *2020 13th CMI Conference on Cybersecurity and Privacy (CMI)-Digital Transformation-Potentials and Challenges (51275)* (pp. 1-6). IEEE.

[7] Brown, B. A., & Heitner, K. L. (2024). Ethical Considerations for Generative AI in Social Science Research. In *Generative AI and Implications for Ethics, Security, and Data Management* (pp. 155-207). IGI Global.

[8] Qian, Y., Siau, K. L., & Nah, F. F. (2024). Societal impacts of artificial intelligence: Ethical, legal, and governance issues. *Societal Impacts*, *3*, 100040.

[9] So, H. J., Seah, L. H., & Toh-Heng, H. L. (2010). Designing collaborative knowledge building environments accessible to all learners: Impacts and design challenges. *Computers & Education*, *54*(2), 479-490.

[10] Stewart, A. F., & Zegras, P. C. (2016). CoAXs: a collaborative accessibility-based stakeholder engagement system for communicating transport impacts. *Research in Transportation Economics*, *59*, 423-433.

[11] Nyanjom, J., Boxall, K., & Slaven, J. (2018). Towards inclusive tourism? Stakeholder collaboration in the development of accessible tourism. *Tourism Geographies*, *20*(4), 675-697.

[12] Fatma, S. (2024). Collaborative Learning: It's Approach and Use in the Learning Process. *As the editors of Transforming Learning: The Power of Educational*, 160.

[13] Di Giovanni, E., Fryer, L., & Raffi, F. (2023). Collaborative Media Accessibility: Actors on the Collaborative Stage. *I-LanD Journal: Identity, Language and Diversity: 1, 2023*, 3-11.

[14] Montes, M., & Popov, V. (2011). Bridging the gap: a new world economic order for development. *Aftermath: A New Global Economic Order*, *3*, 119-47.

[15] Arora, A., & Gambardella, A. (2005). Bridging the gap: Conclusions. *From Underdogs to Tigers: The Rise and Growth of the Software Industry in Brazil, China, India, Ireland and Israel*, 275-302.

[16] Aderibigbe, A. O., Ohenhen, P. E., Nwaobia, N. K., Gidiagba, J. O., & Ani, E. C. (2023). Artificial intelligence in developing countries: bridging the gap between potential and implementation. *Computer Science & IT Research Journal*, *4*(3), 185-199.

[17] Woetzel, J., Garemo, N., Mischke, J., Kamra, P., & Palter, R. (2017). Bridging infrastructure gaps: Has the world made progress. *McKinsey & Company*, *5*.

[18] Agwu, M. E. (2021). Can technology bridge the gap between rural development and financial inclusions?. *Technology Analysis & Strategic Management*, *33*(2), 123-133.

[19] Riel, A., Messnarz, R., & Woeran, B. (2020). Democratizing innovation in the digital era: empowering innovation agents for driving the change. In *Systems, Software and Services Process Improvement: 27th European Conference, EuroSPI*

2020, Düsseldorf, Germany, September 9–11, 2020, Proceedings 27 (pp. 757-771). Springer International Publishing.

[20] Costa, C. J., Aparicio, M., Aparicio, S., & Aparicio, J. T. (2024). The Democratization of Artificial Intelligence: Theoretical Framework. *Applied Sciences*, *14*(18), 8236.

[21] Banifatemi, A., Miailhe, N., Buse Çetin, R., Cadain, A., Lannquist, Y., & Hodes, C. (2021). Democratizing AI for humanity: A common goal. *Reflections on Artificial Intelligence for Humanity*, 228-236.

[22] Xu, C., Sun, Y., & Zhou, H. (2024). Artificial Aesthetics and Ethical Ambiguity: Exploring Business Ethics in the Context of AI-driven Creativity. *Journal of Business Ethics*, 1-22.

[23] Kasaraneni, B. P. (2021). AI-Driven Policy Administration in Life Insurance: Enhancing Efficiency, Accuracy, and Customer Experience. *Journal of Artificial Intelligence Research and Applications*, *1*(1), 407-458.

[24] Balling, L. W., Townend, O., Mølgaard, L. L., Jespersen, C. B., & Switalski, W. (2021). AI-driven insights from AI-driven data. *Hear Rev*, *28*(01), 27-29.

[25] Shaik, A. S., Alshibani, S. M., Jain, G., Gupta, B., & Mehrotra, A. (2024). Artificial intelligence (AI)-driven strategic business model innovations in small-and medium-sized enterprises. Insights on technological and strategic enablers for carbon neutral businesses. *Business Strategy and the Environment*, *33*(4), 2731-2751.

[26] Mulukuntla, S., & Venkata, S. P. (2020). AI-Driven Personalized Medicine: Assessing the Impact of Federal Policies on Advancing Patient-Centric Care. *EPH-International Journal of Medical and Health Science*, *6*(2), 20-26.

[27] Mahjabeen, F., & Islam, M. A. (2024). AI-Driven Sustainability: Innovations in Healthcare, and Manufacturing. *Journal of Multidisciplinary Research*, *10*(01), 1-16.

[28] Ashwini, A., Prabhakar, J. M., & Kadry, S. (2024). 8 Exploring the Applications on Generative AI and LLM. *Generative AI and LLMs: Natural Language Processing and Generative Adversarial Networks*, 155.

[29] Govindan, K. (2022). How artificial intelligence drives sustainable frugal innovation: A multitheoretical perspective. *IEEE Transactions on Engineering Management*, *71*, 638-655.

[30] Ortega-Fernández, A., Martín-Rojas, R., & García-Morales, V. J. (2020). Artificial intelligence in the urban environment: Smart cities as models for developing innovation and sustainability. *Sustainability*, *12*(19), 7860.

[31] Goralski, M. A., & Tan, T. K. (2020). Artificial intelligence and sustainable development. *The International Journal of Management Education*, *18*(1), 100330.

[32] Rehman, S. (2024). Ethical Implications of Genetic Engineering: Balancing Innovation and Responsibility. *Frontiers in Biotechnology and Genetics*, *1*(01), 37-55.

[33] Balasubramaniam, S., & Bharathi, R. (2012). Performance analysis of parallel FIR digital filter using VHDL. *International Journal of Computer Applications*, *39*(9), 1-6.

[34] Shafik, W., Tufail, A., Apong, R. A. A. H. M., & Balasubramaniam, S. Future Directions in Cybersecurity, Digital Forensics and Biometric Systems. In *AI Based Advancements in Biometrics and its Applications* (pp. 238-263). CRC Press.

Index

A

B

C

D

E

F

G

H

I

L

M

N

O

P

Q

R

S

T